PENGU

MILITARY DISPATCHES

ARTHUR WELLESLEY, Duke of Wellington (1769–1852), is generally viewed as Britain's greatest military commander. He fought in some fifty encounters across India and Europe, with almost all battles ending in victory. He finally defeated Napoleon as commander of the Allied forces at Waterloo. He was twice British prime minister.

CHARLES ESDAILE is the author of *The Peninsular War* and *Napoleon's Wars* (both published by Penguin) and is Professor in History at the University of Liverpool.

THE DUKE OF WELLINGTON

Military Dispatches

Edited and Introduced by
CHARLES ESDAILE

PENGUIN BOOKS

For Helen and Mike (quite literally!)

PENGUIN CLASSICS

Published by the Penguin Group
Penguin Books Ltd, 80 Strand, London WC2R ORL, England
Penguin Group (USA) Inc., 375 Hudson Street, New York, New York 10014, USA
Penguin Group (Canada), 90 Eglinton Avenue East, Suite 700, Toronto, Ontario, Canada M4P 2Y3
(a division of Pearson Penguin Canada Inc.)
Penguin Ireland, 25 St Stephen's Green, Dublin 2, Ireland (a division of Penguin Books Ltd)
Penguin Group (Australia), 707 Collins Street, Melbourne, Victoria 3008, Australia
(a division of Pearson Australia Group Pty Ltd)
Penguin Books India Pvt Ltd, 11 Community Centre, Panchsheel Park, New Delhi – 110 017, India
Penguin Group (NZ), 67 Apollo Drive, Rosedale, Auckland 0632, New Zealand
(a division of Pearson New Zealand Ltd)
Penguin Books (South Africa) (Pty) Ltd, Block D, Rosebank Office Park,
181 Jan Smuts Avenue, Parktown North, Gauteng 2193, South Africa

Penguin Books Ltd, Registered Offices: 80 Strand, London WC2R ORL, England

www.penguin.com

Wellington's dispatches were first published, in three volumes, between 1834 and 1839 and revised 1844
This edition, with a new introduction and editorial material, first published in Penguin Classics 2014
001

Selection and editorial material © Charles Esdaile, 2014
All rights reserved

The moral right of the editor has been asserted

Set in 10.25/12.25pt Adobe Sabon
Typeset by Jouve (UK), Milton Keynes
Printed in Great Britain by Clays Ltd, St Ives plc

ISBN: 978-0-141-39431-2

www.greenpenguin.co.uk

Contents

MILITARY DISPATCHES

Preface

In some ways this is a very personal book. In 1985 I was appointed Wellington Papers Research Fellow at the University of Southampton, and the next four years I have always considered not just to be some of the happiest of my whole life, but also the real foundation of my career. As a research student working on the subject of the Spanish army in the Peninsular War, I had always been aware of the published versions of Wellington's dispatches and had, indeed, dipped into them from time to time, but, in my ignorance, I had never considered them to be particularly important from the point of view of the Hispanist which I considered (and still consider!) myself to be. Only when I came to Southampton, then, and was initiated into the mysteries of the Wellington Archive, did I become aware of the extraordinary value that the papers held for my work, the book that eventually came out of my thesis being much enriched by what I found in them, whilst they also provided the basis for the study that I went on to write of the Duke of Wellington and the command of the Spanish army. To have been asked to edit the current work has come, therefore, as a great privilege: it is not often that a scholar has so public an opportunity to pay homage to a source that has had so formative an effect on his development as a historian.

With this sense of privilege, however, also came a sense of foreboding, for a limit of some 120,000 words is but a small compass when it comes to selecting material for publication from the 2,000,000 or more words of the published dispatches. In approaching this task I took the view, first, that at the heart of any work should lie a certain conceptual unity, and, second, that in the case of the Duke of Wellington what those who come to his correspondence for the first time probably require is an account of the military narrative. As I have tried to hint at various points, Wellington's glory was not just that he won battles or conducted successful campaigns, but that he did so in a geographical, social, political and cultural context that was problematic in the extreme, and it is in truth in revealing this complexity that his correspondence is at its most valuable. Yet to wallow in such complexity would not be helpful for the neophyte, while the non-neophyte is likely to be all too well aware of it already, and certainly better aware of it than I can possibly make him in the pages of so slim a volume. Indeed, such would be the problems involved in deciding what to make use of and what to omit that one suspects that it would not be conducive to the good health of the current author: the original editor of Wellington's correspondence, Colonel John Gurwood, ended his days by committing suicide whilst suffering from a state of depression induced in part by overwork. What we have here, then, is essentially a story, namely the story of Wellington's campaigns in the Napoleonic Wars in Europe as recounted at the time by the Duke himself. For those who wish to go further, I hope that the brief section on Further Reading will provide some inspiration, whilst for anyone who has access to them, I can do no better than suggest that they turn to the original work from which the documents published in this book were lifted, J. Gurwood's *The Dispatches of Field Marshal the Duke of Wellington during his Various Campaigns in India, Denmark, Portugal, Spain, the Low Countries and France from 1789 to 1815* (new and enlarged edition; twelve volumes; London, 1852).

Yet taking the decision outlined here has cost me not a little anguish. The view of the Peninsular War that is presented in these pages cannot but be a very English one and yet I have spent my entire career arguing that Anglocentric approaches to the subject are hopelessly inadequate, that the historian of the Peninsular War, indeed, has to perceive the subject from Madrid or Lisbon rather than London or even Wellington's headquarters. Meanwhile, as I intimate above, my work on the Peninsular

War has always essentially been the product of a Hispanist who identifies with Spain and the Spaniards in a manner that would have been utterly incomprehensible to Wellington: as the Duke once said of John Downie, the extraordinary Scottish adventurer who became a Spanish general, I am, I fear, 'Spanish down to my shirt'. To edit the current work, then, has come as a very strange departure for me and one that I am not entirely comfortable with: if one reads Wellington and nothing but Wellington, it is all too easy to infer that, to paraphrase one of his more vitriolic tirades in their respect, the Spaniards never did anything, much less did anything well. Such a view is, of course, wholly unjustified, and, revisionist though I am when it comes to analysing the Spanish national myth, I would wish to dissociate myself from such a stance most completely: much of what the Spaniards did was out of view of Wellington and therefore but imperfectly reflected in his dispatches, but the fact is that many of Spain's soldiers, in particular, fought with the utmost courage in the face of circumstances that even Wellington could not have overcome.

It is, then, with some hesitation that I present this book to the world. Yet I am very glad to have had the chance to prepare it, and the more so as I am writing it in the very midst of the bicentenary of the Peninsular War: 200 years ago this very night Wellington's forces were bivouacking on the banks of the River Pisuerga en route for their great victory of Vitoria. Forty thousand British soldiers – perhaps one in five of those who took part – died in the Peninsular War, and if this book serves in some small way to record their sacrifices then I, and, I hope, their general, will be well pleased.

Finally, some notes of thanks: to Simon Winder for having first come up with the idea; to Anna Hervé and Lin Vasey who have coped with caroline choler with calm and courtesy; to my agent, Bill Hamilton, for having steadied my waverings; to my dear friends and colleagues, Chris Woolgar and Karen Robson, who have these many years managed the Wellington Archives with great aplomb and put up with me with even greater patience; to my military opposite number in Peninsular War 200, Colonel Nicholas Lipscombe, R. A., with whom I have

shared every moment of what has been a very long bicentenary; and, above all, to Alison, Andrew, Helen, Maribel and
Bernadette, without whose love and support no book of mine
would ever see the light.

Charles Esdaile
Liverpool, 9 June 2013

Introduction

In the history of the British army there have been many great
commanders, but the greatest of them all will almost certainly
forever be the Duke of Wellington. Other commanders have
had to deal with greater dangers, incapacitated more enemy
troops, had a greater ability to inspire the love of their men,
learned to co-exist with their political superiors in a more har-
monious fashion, possessed a more attractive manner or been
better coalition generals, but no British general has ever had so
unbroken a record of success, or achieved so much in the face
of such overwhelming numerical superiority on the back of
resources that were so limited. It is, then, quite right that Wellington is beyond doubt the British general with the greatest
public recognition – something that is, perhaps, assured by the
'Duke of Wellington' and 'Iron Duke' public houses to be found
on what sometimes seems to be every street corner – and, for
that matter, the British general who has received the most
extravagant funeral in history. All this being the case, it is, perhaps, fortunate that Wellington also happens to be the British
commander who was the most inclined to put pen to paper.
Though we have no memoirs or autobiography – Wellington
would beyond doubt have regarded writing such a work as being
both utterly improper and totally beneath his dignity – we do
have a mass of private and official correspondence that is quite
incomparable. To quote the early biographer George Gleig:

> It is impossible to imagine an ordeal more trying than that to which
> the character of Arthur, Duke of Wellington has been subjected. All
> his secrets are before the world. Colonel Gurwood's collection of

dispatches . . . gave us such an insight into the mind of the writer
as had never before been obtained into the inner being of any public man. The supplementary volumes published by the present
duke strip off the last rag of covering which clung to it.[1]

Incomparable, but not, alas, accessible: published in various
editions in the nineteenth century, the two works that contain
this material (see below) remain either expensive collectors'
items or the property of more-or-less exclusive research librar-
ies, whilst only one popular edition has ever seen the light of
day, this being Anthony Brett-James' *Wellington at War*, *1794–
1815* (London, 1961). What better way, then, to commemorate
Wellington's most famous victory – the battle of Waterloo of
18 June 1815 – than by remedying this want, and all the more
so as doing so testifies to the extraordinary scale of his achievements and, with them, those of his soldiers.

So well known are the general outlines of Wellington's life
that it seems scarcely necessary to enter into much detail here.
Born in Dublin on 1 May 1769 as the third son of a family
deeply embedded in the Anglo-Irish aristocracy – his father was
the Earl of Mornington – Wellington, or, as he first was, plain
Arthur Wesley (the switch to 'Wellesley' soon decided upon by
the family was little more than a caprice) was educated at Eton
and in France, and in March 1787, having been deemed 'fit for
powder' only, he had entered the British army as an ensign; one
point to note here, meanwhile, is that claims that he was 'Irish'
are difficult to reconcile with the reality of the world of the Prot-
estant ascendancy, let alone with his own views on the subject.
Armed with money, patronage and dedication, the young officer
found advancement no difficulty: by September 1793 he was
both a lieutenant colonel and a member of the Irish parliament.
Sent to fight the French in the campaigns in Flanders and Holland in 1793–5, he was so disgusted by the mismanagement he
witnessed that he briefly considered a career in civil office, but
failure to obtain the necessary preferment soon made him abandon the idea in favour of service with his regiment in India. A
year after his arrival in the subcontinent, where his brother,
Lord Mornington (soon Marquess Wellesley), had just become

governor general of all Britain's extensive territories, war broke out with the Indian state of Mysore, and by January 1799 Wellesley was in the field as, in effect, a corps commander.[2]

In considerable debt, Wellesley had been eager for war. At all events India made his fortune. After playing a prominent role in the capture of Seringapatam, he was made governor of Mysore and spent two years putting down a variety of opponents of British rule, before being given command of the army eventually sent against the polity known as the Mahratha Confederacy. Now a major general, the autumn of 1803 saw him win outstanding victories at Assaye and Argaum, and in the spring of 1805 he returned to England in triumph, whereupon he was elected to the first of a string of 'rotten boroughs' in the Commons, and at the same time driven by his very developed sense of honour to marry Kitty Pakenham, a fellow member of the ascendency whom he had courted prior to his departure to India. Command of a brigade in the army sent to besiege Copenhagen in 1807 followed, as did appointment as the Portland administration's Chief Secretary for Ireland, and by 1808 Wellington had gained the friendship and respect of the up-and-coming Tory politicians and ministers, George Canning and Lord Castlereagh, whilst he had been made a lieutenant general and also become an unofficial military adviser to the Cabinet. When plans emerged to send an expeditionary force to invade the Spanish territories that today make up the state of Venezuela, he was a natural choice for the command, and thus it was that he found himself heading the troops now redirected to the Iberian Peninsula when Spain and Portugal suddenly rose in revolt against Napoleon in the early summer of 1808 (as luck would have it, Wellington's division was still cantoned in southern Ireland at this point and therefore available for these fresh duties).[3]

So much for the curriculum vitae, but what of the man? Hard as one might try, it is difficult to write especially positively of Wellington in this respect. There is, of course, much that one can admire here. Though certainly always much concerned with questions of reputation and honour – hence the anger that he displayed in respect of the fact that in its original form Captain Siborne's famous model of the battle of Waterloo attributed a greater share of the glory for the defeat of Napoleon to the Prussians than he felt proper[4] – the 'Iron Duke' was not much moved by ambition, or, if he was, he was at least careful not to let it either drive his actions or turn his head: in successive campaigns in 1809, 1810, 1811 and 1812, he fell back in more-or-less humiliating retreat rather than copy the Napoleonic model of fighting battles as desperate as they were ill advised for the sake of glory (one thinks here, above all, of Leipzig), whilst, unlike such opponents as Junot and Soult, he did not dream of finding a throne in Spain or Portugal. And, finally as for copying Napoleon and turning his army on the state, for all his complaints at the failings of his civilian superiors, the very idea would have filled him with horror. To quote Gleig again:

> In everything the Duke and Napoleon stood in strong contrast one towards the other. Napoleon could not serve. He never undertook a trust in a subordinate situation which he did not divert to purposes of his own aggrandisement. He never, when advanced to the pinnacle of power, entered into an engagement which he was not prepared, when it suited his own interests, to violate. The Duke was the most perfect servant of his king and country that the world ever saw. He flourished, no doubt, in a condition of society which presented insuperable obstacles to the accomplishment of ambitious projects had he been unwise enough to entertain them, but there is proof in almost every line which he has written ... that, be the condition of society what it might, the one great object of his life would have been to secure the ascendancy of law and order, and to preserve the throne and the constitution of the country unharmed.[5]

Linked to this, of course, was a pronounced sense of duty and public service that kept him on campaign in Portugal, Spain and, latterly, southern France for six years without taking a single day's leave. Then, too, there is the simplicity of his style: the plain cocked hats and frock coats that formed his normal dress were as unaffected as the cottages and farmhouses that were the usual settings for his headquarters. And, finally, there is his undoubted physical courage: whereas Napoleon spent most of the day of Waterloo slouched in a chair at a command post some distance in the rear of his front line, Wellington spent every moment of it at the centre of a storm of enemy fire that killed or wounded almost every single member of his headquarters suite.

So far, so good. The trouble is that many other aspects of the picture are far less flattering. Let us begin with Wellington's relations with his unfortunate wife, Kitty Pakenham. The Duchess of Wellington, as she later became, was famously only married by Wellington out of his sense of duty (he had proposed to her as a young officer, but was turned down by the family on the grounds of his supposed lack of prospects, only for him to commit himself to marrying her come what may). However, time brings change, and when the thrusting young hero of Assaye and Argaum returned to Britain and married his erstwhile sweetheart – extraordinarily enough without actually meeting with her before the wedding service in the London home of the Pakenham family – he found her much changed: her looks had declined and her once sparkling personality had been undermined by years of loneliness and frustration. There ensued for her still more years of loneliness and frustration, and, as Wellington's reputation soared, this in turn produced an ever greater tendency towards depression and introspection. As for her husband, he can possibly be forgiven the string of mistresses with which he indulged himself, not to mention his fondness for the general company of admiring young women, but what is disturbing is the impatience and mental cruelty that he displayed towards his unfortunate wife; the only saving grace to be found in the whole unhappy story is the manner in which, evidently conscience-stricken, he showed her a tenderness at her deathbed that one hopes was something more than just one more gesture towards his goddess, Duty.[6]

Moving on to the public figure rather than the man, we first come to Wellington's relationship with the successive governments which headed the British war effort in the course of the Peninsular War. Unlike Sir John Moore, his predecessor in

Spain, who had been a staunch Whig, Wellington was, like his political masters, a Tory, and had even been a minister in the Portland administration, whilst, as we have seen, from 1809 to 1812, his elder brother, Lord Wellesley, was foreign secretary. Yet neither political loyalties, nor old friendships nor family ties were enough to save the relationship between Wellington's headquarters and London from being very difficult. Always short of money, Wellington insisted on blaming the problem on the government, and for the most part refused point-blank to recognise the very real efforts that it made to support his operations. Nor was it just the issue of money, the British commander also being inclined to fulminate against any aspect of British policy that in any way compromised his position in the Peninsula. A prime example of this was the issue of the Latin American revolutions. When many of Spain's American colonies rose in revolt in 1810, the British government responded by trying to mediate between the rebels and the then Spanish capital of Cádiz. Though arguably misguided, this was by no means indefensible as a policy: a Spain distracted by war in America was a Spain that could not be wholly committed to the war against Napoleon; an America scourged by Spanish troops might be an America that turned to Napoleon; and, finally, a Mexico torn apart by war could not be a Mexico that was a reliable source of silver. Yet mediation also had its defects in that it stirred up anti-British feelings in Spain, whilst it at the same time could hardly be denied that it suited British commercial interests, one of the chief concessions that Cádiz would have been forced to make being to grant the American colonies the right to trade freely with whomsoever they might wish. To all this, Wellington's response was entirely predictable: not only was the London government making his life more difficult than need have been the case, but it was doing so at the behest of 'struggling merchants'. In all this, however, there was great injustice: at base, Wellington was scornful of civilian politicians, whilst he was also frequently incapable of seeing the wider picture, and it is therefore important to recognise that much of his anger should not be taken at face value; to argue, as Fortescue and others have done, that Wellington was waging war weighed down by indifference and incompetence on the home front is therefore very far from the truth.[7] In the words of Rory Muir:

> The ministers have never received much recognition. Liverpool was long remembered chiefly as the butt of Disraeli's jibe 'the arch-mediocrity'; Bathurst receives a scant column in the *Dictionary of National Biography* and even Canning and Castlereagh are famous more for . . . their post-war diplomacy than for their part in the defeat of Napoleon . . . But, if we step back and view the war as a whole, we can see the importance of the ministers. They lack the glamour of the marvellous glittering figure in the foreground but that is no reason to neglect their achievement.[8]

If Wellington's relations with London were often bad, his dealings with his army were not much better. In the safety of his headquarters, he could be relaxed and even genial with the sprigs of nobility with whom he was wont to surround himself, but, beyond its walls a mixture of shyness, intellectual arrogance and aristocratic hauteur produced a demeanour that was at best curt and distant, and at worst intolerant of human frailty and capable of great injustice: a particularly glaring case here is constituted by that of Captain Norman Ramsey, an extremely popular battery commander in the Royal Horse Artillery who had distinguished himself in a very visible fashion at the battle of Fuentes de Oñoro in May 1811, but was temporarily stripped of his command and placed under close arrest by Wellington two days after the battle of Vitoria on account of an honest mistake the British commander deemed to constitute deliberate disobedience of his orders; still worse is that of Lieutenant Colonel Charles Bevan who quite unfairly – the responsibility was rather that of his divisional commander, Sir William Erskine – received the full force of Wellington's wrath in respect of the escape of the French garrison from the beleaguered fortress of Almeida in May 1811 and committed suicide rather than face the disgrace that threatened him.[9] To make matters worse, it has to be said that Wellington's anger did not fall equally on all his subordinates. Regimental officers such as Ramsey and Bevan could be torn to shreds, but, despite frequently being guilty of faults that were far more serious, generals were clearly regarded by him as being protected by their status and usually escaped with no more than a reprimand or even simply a tart remark made in passing. It is perfectly true that Wellington did not have the power to dismiss generals who were guilty of disobedience or incompetence, but he did have the power to request that they should be recalled to Britain. As he was well aware, however, such a step was tantamount to public disgrace unless the man concerned could move straight to another position, and the result was that the British commander used it very sparingly, whilst he was generally careful to maintain a veneer of civility that could be extremely deceptive. When the particularly incompetent Sir James Gordon resigned his short-lived tenure of the post of quartermaster general at the end of 1812 on the grounds of ill health, he seems to have gone home convinced that Wellington was perfectly content with his conduct, and that despite the fact that he had throughout maintained regular contact with the leader of the Whig opposition, Lord Grey, and plied him with damning confidential information which had later found its way into the press.[10]

Even less attractive than the venting of his considerable ire on some hapless regimental officer was Wellington's habit of, first, seeking scapegoats for his frustrations in a manner that took little account of reality, and, second, shifting the responsibility for mistakes on to others. For a good example we need look no further than the siege of Burgos. An episode which only happened at all because Wellington failed to seize the clear opportunity which he was offered to inflict a crushing defeat on the French Army of Portugal in the vicinity of Valladolid, and for which he was manifestly ill-prepared, this degenerated into a series of desperate assaults which made little progress and incurred an ever-growing casualty list. To make matters worse, however, in an evident attempt to avoid the carnage which had led to such appalling scenes before the breaches at Badajoz, the British commander adopted a new style of attack whereby the defenders were to be rushed by small parties of men operating according to the principles of fire and movement. This all sounds very fine, an example indeed of imaginative forward thinking, until one discovers that the assault troops for the most part consisted of small groups of volunteers drawn from several different units who only gathered together minutes before they charged the walls, and therefore had no chance to practice the extremely complicated manoeuvres they found themselves being ordered to embark upon. Inevitably, things went wrong, but, when they did so, the heavy reserves that might just have kept up the impetus of the assault were lacking. Setting aside the question of whose fault it was that Burgos was having to be attacked primarily by infantry rather than gunners in the first place, or, indeed, attacked at all, the responsibility for the repeated failures can be seen to have lain squarely with Wellington and no one else, and yet his correspondence is littered with complaints that his men were not fighting bravely enough. For example, 'I don't much like our operations here, and, though I don't despair of success, my hopes are not very sanguine. The [British] troops have not behaved very well, and the Portuguese troops very badly.'[11] Particularly disturbing, meanwhile, is the case of Major Andrew Lawrie of the Seventy-Ninth Foot. Ordered to lead an escalade on the outer wall of the fortress on the night of 22 September, he made desperate efforts to keep his men on the move and was eventually killed when a French soldier dropped a cannonball on his head, only for Wellington to excoriate him in words that to this day remain deeply shocking:

> . . . the troops ought to have carried the exterior line by escalade on the first trial on the 22d Sept.; and if they had, we had means sufficient to take the place. They did not take the line because [Major Lawrie],the field officer who commanded, did that which is too common in our army. He paid no attention to his orders, notwithstanding the pains I took in writing them, and in reading and explaining them to him twice over. He made none of the dispositions ordered; and instead of regulating the attack as he ought, he rushed on as if he had been the leader of a forlorn hope, and fell, together with many of those who went with him. He had

my instructions in his pocket; and as the French got possession of his body, and were made acquainted with the plan, the attack could never be repeated. When he fell, nobody having received orders what to do, nobody could give any to the troops.[12]

If poor Lawrie was traduced in this fashion, it was in part because Wellington felt that the unfortunate man had behaved in accordance with a certain stereotype – in brief, that of the gentleman-officer for whom gallantry was everything and attention to duty nothing. As he famously wrote, indeed, 'Nobody in the British army ever reads a regulation or an order as if it were to be a guide to his conduct, or in any other manner than an amusing novel, and the consequence is that when complicated arrangements are to be carried into execution . . . every gentleman proceeds according to his fancy.'[13] Such sweeping condemnation, alas, was all too common, and in November 1812 Wellington's behaviour in this respect was to cause great distress and anger when the numerous disorders that ensued during the retreat to Ciudad Rodrigo elicited a General Order that in effect blamed everything that had happened upon the officers of the army. That Wellington's comments were not without some foundation nobody would deny – in an army whose officers were recruited in the rather haphazard fashion that characterised the British service, the presence of a minority of negligent or incompetent officers could not be avoided[14] – but publically to imply that all officers were as bad as each other was harsh, indeed, and the matter would doubtless have festered very badly had the British army not been led to such battlefield glory in 1813, the effect of this being to wipe out the stain of the discredit of the previous winter.[15]

To contempt for many of his officers was added contempt for all of his men. As is well known, Wellington was devoted to the noose, the lash and the punishment parade, scornful of notions of democracy and political progress, obsessed with the concept of order, and inclined to regard the mob – and, by extension, his soldiers – with a mixture of fear, despite and loathing, something that is all too typical here being his description of the raw material of his British troops as the 'scum of the earth': whilst the remark may well have been qualified by the admission that service in the army had in the end made the men 'fine fellows', nothing can hide the prejudice in respect of the lower classes that it reveals. Under Wellington, indeed, few members of the rank and file could expect much in the way of reward. Recommending deserving sergeants for a commission was not unknown to him – in fact, he did so on a number of occasions when he wished to grant a mark of favour to regiments that had particularly distinguished themselves in one battle or another – but he did not like the idea, and was famously inclined to caution against it on the grounds that the men concerned were unable to fit in with the society in which they found themselves and ended up ruining themselves by turning to drink.[16] One can, perhaps, go too far here: Wellington could recommend men for promotion, but could not actually commission men himself. As he complained, 'I, who command the largest British army that has been employed against the enemy for many years, and who have upon my hands certainly the most extensive and difficult concern that was ever imposed on any British officer, have not the power of making even a corporal!'[17] Yet for Wellington to protest in this fashion was to beg the question: whilst he might well have been happy to make common soldiers corporals, one cannot but wonder how many of those corporals might one day have been elevated to the ranks of the officer corps. That said, at least in this instance his position had a certain logic: much though it might be wished that the situation was otherwise, a considerable number of factors ranging from want of education to the need for an officer to have at least some private means made the position of the ex-ranker very hard, whilst, however lamentable, dislike of the lower classes was understandable enough for a man of Wellington's time and background. But in other cases one rather sees what looks like mere caprice: for example, as is well known, throughout the Peninsular War and the campaign of Waterloo Wellington had a troubled relationship with his artillery, but the root cause of his dissatisfaction had little to do with the men actually serving with the army, and it is therefore disturbing to see him, as at Waterloo, seemingly taking out his frustrations by damning his gunners with faint praise and depriving their officers of the brevet promotions which they might ordinarily have expected.[18]

If other elements of the army suffered less harshly than the artillery, it cannot be denied that, viewed from today's perspective, Wellington's style of command seems distinctly unattractive. In the first place, the use of initiative was frowned upon, sometimes being reprimanded even when it demonstrably led to positive results. And, in the second, subordinates were never briefed as to exactly what he intended, and, whilst this is not enough to excuse disobedience of a direct order, it does mean that sometimes operations miscarried, the most glaring example of such a case being constituted by the attack mounted by Sir Thomas Graham in the battle of Vitoria. In so far as can be ascertained, at the time of drawing up the orders for the movement of the four columns into which Wellington divided up the Anglo-Portuguese army – orders which are bereft of any preamble giving a general overview of how the battle would be fought – his intention was essentially to orchestrate a concentric advance that would have cut off the entire French army in its position west of the city of Vitoria. As Sir Charles Oman says, 'Reading [Wellington's] directions to Graham, Hill and Dalhousie, and looking at the way they work out on the map and the allocation of forces in each column, it would seem that . . . he planned a complete encircling scheme which should not only accomplish what he actually did accomplish, but much more.'[19] In the event, however, Graham's column went astray in that, rather than pushing straight down its axis of advance along the Bilbao road and seizing Vitoria itself, which is what Wellington's battle plan called for, it allowed itself to get bogged down in fighting around the villages of Gamarra Mayor and Gamarra Menor. Reading Wellington's orders, however, this is quite understandable:

The column under the Earl of Dalhousie and that under Sir T. Graham are to regulate their movements by those of the two columns of the army on the right, the advance of which they are to endeavour to facilitate; but they are not to forego the advantage of being able to turn the right of the enemy's position, and the town of Vitoria, by moving to their left flank, in the event of being required to do so. This latter part of the instruction is applicable more particularly to the column under the orders of Lieut. Gen. Sir T. Graham.[20]

To say that this paragraph must have been extremely perplexing for Graham, who at the beginning of the battle was many miles from Wellington's headquarters even as the crow flies, let alone by means of the winding mountain roads any courier would have had to follow, is an understatement. Was he to attack Vitoria head-on or was he rather to veer south-eastwards so as (or so must one suppose) to cut the main road to France at some point to the north-east of the city? Either interpretation must have seemed defensible, and in the event Graham clearly felt that the shift to his left was by far the safer of the two. Yet it was a decision that saved the French army, for, cut though the main road eventually was, the failure to take the city of Vitoria meant that the invaders' only other escape route, the road to Pamplona via Salvatierra, was left open. Still worse, having plumped for the course of action that he did, Graham was so undermined by doubt that he did not even press home his attack very effectively: in the end it was not Graham's troops that cut the road to France but rather the Spanish division of General Longa, whereas a determined push might well have been enough to allow Graham to get across the river and move on Vitoria from the north-east, thereby ensuring a much more satisfactory end to the battle.[21]

From here we might move on to a more general point. As Oman remarks, 'It is certain that Wellington never trained a general who proved himself a first-rate exponent of the art of war, but his system . . . was not calculated to foster initiative or self-reliance among his lieutenants.'[22] Given the quality of some of Wellington's generals, this is understandable enough (see over), but it cannot but be felt that his own attitude contributed greatly to his problems. To quote the cavalry brigadier Robert Long: 'A great deal of mischief arises . . . from the absurd mystery and secrecy observed upon occasions which

produce considerable embarrassment to executive officers
without a corresponding advantage to the service. To ask
where to go [or] to halt is high treason; consequently, your
ignorance upon these subjects prevents your taking such steps
as might anticipate embarrassment of various descriptions. If
general officers are not entitled to some degree of confidence,
they are, and must be, ciphers in the army.'[23] All that can be
said here is that, as witness the impromptu 'o-group' that he
held in the positions of the Light Division on the eve of the battle of the River Nivelle in November 1813, it is just possible that
Wellington learned from his mistakes.[24]

There is, then, much to criticise. Yet at the same time there
is also much that can be excused. In the Peninsular War, especially, Wellington faced a trial such as has been faced by few
other British generals. Setting aside the many personal issues
involved – Wellington was after all away from Britain for almost
six years, whilst the many thousands of pages of correspondence drafted in his own hand, frequently in conditions of great
discomfort, testify to a workload that is scarcely imaginable –
there were the many deficiencies of his own forces, including,
not least, the manner in which Horse Guards (the headquarters
of the British army) repeatedly inflicted generals on him who
were barely competent and could scarcely be relied upon (perhaps the worst of these was the mentally unstable Sir William
Erskine, but there were several others including Lord Dalhousie, who was elevated to the command of a de facto corps at
Vitoria; the pioneer of light-infantry tactics William Stewart;
and the cavalry commander John Slade).[25] Also a problem was
the issue of loyalty: on the many occasions when things went
wrong or when Wellington engaged in tactics of a Fabian
nature – good examples include the retreats to Lisbon and
Ciudad Rodrigo – there were plenty of officers who leaped to
put pen to paper and write letters home that were full of criticism. Then there was the country's inability to supply the
Anglo-Portuguese army adequately; the endless drunkenness
and plundering engaged in by the rank and file; the manner in
which many officers thought nothing of applying for home leave
at the slightest opportunity; the reluctance of the Portuguese

authorities to acquiesce in the admittedly very grim recipe that
was prescribed for the defence of their country in 1810; the
behaviour of the Spaniards, whose many difficulties were only
partly sufficient to excuse an attitude that was difficult and
obstructive; the gratuitous advice lavished upon Wellington by
such worthies as the sometime hero of the French Revolution,
General Dumouriez ... If the British commander was frequently testy, if he clearly felt that he was surrounded by fools
and incompetents, it is therefore scarcely to be wondered at. In
the words of Richard Holmes, 'All this reinforced his tendency
to trust almost nobody and to do everything himself, producing
the symptoms of what we would today call a control freak.'[26]

And, of course, if there is much that can be excused, there is
also much that can be admired. For all Wellington's faults,
indeed, nothing can conceal the key fact that he was a military
genius. Even here one might cavil at taking the idea too far: as
Jeremy Black has pointed out, Wellington's victories in part
stand out as much as they do because of failure elsewhere, total
victory at Waterloo, for example, being matched by total failure at New Orleans, whilst the excellent quality of the infantry
that won him battle after battle was the product of reforms
that not only had nothing to do with him, but were the work of
men – above all, the Duke of York and Sir John Moore – who
were of a far more enlightened stamp than he was.[27] Admit this
though we might, however, there is no denying that Wellington's achievements were quite extraordinary. First of all, and
all the more so as it is sometimes overlooked, there is the vital
contribution that he made in respect of the organisation of the
Peninsular army. In 1808 the British troops sent out to Portugal
had been formed into brigades and divisions that were entirely
ad hoc in nature and this continued to be the case into 1809.
However, prior to the campaign of Talavera, Wellington introduced a new structure that was to prove crucial to his success.
In brief, each infantry division was now to consist of two or
three brigades of four battalions apiece. This was conventional
enough – the very same pattern was to be found in the French
army, for example – but Wellington introduced a detail that
was absolutely unique. Thus, several battalions armed with

rifles were split up and their companies attached to a number of infantry brigades at a rate of one apiece. This may seem a matter so arcane as to warrant little comment, but in fact it made a crucial difference in that it allowed British brigade commanders to deploy a significantly larger number of skirmishers than their French opponents (otherwise, like their French opponents, they would have been restricted solely to the light companies that formed a part of their line battalions). Given, first, that the Portuguese brigade that from 1810 formed a part of each infantry division could deploy a full battalion of light infantrymen – the brown-uniformed *caçadores* – in addition to the light companies integral to their two line infantry battalions, and, second, that two of the nine infantry divisions that eventually made up the Peninsular army – the elite Light Division and the Seventh Division – were wholly made up of troops who could fight in open order, the result was that Wellington's battle line was given a significant advantage over its opponents: no more could France's skirmishers dominate the battlefield in the manner that they had done in such clashes as Jena and Auerstädt. To quote Rory Muir, 'A typical infantry division of Wellington's army could more than match any screen of skirmishers thrown out by the French. For example, the 6,700 men of Leith's division at Salamanca included almost 1,000 light infantry: light companies from the eight British line battalions, two companies of the Brunswick-Oels [Jäger] and the whole of the Eighth Caçadores.'[28]

For all his conservatism, then, it is quite clear that Wellington was not at all reactionary when it came to how his army should fight on the battlefield. Whereas it might be assumed that a man of his views might favour – indeed, even insist on – the use of rigid close-order tactics that ensured that the common soldiers – a group that, as we have seen, he held in the most absolute contempt – were at all times kept under the close control of their officers and denied any opportunity of thinking for themselves, in fact he stands revealed as a pragmatist: whilst he may not have been in the forefront of the movement that saw battalion after battalion of line infantry converted into light infantry units and the British army's unique force of riflemen expanded to a strength of seven battalions, he did not stand in its way and was happy to put it to good use. Such flexibility is also on show in Wellington's handling of his artillery. Thus, for a considerable part of the Peninsular War, the Anglo-Portuguese army had relatively few guns, whilst most of the ones that it did have were light six-pounders of limited range and hitting power. Realising that the result was that his batteries risked being swamped by the eight-pounders used by the French, he avoided turning his guns into easy targets by concentrating them in 'grand batteries', instead keeping them spread out in individual batteries and, on occasion, even sections, with orders to reserve their fire until the sector of the line they were stationed in was actually attacked. Such a policy might seem old fashioned – a rejection, indeed, of the new methods of waging war pioneered by the French army, and, with it, a reversion to the norms of the eighteenth century. Yet this was very far from the truth. While equipped with the very limited resources of the first part of the war, Wellington used his guns in a manner that suited their capacities, but, when the situation changed, his approach changed with it. Thus, in the winter of 1812–13 the Anglo-Portuguese army was reinforced with several new batteries of artillery, while many of its guns were now powerful nine-pounders rather than the singularly unimpressive three-pounders and six-pounders of 1808–9, the result being that at Vitoria we see a very different style of battle and, in particular, the organisation on the battlefield of a grand battery that eventually numbered over seventy guns.[29]

In any consideration of Wellington's generalship, then, pragmatism is a strength that should be placed well to the fore. Next must come a quality that can best be described as strategic vision. At almost every moment, then, he had a clear concept of how the war should be fought. Let us begin here with the defence of Portugal, the vital base on which everything else depended. According to Sir John Moore, this could not be held against an invader, and yet, right from the beginning, Wellington saw, that so long as matters were arranged in the necessary fashion, Portugal could be rendered not just defensible but impregnable. The full scheme, admittedly, took a little time to

emerge, but by the time that it faced its greatest challenge in
1810, all its elements were in place, namely an expanded and
revivified Portuguese regular army; a large force of militia
and home guards who could close in around an invading army
and deny it both intelligence and supplies; a scorched-earth policy that would devastate those areas through which any invaders
passed; and, finally, the construction of a series of defensive
lines blocking any access to the city of Lisbon. If this was a concept that was all but unbeatable, Wellington was equally
devastating on the attack. Here we can turn to the offensives
that he launched in the interior of Spain in 1812 and 1813.
Learning from his experiences during the Talavera campaign of
1809 that any attempt to launch a serious challenge to the Bonaparte kingdom of Spain would be likely to meet with massive
retribution on the part of the invaders, he so arranged matters
that when he repeated the experiment the French now found
themselves assailed on all sides by diversionary operations, of
which the most important relied on and exploited British control of the sea (a more superficial view is that the victories of
Salamanca and Vitoria were the product of a unique combin-
ation of regular and irregular warfare, but this takes matters a
little too far in so far as it relates to the Spanish guerrillas:
whilst Wellington was certainly aware of the *partidas* and
ready to seize upon any advantage that they might give him, he
was certainly not prepared to rely upon them, nor still less
make them an integral part of his operations).[30]

If Wellington was a strategic genius, he was also a master of
the art of making war at the operational level. As witness several excellent examples from the campaigns of 1813–14, then,
time and again French commanders found themselves being
outmanoeuvred, or even taken completely by surprise. First,
there is the march to Vitoria, Wellington conducting this in
such a way that the troops of Joseph Bonaparte were repeatedly outflanked and thereby forced to abandon position after
position without a fight, the result being that his opponents
arrived on the battlefield not just vulnerable to an attack from
the north as well as the west, but also badly demoralised (a further feature in this campaign was the rapid switch of the main

British base in the Peninsula from Lisbon to Santander, and, with it, an enormous reduction in the length of the Anglo-Portuguese army's line of communications). Second, there is the invasion of France on 7 October 1813, Wellington opting to cross the river that marked the border – the Bidássoa – by having his troops wade its very lowest reaches at low tide, thereby taking the powerful defensive positions that guarded the main crossings in the flank. And, third, there was the passage of the River Adour on 22 February 1814, whereby the difficult target of Bayonne was invested without resistance thanks to a surprise crossing of the river in the very dangerous waters at its mouth, whilst the main French army was drawn off far to the east. If these episodes are highlights of Wellington's command of the operational art, there are many other instances of the competent management of difficult situations, good examples that come to mind in this respect being the campaign of El Bodón in September 1811, the evacuation of Old and New Castile in the autumn of 1812 and the concentration of the badly wrong-footed Anglo-Dutch army at Quatre Bras in the wake of Napoleon's invasion of Belgium in June 1815. By contrast, meanwhile, there are very few instances where Wellington himself was caught out by his opponents: the Waterloo campaign is one, Marmont's counter-attack on the River Duero in July 1812 another and Soult's attempt to relieve Pamplona a year later a third. And only once can an instance be discovered in which Wellington's touch appears to have deserted him, this being the offensive that eventually led to the siege of Burgos: in the circumstances what was needed was a rapid thrust that would inflict a heavy defeat on the French forces that had advanced on Valladolid under Clausel, but the initial opportunity to do this was bungled by his subordinates, whilst Wellington thereafter showed a most uncharacteristic lethargy that was almost certainly the product of serious doubts as to the viability of his strategic situation.[31]

What makes the Burgos campaign all the more extraordinary is that in normal circumstances a particular strength of Wellington's was his ability to stick with a plan of action once he had adopted it and follow it through to its logical conclusions

no matter what the consequences. Consider, for example, the
refusal to succour the beleaguered Spanish fortress of Ciudad
Rodrigo in the summer of 1810 and, for that matter, the retreat
into central Portugal that followed. These actions, Wellington
knew, would cause outrage in political and military circles in
Spain and Portugal alike, dismay his own subordinates and
unsettle opinion back in Britain, whilst also inflicting the most
terrible consequences on the inhabitants of Beira. But nothing
would shake him from his course, and so the Anglo-Portuguese
army continued to retreat, first to Buçaco and then to the Lines
of Torres Vedras. And consider, too, Wellington's refusal to
commit his army to the support of the Spanish offensive that
led to the battle of Ocaña in November 1809: if this decision
was welcome to his army and the British government, both of
which had been left very wary of any further co-operation with
the Spaniards by the campaign of Talavera, Spanish fury knew
no bounds. In short, there was great strength of character in
Wellington's campaigning, and, mixed in with this, a streak of
real ruthlessness. Setting aside his readiness to see 100,000 or
more Portuguese civilians die of hunger or exposure in the service of his scheme for the defence of Portugal in 1810, the best
example of this tendency is probably the notorious Frasnes
memorandum. Stripping a complicated story down to its essen-
tials, what happened is that Wellington, who had in his own
words been 'humbugged' by Napoleon and was scrabbling to
get his scattered forces into position, persuaded Blücher to
make a stand at the town of Ligny by sending him a document –
the said Frasnes memorandum – that conveyed an impression
of the situation of the Anglo-Dutch army that was at best
extremely misleading, if not wholly mendacious.[32]

In so far as the conduct of campaigns, then, Wellington
was a dangerous opponent. However, if that was the case, on
the battlefield he was absolutely deadly. In the Peninsula he
triumphed, generally resoundingly so, over every French commander that came against him (a list that includes Victor,
Masséna, Marmont and Soult, all of whom numbered among
Napoleon's foremost subordinates), while at Waterloo he held
off Napoleon himself for a full day at the head of an army that

was not remotely comparable to the troops he had headed in Spain and Portugal. As for what lay at the root of this remarkable record, we may speak of three main factors. In the first place, there was Wellington's understanding of the strengths and weaknesses of the forces he commanded: if he on the one hand reinforced the skirmish line and restricted his gunners to the task of close support, he on the other held back the notoriously undisciplined British cavalry, the latter never being made use of in formations larger than a brigade and almost always employed in nothing more than local counter-attacks. In the second place, there was Wellington's use of ground, the best-known feature of this being the exploitation of reverse slopes as a means of keeping his men sheltered from French observation and fire alike, although we also should not forget the employment of villages, chateaux and farmhouses as improvised bastions or outworks. And, in the third place, there was, as we have seen, his belief that the best place to lead his army was in the very midst of the front line, this allowing him, as at Salamanca and Waterloo, personally to influence the flow of battle by ordering up reserves, launching surprise attacks or suddenly appearing at one crisis point or another to animate officers and men alike.[33]

To conclude, therefore, it is evident that Wellington's icy manner reflected a cool detachment that allowed him constantly to out-think the enemy, to exploit any accident of ground to the full, to maximise the strong points of his own forces and to get the best out of his officers and men: liked he may not have been, but respect and confidence he inspired in abundance. What is more, these talents could be turned, as the French learned to their cost at Salamanca, as much to the service of the attack as they could to that of the defence: whilst the stereotype that is fixed in our minds is that of French columns gallantly charging British lines, from 1812 onwards the majority of the battles fought by the Anglo-Portuguese army saw it on the attack, albeit frequently using much the same methods as it had done when confined to the defensive.

In Wellington, then, Britain truly had one of the great generals of all time, but what of his writings? We here come to one

of the most extraordinary archival resources to have been gen-
erated by the Britain of the nineteenth century: looking at the
sheer extent of the Wellington Papers, indeed, it is difficult to
imagine how their progenitor found time to wage war on the
French. Of what, however, do the many thousands of items
which make up his personal archive consist? A facile answer, of
course, would simply be Wellington's correspondence, but this
masks the important distinction that existed between 'official'
and 'unofficial' sources. Thus, 'official' documents were formal
communications usually called either dispatches or memoranda, of which the former constituted reports designed to
keep the government informed as to the progress of operations
in the Peninsula and at the same time act as a historical record
of events, and the latter responses to specific queries that Wellington had been asked to report on; to these categories could
be added the letters of serving members of the government
(usually the prime minister or the secretary of state for war and
the colonies) written in response to the dispatches sent to London by Wellington and the instructions which laid out his
orders, a secondary level of correspondence being constituted
by the similar documents that passed to and fro between Wellington and his subordinate commanders together with the
General Orders regularly issued from his headquarters, not to
mention the many letters written to the British ambassadors in
Lisbon and, as appropriate, Seville, Cádiz and Madrid. What
all these documents had in common was the possibility of publication in the official *London Gazette*, the result being they
were very much written with that in mind, one of the most
important principles here being that nothing should appear in
them that was not absolutely verifiable as fact by their authors.
However, 'official' was not the only category of document. On
the contrary, letters could be excluded from publication by vir-
tue of the simple act of marking them as being 'private', the net
result being the creation of a safe space in which correspond-
ents could express themselves far more freely, range over a far
wider range of issues and engage in speculation or simple
gossip, whilst there were, of course, a great many letters that

Wellington wrote as a private citizen, most notably to his four brothers, Richard, Gerald, William and Henry.[34]

Moving on from the form of Wellington's papers to their extent and content, the student who comes upon them for the first time cannot but be overwhelmed by their extent and content. The sheer number of letters written by the general beggar belief, and all the more so as they were invariably drafted by his own hand, and that at the end of a day which could have involved many miles of hard riding or fighting a desperate battle; meanwhile, as this work will reveal all too quickly, they also in many instances stretch to many pages and were often turned out at a rate of anything between five and ten a day. To quote Anthony Brett-James:

> The twelve volumes of *Dispatches* contain close on two and one half million words, most if not all of them written in Wellington's own hand. To these may be added half as many from the *Supplementary Despatches*. It is extraordinary that, in an age when a military commander disposed of no wireless, telephone, dictaphone, jeep, staff car, helicopter, armoured car or personal aircraft, he should have been able to get through so immense a volume of paper work and administration.[35]

As to the content, this is even more extraordinary. Ranging, as it does, from the political situation back in England through the conduct of the campaign, the myriad problems of Anglo-Spanish relations and the supply and discipline of the British army to the misconduct of individual officers, the letters constitute a unique record of one of the longest campaigns in British military history, of the British war effort in the struggle against Napoleon and, finally, of the internal workings of the British army at a moment when it was poised between the norms of two very different periods in its development. On top of all that, meanwhile, there is the insight that it provides into the mind of the greatest military commander that Britain has ever produced. To quote Brett-James once again, 'As one reads through the twelve portly volumes of Gurwood's edition of the

Dispatches, one cannot but be amazed by the variety of knowledge, the clarity of exposition, the attention to detail, the relentless supervision or inspiration of such manifold activities – military, administrative and diplomatic.'[36]

Here, then, is the Duke of Wellington as commander and the Duke of Wellington as author. Both figures are towering presences, but the one is probably much better known than the other. It is therefore very good to have this opportunity to highlight a pair of works – John Gurwood's *The Dispatches of Field Marshal the Duke of Wellington during his Various Campaigns in India, Denmark, Portugal, Spain, the Low Countries and France from 1789 to 1815* and the 2nd Duke of Wellington's *Supplementary Despatches, Correspondence and Memoranda of Field Marshal Arthur, Duke of Wellington* – that in their own way remain classics of nineteenth-century literature and, in the former instance, as the first such work ever to be produced in Britain, set the pattern for many future volumes. Yet in the end the commander and the author are not separate figures, but rather one and the same: whichever we look at, then, we see the same steely figure of austerity and rectitude that has come down to us as the 'Iron Duke'.

NOTES

1. G. R. Gleig, *The Life of Arthur, First Duke of Wellington* (London, 1862), p. 611.

2. Wellington's early life is covered by a host of biographies, of which the best is R. Muir, *Wellington: The Path to Victory, 1769–1814* (London, 2013).

3. The best guide to Wellington's campaigns in India is J. Weller, *Wellington in India* (London, 1972); meanwhile, for a general discussion of the period 1799–1808, see H. J. Davies, *Wellington's Wars: The Making of a Military Genius* (London, 2012), pp. 40–89.

4. P. Hofschroer, *Napoleon's Smallest Victory: The Duke, the Model-Maker and the Secret of Waterloo* (London, 2004). In this work, the author goes much too far – the evidence that Wellington went out of his way to persecute Siborne, for example, is less

than convincing – but it is at least clear that Wellington did not respond favourably to the model.

5.   Gleig, *Life of Arthur, First Duke of Wellington*, p. 613.

6.   For the story of Arthur Wellesley and Kitty Pakenham, see J. Wilson, *A Soldier's Wife: Wellington's Marriage* (Littlehampton, 1987).

7.   For the most recent exposition of this thesis, see J. Moon, *Wellington's Two-Front War: The Peninsular Campaigns at Home and Abroad, 1808–1814* (Norman, Oklahoma, 2011).

8.   R. Muir, *Britain and the Defeat of Napoleon* (London, 1996), p. 381.

9.   For Norman Ramsey, see N. Lipscombe, *Wellington's Guns: The Untold Story of Wellington and his Artillery in the Peninsula and at Waterloo* (Oxford, 2013), pp. 285–8; meanwhile, a full account of the Bevan affair may be found in A. Hunter, *Wellington's Scapegoat: The Tragedy of Lieutenant-Colonel Charles Bevan* (London, 2003).

10. Gordon has been much criticised for his actions, and there is no doubt that supplying Grey with confidential information that could have been used against Wellington and the British government was in and of itself an act of grave disloyalty. In fairness to Gordon his letters, which may be consulted in the papers of Lord Grey at the University of Durham, are rarely directly critical of Wellington and in fact express much sympathy for his difficulties. For all this, see R. Muir, 'Politics and the Peninsular army', in C. M. Woolgar (ed.), *Wellington Studies, IV* (Southampton, 2008), pp. 72–3, and R. McGuigan, 'Wellington's generals in Portugal, Spain and France, 1809–1814', in R. Muir et al (eds.), *Inside Wellington's Peninsular Army, 1808–1814* (Barnsley, 2006), pp. 178–9.

11. Lord Wellington to Lord Bathurst, Villa Toro, 4 October 1812, Second Duke of Wellington (ed.), *Supplementary Despatches, Correspondence and Memoranda of Field Marshal Arthur, Duke of Wellington* (London, 1858–72), VI, p. 440.

12. Lord Wellington to Lord Liverpool, Ciudad Rodrigo, 23 November 1812, J. Gurwood (ed.), *The Dispatches of Field Marshal the Duke of Wellington during his Various Campaigns in India, Denmark, Portugal, Spain, the Low Countries and France from 1789 to 1815* (London, 1852), VI, pp. 174–5.

13. Lord Wellington to H. Torrens, Freneda, 6 December 1812, ibid., VI, p. 201. Freneda is today called Fresnada.

14. For a recent discussion of the quality of the officer corps at regimental level, see A. Bamford, *Sickness, Suffering and the Sword:*

The British Regiment on Campaign, 1808–1815 (Norman, Oklahoma, 2013), pp. 60–83.

15. Even as it was, for many officers the incident remained a painful memory. Writing in the late 1820s, for example, Jonathan Leach of the Ninety-Fifth complained, 'That many regiments were guilty of great irregularities and did fall to pieces and lose their discipline during this disastrous defeat was too true, but it was no less so that many others maintained their order, good spirit and discipline throughout the retreat and left no men who were not either too badly wounded . . . to be brought on or were actually expiring from sickness, excessive fatigue, cold, wet and want of food. The charge was therefore thought by many people too sweeping' (*Rough Sketches in the Life of an Old Soldier during a Service in the East Indies, at the Siege of Copenhagen in 1807, in the Peninsula and the South of France in the Campaigns from 1808 to 1814 with the Light Division, in the Netherlands in 1815, including the Battles of Quatre Bras and Waterloo, with a Slight Sketch of the Three Years passed by the Army of Occupation in France* (London, 1831), p. 298).

16. e.g. Earl of Stanhope, *Notes of Conversations with the Duke of Wellington, 1831–1851* (London, 1889), pp. 13, 18.

17. H. Maxwell, *The Life of Wellington* (London, 1899), II, pp. 122–3.

18. Lipscombe, *Wellington's Guns*, pp. 389–98.

19. C. Oman, *A History of the Peninsular War* (Oxford, 1902–30), VI, p. 447.

20. 'Instructions for the movements of the army on the 21st June', Gurwood, *Dispatches*, VI, p. 536.

21. For an interesting view of the battle that is inclined to take issue with Wellington, see J. Meyer, 'The battle of Vitoria: a critical view', *Consortium on Revolutionary Europe Proceedings*, xx (1990), pp. 674–80.

22. C. Oman, *Wellington's Army, 1809–1814* (London, 1913), p. 151.

23. T. McGuffie (ed.), *Peninsular Cavalry General: The Correspondence of Lieutenant General Robert Ballard Long* (London, 1951), pp. 237–8.

24. For the gathering prior to the battle of the River Nivelle, see G. C. Moore-Smith (ed.), *The Autobiography of Sir Harry Smith, 1787–1819* (London, 1910), pp. 142–4. Note, however, that at Waterloo, Wellington's second-in-command, Lord Uxbridge, had no knowledge whatsoever of his intentions.

25. Even Wellington's better generals were not always to be relied

on: one thinks here of Craufurd's recklessness at the River Coa or the moral collapse experienced by Beresford when he found himself in command of a field army at Albuera.

26. R. Holmes, *Wellington: The Iron Duke* (London, 2002), p. 169.

27. See J. Black, 'Wellington in the context of long-term military history', in C. M. Woolgar (ed.), *Wellington Studies, II* (Southampton, 1999), pp. 35–6.

28. R. Muir, 'Wellington and the Peninsular War: the ingredients of victory', in Muir, *Inside Wellington's Peninsular Army*, p. 30. For an interesting essay on Wellington's use of light infantry, see A. Harman, ' "They decide not nor are they chiefly relied upon in battle": British rifles and light infantry in the Peninsular War', in P. G. Griffith (ed.), *Modern Studies of the War in the Peninsula, 1808–1814* (London, 1999), pp. 265–98.

29. For Wellington's artillery tactics, see B. P. Hughes, *Open Fire! Artillery Tactics from Marlborough to Wellington* (Chichester, 1983), pp. 62–74. The one area concerning artillery or, indeed, any other part of his army, where Wellington did adopt a wholly conservative position concerned the use of rockets. Offered a battery armed with such weapons for the campaign of 1813, Wellington accepted it, but told the secretary of state for war and the colonies, Lord Bathurst, that he had only done so because he wanted its horse teams. One suspects that this was a joke, but the fact is that, despite having encountered rockets in India, he was clearly no fan of the new weapon at this time. Yet, once again, what comes over is not principle but pragmatism: as he also told Bathurst, 'I do not want to set fire to any town, and I do not know any other use of the rockets' (Lord Wellington to Lord Bathurst, St Jean de Luz, 22 November 1813, Gurwood, *Dispatches*, VII, p. 158).

30. For a classic statement of the 'regular and irregular warfare' thesis, see D. G. Chandler, 'Wellington and the guerrillas', in D. G. Chandler (ed.), *On the Napoleonic Wars* (London, 1994), pp. 166–81; more nuanced is C. J. Esdaile, 'Wellington and the Spanish guerrillas: the campaign of 1813', *Consortium on Revolutionary Europe Proceedings*, xxi (1991), pp. 298–306. Meanwhile, Wellington's use of seapower may be studied in C. D. Hall, *Wellington's Navy: Seapower and the Peninsular War, 1807–1814* (London, 2004).

31. The brief campaign that preceded the siege of Burgos is not an episode that has received much coverage, whilst even writers of so solid a stamp as Oman have expressed their bewilderment as

to what was going on. For a detailed analysis, see C. J. Esdaile and P. Freeman, *The Siege: Burgos, 1812* (forthcoming).

32. Whether this incident actually occurred is uncertain as the only version of the Frasnes memorandum known to exist is one that was published by a Prussian military historian in 1876. If it did, however, the consequences of Blücher not having stood and fought at Ligny are too awful to contemplate. What is more serious, perhaps, is the allegation that the historical record was systematically doctored by both the insertion of fake documents and the suppression of a variety of real ones in defence of Wellington's reputation, and, in particular, the thesis that he was aware of the French advance at least twelve hours before the news is supposed to have disrupted the Duchess of Richmond's ball. At best, however, the evidence of a conspiracy is circumstantial, whilst, as for Wellington himself, the most that can be said is that, first, he was badly deceived by Napoleon, and, second, that even if he knew of Napoleon's advance much earlier than was actually the case, he took rather longer than might have been expected to make up his mind that it was not a feint but rather very much the real thing. What is certainly untrue is the suggestion implicit in Hofschroer's thesis that Wellington deliberately exposed the Prussians to defeat so as to reduce their share of the glory: convinced as the British commander was of the many failings of his 'infamous army', it is most unlikely that he would ever deliberately have risked fighting Napoleon essentially on his own. See P. Hofschroer, *1815: The Waterloo Campaign, I: Wellington, his German Allies and the Battles of Ligny and Quatre Bras* (London, 1998), pp. 331–51, and Davies, *Wellington's Wars*, pp. 231–5.

33. A major issue here is one of physical fitness. At Waterloo the 46-year-old Napoleon was fat and out of condition, whereas the 46-year-old Wellington was still as lean as he had ever been.

34. For a general discussion of the official correspondence, see C. M. Woolgar, 'Writing the dispatch: Wellington and official communication', in Woolgar, *Wellington Studies, II*, pp. 1–26.

35. A. Brett-James, *Wellington at War, 1794–1815: A Selection of his Wartime Letters* (London, 1961), pp. xxxv–xxxvi.

36. Ibid., p. xxix.

Further Reading

The literature on the Napoleonic Wars, the Peninsular War, Waterloo, the British army of the Napoleonic period and the life and times of the Duke of Wellington is overwhelming. In consequence, these notes can only encapsulate a few suggestions. Let us begin, however, with the Napoleonic Wars. Here those wishing for a detailed international history will be satisfied with my *Napoleon's Wars: An International History* (London, 2007), but for a lighter touch, see G. Rothenberg, *The Napoleonic Wars* (London, 2000). Equally, with respect to the Peninsular War, the most detailed overview is constituted by my *The Peninsular War: A New History* (London, 2002), but readers who want only an outline guide to the campaigns will be happier with D. Gates, *The Spanish Ulcer: A History of the Peninsular War* (London, 1986), though the numerous problems with the latter's maps mean that this is best consulted in conjunction with the truly sumptuous N. Lipscombe, *The Peninsular-War Atlas* (London, 2010). Last but not least, for those with access to them, the seven volumes of C. Oman, *A History of the Peninsular War* (Oxford, 1902–30) will be found to be indispensable.

For many British readers, of course, however unfortunate this may be, the term 'Peninsular War' will forever be associated with the campaigns of Sir John Moore and the Duke of Wellington. In consequence, there are numerous works that are billed as histories of the Peninsular War which in fact are nothing more than studies of the campaigns of the British army and its Portuguese allies. This is not, of course, to say that such books are necessarily bad, but, as is the case with the current volume, it does have to be remembered that they cover only a part of the conflict (it is very sobering here to remember that, according to the detailed lists of officer casualties drawn up in the early twentieth century by the French scholar Aristide Martinien, of the *c.* 37,000 French soldiers who died in combat in the Peninsular War, some 71 per cent fell in actions in which not a single British soldier was involved). At the same time, it has also to be said that the authors of such works almost never have access to Spanish or Portuguese, the consequence being that their works are invariably extremely Anglocentric. Nevertheless, if all that is wanted is an account of the operations of Moore and Wellington, they are an obvious place to go, the best examples of such works probably being J. Weller, *Wellington in the Peninsula* (London, 1962) and M. Glover, *The Peninsular War: A Concise Military History* (London, 1974). Also worth noting, meanwhile, are the numerous accounts of individual battles and campaigns, the best of which by far are G. Dempsey, *Albuera, 1811: The Bloodiest Battle of the Peninsular War* (Barnsley, 2008), and R. Muir, *Salamanca, 1812* (London, 1996). Finally, there is also another atlas I might mention in the shape of I. Robertson, *An Atlas of the Peninsular War* (London, 2010): wildly mistitled though this is, there is no doubt that its maps are a visual feast.

On the battle of Waterloo there is also an enormous literature. Standard 'British' views, of course, abound, including J. Naylor, *Waterloo* (London, 1963) and D. Howarth, *A Near-Run Thing: The Day of Waterloo* (London, 1968), while for two accounts that are as short as they are elegant, see J. Black, *The Battle of Waterloo: A New History* (London, 2010) and A. Roberts, *Waterloo: Napoleon's Last Gamble* (London, 2010). For the Prussians, see the tendentious P. Hofschroer, *1815: The Waterloo Campaign: The German Victory* (London, 1999), whilst the experience of the French army is dealt with by A. Field, *Waterloo: The French Perspective* (Barnsley, 2012). Finally, for two views that attempt a transnational perspective, see A. G. J. Chalfont, *Waterloo: Battle of Three Armies* (London, 1979) and A. Barbero, *The Battle: A New History of the Battle of Waterloo* (London, 2006).

The British army of the Napoleonic Wars is covered by many historians, many of them anxious to show that Wellington's famous comments about his men being the 'scum of the earth' were not merited. At the head of the list, at least in so far as the Peninsular War is concerned, must come C. Oman, *Wellington's Army, 1809–1814* (London, 1913), whilst general works also include M. Glover, *Wellington's Army in the Peninsula, 1808–14* (Newton Abbot, 1977) and P. Haythornthwaite, *The Armies of Wellington* (London, 1994). For social aspects of the army, meanwhile, see R. Holmes, *Redcoat: The British Soldier in the Age of Horse and Musket* (London, 2002), P. Haythornthwaite, *Redcoats: The British Soldiers of the Napoleonic Wars* (Barnsley, 2012) and E. Coss, *All for the King's Shilling: The British Soldier under Wellington, 1808–1814* (Norman, Oklahoma, 2010).

Last but not least, we come to the subject of Wellington himself. The definitive account, at least as far as the close of the Peninsular War, is now beyond doubt, R. Muir, *Wellington: The Path to Victory, 1769–1814* (London, 2013), but there are also several shorter works that concentrate on the military side of things, these including G. Corrigan, *Wellington: A Military Life* (London, 2001), R. Holmes, *Wellington: The Iron Duke* (London, 2002) and L. James, *The Iron Duke: A Military Biography of Wellington* (London, 1992). Finally, for a more analytical treatment, see H. J. Davies, *Wellington's Wars: The Making of a Military Genius* (London, 2012).

A Note on the Text

The letters in this volume have been selected from J. Gurwood (ed.), *The Dispatches of Field Marshal the Duke of Wellington during his Various Campaigns in India, Denmark, Portugal, Spain, the Low Countries and France from 1789 to 1815* (London, 1852), with one exception (see Sources, pp. 401–5), and the nineteenth-century spelling and punctuation have been retained so that the reader has the flavour of the original. Thus, we find: honor, labor and neighbourhood; to-day, to-morrow; antient, reconnaitre; and two words where we now use one, e.g. any one, every thing, head quarters. The footnotes are from Gurwood's text, as are the multiple asterisks on p. 162. The original text uses -is- spellings (e.g. organise, organisation) except in three instances which have been standardised (pp. 14, 31, 76)., but titles given as Visc. and Visct. have not been altered. A few instances of minor punctuation mistakes have been silently corrected.[1] Where Gurwood's text covered the identity of some officers and units by using long dashes, the names have been supplied in square brackets.

The maps use modern place name spellings.

NOTE

1   These are one comma changed to a full stop (in the middle of a sentence) and H. R, H. changed to H. R. H.; two missing full stops added; a missing accent and a missing hyphen (co oper-ated) added; and spaced hyphens in table headings closed up (non – commissioned). Titles given as Visc. and Visct. have not been changed.

Short Biographies of Recipients

ABERDEEN: George Hamilton-Gordon, 4th Earl of Aberdeen (1784–1860). A prominent Scottish landowner, Aberdeen was the elder brother of a favourite aide de camp of Wellington's who was killed at Waterloo. Until 1812 he concerned himself entirely with a strong interest in the classical world and the improvement of his Scottish estates, but in 1812 he entered the diplomatic service following the tragic death of his young wife. Quickly securing the post of ambassador to Vienna, he thereafter enjoyed a long career in public life, serving as foreign secretary (1828–30, 1841–6), secretary of state for war and the colonies (1835–6) and prime minister (1852–5).

BATHURST: Henry Bathurst, 3rd Earl Bathurst (1762–1834). After occupying a series of minor posts in the cabinets of William Pitt, the Duke of Portland and Spencer Perceval, Bathurst became Secretary of State for War and the Colonies in the Liverpool administration in May 1812.

BERESFORD: William Carr Beresford, 1st Viscount Beresford, 1st Duke of Campo Maior (1768–1856). The illegitimate son of the Marquess of Waterford, by 1808 Beresford had seen service in Corsica, India, Egypt, the Cape Colony and South America. Having served as a brigade commander in the campaign of La Coruña, in March 1809 he was appointed commander-in-chief of the Portuguese army and within a year had made it the equal of Wellington's British troops in training and discipline. As a field commander, however, he was less effective, as witness the state of nervous collapse to which he was reduced in the battle of La Albuera.

BOURKE: Sir Richard Bourke (1777–1855). In 1808 a lieutenant colonel attached to the quartermaster general's department, Bourke was posted to Portugal in 1809, and his knowledge of Spanish quickly saw him sent to the headquarters of Cuesta's Army of Extremadura as liaison officer. In the wake of the Talavera campaign, however, he went home to care for his wife, who had fallen gravely ill. Returning to the Peninsula in 1812, he took over from Sir Howard Douglas as British military agent in the city of La Coruña, occupying this post to the end of the war. A humane and enlightened individual of progressive views who favoured many radical causes, after 1814 he enjoyed a long and distinguished service career whose high point was his governorship of New South Wales (1831–7).

BURRARD: Sir Harry Burrard, 1st Viscount Lymington, (1755–1813). Competent and well liked, Burrard had commanded a brigade in the campaign in Holland in 1799, and in 1808 he was appointed second-in-command of the British forces that were being sent to Portugal, his immediate superior being Sir Hew Dalrymple. Arriving in Portugal on the eve of the battle of Vimeiro, Burrard, who all agree was an extremely affable individual, behaved with great courtesy towards Wellington and allowed him to fight the battle alone, but after the victory he imposed his authority and forbade any pursuit of the enemy. Though exonerated from any wrongdoing by the subsequent commission of inquiry, he was never given a further command.

CASTLEREAGH: Robert Stewart, 2nd Marquess of Londonderry (1769–1822). A leading Tory politician of the Revolutionary and Napoleonic era, Stewart is usually known by his courtesy title of Viscount Castlereagh (he did not succeed to the Marquessate of Londonderry until 1820). Secretary of State for War and the Colonies when the Peninsular War broke out in 1808, Castlereagh was friendly with Wellington, and did all he could to promote his interests with regard to the campaign of Vimeiro. Traditionally, he was thought to have played a major role in having Wellington reappointed to the command of the British forces in Portugal in April 1809, but it is now believed that it was rather George Canning who took the lead. Forced to resign from the Cabinet in September of the same year, Castlereagh returned to government in 1812 as foreign secretary, and as such became a leading figure in the diplomacy of the final years of the Napoleonic era and their immediate aftermath.

COOKE: Edward Cooke (1755–1820). A scion of a family of Buckinghamshire gentry, Cooke secured a series of posts in the government of Ireland and was a long-serving member of the pre-1801 Irish parliament. Staunch support of British policy in Ireland having won him the patronage of Lord Castlereagh, he was rewarded with the post of undersecretary of state for war and the colonies in the administrations of William Pitt (1804–6), and Lord Portland (1807–9), and then in 1812 with that of undersecretary of state at the Foreign Office.

CUESTA: Gregorio García de la Cuesta (1740–1812). A Spanish officer with a long record of distinguished service, particularly in the so-called 'War of the Convention' of 1793–5, Cuesta succeeded to the command of the Army of Extremadura in December 1808. Though bold and vigorous by nature, he was a mediocre commander and in March 1809 led his troops to a heavy defeat at Medellín. Wellington's chief Spanish counterpart during the campaign of Talavera, he was frequently at odds with the British commander, but in the battle itself he did very well, sending his allies a considerable amount of support at precisely the time that it was needed. Still suffering from the effects of a serious fall from his horse at Medellín, on 12 August he suffered a major stroke and had to retire from active service.

DALHOUSIE: George Ramsey, 9th Earl of Dalhousie (1770–1838). A Scottish aristocrat who had entered the army in 1788, Dalhousie saw service in the West Indies, Holland, Egypt and Walcheren before arriving in Spain in September 1811 as a lieutenant general. Given the command of the Seventh Division, however, he proved a failure, making a series of costly mistakes in the retreat from Burgos and the battles of Vitoria and the Pyrenees. He was later a singularly unsuccessful governor of what was then known as British North America.

FRERE: John Hookham Frere (1769–1846). A close friend of George Canning's from his days at the University of Cambridge,

Frere had taken a major role in the anti-Jacobin polemics of the 1790s, served for some time as a Tory MP and spent two years in Madrid as ambassador during the Peace of Amiens. Sent to Spain in October 1808 as Britain's first ambassador to the Patriot government, his efforts to persuade Sir John Moore to march to the defence of Madrid in the wake of the battles of Gamonal and Tudela attracted much criticism, and he was recalled to London, thereafter retiring into private life.

GORDON: Sir James Willoughby Gordon, 1st Baronet Gordon (1772–1851). After serving in a series of staff roles at the Horse Guards, in 1809 Gordon attained the post of commissary-in-chief to the British army. In May 1812 the patronage of the Prince of Wales, of whom he was a favourite, secured him appointment as Wellington's chief of staff, but he did not prove a success, and there was general relief when he returned to England on health grounds at the end of the year.

GRAHAM: Thomas Graham, 1st Baron Lynedoch (1748–1843). A minor Scottish nobleman, like many other lairds Graham took the opportunity afforded by the French Revolutionary Wars to increase both his standing in London and his patronage in the local community by raising a new regiment. That said, however, there is no doubting either his personal courage or his hatred of the French Revolution, and in 1809 his services obtained for him the rank of major general. Sent to Cádiz to take command of the Anglo-Portuguese division that had been sent to help secure the city against the French, he distinguished himself at the battle of Barrosa in March 1811. However, given a prominent role as a de facto corps commander in the campaigns of 1813, he proved something of a disappointment, while his handling of the British force sent to Holland in 1814 was little short of disastrous.

HARDINGE: Henry Hardinge, 1st Viscount Hardinge (1785–1856). The son of a Durham parson, Hardinge entered the army in 1799 and by 1808 had secured attachment to the quartermaster general's department, in which capacity he served in the campaigns of both Vimeiro and La Coruña. Seconded to the Portuguese army in 1809, he served as Beresford's deputy quartermaster general for most of the war, and particularly distinguished himself at the battle of Albuera in 1811. Remaining in the army after 1815, he enjoyed a highly distinguished military and political career, serving variously as chief secretary for Ireland (1830, 1834–5), secretary at war (1828–30, 1841–4), governor general of India (1844–8), master general of the ordnance (1852) and commander-in-chief (1852–6).

HOPE: Sir John Hope, 4th Earl of Hopetoun (1765–1823). A Scottish aristocrat, Hope entered the army in 1784 and in 1802 reached the rank of major general, having previously seen service in the West Indies, Holland and Egypt. Sent to Portugal with Sir John Moore in the summer of 1808, he played a prominent role in the campaign of La Coruña, but did not return to the Peninsula until the autumn of 1813. Appointed to the post of commander of the left wing of the Anglo-Portuguese army, he distinguished himself at the battles of the River Nivelle and the River Nive, and was given charge of the siege of Bayonne, only to be taken prisoner in a French sortie.

LIVERPOOL: Robert Banks Jenkinson, 2nd Earl of Liverpool (1770–1828). A Tory MP from a very early age, Jenkinson was originally known as Lord Hawkesbury and served under this name in every British government bar that of the 'Talents' from 1801 to 1809. Now Lord Liverpool, in September 1809 he became secretary of state for war and the colonies in the Perceval administration, and succeeded Perceval as prime minister when the latter was assassinated in May 1812.

PAGET: Sir Edward Paget (1775–1849). The fourth son of the 1st Earl of Uxbridge, Paget commanded the reserve at the battle of La Coruña and later lost an arm in the battle of Oporto. Sent back to England to recuperate, he did not return to the Peninsula until the summer of 1812. Given command of Wellington's cavalry, he was captured by the French during the retreat to Ciudad Rodrigo in November, and played no further part in the war. Staying on in the army after 1815, he served in a number of prestigious colonial appointments including that of commander-in-chief in India. He is often confused with his brother, Henry Paget, 2nd Earl of Uxbridge, who served with distinction in the campaign of La Coruña but never returned to the Peninsula on account of his elopement with the wife of Wellington's younger brother, Henry Wellesley.

RICHMOND: Charles Lennox, 4th Duke of Richmond (1764–1819). A close personal friend of Wellington's, famous as a duellist and cricketer alike, Richmond became lord lieutenant of Ireland in 1807. In 1815 he attached himself to Wellington's command in Belgium in an unofficial capacity and was present on the field at Waterloo until Wellington requested him to return to Brussels on the grounds that the danger was so great that it should not be endured by anyone except those whose duty forced them to brave it. His chief claim to fame, then, is the fact that it was his wife who put on the ball at which Wellington spent the evening of 15 June.

STUART: Charles Stuart, 1st Baron de Rothesay (1779–1845). A career diplomat who had joined the diplomatic service in 1801 and had experience in both Austria and Russia, Stuart was appointed as special envoy to Patriot Spain in the autumn of 1808, and went on to become ambassador to Portugal and, very unusually, a member of the Council of Regency that had been established to rule the country in the absence of its royal family in Brazil. In 1814 he was appointed ambassador to France, and escorted Louis XVIII into exile at the onset of the Hundred Days.

VILLIERS: John Charles Villiers, 3rd Earl of Clarendon (1757–1838). A scion of a family of impeccable aristocracy who had served for some years as a Tory MP, Villiers was appointed ambassador to Portugal in November 1808, and occupied the position with reasonable success, until he was replaced by Charles Stuart in January 1810.

WELLESLEY, H.: Henry Wellesley, 1st Baron Cowley (1773–1847). The youngest brother of the Duke of Wellington, Henry Wellesley was a career diplomat who by 1808 had served in a variety of posts in Sweden and India. Appointed ambassador to Spain in 1810, he saw out the rest of the Peninsular War in Cádiz and Madrid, and played a key role in Anglo-Spanish relations.

List of Maps

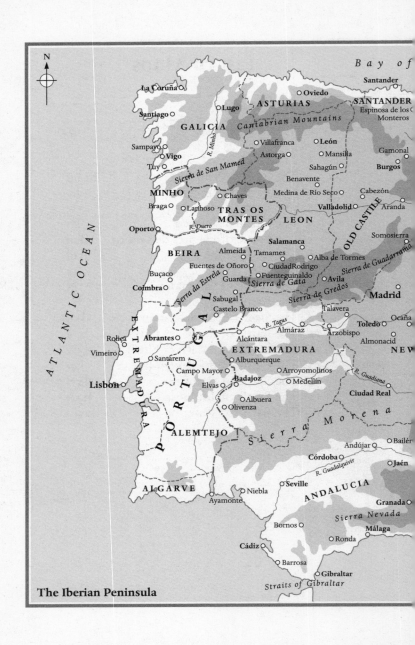

The Iberian Peninsula

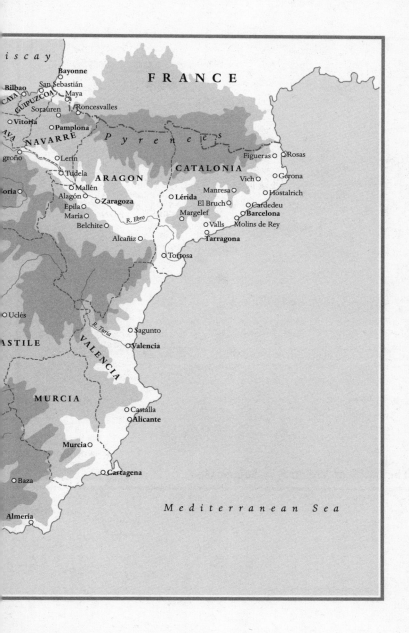

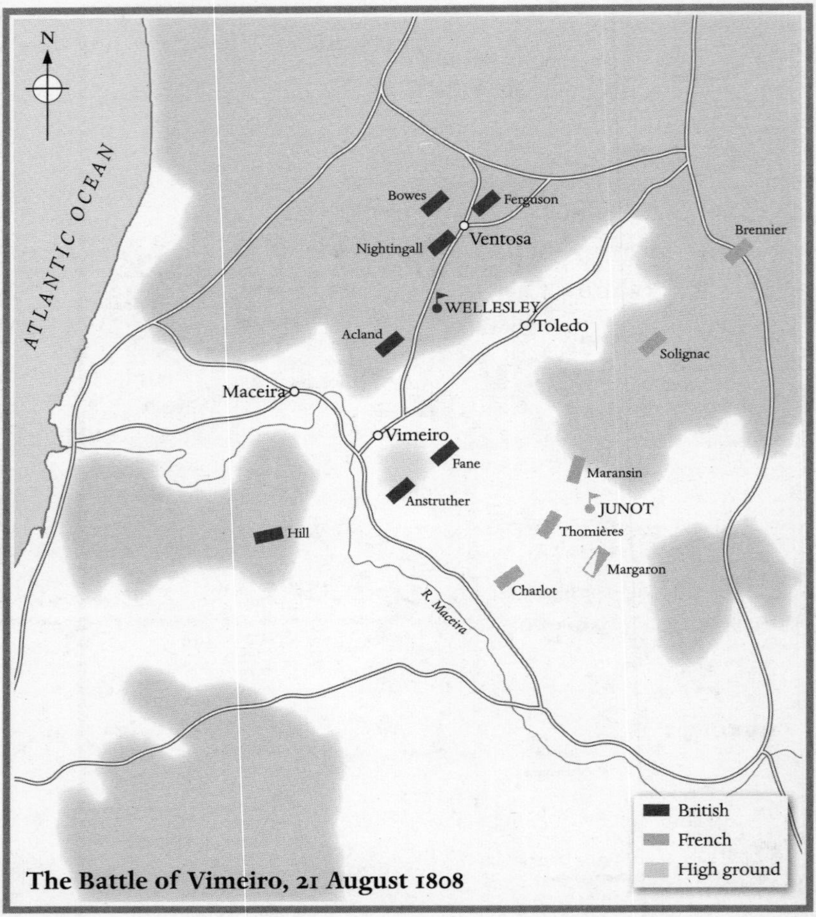
N
ATLANTIC OCEAN
Bowes
Ferguson
Nightingall
Ventosa
Brennier
WELLESLEY
Toledo
Acland
Solignac
Maceira
Vimeiro
Fane
Maransin
Anstruther
JUNOT
Hill
Thomières
Margaron
Charlot
R. Maceira
British
French
High ground
The Battle of Vimeiro, 21 August 1808

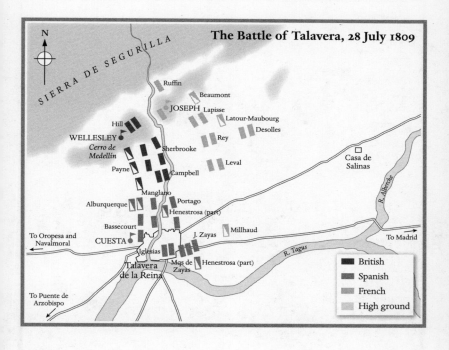

The Battle of Talavera, 28 July 1809

N

SIERRA DE SEGURILLA

Ruffin

Beaumont

JOSEPH Lapisse

Latour-Maubourg

Hill Desolles

WELLESLEY Rey

Cerro de Sherbrooke
Medellín

Payne Leval

Campbell

Casa de
Salinas

Manglano

Alburquerque Portago

Henestrosa (part)

Bassecourt

CUESTA J. Zayas Millhaud

To Oropesa and To Madrid
Navalmoral

Iglesias

R. Alberche

Talavera Mqs de Henestrosa (part)
de la Reina Zayas

R. Tagus

To Puente de
Arzobispo

British
Spanish
French
High ground

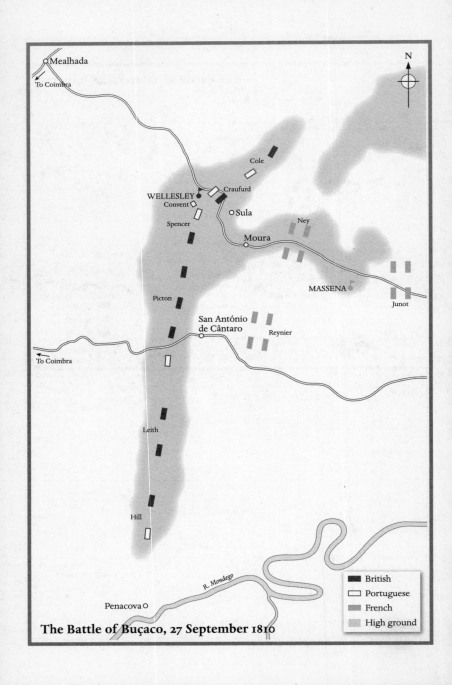

Mealhada

To Coimbra

N

Cole

Craufurd

WELLESLEY

Convent

Sula

Spencer

Ney

Moura

Picton

MASSENA

Junot

San António
de Cântaro

Reynier

To Coimbra

Leith

Hill

R. Mondego

British

Portuguese

French

High ground

Penacova

The Battle of Buçaco, 27 September 1810

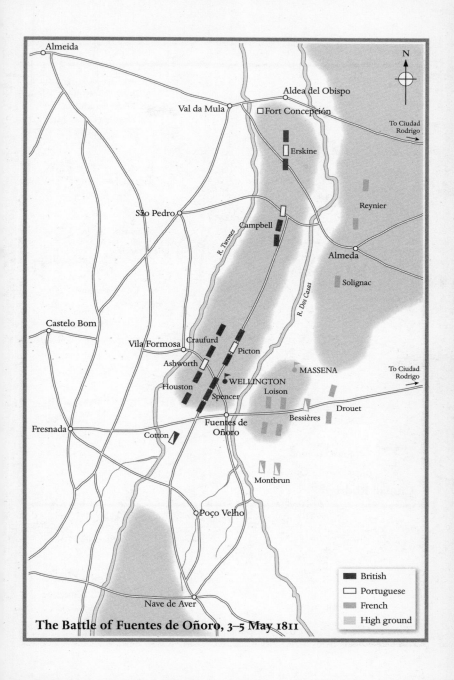

Almeida

Aldea del Obispo

Val da Mula

☐ Fort Concepción

To Ciudad
Rodrigo →

Erskine

Reynier

São Pedro

Campbell

Almeda

R. Turones

Solignac

R. Dos Casas

Castelo Bom

Craufurd

Vila Formosa

Picton

MASSENA

To Ciudad
Rodrigo →

Ashworth

●WELLINGTON

Loison

Houston

Spencer

Drouet

Bessières

Fresnada

Fuentes de
Oñoro

Cotton

Montbrun

Poço Velho

British
Portuguese
French
High ground

Nave de Aver

The Battle of Fuentes de Oñoro, 3–5 May 1811

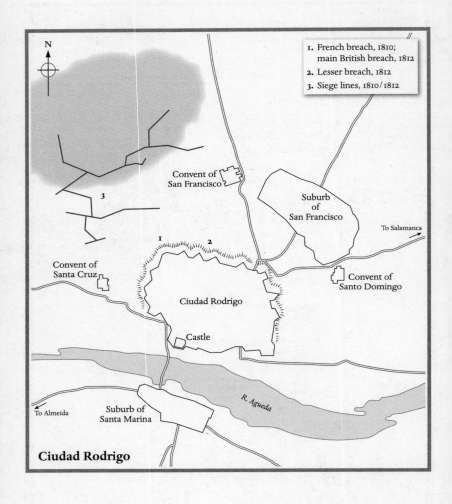

Ciudad Rodrigo

1. French breach, 1810; main British breach, 1812
2. Lesser breach, 1812
3. Siege lines, 1810/1812

Convent of San Francisco

Suburb of San Francisco

To Salamanca

Convent of Santa Cruz

Convent of Santo Domingo

Ciudad Rodrigo

Castle

R. Agueda

To Almeida

Suburb of Santa Marina

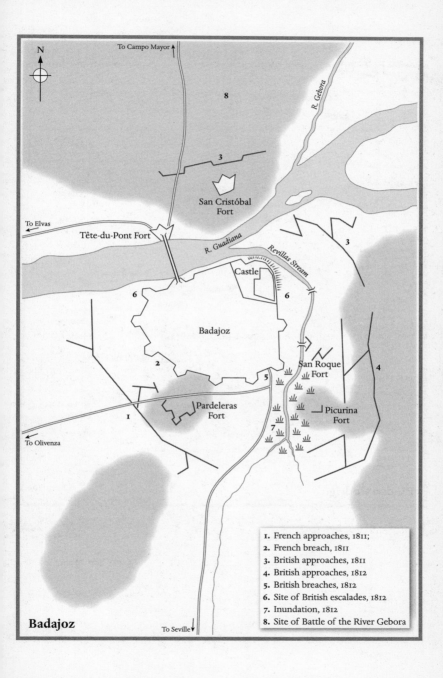

Badajoz

1. French approaches, 1811;
2. French breach, 1811
3. British approaches, 1811
4. British approaches, 1812
5. British breaches, 1812
6. Site of British escalades, 1812
7. Inundation, 1812
8. Site of Battle of the River Gebora

N

To Campo Mayor

R. Gebora

San Cristóbal Fort

To Elvas

Tête-du-Pont Fort

R. Guadiana

Revillas Stream

Castle

Badajoz

San Roque Fort

Pardeleras Fort

Picurina Fort

To Olivenza

To Seville

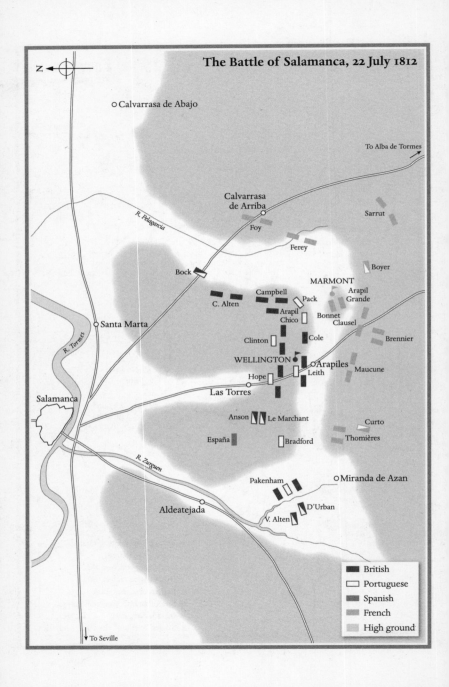

The Battle of Salamanca, 22 July 1812

N

o Calvarrasa de Abajo

To Alba de Tormes

R. Pelagarcia

Calvarrasa
de Arriba

Foy

Sarrut

Ferey

Boyer

Bock

MARMONT

Campbell

Pack

Arapil
Grande

C. Alten

Arapil
Chico

Bonnet

Clausel

Clinton

Cole

Brennier

WELLINGTON

Santa Marta

R. Tormes

Arapiles

Leith

Maucune

Hope

Las Torres

Anson   Le Marchant

Curto

España   Bradford

Thomières

Salamanca

R. Zurguen

Pakenham

o Miranda de Azan

D'Urban

Aldeatejada

V. Alten

To Seville

	British
	Portuguese
	Spanish
	French
	High ground

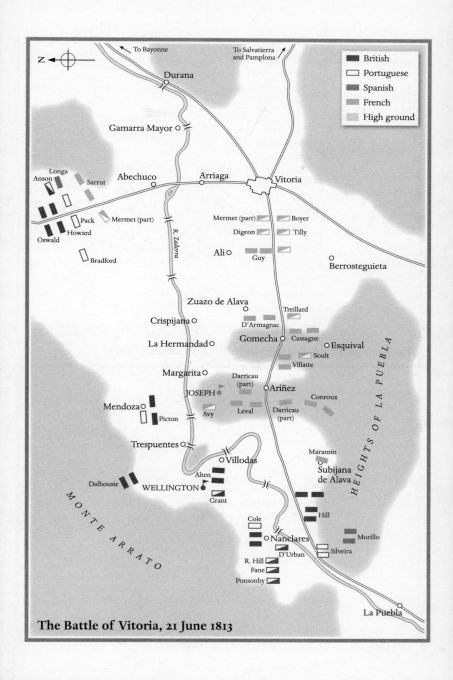

The Battle of Vitoria, 21 June 1813

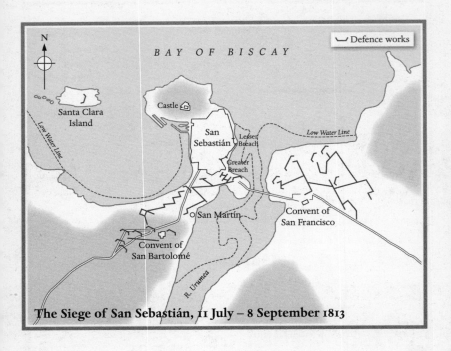

The Siege of San Sebastián, 11 July – 8 September 1813

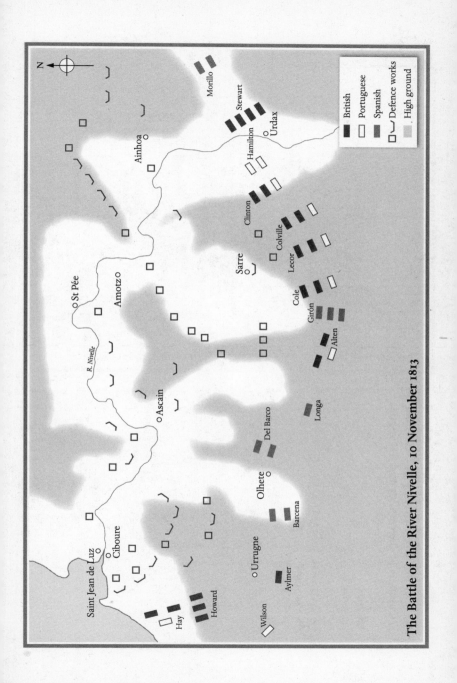

The Battle of the River Nivelle, 10 November 1813

N

Morillo
Stewart
Urdax
Hamilton
Ainhoa
Clinton
Colville
Sarre
Lecor
Cole
Girón
Alten
Amotz
St Pée
R. Nivelle
Longa
Ascain
Del Barco
Olhete
Barcena
Ciboure
Urrugne
Aylmer
Saint Jean de Luz
Wilson
Hay
Howard

British
Portuguese
Spanish
Defence works
High ground

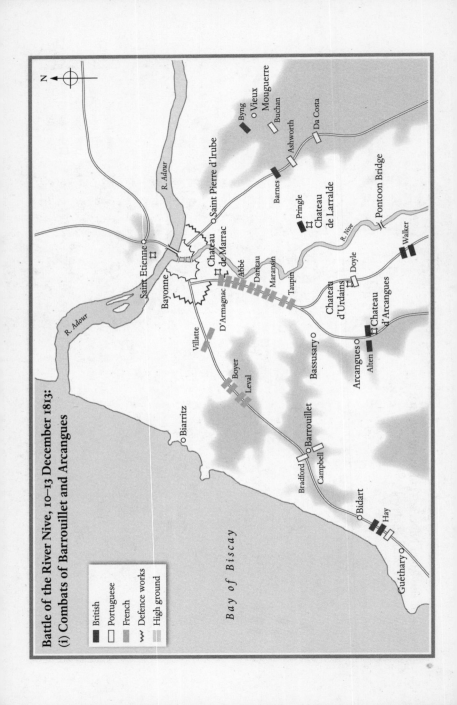

**Battle of the River Nive, 10–13 December 1813:
(i) Combats of Barrouillet and Arcangues**

N

Byng

○ Vieux
Mouguerre

Buchan

Da Costa

Ashworth

Barnes

Pringle

Chateau
de Larralde

Pontoon Bridge

R. Nive

Walker

R. Adour

Saint Pierre d'Irube

Chateau
de Marrac

Abbé

Darieau

Maransin

Taupin

Doyle

Saint Etienne

Chateau
d'Urdains

Chateau
d'Arcangues

Bayonne

D'Armagnac

R. Adour

Villatte

Bassusary ○

Arcangues ○

Alten

Boyer

Leval

○ Biarritz

Barrouillet

Bradford

Campbell

Bidart

Hay

Guéthary ○

Bay of Biscay

British

Portuguese

French

Defence works

High ground

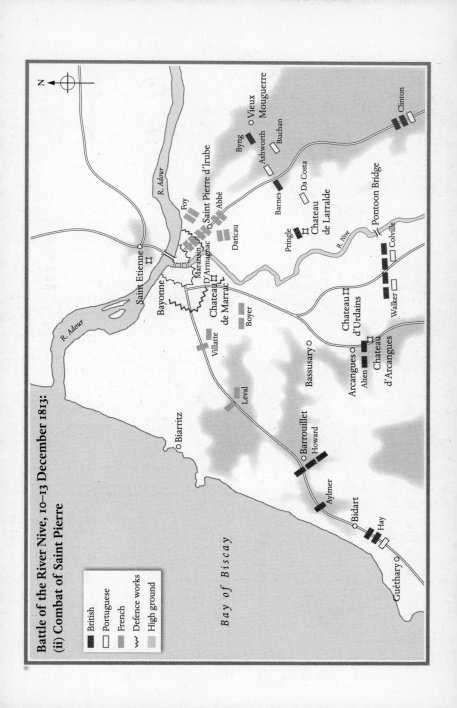

Battle of the River Nive, 10–13 December 1813:
(ii) Combat of Saint Pierre

N

British
Portuguese
French
Defence works
High ground

R. Adour

Vieux Mouguerre

Byng
Ashworth
Buchan
Da Costa
Barnes
Chateau de Larralde
Pringle
Clinton

Foy
Saint Pierre d'Irube
Abbé
Daricau

Pontoon Bridge

R. Nive

Colville

Maransin
D'Armagnac

Saint Etienne

Walker

Chateau d'Urdains

Bayonne

Chateau de Marrac
Boyer

Arcangues
Alten
Chateau d'Arcangues

Villatte

Bassusary

R. Adour

Leval

Biarritz

Barrouillet
Howard

Bay of Biscay

Aylmer
Bidart

Hay

Guéthary

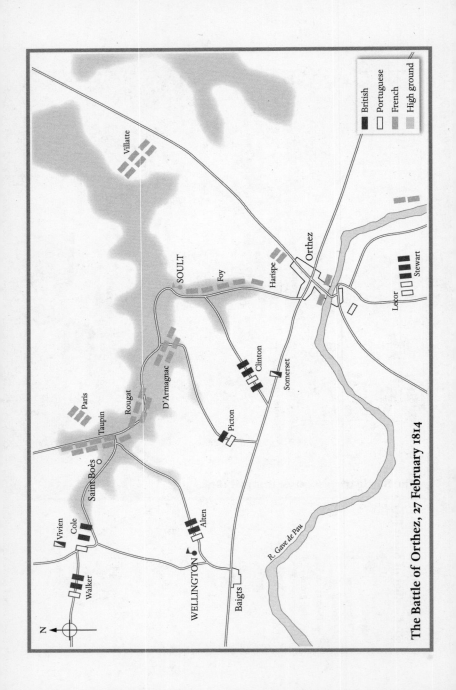

The Battle of Orthez, 27 February 1814

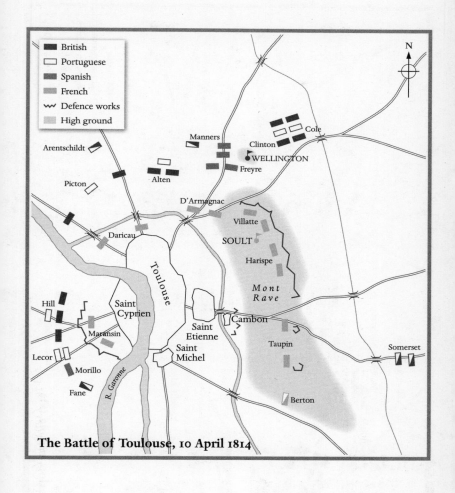

The Battle of Toulouse, 10 April 1814

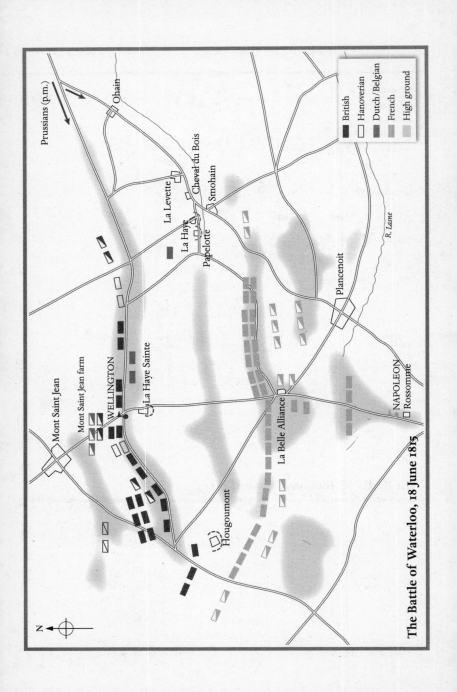

The Battle of Waterloo, 18 June 1815

Legend:
- British
- Hanoverian
- Dutch/Belgian
- French
- High ground

Labels: Prussians (p.m.), Ohain, La Levette, Cheval du Bois, Smohain, La Haye, Papelotte, Plancenoit, R. Lasne, Mont Saint Jean, Mont Saint Jean farm, WELLINGTON, La Haye Sainte, La Belle Alliance, Hougoumont, NAPOLEON, Rossomme

N

Military Dispatches

ONE

THE CAMPAIGNS OF 1808

The beginning of the Duke of Wellington's rise to fame may be dated very precisely. Having just been taken over by her supposed ally, France, in May 1808 Spain rose in revolt against the large numbers of troops that had been sent to occupy her soil by Napoleon. The British government, eager to turn this event to its advantage, resolved to send an army to the Peninsula under Sir Arthur Wellesley. Initially, the plan was to send the men concerned to northern Spain, but for a variety of reasons they were diverted to Portugal, the Spanish uprising having inspired a second insurrection in that country. No sooner had Wellesley sailed from Cork on 13 July than news arrived from Portugal that the French garrison there was much larger than had originally been reported. Further troops were therefore ordered out, but this in turn meant that the British force stood to become too large to be commanded by so junior a general as Wellesley, the latter being superseded by the governor of Gibraltar, Sir Hew Dalrymple. Determined to make what use he could of the opportunities that had been offered him, on 9 August Wellesley marched southwards from his landing place at Mondego Bay, and, having first gained a minor victory at Roliça, on 21 August defeated the French governor of Portugal, General Jean Andoche Junot, at Vimeiro. In this action Wellesley demonstrated many of the qualities that made him such a great battlefield commander, just as his infantry clearly demonstrated the superiority of its tactical system, but the result was nonetheless immense frustration. Had a general advance been ordered at the end of the battle, the result must have been total disaster for the French. But Wellesley's period of grace had run out, for a representative of Dalrymple turned up at just the wrong moment and refused to sanction the slightest forward movement, believing, first, that Wellesley was a rash commander who had only risen to prominence because of his political connections, and, second, that the French were receiving reinforcements. Still worse, when Junot sensibly decided that his best hope was to sue for peace, he was offered terms that were absurdly generous: he and his men were to be embarked for a French port in British ships and allowed to depart with their cannon, baggage and personal possessions without having to lay down their arms even in form. Formalised in the so-called Convention of Sintra, these terms caused considerable controversy. From King George III downwards, almost every sector of public opinion was appalled at the opportunity that appeared to have been thrown away, and on 21 September Dalrymple was recalled to London to account for his conduct, an equally disgusted Wellesley having already sailed for home. In view of the furore this might have been the end of Wellesley's career, but, such were his political connections that, whereas the inquiry set up to look into the matter damned Dalrymple with such faint praise that it was clear that he would never be offered a command again, the victor of Vimeiro escaped unscathed.

To Visct. Castlereagh.

Coruña, 21st July, 1808.

I arrived here yesterday, and I propose to go to sea again this day, to meet the fleet, which however has not yet appeared off the coast.

Since my arrival I have had frequent conversations with the Junta; and Mr Stuart, who arrived also yesterday, will send by this conveyance to Mr Canning an account of all the intelligence which we have received from them respecting the present situation of affairs in Spain. The general result, however, appears to me to be, that the whole of the Spanish nation, with the exception of the provinces of Biscay and Navarre, and those in the neighbourhood of Madrid, are in a state of insurrection against the French; that several French detachments in different parts of the country had been destroyed, viz., a corps under Lefebre, which had been attacked four times, near Zaragoza, in Aragon, particularly on the 16th and 24th June, a corps which I believe to have been under the command of Dupont; and it is said that Dupont was taken prisoner in an action fought between Andujar and La Carolina, before the 23rd June; and two corps defeated in Catalonia before the 19th June, one on its march to Montserrat, and the other to Zaragoza. The Catalonians have also got possession of the fort of Figueras, in the neighbourhood of Rosas, and have blockaded the French troops in Barcelona. As, however, the communication, which was never very perfect between one province and the others, has been impeded by the march and position of the French armies, and particularly by their late success at Rio Seco, to which I shall presently refer, the Junta have no official accounts of any of these actions; but they give credit to those they have received, copies of which will be transmitted to Mr Canning by Mr Stuart. He will also send the account which the Junta have received of the action at Rio Seco. The army of Castille and Galicia united was posted at that place, which is in the province of Valladolid; and their intention, as is stated, was either to have attacked the French corps under Marshal Bessières at Burgos, or to have marched upon Madrid. But I suspect that they would have confined their operations to the arrangement of the insurrection towards Madrid, and to cutting off the communication between the French troops stationed there and in Biscay and Navarre. It is said that they intended to attack Marshal Bessières on the 16th, but he attacked them on the 14th: his infantry was at first defeated by the Spaniards, with the loss of 7000 men; but afterwards his cavalry fell upon the left wing of the Spanish army, which consisted of the peasants of Castille, and defeated it.

I understand that the Spanish army, which consisted of 50,000 men, lost about 7000 men and 2 pieces of cannon; and

that they had taken and still retain 6 pieces belonging to the
French. The Spaniards retired either on that night or on the
next day to Benavente on the Esla. The worst of this action is,
that it has given the French possession of the whole course of
the Douro, and by obliging the Galician troops to retire from
Rio Seco, it has interrupted the communication between this
province and those to the southward and eastward.

I understood that the Junta were much alarmed when they
received the account of this defeat; but the arrival of the money
yesterday has entirely renewed their spirits; and I did not see
either in them or in the inhabitants of this town any symptom
either of alarm or doubt of their final success. The capture of
Santander by the French is not considered an event of any
importance; and it is said here that a corps was actually on its
march from the Asturias to retake that place.

It is impossible to convey to you an idea of the sentiment
which prevails here in favor of the Spanish cause. The difference between any two men is whether the one is a better or a
worse Spaniard, and the better Spaniard is the one who detests
the French most heartily. I understand that there is actually no
French party in the country; and at all events I am convinced
that no man now dares to show that he is a friend to the French.
The final success must depend upon the means of attack and
defence of the different parties, of the amount of which it is
impossible for me at present to form an opinion. If it be true
that the several French corps which I have above enumerated
have been cut off, it is obvious that Buonaparte cannot carry
on his operations in Spain, excepting by the means of large
armies; and I doubt much whether the country will afford subsistence for a large army, or whether he will be able to supply
his magazines from France, the roads being so bad and the
communications so difficult. If this be true, his object must be
to gain possession of the northern provinces, and this can be
done only by the invasion and possession of the Asturias. I
think, therefore, that our government ought to direct its attention particularly to that important point, and to endeavor to
prevail upon the Asturians to receive a body of our troops. I
consider this point so important, that I should not be surprised

if Buonaparte, finding that he cannot penetrate by land, should make an effort to reach the Asturias by sea; and I should therefore recommend to you to reinforce the squadron which is here, and let it cruise between Cape Ortegal and Santander. It might come here in case of a gale from the northward.

I suggested to the Junta to fit out the ships at Ferrol for this service; but they said it would divert their attention and their means from other more important objects; and that, although they were aware of its importance, they would prefer relying, for the naval defence which they might require, on the assistance to be received from Great Britain.

It will be necessary that you should assist all the Spanish provinces with money, arms, and ammunition. Notwithstanding the recent defeat of the Galician army, the Junta have not expressed any anxiety to receive the assistance of British troops; and they again repeated this morning that they could put any number of men into the field, if they were provided with money and arms; and I think that this disinclination to receive the assistance of British troops is founded in a great degree on the objection to give the command of their troops to British officers.

The Junta here have expressed a great wish to unite in a general Cortes with the other provinces; but, in addition to the difficulties which must attend the adoption of this measure, from the position of the French armies, I understand that there are others referable to the desire which each of the kingdoms of which Spain is composed has, that the Cortes should be established within itself.

If the French should be obliged to quit Madrid, it is probable that this difficulty would be overcome; and till that period, or until the strength of the French army shall have been driven from the centre of Spain, I am not quite certain that it is not as well that each of the kingdoms should be governed by its own Junta. I am convinced that the general zeal and exertion of each are greater, at present, than would be manifested if the whole Kingdom were under the direction of one body.

In respect to my own operations, I find that Junot has collected, it is supposed, 12,000 men at Lisbon; and the French still hold Almeida, and other points in Portugal, with 3000 more. The 3 northern provinces of Portugal are in a state of insurrection, and there is a Portuguese army at Oporto, to join which 2000 Spanish troops have marched from Galicia, and they will arrive there about the 24th or 25th.

From the intelligence which I have received here, I can form no opinion whether I shall be joined by Gen. Spencer or not. Mr Stuart heard from the *Brilliant*, on his passage, that Gen. Spencer had left Cadiz, after the Spaniards had got possession of the French fleet, and had gone to Ayamonte, at the mouth of the Guadiana, to stop the progress of a French corps which was coming by that route from Portugal into Andalusia. They had heard nothing here of this movement; but they had heard a report that 5000 British troops had been in Gen. Castaños' army, and had behaved remarkably well, but on what occasion, and what troops, they did not know.

I understand that there is a Spanish corps of 20,000 men in Estremadura, at Almaraz, on the Tagus, which corps will impede the communication between Junot and the army at Madrid; and it may be reasonably expected that the number of French now in Portugal will be the number which we shall have to contend with. The Junta express great anxiety respecting my operations in Portugal, and have strongly recommended me not to attempt to land at Lisbon, or in the neighbourhood of the French army. They urge, as an objection to this measure, that I shall thereby entirely lose the advantage of the co-operation of the Spanish and Portuguese forces at Oporto, who will not be able to approach Lisbon till they have heard that I have disembarked; and they recommend that I should disembark at Vigo or Oporto, and bring the allies with me to Lisbon. It is impossible for me to decide upon this or any other measure till I shall know more of the situation of affairs. I should have no doubt of success, even without Gen. Spencer's assistance, or that of the allies, if I were once ashore; but to effect a landing in front of an enemy is always difficult, and I shall be inclined to land at a distance from Lisbon.

I now intend to look for the fleet this night, and if we should not find it, I shall leave one of Capt. Hotham's squadron upon the rendezvous, with directions for Malcolm to follow me, and go in the *Crocodile* to Oporto, where I shall be able to decide upon the measures which I shall adopt.

To Visct. Castlereagh.

H. M. S. *Crocodile*, off Oporto, 25th July, 1808.

I avail myself of the opportunity of the return of the *Peacock* to England, to inform you that I sailed from Coruña, as I told you I should, on the night of the 21st, and joined the fleet the next day, and arrived here yesterday, in the *Crocodile*: the fleet are now coming on.

All the provinces to the north of the Tagus, with the exception of the country immediately about Lisbon, are in a state of insurrection against the French, and the people are ready and desirous to take arms, but, unfortunately, there are none in the country; indeed, I may say, none to arm the troops which the Bishop of Oporto and the Junta of this place have assembled. They have at present a corps of about 5000 men, regular troops and militia, including 300 cavalry at Coimbra, armed with 1000 muskets got from the fleet, fowling pieces, &c., and 12,000 peasantry, mostly unarmed, I believe. The regular troops are composed of detachments of different corps, and cannot in any respect be deemed an efficient force. Besides these, there are 300 Spanish infantry, about 1500 regular Portuguese infantry, and some militia volunteers and peasantry, here.

The corps of Spanish infantry, which had commenced its march from Galicia, as I informed you in my last letter, is not yet arrived. It was stopped on the frontier, because there were no orders at Braganza to allow it to enter the country; and, although the Bishop expects it, the Portuguese officers appear to think that the success of the French against the Spanish army on the 14th has diverted this corps from the cause in this country. Under all the circumstances, I have determined to take forward the Portuguese corps now at Coimbra, and to collect

every thing else upon this place. The Bishop is much alarmed
respecting the success of the French in the province of Valladolid. It is reported here that there has been a second action; and
I saw a letter last night from the Bishop of Santiago, stating
that Gen. Cuesta, the Castillian Commander in Chief, had
informed him that he had gained a victory in this action, and
had actually in his camp 1500 horses taken from the French
cavalry; and it is, at the same time, reported that the French are
actually in Benavente. It is impossible to learn the truth.

I have received a letter from Sir C. Cotton, of the 9th inst.,
in which he advises me to leave the fleet to windward, and to
go down to the Tagus to confer with him. He has occupied a
post with 400 marines at Figueira on the Mondego, in front of
Coimbra, at which place, or at Peniche, he thinks it will be
most advisable for me to land. I therefore propose to send the
fleet to the Mondego to make all the arrangements for landing;
to go down to communicate with the Admiral; and by the time
I shall have returned, all will be ready to go on shore, either at
the Mondego or Peniche, or farther to the southward if the
Admiral thinks it advisable.

I have heard nothing positive of Gen. Spencer, excepting that
he was with Sir C. Cotton in the beginning of this month, his
corps having been landed, merely to preserve the health of the
men, near Cape St Mary's. I conclude, therefore, that I shall
find him with the fleet off the Tagus. The French corps is concentrated at or about Lisbon, and is said to consist of from
13,000 to 14,000 men. Sir C. Cotton says they are adding to
the fortifications of the town, of a citadel within the town, and
of Fort St Julian.

The measures to be adopted for this country are to supply it
with arms and money. I saw a statement last night, from which
it appears that they could get together 38,000 men with ease, if
they had arms or money to pay them. If I should find the troops
at Coimbra to be worth it, I propose to arm them.

To Visct. Castlereagh.

H. M. S. *Donegal*, off Figueira, 1st Aug. 1808.

I have the honor to inform you, that when on my passage from the fleet to the mouth of the Tagus, I fell in with H. M. S. *Plantagenet*, on the 26th July, in which was embarked Capt. Cooke, of the Coldstream Guards, who delivered to me the dispatches from Gen. Spencer, of which I enclose copies, by which I was informed that that officer had landed at Puerto de Sta Maria, and had determined to remain in the province of Andalusia. After consulting with Sir C. Cotton upon the situation of affairs in Portugal and Spain, I thought it proper to send Gen. Spencer orders to re-embark his whole corps and to join me, unless he should be engaged in any active operation, the relinquishment of which he should deem detrimental to the cause of the Spaniards. As Gen. Spencer, in his letter, and more particularly in a verbal message by Capt. Cooke, represented the great distress for money which was felt by the Junta of Seville, I desired him to draw upon England for £100,000, and to pay that sum to the person they should appoint to receive it.

I have the honor to enclose copies of the letters which I have written to Gen. Spencer upon this occasion, in which the reasons which induced me to give these orders are sufficiently detailed; and they will, I hope, justify me for having given them, without being under the necessity of troubling your Lordship with my reasons for thinking that it was probable that Dupont was not sufficiently strong for Gen. Castaños; that Gen. Spencer's corps was useless at Cadiz, while the operations of mine in Portugal were cramped for want of its assistance; that a junction of the two corps was necessary to enable either to perform any effectual service; and that, in the general situation of affairs in Spain, as well as in Portugal, it was most important to drive the French out of Portugal.

The orders which I gave appeared to me to be entirely in conformity with the intentions and object of His Majesty's government, and to be consistent with those which your Lordship gave to the General in your letter of the 30th June; and although it appears by your Lordship's dispatch of the 15th July, which I received here from Lord Burghersh on the 30th, that it was His Majesty's intention to assist the Spanish nation with a body of his troops in Andalusia, I did not think it proper to recall those which I had sent to Gen. Spencer on the 26th. The second orders would not have reached him till the 3d or 4th of Aug., when he would have carried the first into execution, and would probably be far advanced on his passage; and I received accounts on my arrival here, on the same day, to which I gave credit, that Gen. Castaños had defeated Gen. Dupont on the 20th inst., and there was no longer any immediate necessity for the assistance of the British corps in that quarter of Spain. These accounts have been still further confirmed by others arrived this day, from which it appears that Gen. Dupont, and all the French troops to the southward of the Sierra Morena, had surrendered, on condition, that they should be sent to France by sea.

The information of the state of the enemy's force in Portugal, communicated to me by Gen. Spencer (which, however exaggerated the accounts he had received may be, deserve attention), and the expectation held out by your Lordship, that a reinforcement would arrive here at an early period, have necessarily induced me to delay the commencement of the operations of the troops under my command till the arrival of the corps from England, or of Gen. Spencer. The General will have received my letter of the 26th, I hope, on the 28th, and I expect that he will be ready to sail by the 31st. The length of his passage to the Tagus, and to this place, must then depend upon the winds, which have blown from the southward since the 28th.

The enemy's position in the neighbourhood of the Tagus appears so strong, that it is considered impracticable to make a landing in that quarter, without diverting the attention by an attack to the northward. The plans of attack on Cascaes Bay would fail, because it is stated to be impossible to approach the coast sufficiently with the large ships to silence the Fort of Cascaes, and the other works erected for the defence of the bay;

and although the ships of war might be able to pass Fort St Julian, the Fort Bugio, and the other works by which the entrance of the Tagus is defended, it is not imagined that these forts could be silenced by their fire, so as to enable the troops to land at Paco d'Arcos, as was proposed. Between Cascaes and the Cape Roca, and to the northward of Cape Roca, there are small bays, in which small bodies of men could be disembarked in moderate weather. But the surf on the whole of the coast of Portugal is great, and the disembarkation in these bays of the last divisions of the troops, and of their necessary stores and provisions, would be precarious, even if a favorable moment should have been found for the disembarkation of the first. The vicinity of the enemy, and the want of resources in the country in the neighbourhood of the Rock of Lisbon, for the movement of the necessary stores and provisions for the army, would increase the embarrassment of a disembarkation in that quarter. All these considerations, combined with a due sense of the advantages which I shall derive from the co-operation of the Portuguese troops, have induced me to decide in favor of a landing to the northward.

There is no place to the northward of Lisbon which would at all answer for a place of disembarkation nearer than Mondego, excepting possibly Peniche. But the fort upon that peninsula is strong, and is occupied by the enemy with a sufficient garrison, and could not be taken without heavy ordnance; and the ordnance and ammunition, which your Lordship informed me in your dispatch of the 30th June was to sail from the river on that day, has not yet arrived.

I shall consider the possession of the harbour and city of Lisbon as the immediate object of our operations, which must be attained by that of the forts by which the entrance of the Tagus is guarded. It is probable that it will be necessary to attack two of these forts, Cascaes and St Julian, with heavy ordnance; and it is obvious that the enemy will not allow us to undertake those operations till he shall have been driven from the field.

The positions which he would take for the defence of these posts must be all turned from the heights to the northward of

Lisbon, and, indeed, unless prevented by our possession of these heights, the enemy would have it in his power to renew the contest in different positions, until he should be driven into Lisbon or retire. The last will be rendered difficult, if not impossible, excepting in boats across the Tagus, by the adoption of the line of attack by the heights to the northward, which I also prefer, as being more likely to bring the contest to the issue of a battle in the field.

I have this day commenced my disembarkation in the river of Mondego, because I was apprehensive that any further delay might tend to discourage the country, and because I shall experience greater facilities in making the arrangements for the movement and supply of the army when it shall be on shore than while it shall continue afloat. The landing is attended with some difficulties even here, and would be quite impossible if we had not the cordial assistance of the country, notwithstanding the zeal and abilities of the officers of the navy; and in all probability Gen. Spencer and the reinforcements from England will arrive before the troops at present here shall be on shore: if either should arrive, I propose to commence my march.

I have the honor to inform your Lordship that I have issued 5000 stands of arms for the purpose of arming the Portuguese regular troops, who, it is intended, should co-operate with the British army in the attack on the French in this country.

To Visct. Castlereagh.

H. M. S. *Donegal*, 1st Aug. 1808.

I have nothing to add to my public letter of this date, excepting to tell you I have reason to believe Gen. Spencer's account of the French force in Portugal is exaggerated. I intended to make the attack with my own corps, aided by the Portuguese, if it should have turned out that he could not join me, according to my orders of the 26th July, until I received your letter of the 15th, in which you announce the reinforcements; and I shall now march on, of course, as soon as one of the corps shall arrive.

Pole and Burghersh have apprised me of the arrangements for the future command of this army; and the former has informed me of your kindness towards me, of which I have experienced so many instances, that I can never doubt it in any case. All that I can say upon that subject is, that whether I am to command the army or not, or am to quit it, I shall do my best to insure its success; and you may depend upon it that I shall not hurry the operations, or commence them one moment sooner than they ought to be commenced, in order that I may acquire the credit of the success.

The government will determine for me in what way they will employ me hereafter, whether here or elsewhere. My opinion is, that Great Britain ought to raise, organise, and pay an army in Portugal, consisting of 30,000 Portuguese troops, which might be easily raised at an early period; and 20,000 British, including 4000 or 5000 cavalry. This army might operate on the frontiers of Portugal in Spanish Estremadura, and it would serve as the link between the kingdoms of Galicia and Andalusia: it would give Great Britain the preponderance in the conduct of the war in the Peninsula; and whatever might be the result of the Spanish exertions, Portugal would be saved from the French grasp. You know best whether you could bear the expense, or what part of it the Portuguese government would or could defray. But if you should adopt this plan, you must send everything from England; arms, ammunition, clothing, and accoutrements, ordnance, flour, oats, &c. These articles must find their way to the frontier, partly by the navigation of the Douro and Tagus, and partly by other means.

P. S. The ground I have for believing that Castaños has beaten Dupont is, that I have read a copy of his dispatch to the Junta of Seville, published in the Coimbra gazette. Its purport is nearly what I have stated in my dispatch, excepting only that Dupont may have surrendered with his army, and that the French force in the Sierra Morena, not engaged in the action of the 20th, may have capitulated, on condition of being sent to France by sea. I do not understand Portuguese well enough to

say whether this is not the case, and somebody has taken away
the gazette.

2d P. S. You will observe that I have exceeded my authority
in ordering Spencer to draw for £100,000 upon England, and
to advance that sum to the Junta at Seville; of which act I hope
you will see the propriety, and that you will send me an approbation of it. I must mention, however, that since I did it, I have
heard that Sir H. Dalrymple had refused to advance them any
money, although he had an authority.

To Lieut. Gen. Sir H. Burrard, Bart.

Lavos, 8th Aug. 1808.

Having received instructions from the Sec. of State, that you
were likely to arrive on the coast of Portugal with a corps of
10,000 men, lately employed in the north of Europe under the
orders of Sir J. Moore, I now submit to you such information
as I have received regarding the general state of the war in Portugal and Spain, and the plan of operations which I am about
to carry into execution, in obedience to the orders of the Sec. of
State.

The enemy's force at present in Portugal consists, as far as I
am able to form an opinion, of from 16,000 to 18,000 men, of
which number there are about 500 in the Fort of Almeida,
about the same number in Elvas, about 600 or 800 at Peniche,
and 1600 or 1800 in the province of Alentejo, at Setuval, &c.;
the remainder are disposable for the defence of Lisbon, and are
in the forts of St Julian and Cascaes, in the batteries along the
coast as far as the Rock of Lisbon, and in the old citadel of
Lisbon, to which the enemy have lately added some works.

Of the force disposable for the defence of Lisbon, the enemy
have lately detached a corps of about 2000 men under Gen.
Thomière, principally, I believe, to watch my movements, which
corps is now at Alcobaça; and another corps, of 4000 men,
under Gen. Loison, was sent across the Tagus into Alentejo, on

the 26th of last month: the object of which detachment was to disperse the Portuguese insurgents in that quarter; to force the Spanish corps, consisting of about 2000 men, which had advanced into Portugal as far as Evora from Estremadura, to retire; and thus to be enabled to add, to the force destined for the defence of Lisbon, the corps of French troops which had been stationed at Setuval and in the province of Alentejo. At all events, Loison's corps will return to Lisbon, and the French corps disposable for the defence of that place will probably be about 14,000 men, of which at least 3000 must be left in the garrison and forts on the coast and in the river.

The French army under Dupont in Andalusia surrendered, on the 20th of last month, to the Spanish army under the command of Gen. Castaños; so that there are now no French troops in the south of Spain.

The Spanish army of Galicia and Castille, to the northward, received a check at Rio Seco, in the province of Valladolid, on the 14th July, from a French corps supposed to be under the command of Gen. Bessières, which had advanced from Burgos.

The Spanish troops retired on the 15th to Benavente, and I understand there has since been an affair between the advanced posts in that neighbourhood; but I am not certain of it, nor am I acquainted with the position of the Spanish army, or of that of the French, since the 14th July. When you shall have been a short time in this country, and shall have observed the degree to which the deficiency of real information is supplied by the circulation of unfounded reports, you will not be surprised at my want of accurate knowledge upon these subjects.

It is, however, certain that nothing of importance has occurred in that quarter since the 14th July, and from this circumstance I conclude that the corps of Marshal Bessières attacked the Spanish army at Rio Seco, solely with a view to cover the march of King Joseph Bonaparte to Madrid, where he arrived on the 21st July.

Besides the defeat in Andalusia, the enemy, as you may probably have heard, have been beaten off in an attack upon Zaragoza, in Aragon; in another upon the city of Valencia (in both of which actions it is said that they have lost many men);

and it is reported, that in Catalonia two of their detachments
have been cut off, and that they have lost the Fort of Figueras
in the Pyrenees, and that Barcelona is blockaded: of these
last mentioned actions and operations I have seen no official
accounts, but the report of them is generally circulated and
believed. At all events, whether these reports are founded or
otherwise, it is obvious that the insurrection against the French
is general throughout Spain; that large bodies of Spaniards are
in arms (among others, in particular, an army of 20,000 men,
including 4000 cavalry, at Almaraz, on the Tagus, in Estremadura); that the French cannot carry on their operations by
means of small corps. I should imagine from their inactivity,
and from the misfortunes they have suffered, that they have not
the means of collecting a force sufficiently large to oppose the
progress of the insurrection and the efforts of the insurgents,
and to afford support to their different detached corps; or that
they find they cannot carry on their operations, with armies so
numerous as they must find it necessary to employ, without
magazines.

In respect to Portugal, the whole Kingdom, with the exception of the neighbourhood of Lisbon, is in a state of insurrection
against the French; their means of resistance are, however, less
powerful than those of the Spaniards. Their troops have been
completely dispersed, their officers had gone off to Brazil, and
their arsenals pillaged, or in the power of the enemy. Their
revolt, under the circumstances in which it has taken place, is
still more extraordinary than that of the Spanish nation. The
Portuguese may have, in the northern parts of the Kingdom,
about 10,000 men in arms, of which number 5000 are to march
with me towards Lisbon; the remainder, with a Spanish detachment of about 1500 men, which came from Galicia, are
employed in a distant blockade of Almeida, and in the protection of Oporto, which is at present the seat of government. The
insurrection is general throughout Alentejo, and Algarve to the
southward, and Entre Minho e Douro, and Tras os Montes,
and Beira, to the northward; but for want of arms the people
can do nothing against the enemy.

Having consulted Sir C. Cotton, it appeared to him and to

me, that the attack proposed upon Cascaes Bay was impracticable, because the bay is well defended by the Fort of Cascaes, and the other works constructed for its defence, and the ships of war could not approach sufficiently near to silence them. The landing in the Paço d'Arcos in the Tagus could not be effected without silencing Fort St Julian, which appeared to be impracticable to those who were to carry that operation into execution.

There are small bays within, and others to the northward of the Rock of Lisbon, which might admit of landing troops; but they are all defended by works which must first have been silenced: they are of small extent, and but few men could have landed at the same time: there is always a surf on them, which affects the facility of landing at different times so materially, as to render it very doubtful whether the troops first landed could be supported in sufficient time by the others; and whether the horses for the artillery and cavalry, and the necessary stores and provisions, could be landed at all. These inconveniences attending a landing in any of the bays near the Rock of Lisbon would have been aggravated by the neighbourhood of the enemy to the landing place, and by the exhausted state of the country in which the troops would have been landed.

It was obviously the best plan, therefore, to land in the northern parts of Portugal, and I fixed upon Mondego bay, as the nearest place which afforded any facility for landing excepting Peniche; the landing place of which peninsula is defended by a fort occupied by the enemy, which it would be necessary to attack regularly, in order to place the ships in safety. A landing to the northward was further recommended, as it would insure the co-operation of the Portuguese troops on the expedition to Lisbon. The whole of the corps placed under my command, including those under the command of Gen. Spencer, having landed, I propose to march on Wednesday. I shall take the road by Alcobaça and Obidos, with a view to keep up my communication by the sea coast, and to examine the situation of Peniche; and I shall proceed towards Lisbon by the route of Mafra, and by the hills to the northward of that city.

As I understood from the Sec. of State that a body of troops

under the command of Brig. Gen. Acland may be expected on
the coast of Portugal before you will arrive, I have written to
desire that he will proceed from hence along the coast of Portugal to the southward; and I propose to communicate with
him by the means of Capt. Bligh, of the *Alfred*, who will attend
the movements of the army, with a few transports, having on
board provisions and military stores. I intend to order Brig.
Gen. Acland to attack Peniche, if I should find it necessary to
obtain possession of that place; and if not, I propose to order
him to join the fleet stationed off the Tagus, with a view to disembark in one of the bays near the Rock of Lisbon, as soon as
I shall approach sufficiently near to enable him to perform that
operation.

If I imagined that Gen. Acland's corps was equipped in such
a manner as to be enabled to move from the coast, I should
have directed him to land at Mondego, and to march upon
Santarem, from which situation he would have been at hand
either to assist my operations or to cut off the retreat of the
enemy, if he should endeavor to make it either by the north of
the Tagus and Almeida, or by the south of the Tagus and Elvas.
But as I am convinced that Gen. Acland's corps is intended to
form part of some other corps, which is provided with a commissariat; that he will have none with him; and, consequently,
that his corps must depend upon the country; and as no reliance can be placed upon the resources of this country, I have
considered it best to direct the General's attention to the sea
coast. If, however, the command of the army remained in my
hands, I should certainly land the corps which has been lately
under the command of Sir J. Moore at Mondego, and should
move it upon Santarem.

I have the honor to enclose a return of the troops under my
command, and the copy of a letter which I have written to
Capt. Malcolm, of the *Donegal*, in which the mode of dispos-
ing the transports is stated.

To Visct. Castlereagh.

Lavos, 8th Aug. 1808.

My dispatch contains the fullest information upon every subject, and I have nothing to add to it. I have had the greatest difficulty in organising my commissariat for the march, and that department is very incompetent, notwithstanding the arrangements which I made with Huskisson upon the subject. This department deserves your serious attention. The existence of the army depends upon it, and yet the people who manage it are incapable of managing anything out of a counting house.

I shall be obliged to leave Spencer's guns behind for want of means of moving them; and I should have been obliged to leave my own, if it were not for the horses of the Irish Commissariat. Let nobody ever prevail upon you to send a corps to any part of Europe without horses to draw their guns. It is not true that horses lose their condition at sea.

I have just heard that Joseph Buonaparte left Madrid for France, accompanied by all the French, on the 29th of last month.

I have received your private letter of the 21st July, for which I am much obliged to you. I shall be the junior of the Lieut. Generals; however, I am ready to serve the government wherever and as they please.

To Visc. Castlereagh.

Caldas, 16th Aug. 1808.

I marched from Lavos on the 10th, and was joined at Leiria on the 12th by the Portuguese troops under Gen. B. Freire, consisting of between 5000 and 6000 men. But I am concerned to inform your lordship that they have not accompanied me any farther. Since my arrival in this country, Gen. B. Freire, and the other Portuguese officers, had expressed a wish that the British Commissariat should support the Portuguese troops from the British stores during the campaign; particularly in a meeting which I had with them at Oporto on the night of the 24th July, and in another at Monte Mór o Velho on the 7th inst.; and upon both these occasions I told them explicitly that it was impossible to supply their wants from the British stores; that those stores were formed with a view to the consumption of the British only, and that but during a short time; and that it was a proposition of a novel nature to require an army landing from its ships not only to supply its own consumption of bread, but likewise that of the army of the state to whose assistance it had been sent. I told the Portuguese officers, however, that I believed I should not have occasion to call upon the country to supply bread during my march towards Lisbon; but that I should require beef, wine, and forage, all of which the Bishop of Oporto engaged should be supplied to me.

Before I marched to Leiria, the Portuguese officers earnestly urged my early advance, to secure a magazine which had been formed at that place, as I understood, for the use of the British troops, and my advance certainly saved it from the enemy. But I received no supply from the magazine, which was left entire for the use of the Portuguese army. On the evening, however, of the arrival of the Portuguese army at Leiria, some very extraordinary messages were sent to me respecting their supplies; and in a conversation which I had with him that night, Gen. Freire expressed his anxiety upon the subject. The plan of the march for the next morning was communicated to him, and the hour for the departure of the Portuguese troops was fixed. Instead of making the march, however, as had been agreed upon, I received from Gen. Freire a proposition for a new plan of operations, which was to take the Portuguese troops to a distance from the British army, by Thomar, towards Santarem, unless I should consent to feed the whole of them; and the pretext for the adoption of this plan was the probable want of supplies on the road which I had proposed to take, and their great plenty in the proposed quarter; and that the Portuguese troops would be in a situation to cut off the retreat of the French from Lisbon.

In my reply, I pointed out the inefficiency and danger of this plan, and requested the General to send me 1000 infantry, all his cavalry, and his light troops, which I engaged to feed; and I recommended to him either to join me himself with the remainder, or at all events to remain at Leiria, or at Alcobaça, or somewhere in my rear, where at least his own troops would be in safety. He has sent me the troops which I have required, to the amount of 1400 infantry, and 260 cavalry; but he has announced to me that he intends to persevere in his proposed plan of operations for the remainder of his army, notwithstanding that I have informed him that I have found resources in the country fully adequate to the subsistence of his troops.

I have been thus particular in detailing to your Lordship the circumstances which have attended, for I am certain they have not occasioned, the separation of the Portuguese army from that of His Majesty. There must have been in the magazine at Leiria bread for the Portuguese troops for 2 days. I found at Alcobaça a sufficiency to last them one day, and more might have been procured; and this town would have afforded ample supplies.

Gen. Freire has been apprised of this state of the resources, and yet he perseveres in his plan; and I acknowledge that I can attribute it only to his apprehensions, which, however, he has never hinted to me, that we are not sufficiently strong for the enemy. I am convinced that he can have no personal motive for his conduct, as I have been always on the most cordial good terms with him; I have supplied him with arms, ammunition, and flints, and have done every thing in my power for his army; and only on the day before he communicated to me the alteration of his plan for the march of his army he voluntarily placed himself and his troops under my command.

Having found the resources of the country more ample than I expected, I should certainly have undertaken to feed his army according to his desire; as I consider it of importance, on political rather than on military grounds, that the Portuguese troops should accompany our march; only that I have found the British Commissariat to be so ill composed as to be incapable of distributing even to the British troops the ample supplies which have been procured for them; and I did not wish to burden them with the additional charge of providing and distributing supplies to the Portuguese army. Besides, as I have above explained to your Lordship, I do not believe the motive stated is that which has caused the determination to which I have adverted.

I marched from Leiria on the 13th, and arrived at Alcobaça on the 14th, which place the enemy had abandoned in the preceding night; and I arrived here yesterday. The enemy, about 4000 in number, were posted about 10 miles from hence at Roliça; and they occupied Obidos, about 3 miles from hence, with their advanced posts. As the possession of this last village was important to our future operations, I determined to occupy it; and as soon as the British infantry arrived upon the ground, I directed that it might be occupied by a detachment consisting of 4 companies of riflemen of the 60th and 95th regts.

The enemy, consisting of a small piquet of infantry and a few cavalry, made a trifling resistance and retired; but they were followed by a detachment of our riflemen to the distance of 3 miles from Obidos. The riflemen were there attacked by a superior body of the enemy, who attempted to cut them off from the main body of the detachment to which they belonged, which had now advanced to their support; larger bodies of the enemy appeared on both the flanks of the detachments; and it was with difficulty that Major Gen. Spencer, who had gone out to Obidos when he heard that the riflemen had advanced in pursuit of the enemy, was enabled to effect their retreat to that village. They have since remained in possession of it, and the enemy have retired entirely from the neighbourhood.

In this little affair of the advanced post, which was occasioned solely by the eagerness of the troops in pursuit of the enemy, I am concerned to add that Lieut. Bunbury, of the 2d batt., 95th regt., was killed, and the Hon. Capt. Pakenham wounded, but slightly; and we have lost some men, of whose numbers I have not received the returns.

Besides the corps of about 4000 men, commanded by Gens.

Laborde and Thomière, which is retiring in front of the army by the sea road towards Lisbon, there is another corps, consisting of about 5000 men, assembled at Rio Maior, under Gen. Loison, which I conclude will retire by the great Lisbon road, and they will probably join near Lisbon with whatever troops can be spared from the defence of the fortifications.

Loison's corps has lately been employed in Alentejo against a Spanish detachment of about 1000 men, and the Portuguese insurgents in that quarter, and with a view to the relief of Elvas. I understand that it has suffered much in the expedition, as well by the fatigue of the marches which it has made as by the opposition it has met with.

When I was at Alcobaça I communicated with Capt. Bligh, of the *Alfred*, who was detained off Nazareth with a convoy of victuallers and ordnance store ships, and he landed a supply, which I hope to receive this evening; and he is now off Peniche, where I intend, if possible, to communicate with him to-morrow morning.

To Visct. Castlereagh.

Villa Verde, 17th Aug. 1808.

The French Gen. Laborde having continued in his position at Roliça, since my arrival at Caldas on the 15th inst., I determined to attack him in it this morning. Roliça is situated on an eminence, having a plain in its front, at the end of a valley, which commences at Caldas, and is closed to the southward by mountains, which join the hills forming the valley on the left. Looking from Caldas, in the centre of the valley, and about 8 miles from Roliça, is the town and old Moorish fort of Obidos, from whence the enemy's piquets had been driven on the 15th; and from that time he had posts in the hills on both sides of the valley, as well as in the plain in front of his army, which was posted on the heights in front of Roliça, its right resting upon the hills, its left upon an eminence on which was a windmill, and the whole covering 4 or 5 passes into the mountains on his rear.

I have reason to believe that his force consisted of at least 6000 men, of which about 500 were cavalry, with 5 pieces of cannon; and there was some reason to believe that Gen. Loison, who was at Rio Maior yesterday, would join Gen. Laborde by his right in the course of the night.

The plan of attack was formed accordingly; and the army, having broken up from Caldas this morning, was formed into 3 columns. The right, consisting of 1200 Portuguese infantry, 50 Portuguese cavalry, destined to turn the enemy's left, and penetrate into the mountains in his rear. The left, consisting of Major Gen. Ferguson's and Brig. Gen. Bowes' brigade of infantry, 3 companies of riflemen, a brigade of light artillery, and 20 British and 20 Portuguese cavalry, was destined, under the command of Major Gen. Ferguson, to ascend the hills at Obidos, to turn all the enemy's posts on the left of the valley, as well as the right of his post at Roliça. This corps was also destined to watch the motions of Gen. Loison on the enemy's right, who, I had heard, had moved from Rio Maior towards Alcoentre last night. The centre column, consisting of Major Gen. Hill's, Brig. Gen. Nightingall's, Brig. Gen. C. Craufurd's, and Brig. Gen. Fane's brigades (with the exception of the riflemen detached with Major Gen. Ferguson), and 400 Portuguese light infantry, the British and Portuguese cavalry, a brigade of 9 pounders, and a brigade of 6 pounders, was destined to attack Gen. Laborde's position in the front.

The columns being formed, the troops moved from Obidos about 7 o'clock in the morning. Brig. Gen. Fane's riflemen were immediately detached into the hills on the left of the valley, to keep up the communication between the centre and left columns, and to protect the march of the former along the valley, and the enemy's posts were successively driven in. Major Gen. Hill's brigade, formed in three columns of battalions, moved on the right of the valley, supported by the cavalry, in order to attack the enemy's left; and Brig. Gens. Nightingall and Craufurd moved with the artillery along the high road, until at length the former formed in the plain immediately in the enemy's front, supported by the light infantry companies, and the 45th regt. of Brig. Gen. Craufurd's brigade; while the 2 other regiments of this brigade (the 50th and 91st), and half of the 9 pounder brigade, were kept up as a reserve in the rear.

Major Gen. Hill and Brig. Gen. Nightingall advanced upon the enemy's position, and at the same moment Brig. Gen. Fane's riflemen were in the hills on his right, the Portuguese in a village upon his left, and Major Gen. Ferguson's column was descending from the heights into the plain. From this situation the enemy retired by the passes into the mountains with the utmost regularity and the greatest celerity; and notwithstanding the rapid advance of the British infantry, the want of a sufficient body of cavalry was the cause of his suffering but little loss on the plain. It was then necessary to make a disposition to attack the formidable position which he had taken up.

Brig. Gen. Fane's riflemen were already in the mountains on his right; and no time was lost in attacking the different passes, as well to support the riflemen as to defeat the enemy completely.

The Portuguese infantry were ordered to move up a pass on the right of the whole. The light companies of Major Gen. Hill's brigade, and the 5th regt., moved up a pass next on the right; and the 29th regt., supported by the 9th regt., under Brig. Gen. Nightingall, a third pass; and the 45th and 82d regts., passes on the left. These passes were all difficult of access, and some of them were well defended by the enemy, particularly that which was attacked by the 29th and 9th regts. These regiments attacked with the utmost impetuosity, and reached the enemy before those whose attacks were to be made on their flanks.

The defence of the enemy was desperate; and it was in this attack principally that we sustained the loss which we have to lament, particularly of that gallant officer, the Hon. Lieut. Col. Lake, who distinguished himself upon this occasion. The enemy was, however, driven from all the positions he had taken in the passes of the mountains, and our troops were advanced in the plains on their tops. For a considerable length of time the 29th and 9th regts. alone were advanced to this point, with Brig. Gen. Fane's riflemen at a distance on the left, and they were afterwards supported by the 5th regt., and by the light companies of Major Gen. Hill's brigade, which had come upon their right, and by the other troops ordered to ascend the mountains, who came up by degrees.

The enemy here made 3 most gallant attacks upon the 29th and 9th regts., supported as I have above stated, with a view to cover the retreat of his defeated army, in all of which he was, however, repulsed; but he succeeded in effecting his retreat in good order, owing principally to my want of cavalry; and, secondly, to the difficulty of bringing up the passes of the mountains, with celerity, a sufficient number of troops and of cannon to support those which had first ascended. The loss of the enemy has, however, been very great, and he left 3 pieces of cannon in our hands.

I cannot sufficiently applaud the conduct of the troops throughout this action. The enemy's positions were formidable, and he took them up with his usual ability and celerity, and defended them most gallantly. But I must observe, that although we had such a superiority of numbers employed in the operations of this day, the troops actually engaged in the heat of the action were, from unavoidable circumstances, only the 5th, 9th, 29th, the riflemen of the 95th and 60th, and the flank companies of Major Gen. Hill's brigade; being a number by no means equal to that of the enemy. Their conduct therefore deserves the highest commendation.

I cannot avoid taking this opportunity of expressing my acknowledgments for the aid and support I received from all the General and other officers of this army: I am particularly indebted to Major Gen. Spencer for the advice and assistance I received from him; to Major Gen. Ferguson, for the manner in which he led the left column; and to Major Gen. Hill, and Brig. Gens. Nightingall and Fane, for the manner in which they conducted the different attacks which they led.

I derived most material assistance also from Lieut. Col. Tucker and Lieut. Col. Bathurst, in the offices of D. A. and D. Q. M. Gen., and from the officers of the Staff employed under them. I must also mention that I have every reason to be satisfied with the artillery under Lieut. Col. Robe. I have the honor to enclose herewith a return of killed, wounded, and missing.

To Visc. Castlereagh.

Vimeiro, 22d Aug. 1808.

After I wrote to you yesterday morning, we were attacked by the whole of the French army, Sir H. Burrard being still on board the ship, and I gained a complete victory. It was impossible for troops to behave better than ours did; we only wanted a few hundred more cavalry to annihilate the French army.

I have sent my report upon this action to Sir H. Burrard, who will send it home. You will see in it that I have mentioned Col. Burne, of the 36th regt., in a very particular manner; and I assure you that there is nothing that will give me so much satisfaction as to learn that something has been done for this old and meritorious soldier. The 36th regt. are an example to this army.

Sir Harry did not land till late in the day, in the midst of the attack, and he desired me to continue my own operations; and as far as I am personally concerned in the action, I was amply rewarded for any disappointment I might have felt in not having had an opportunity of bringing the service to a close, by the satisfaction expressed by the army that the second and more important victory had been gained by their old General. I have also the pleasure to add, that it has had more effect than all the arguments I could use to induce the General to move on, and I believe he will march to-morrow. Indeed, if he does not, we shall be poisoned here by the stench of the dead and wounded; or we shall starve, everything in the neighbourhood being already eaten up.

From the number of dead Frenchmen about the ground, and the number of prisoners and wounded, I should think their loss could not be far short of 3000 men. The force which attacked us was very respectable, and probably not short of 14,000 men, including 1300 dragoons and artillery, and 300 chasseurs à cheval.

Sir Hew Dalrymple arrived last night, and will land this morning.

To the Duke of Richmond.

Camp at Vimeiro, 22nd Aug. 1808.

Sir H. Burrard came here on the night of the 20th, but did not land, and, as I am the most fortunate of men, Junot attacked us yesterday morning with his whole force, and we completely defeated him. You will see the account of the action. The French have lost not less than 3000 men.

Since I wrote to you last, I came here to facilitate Anstruther's landing and junction, which took place on the 20th, in the morning. In the evening Acland came up from the Tagus, and I landed him immediately, and he joined us before the action yesterday morning; but Sir Harry did not come up till the action was nearly over.

Although we had, when Acland joined, not less than 17,000 men, and between 6000 and 7000 Portuguese in our neighbourhood, Sir Harry did not think these sufficient to defeat 12,000 or 14,000 Frenchmen, but determined to wait for Moore's corps, notwithstanding all that I could urge upon the subject. The action of yesterday has, however, had more effect than all my eloquence, and I believe he will march on to-morrow. If he would have allowed me to move that part of the army yesterday evening, which had not been engaged in the morning, the French would not have stopped till they reached Lisbon.

To Charles Stuart, Esq.

Ramalhal, 25th Aug. 1808.

Since I wrote to you last we have been very actively employed in this quarter, and with some success.

On the 17th inst. I attacked and defeated Laborde's corps,

consisting of about 6000 men, in the neighbourhood of Roliça, about 6 or 7 miles to the south of Obidos. On the following day, the French troops under Gen. Junot, Gen. Loison, and Gen. Laborde, joined in the neighbourhood of Torres Vedras, to the amount of from 12,000 to 14,000 men. I marched on the same day towards Lourinha, to protect the landing of a brigade of infantry under Gen. Anstruther, which brigade joined me on the 20th at Vimeiro, near Maceira; and I was joined by another brigade of infantry, under Gen. Acland, early in the morning of the 21st, which brigade had landed in the course of that night. The French army attacked me in my position at Vimeiro, on the 21st, at about 8 in the morning; and it was completely defeated, with the loss of 13 pieces of cannon, and a vast number of killed, wounded, and prisoners. Sir H. Burrard, who had come into the roads of Maceira on the night of the 20th, landed during the action on the morning of the 21st; and if I had not been prevented, I should have pursued the enemy to Torres Vedras on that evening, and, in all probability, the whole would have been destroyed.

On the 22d, in the morning, Sir H. Dalrymple arrived; and in the evening Gen. Kellermann came in with a proposition to suspend hostilities, with a view to make a Convention for the evacuation of Portugal by the French.

In the agreement which Sir Hew entered into upon this occasion there was an article stipulating that the Russians should be allowed to use the port of Lisbon as a neutral port, which was referred to the Admiral, who has refused to consent to it; and the General has this day given notice to Junot that the suspension of arms will be at an end on the 28th at noon, unless a Convention for the evacuation of Portugal by the French, by sea, should be agreed upon before that day.

This is the general outline of the state of affairs here. Sir J. Moore's corps is in the roads of Maceira, and I believe is to be landed. Besides this, we have 6000 Portuguese troops at Lourinha; and I believe there is a detachment of Spanish and Portuguese troops about Santarem and Abrantes.

The retreat of the French is, however, open through Alentejo towards Elvas; and I have but little doubt that if we should not get them out of Portugal by sea, they will secure themselves in Elvas and Almeida, and we shall have the pleasure of attacking those places regularly, or of blockading them in the autumn. If we should be able to get them away by sea, it will be possible to push our troops into Spain at an early period. I request you to furnish Col. Doyle with such information from this letter as may be useful to him.

The French troops are now assembled at Cabeça de Montachique, and extending towards Mafra. We are behind Torres Vedras, which town is not occupied by either party.

To the Duke of Richmond.

Ramalhal, 27th Aug. 1808.

I wrote to you after the battle of the 21st. On the 22d, in the morning, Sir H. Dalrymple arrived; and on that evening Gen. Kellermann came in to ask for a suspension of hostilities, to give time for the negotiation of a Convention for the evacuation of Portugal by the French by sea. Sir Hew consented to this, and desired me to sign it, notwithstanding that I neither negotiated nor approved of it.

This agreement contained many improper stipulations; among others, it gave the French 48 hours' notice of an intention to put an end to it. It likewise contained a stipulation in respect to the Russians which ought never to have been admitted; and it was in other respects objectionable on account of its French *verbiage*. I have not got a copy of it. The objections to it have, however, since been considerably removed, by the refusal of the Admiral to consent to the stipulation respecting the Russians, and by the determination of the suspension of hostilities to-morrow at 12 o'clock, unless Murray, who is negotiating the Convention, should be of opinion that an additional period of 24 hours is necessary to enable him to perform his work. I am ready to march in the evening, and Sir J. Moore next day; and, whether there is a Convention or not, I hope to be in Lisbon by the beginning of September.

I approve of allowing the French to evacuate the country, for I am convinced that, if we did not, we should be obliged to attack Elvas, Fort la Lippe, Almeida, and Peniche, regularly, or blockade them, and thus the autumn would pass away; and it is better to have 10,000 or 12,000 additional Frenchmen on the northern frontier of Spain, and the English army in Spain, than the Frenchmen in Portugal, and the English blockading them in strong places. This necessity would have been avoided, if Sir H. Burrard would or could have carried on with Sir J. Moore's corps the operations upon Santarem, which I recommended to him, by which the French would certainly have been cut off from Elvas and Almeida.

The French got a terrible beating on the 21st. They did not lose less, I believe, than 4000 men; and they would have been entirely destroyed, if Sir H. Burrard had not prevented me from pursuing them. Indeed, since the arrival of the great generals, we appear to have been palsied, and every thing has gone on wrong.

I am getting plans done for you of both the battles of the 17th and 21st, and I will write to you if any thing further should occur. I am not very well pleased, between ourselves, with the way in which things in this country are likely to go on, and I shall not be sorry to go home, if I can do so with propriety; in which case I shall soon see you. But I don't like to desire to go, lest it should be imputed to me that I am unwilling to serve where I don't command.

P. S. I have heard nothing of Ireland since I left it. Pray, remember me most kindly to the Duchess, and Louisa, &c., and Lady Edward. Lord FitzRoy has been very useful to me; and I have this day lent him to Sir H. Dalrymple, to go to the French head quarters.

To Visc. Castlereagh.

Zambujal, 12 miles N. of Lisbon, 5th Sept. 1808.

Your brother Charles communicated to me your letter of the
20th Aug. to Sir H. Dalrymple, of which Sir Hew himself communicated to me different parts yesterday; and I proceed to give
you my opinion on the points to which it relates. I must apprise
you, however, that our information here of the state of affairs in
Spain is very defective; that we, or at least I, do not know what
is the position, what are the numbers, what are the means, or
what ought to be the objects of the French army in Spain; and I
am equally ignorant of the state of the force of the Spaniards.

I rather believe, however, that the French army in Spain now
consists of about 40,000 men, of which number about 5000 are
cavalry, and that they are under the command of Marshal
Bessières, and are stationed somewhere about Vitoria, in Biscay. The probability that they will be reinforced must depend
upon the state of affairs in the other parts of Europe, of which
I have no knowledge whatever; but if the attention of the
French government is not called to other quarters, we must
expect that the French army in Spain will be increased at an
early period to a very large amount.

The amount of the force with which operations can be carried on in Spain is another and a very material consideration,
which bears upon the whole question; and, from all that I have
heard of the state of the resources in the country, I should doubt
whether it will be practicable to carry on operations in Spain
with a larger corps than 40,000 men. There may be other *corps
de rèserve*, and employed in operations on other lines, or on the
same line, in the protection of convoys from France, &c.; but it
is not probable that the corps in front will exceed 40,000 men.
You must consider this, however, as a mere matter of opinion,
founded upon general information of the state of the resources
in Spain, in which I may be much mistaken.

The next point for consideration is the force of the Spaniards: I really know of nothing that they have in the shape of an

army capable of meeting the French, excepting that under Gen. Castaños. Gen. Cuesta has some cavalry in Castille; Gen. Galluzzo some more in Estremadura; and Blake's army of Galicia may in time become an efficient corps. But those armies of peasantry, which in Murcia, Valencia, and Catalonia, have cut up French corps, must not be reckoned upon (at least at present) as efficient armies to meet the French troops in the field. It is most probable that they will not, and indeed cannot, leave their provinces; and if they could, no officer could calculate a great operation upon such a body.

I doubt not that, if an accurate report could be made upon their state, they want arms, ammunition, money, clothing, and military equipments of every description; and although such a body are very formidable and efficient in their own country, and probably equal to its defence, they must not be reckoned upon out of it; and in any case it is impossible to estimate the effect of their efforts. In some cases equal numbers will oppose with success the French troops; in others, 1000 Frenchmen, with cavalry and artillery, will disperse thousands of them, and no reliance can be placed on them in their present state.

The result, then, of my information of the present state of the Spanish force to be opposed to the French, is, that there are about 25,000 men under Castaños, now ready, and about the same number under Blake in Galicia, upon whom you may reckon as efficient troops. All the rest may become so, and may be useful in different ways even at present, but you must not found the arrangement for a great military operation on their utility or efficiency. I understand that government had promised 10,000 men to Castaños, and I have no doubt whatever that a corps well equipped, consisting of about 15,000 men, including a proportion of British cavalry and artillery, would be highly useful to him. This would make his army 40,000 men, of which the British corps would be the best troops that could be found anywhere; and this army, aided by the insurrection from the other kingdoms of Spain, would be the operating army against what I have supposed to be the French operating army. This British corps should advance from Portugal, to which kingdom it would be in the mean time a defence.

You should leave in Portugal a British corps of 5000 men, to be stationed at and in the neighbourhood of Lisbon, with probably a small garrison in Elvas. The object in stationing this corps in Portugal is to give strength to the government which you will establish here, and to render it independent of the factions and intrigues by which it will be assailed on all sides. You ought to send to Lisbon, in the quality of the King's Ambassador, a discreet person, who could superintend the management of the affairs of this country, particularly the expenditure of the money which you must supply for its wants, and its application to the purposes for which it will be given, viz., to provide a military defence.

The next consideration is the employment of the remainder of the army now in Portugal, amounting by estimate to about 10,000 men, with an additional corps of 10,000 men assembled and ready in England, and some cavalry. I acknowledge that I do not think the affairs in Spain are in so prosperous a state as that you can trust, in operations within that kingdom, the whole disposable force which England possesses, without adopting measures of precaution, which will render its retreat to the sea coast nearly certain. Besides this, I will not conceal from you that our people are so new in the field, that I do not know of persons capable of supplying, or, if supplied, of distributing the supplies, to an army of 40,000 men (British troops) acting together in a body. Even if plenty could be expected to exist, we should starve in the midst of it, for want of due arrangement. But the first objection is conclusive. We may depend upon it that whenever we shall assemble an army the French will consider its defeat and destruction their first object, particularly if Buonaparte should be at the head of the French troops himself; and if the operations of our army should be near the French frontier, he will have the means of multiplying, and will multiply, the numbers upon our army in such a degree as must get the better of them. For the British army, therefore, we must have a retreat open, and that retreat must be the sea.

Our operations carried on from Portugal and the north of Spain would, as you truly observe, involve us in a line of operations much too long. The retreat would be difficult, if not impossible. This objection, you will say, would apply equally to the corps of 15,000 men proposed to be employed with Castaños. 1st, I conceive that there is a great deal of difference between the risk of the loss of such a corps as this, and that of the loss of the whole of the disposable force of Great Britain. 2dly, it does not follow that, because the whole British army could not make its retreat into Portugal, a corps of 15,000 could not. 3dly, it does not follow that this corps of 15,000 men would necessarily retreat upon Portugal; being a part of Castaños' army, it might retire with his troops into Andalusia, leaving the frontiers of Portugal to be defended by the Portuguese and the British corps of 5000 men, till those, or a part of them, would again be brought round to the Tagus, or could enter Portugal by Algarve. I conclude, then, that although this corps might be risked, and its retreat to the sea should be considered in some degree *en l'air*, that of the whole disposable force of Great Britain ought to be, and must be, saved.

The only efficient plan of operations in which the British troops can be employed, consistently with this view, is upon the flank and rear of the enemy's advance towards Madrid, by an issue from the Asturias. If it be true, as is stated by the Asturian deputies in London, that their country is remarkably strong, and that it is secure from French invasion; if it be true that the ports of Santander and Gijon, the former particularly, are secure harbours in the winter; and if the walls can give to both, or either, the means of making an embarkation, even if the enemy should be able to retreat through the mountains; the Asturias is the country we should secure immediately, in which we should assemble our disposable force as soon as possible, and issue forth into the plains, either by Leon or the pass of Reynosa. The army could then have a short, although probably a difficult communication with the sea, which must be carried on by mules, of which there are plenty in the country; it could co-operate with Blake's Galician army, and could press upon the enemy's right flank and rear, and turn his position upon the Ebro, which it is evident he intends to make his first line. To secure the Asturias as soon as possible, you may depend upon it, is your first object in Spain, and afterwards to assemble within that country your whole disposable force, after marching the detachment to Castaños.

There are some points of detail which must be attended to in

these arrangements. The army now in this country might either
be marched into Leon, or it might be embarked and trans-
ported to Gijon or Santander. The latter would be the quickest
operation; by the adoption of the former, its artillery, in its
present form, might accompany it; but it must be recollected,
that if the artillery should be kept in its present form, in case of
retreat it must be left behind in the plains; as I understand there
is no carriage-road across the mountains of Asturias.

The troops, then, now in this country ought to be embarked in
the Tagus, and sent to the Asturias; and ordnance carriages ought
to be sent from England without loss of time, which can be taken
to pieces, and carried by hand, or when put together can be drawn
by horses. The reports, which will be made by the officers sent to
those countries, will state whether cavalry can pass through them:
I should think they might; as I see that wherever a mule can go a
horse can likewise. If so, the cavalry from England should likewise
be landed in Asturias; if not, the cavalry should be landed at
Coruña or Ferrol, and join the army in the plains, through the
passes of Galicia, which we know are practicable for cavalry.

There remains now to be considered only the operations of
the Sicilian corps, consisting of 10,000 men. In the present
state of affairs the government will probably not deem it expedient to remove this corps from the Mediterranean. If the
Spaniards should be able to make any head against the French
on the left of their line in Catalonia, and on the Lower Ebro,
this corps might reinforce that part of the Spanish insurrection,
keeping its retreat always open to the sea. This, however, would
be very difficult, the French being in possession of Barcelona;
and probably the siege of that place, aided by the insurgents of
Catalonia, would be the most this corps would perform. And
whether the operation should be successfully included, or the
corps should be forced to re-embark in consequence of the
approach of the stronger French force, it would materially aid
the operations of the troops in the centre of Spain.

The result of all these operations, which must for the present
be distinct, would be to confine the French to their line of the
Ebro for the present, and eventually to oblige them to retire
upon their own frontier. Time would be gained for the further

organisation of the Spanish government and force; by the judicious and effectual employment of which the British government would be enabled to withdraw its troops from Spain, to employ them in other parts of Europe. As for preventing the retreat of the French from Spain, it is quite out of the question. They have possession of all the fortresses on this side of the Pyrenees, through which mountains there are not less than 40 passes by which troops could march. Besides, if it were possible under these circumstances to place an army in their rear, with the object of cutting them off from France, you might depend upon it that all France would rise as one man for their relief, and the result would be the loss of the army which should be so employed.

In respect to your wish, that I should go into the Asturias to examine the country, and form a judgment of its strength, I have to mention to you that I am not a draftsman, and but a bad hand at description. I should have no difficulty in forming an opinion, and a plan for the defence of that country, provided I was certain that it would be executed. But it would be an idle waste of my time, and an imposition upon you, if I were to go into that country with the pretence of giving you, or any General officer you should employ there, an idea of the country; and it would be vain and fruitless to form a plan for the defence of the country which would depend upon the execution of another. Indeed, this last would only bring disgrace upon me, and would disappoint you. Under these circumstances, I have told Sir H. Dalrymple that I was not able to perform the duty in which you had desired I should be employed; that I was not a topographical engineer, and could not pretend to describe in writing such a country as the Asturias; and he appeared to think that some of the gentlemen of the Q. M. G.'s department might be more usefully employed on this service. I hope you will not believe that I feel any disinclination to performing any service in which you may think I can be of use to you; and that I have discouraged the idea of employing me on that proposed, solely from my incapacity of performing it as it ought to be performed, and from a certainty that you were not aware of the nature of the service which you required from me when you wrote to Sir H. Dalrymple.

TWO

THE CAMPAIGNS OF 1809

The campaign of 1808 was not ended by the departure of Dalrymple and Wellesley for London. On the contrary, now commanded by Sir John Moore, the army that had triumphed at Vimeiro entered Spain in support of the Spanish forces that had been battling the French since May. In the long term, this intervention was a success: in brief, by launching a surprise offensive in Old Castile, Moore was able to save southern and western Spain from the enormous reinforcements with which Napoleon had flooded the Peninsula following the humiliating defeat suffered by General Dupont at Bailén in July. However, at the time, the reality seemed very different: Moore was forced to engage in a long and difficult retreat to the Galician port of La Coruña in the course of which the discipline of much of his army broke down, the result being that the countryside through which his men passed was ravaged by bands of marauders. A rearguard action outside La Coruña which cost Moore his life saved a certain amount of face, while the bulk of the army did get home safely enough. That said, the political consensus that had sustained intervention in the Peninsula was shattered and Anglo-Spanish relations left in ruins. So bad was the situation that for a time it seemed that Britain might leave the Spaniards and Portuguese to their own devices, but, bolstered by a memorandum from Wellesley in which he outlined a coherent strategy for continuing the struggle, the British government held firm, and in April 1809 a thoroughly rehabilitated Wellesley was dispatched to Portugal at the head of a large force of troops. In that country the first months of 1809 had witnessed a fresh crisis in that a large part of the army that had pursued Moore into Galicia had crossed the frontier under Marshal Soult and occupied Oporto, but by the time that Wellesley arrived the invaders had lost all momentum and adopted a defensive posture. There followed a campaign of great brilliance. Closing in on Oporto, on 12 May the British commander managed to take Soult by surprise and get his men across the Douro. Within hours the entire French army was in full retreat, and there followed a long chase through the mountains of northern Portugal from which the invaders only escaped by abandoning all their artillery and baggage. With Soult out of the way, Wellesley turned south to attack the French forces threatening the Portuguese frontier further south under Marshal Victor. Joining with the Spanish Army of Extremadura commanded by Gregorio García de la Cuesta, in July Wellesley launched an offensive in the Tagus valley. At this point, however, everything went wrong. Thus, the British experienced serious logistical problems; relations with the Spanish commander became ever more problematic; albeit through no fault of Wellesley, major opportunities to secure a rapid victory were squandered; and a Spanish army that was supposed to be advancing on Madrid from the south failed to tie down the French forces facing it in the manner that had been expected. In a fierce battle at Talavera de la Reina, Wellesley and Cuesta inflicted a costly defeat on the French forces that the changed circumstances of the campaign had allowed to converge on them, but then disaster struck. Augmented by the French troops that had been garrisoning Galicia and Old Castile, the troops of Marshal Soult burst through the Sierra de Gredos and placed themselves across the Allied lines of communication. This predicament was resolved by the British and Spanish armies retiring across the River Tagus and seeking safety in the mountains to the south, but to all intents and purposes the campaign was over: now ennobled as Lord Wellington in recognition of the victory of Talavera, Wellesley refused to engage in any further co-operation with the Spaniards, and withdrew his army first to the area of Badajoz and Merida and then across the frontier into Portugal. As with its predecessor, then, the campaign of 1809 ended in bitterness and frustration.

Memorandum on the defence of Portugal.

London, 7th March, 1809.

I have always been of opinion that Portugal might be defended, whatever might be the result of the contest in Spain; and that in the mean time the measures adopted for the defence of Portugal would be highly useful to the Spaniards in their contest with the French.

My notion was, that the Portuguese military establishments, upon the footing of 40,000 militia and 30,000 regular troops, ought to be revived; and that, in addition to these troops, His Majesty ought to employ an army in Portugal amounting to about 20,000 British troops, including about 4000 cavalry. My opinion was, that even if Spain should have been conquered, the French would not have been able to overrun Portugal with a smaller force than 100,000 men; and that, as long as the contest should continue in Spain, this force, if it could be put in a state of activity, would be highly useful to the Spaniards, and might eventually have decided the contest.

It is obvious, however, that the military establishments of Portugal could not be revived without very extensive pecuniary assistance and political support from this country; and the only mode in which it appeared to be safe, or even practicable, to give this assistance and support, or to interfere at all in a military way in the concerns of Portugal, was to trust the King's Ambassador at Lisbon to give or withhold such sums as he might think necessary for the support of military establishments only, and to instruct him to see that the revenues of Portugal, whatever they might be, were in the first instance applied to the same objects. By the operation of these powers and instructions, it is probable that he would have had a complete control over the measures of the Portuguese government; and we might have expected by this time to have in the field an efficient Portuguese army.

As it was not possible, however, to adopt these measures at that time, and as the attention of the government has necessarily been drawn to other objects, it is probable that the military establishments of Portugal have made but little progress; and in considering the extent of the British force required for the defence of that country, and the other measures to be adopted, the small extent of the Portuguese force, and the probability of an early attack by the enemy, must be considered on the one hand; and, on the other, the continuance of the contest in Spain, and the probability that a very large French force will not be disposable in a very short period of time for the attack upon Portugal.

I would still recommend the adoption of the political measures above suggested, with a view to the revival of the military establishments in Portugal. It is probable that the expense of these measures will not in this year exceed a million sterling. But if they should succeed, and the contest should continue in Spain and in Portugal, the benefit which will accrue from them will be more than adequate to the expense incurred.

The British force employed in Portugal should, in this view of the question, not be less than 30,000 men, of which number 4000 or 5000 should be cavalry; and there should be a large body of artillery.

The extent of force in cavalry and artillery, above required, is because the Portuguese military establishments must necessarily be deficient in these two branches; and British or German cavalry and artillery must be employed with the Portuguese infantry.

The whole of the army in Portugal, Portuguese as well as British, should be placed under the command of British officers. The Staff of the army, the Commissariat in particular, must be British; and these departments must be extensive in proportion to the strength of the whole army which will act in Portugal, to the number of detached posts which it will be necessary to occupy, and in a view to the difficulties of providing and distributing supplies in that country. In regard to the detail of these measures, I recommend that the British army in Portugal should be reinforced as soon as possible with some companies of British riflemen, with 3000 British or German cavalry; that the complement of ordnance with that army should be made 30 pieces of cannon, of which 2 brigades of 9 pounders; that these pieces of ordnance should be completely horsed; that 20 pieces of brass (12 pounders) ordnance upon travelling carriages should be sent to Portugal, with a view to the occupation of certain positions in the country; that a corps of engineers for an army of 60,000 men should be sent there, and a corps of artillery for 60 pieces of cannon.

I understand that the British army now in Portugal consists of 20,000 men, including cavalry. It should be made up of 20,000 infantry at least, as soon as possible, by additions of riflemen and other good infantry, which by this time may have been refitted after the campaign in Spain. The reinforcements may follow, as the troops shall recover from their fatigues.

The first measures to be adopted are to complete the army in Portugal with its cavalry and artillery, and to horse the ordnance as it ought to be. As soon as this shall be done the General and Staff officers should go out; as it may be depended upon that as soon as the newspapers shall have announced the departure of officers for Portugal, the French armies in Spain will receive orders to make their movements towards Portugal, so as to anticipate our measures for its defence. We ought therefore to have every thing on the spot, or nearly so, before any alarm is created at home respecting our intentions.

Besides the articles above enumerated, 30,000 stands of arms, clothing, and shoes, for the Portuguese army, should be sent to Lisbon as soon as possible.

To Visct. Castlereagh.

Lisbon, 24th April, 1809.

Having heard from the Admiral that he intends to send the *Statira* to England at an early hour to-morrow morning, I shall not suffer that opportunity to pass by without writing to you, although I have but little to tell you.

I arrived here on Saturday, and found that Sir J. Cradock

and Beresford had moved up the country to the northward with the troops under their command respectively, the former to Leiria, and the latter to Thomar. Sir J. Cradock does not, however, appear to have entertained any decided intention of moving forward; on the contrary, indeed, he appears, by his letters to Mr Villiers, to have intended to go no farther, till he should hear that Victor's movements were decided; and, therefore, I consider affairs in this country to be exactly in the state in which, if I found them, it was the intention of the King's ministers that I should assume the command; and accordingly I propose to assume it as soon as I shall communicate with Sir J. Cradock. I have written to him and to Gen. Beresford, to apprise them that I conceive advantages will result from our meeting here, and I expect them both here as soon as possible.

In respect to the enemy, Soult is still at Oporto, and he has not pushed his posts to the southward farther than the river Vouga. He has nothing in Tras os Montes, since the loss of Chaves, of which you have been most probably apprised; but he has some posts on the river Tamaga, which divides that province from Minho; and it is supposed that he wishes to secure for himself the option of retreating through Tras os Montes into Spain, if he should find it necessary.

Gen. Silveira, with a Portuguese corps, is in Tras os Montes; but I am not acquainted with its strength or its composition.

Gen. Lapisse, who commands the corps which it was supposed, when I left England, was marching from Salamanca into Portugal, has turned off to his left, and has marched along the Portuguese frontier to Alcantara, where he crossed the Tagus, and thence he went to Merida, on the Guadiana, where he is in communication with, indeed I may say part of, the army of Victor. He has an advanced post at Montijo, nearer to the Portuguese frontier than Merida. Victor has continued at Medellin since the action with Cuesta. He is either fortifying himself at that post, or making an entrenched camp there. Cuesta is at Llerena, collecting a force again, which it is said will soon be 25,000 infantry, and 6000 cavalry, a part of them good troops. I know nothing of the Marques de la Romana, or of anything to the northward of Portugal.

I intend to move upon Soult as soon as I can make some arrangement on which I can depend for the defence of the Tagus, either to impede or delay Victor's progress, in case he should come in while I am absent. I should prefer an attack upon Victor in concert with Cuesta, if Soult was not in possession of a fertile province of this kingdom and of the favorite town of Oporto, of which it is most desirable to deprive him; and if any operation upon Victor, connected with Cuesta's movements, would not require time to concert it, which may as well be employed in dislodging Soult from the north of Portugal, and to bring the British army to the Eastern frontier.

If the light brigade should not have left England when you receive this letter, I trust that you will send them off without loss of time; and I request of you to desire the officer commanding them to endeavor to get intelligence as he shall go along the coast, particularly at Aveiro, and the mouth of the Mondego; and I wish that he should stop at the latter place for orders, if he should find that the British army is engaged in operations to the northward, and that he should have already received orders at Aveiro. The 23d light dragoons might also receive orders to a similar purport. The hussars, I conclude, will have sailed before this time.

We are much in want of craft here, now that we are going to carry on an operation to the northward. Constant convoys will be necessary, and the Admiral does not appear to have the means in his power of supplying all that is required of him. The 24th regt. arrived this day.

To Don Gregorio Cuesta.

Villa Franca, 29th April, 1809.

I had the honor of receiving yesterday your Excellency's letter of the 23rd April, and I assure your Excellency that it will give me great satisfaction to co-operate with your Excellency, as far as it may be in my power, to defeat those forces of the enemy which threaten the cities of Seville and Lisbon.

Your Excellency must be aware of the state of the Portuguese army; a commencement has only lately been made to organise and discipline it: and although I have the utmost reliance on the valor, the zeal, and the loyalty of the troops of Portugal, I cannot at this moment consider them in such a state of discipline as to confide to their exertions the safety of Portugal, especially committed to my care, against the further attempts which may be made upon it by the disciplined troops of France, which have already invaded, and are in possession of, an important part of this kingdom. Under these circumstances, my attention has necessarily been directed, in the first instance, to remove from Portugal the further evils with which both Spain and Portugal are threatened by Marshal Soult; and the greatest part of the army under my command is now on its march for that purpose. A small detachment of British troops, with one of Portuguese troops, will remain upon the Tagus, to watch the movements of the enemy, and to guard the passages of that river, in case the enemy should direct his attack upon this country.

If I should succeed in removing Marshal Soult from the north of Portugal, I intend to go forthwith with all the troops under my command (consisting of about 25,000, of which nearly 4000 will at that time be cavalry), to the Eastern frontier of Portugal, in the neighbourhood of Elvas; and I shall be happy to co-operate with you in any plan which may be agreed upon for the attack of Marshal Victor. In the mean time, a detachment of the garrison of Elvas has been directed to take the field, in co-operation with a similar detachment of the garrison of Badajoz, to act as a corps of observation in that quarter; but I cannot avoid taking this opportunity of recommending that this corps should not be exposed to the attack of the enemy, or to be cut off from the garrisons to which the parts of it respectively belong.

In the present situation of affairs, all that we can require is time; and that we should not lose our men, or any of the valuable positions which we still possess. In a short time we shall all be enabled to co-operate in a vigorous attack upon the enemy; and till that period shall arrive, it is not very material whether he acquires a little more of the open country, provided we do not lose any of the men who are destined to defend the valuable points and positions which remain in our hands.

Your Excellency is mistaken respecting the position of Sir R. Wilson's corps. He has been removed to the neighbourhood of the Douro, to confine himself to that quarter. I consider the position of Alcantara, however, to be so important at this moment, in respect both to the defence of Portugal and to our future designs upon Marshal Victor, that I shall give directions that it should be occupied by a Portuguese corps, if it should be possible to form one fit for that purpose. I shall be obliged to your Excellency, if you will give directions that any Portuguese or British corps, which may go to Alcantara, may be received there.

I have written to your Excellency a long letter in English, understanding that you have under your command officers in your confidence who can explain it to you, in which I have taken the liberty of giving my opinions with great freedom. I hope that your Excellency will receive them, as they are intended, as a mark of my sincere desire to be of use to you, as far as is in my power at present; which I hope and believe, from the situation of the enemy, I shall have still better opportunities of proving to you before much time shall elapse.

To Marshal Beresford.

Oporto, 12th May, 1809.

I wrote to you at 12, to inform you that the enemy had left this town, excepting their small guards, and that my troops are passing over.

As soon as one battalion, the Buffs, had passed, the enemy made a most furious attack upon them, which they continued for about 2 hours. We threw over reinforcements as fast as we could; but the most we could do was to send over the remainder of Hill's brigade and the Portuguese battalion, which corps defended themselves most gallantly, and we ended by obtaining a complete victory. We have taken some pieces of cannon, how many I cannot say, many prisoners, killed vast numbers; and the infantry went off towards Valongo and Amarante in the utmost confusion. Some of the cavalry went the same way. I am much afraid that we shall not be able to march till the day after to-morrow.

I have received your letter of the 9th. Keep Villa Real if you can do so with safety, and depend upon my being close upon the heels of the French. I shall state my movements exactly as soon as I can.

To Visct. Castlereagh.

Montealegre, 18th May, 1809.

When I determined upon the expedition to the north of Portugal against Marshal Soult, I was in hopes that the Portuguese General, Silveira, would have been able to hold his post upon the Tamaga till he should be reinforced; by which, and by the possession of Chaves, the enemy's retreat would have been cut off, excepting across the Minho; and I intended, if successful, to press him so hard, that the passage of that river would have been impracticable. The loss of the bridge of Amarante, however, on the 2d inst., altered our prospects. I had then no hopes that Marshal Beresford, who marched towards the upper part of the Douro on the 5th, and arrived at Lamego on the 10th, would be able to effect more than confine the enemy on that side, and oblige him to retire by Chaves into Galicia, rather than by Villa Real into Castille. General Beresford, however, having obliged the enemy's posts at Villa Real and Mezam Frio to fall back with some loss, and having crossed the Douro, drove in Gen. Loison's outposts at the bridge of Amarante, and again acquired possession of the left bank of the Tamaga on the

12th, the day on which the corps under my command forced the passage of the Douro at Oporto.

Loison retired from Amarante on the morning of the 13th, as soon as he had heard of the events at Oporto of the preceding day, and met the advanced guard of the French army at a short distance from the town, which Gen. Beresford immediately occupied. I was unable to commence the pursuit of the enemy till the morning of the 13th, when the Hanoverian legion moved to Valongo, under Major Gen. Murray. On that evening I was informed that the enemy had, in the morning, destroyed a great proportion of his cannon in the neighbourhood of Penafiel, and had directed his march towards Braga. This appeared to be the probable result of the situation in which he found himself, in consequence of Gen. Beresford's operations upon the Tamaga; and as soon as I had ascertained that the fact was true, I marched on the morning of the 14th, with the army in two columns, towards the river Minho. At the same time I directed Gen. Beresford upon Chaves, in case the enemy should turn to his right; and Major Gen. Murray to communicate with Gen. Beresford, if he should find, as reported, that Loison remained in the neighbourhood of Amarante.

On the evening of the 14th I was certain, from the movements of the enemy's detachments in the neighbourhood of Braga, that he intended to direct his retreat upon Chaves or Montealegre; and directed Gen. Beresford, in case of the latter movement, to push on for Monterey, so as to stop the enemy if he should pass by Villa de Rey. Gen. Beresford had anticipated my orders to march his own corps upon Chaves, and had already sent Gen. Silveira to occupy the passes of Ruivaes and Melgaço, near Salamonde, but he was unfortunately too late.

I arrived at Braga on the 15th (Gen. Murray being at Guimaraens, and the enemy about 15 miles in our front), and at Salamonde on the 16th. We had there an affair with their rear guard. The Guards, under Lieut. Gen. Sherbrooke and Brig. Gen. Campbell, attacked their position, and having turned their left flank by the heights, they abandoned it, leaving a gun and some prisoners behind them. This attack was necessarily made at a late hour in the evening.

On the 17th we moved to Ruivaes (waiting to see whether the enemy would turn upon Chaves or continue his retreat upon Montealegre), and on the 18th to this place. I here found that he had taken a road through the mountains towards Orense, by which it would be difficult, if not impossible, for me to overtake him, and on which I had no means of stopping him.

The enemy commenced his retreat, as I have informed your Lordship, by destroying a great proportion of his guns and ammunition. He afterwards destroyed the remainder of both and a great proportion of his baggage, and kept nothing excepting what the soldiers or a few mules could carry. He has left behind him his sick and wounded; and the road from Penafiel to Montealegre is strewed with the carcases of horses and mules, and of French soldiers, who were put to death by the peasantry before our advanced guard could save them. This last circumstance is the natural effect of the species of warfare which the enemy have carried on in this country. Their soldiers have plundered and murdered the peasantry at their pleasure; and I have seen many persons hanging in the trees by the sides of the road, executed for no reason that I could learn, excepting that they have not been friendly to the French invasion and usurpation of the government of their country; and the route of their column, on their retreat, could be traced by the smoke of the villages to which they set fire. We have taken about 500 prisoners. Upon the whole the enemy has not lost less than a fourth of his army, and all his artillery and equipments, since we attacked him on the Vouga.

I hope your Lordship will believe that no measure which I could take was omitted to intercept the enemy's retreat. It is obvious, however, that if an army throws away all its cannon, equipments, and baggage, and everything which can strengthen it, and can enable it to act together as a body; and abandons all those who are entitled to its protection, but add to its weight and impede its progress; it must be able to march by roads through which it cannot be followed, with any prospect of being overtaken, by an army which has not made the same sacrifices.

It is impossible to say too much of the exertions of the

troops. The weather has been very bad indeed. Since the 13th the rain has been constant, and the roads in this difficult country almost impracticable. But they have persevered in the pursuit to the last, and have been generally on their march from day-light in the morning till dark. The brigade of Guards were at the head of the column, and set a laudable example; and in the affair with the enemy's rear guard, on the evening of the 16th, they conducted themselves remarkably well.

To Marshal Beresford.

Plasencia, 17th July, 1809.

The infantry of the army moved this day, and the whole will cross the Tietar to-morrow, to co-operate with Cuesta in an attack upon the French upon the Alberche. It is not quite certain yet whether they intend to retire, or to wait for us, but I am inclined to think they will do the former.

I have ordered Gen. Lightburne, and the 2d batt. 5th regt., and 2d batt. 58th regt., to be prepared to obey any orders they may receive from you. Having been in camp for a fortnight, at Alcantara (Lisbon), I conclude that they are now prepared to move. I have ordered the other troops to join me by Abrantes, and I shall be obliged to you if you will arrange that this brigade, which is to join you, should proceed by any other road. You must take care of their subsistence on the road; and I beg you to recollect that they are young troops, unaccustomed to war, and I shall be obliged to you if you will not march them more than 3 or 4 leagues in a day. They will be subsisted to the 24th Aug., before they leave Lisbon.

I asked Cuesta to secure for me the passes of Baños and Perales, and he has occupied the former, but has left the latter to be occupied by the Duque del Parque. I wish that you would send somebody to see how the pass is occupied, and that, at all events, you should have an eye to that pass. It will make me quite secure, and will render me the greatest service that, in their present situation, the Portuguese troops could render. I don't think that the French would like to venture through that pass in the existing situation of their affairs. The bridges of Alcantara and Almarez being irreparable, they would be in a *cul de sac*, and would have no *exit*, excepting through a desert on the frontier of Portugal.

P. S. If you don't like to have —, you may leave him at Lisbon.

To the Rt. Hon. J. H. Frere.

Talavera de la Reyna, 24th July, 1809.

I conclude that Gen. Cuesta apprised the government of the success of the first operations of the combined armies. We intended to attack the enemy this morning at daylight in his position on the Alberche, and all the arrangements were made and the columns formed for that purpose; but the enemy retired to Sta Olalla in the course of last night. Gen. Cuesta has since marched to Cevolla; and I do not know whether he intends to halt there, or what are to be his future operations.

I have been obliged to intimate to him, since my arrival here, that I should consider that I had performed the engagement which I had made with him as soon as I should have removed the enemy from the Alberche, and should thereby have given him possession of the course of the Tagus, and should have laid open to him the communication with La Mancha and with Gen. Venegas' corps, and that I could attempt no further operation till I should be made certain of my supplies, by being furnished with proper means of transport and the requisite provisions from the country.

This intimation has become still more necessary within the last 2 days, in which I am concerned to say that, although my troops have been on forced marches, engaged in operations with the enemy, the success of which I must say depended upon them, they have had nothing to eat, while the Spanish army have had plenty; notwithstanding that I have returns of engagements made by the alcaldes of villages in the Vera de Plasencia to furnish this army before the 24th of this month with 250,000 rations.

I certainly lament the necessity which obliges me to halt at present, and will oblige me to withdraw from Spain, if it should continue. There is no man that does not acknowledge, even Gen. Cuesta himself acknowledges, the justice and propriety of my conduct in halting now, or in eventually withdrawing; and I can only say, that I have never seen an army so ill-treated in any country, or, considering that all depends upon its operations, one which deserved good treatment so much.

It is ridiculous to pretend that the country cannot supply our wants. The French army is well fed, and the soldiers who are taken in good health, and well supplied with bread, of which indeed they left a small magazine behind them. This is a rich country in corn, in comparison with Portugal, and yet, during the whole of my operations in that country, we never wanted bread but on one day on the frontiers of Galicia. In the Vera de Plasencia there are means to supply this army for four months, as I am informed, and yet the alcaldes have not performed their engagements with me. The Spanish army has plenty of every thing, and we alone, upon whom every thing depends, are actually starving.

I am aware of the important consequences which must attend the step which I shall take in withdrawing from Spain. It is certain that the people of England will never hear of another army entering Spain after they shall have received the accounts of the treatment we have met with; and it is equally certain that without the assistance, the example, and the countenance of a British army, the Spanish armies, however brave, will never effect their object. But no man can see his army perish by want without feeling for them, and most particularly must he feel for them when he knows that they have been brought into the country in which this want is felt by his own act, and on his own responsibility, and not by orders from any superior authority. I shall be obliged to you if you will make known to the government my sentiments upon this subject.

I have reason to believe that the enemy are in full march towards Madrid. They had their rear guard in Sta Olalla this day; and I have just heard that Gen. Cuesta was marching to that place instead of to Cevolla. I am only afraid that he will get himself into a scrape: any movement by me to his assistance is quite out of the question. I advised him to secure his communications with Venegas and the course of the Tagus, while measures should be taking to supply the British army with means of transport. If the enemy should discover that we are not with him, he will be beaten, or must retire. In either case he may lose all the advantages which might have been derived from our joint operations, and much valuable time, by his eager desire to enter Madrid on an early day. The enemy will make this discovery to-day, if Cuesta should risk any attempt upon their rear guard at Sta Olalla.

To Visc. Castlereagh.

Talavera de la Reyna, 24th July, 1809.

According to the arrangement which I had settled with Gen. Cuesta, the army broke up from Plasencia on the 17th and 18th inst., and reached Oropesa on the 20th, where it formed a junction with the Spanish army under his command.

Sir R. Wilson had marched from the Venta de Bazagona on the Tietar, with the Lusitanian Legion, a battalion of Portuguese cacadores, and 2 Spanish battalions, on the 15th. He arrived at Arenas on the 19th, and at Escalona on the Alberche on the 23d.

Gen. Venegas had also been directed to break up from Madridejos on the 18th and 19th, and to march by Tembleque and Ocaña to Fuentidueña on the Tagus, where that river is crossed by a ford, and thence to Arganda, where he was to arrive on the 22d and 23d.

The combined armies moved on the 22d from Oropesa, and the advanced guards attacked the enemy's outposts at Talavera.

Their left was turned by the 1st hussars and the 23d light dragoons, under Gen. Anson, and directed by Lieut. Gen. Payne, and by the division of infantry under the command of Major Gen. Mackenzie, and they were driven in by the Spanish advanced guard under the command of Gen. Zayas and the Duque de Alburquerque. We lost 11 horses by the cannonade from the enemy's position on the Alberche, and the Spaniards had some men wounded.

The columns were formed for the attack of this position yesterday, but the attack was postponed till this morning, by desire of Gen. Cuesta, when the different corps destined for the attack were put in motion. But the enemy had retired at about one in the morning to Sta Olalla, and thence towards Torrijos, I conclude, to form a junction with the corps under Gen. Sebastiani. I have not been able to follow the enemy as I could wish, on account of the great deficiency in the means of transport with this army, owing to my having found it impossible to procure even one mule or a cart in Spain.

I enclose the copy of a letter which I thought it proper to address upon this subject to Major Gen. O'Donoju, the Adj. Gen. of the Spanish army, as soon as I found that this country could furnish no means of this description; and I have since informed Gen. Cuesta, that I should consider the removal of the enemy from his position on the Alberche as a complete performance on my part of the engagement into which I had entered with him in his camp on the 11th inst., as that operation, if advantage was duly taken of it, would give him possession of the course of the Tagus, and would open his communication with La Mancha and with Venegas.

Within these 2 days I have had still more reason for adhering to my determination to enter into no new operation, but rather to halt, and even to return to Portugal, if I should not be supplied as I ought, as, notwithstanding His Majesty's troops have been engaged in very active operations, the success of which depended no less upon their bravery and exertions than upon the example they should hold out and the countenance they should give to the Spanish troops, they have been in actual want of provisions for these last 2 days; and even if I should have been willing, under such circumstances, to continue my co-operation with Gen. Cuesta, I am unable to do so with any justice to the troops. Gen. Cuesta is, I believe, fully sensible of the propriety of my determination, and I understand that he has urged the Central Junta to adopt vigorous measures to have our wants supplied. It is certain that at the present moment the people of this part of Spain are either unable or unwilling to supply them; and in either case, and till I am supplied, I do not think it proper, and indeed I cannot, continue my operations in Spain.

I ought probably to have stipulated that I should be supplied with the necessary means of transport before the army entered Spain. I did require and adopted the measures necessary to procure these means, which I conceived would have answered, considering the large supplies of the same kind which the army under the command of the late Sir J. Moore had procured; and as I could not engage to enter upon any operations in Spain which should not be consistent with the defence of Portugal, I did not think it proper to make any stipulation for the advantage of the troops, which stipulation after all did not appear necessary, in order to enable me to procure what I wanted.

I have great hopes, however, that before long I shall be supplied from Andalusia and La Mancha with the means which I require, and I shall then resume the active operations which I have been compelled to relinquish.

To the Rt. Hon. J. Villiers.

Talavera de la Reyna, 29th July, 1809.

The enemy having collected all the troops he had in this part of Spain, attacked us here on the 27th. The battle lasted till yesterday evening, when we beat him in all parts of our line; and he retreated in the evening and night, leaving in our hands 20 pieces of cannon, ammunition, waggons, prisoners, &c. The battle was a most desperate one. Our loss has been very

great, that of the enemy larger. The attack was made principally upon the British, who were on the left; and we had about
two to one against us; fearful odds! but we maintained all our
positions, and gave the enemy a terrible beating. The Spanish
troops that were engaged behaved well; but there were very
few of them engaged, as the attack was made upon us.

I have received your letters of the 19th and 22d July. I shall
send the Commissariat an extract of your letter respecting the
want of bills; it is strange that there should be any want of this
kind. I rather believe that a Commissary, Mr Nelson, has been
sent to Ciudad Rodrigo, to settle our accounts and pay our
debts there, notwithstanding that 2 gentlemen have been sent
to Lisbon for the same purpose. I shall write also to the Commissary Gen. upon this subject.

The demands of the Portuguese upon our funds are so very
large, as well on account of debts as of subsidy, that I do not
know how to answer them; but I will see what can be done in
respect to this debt on bills. I wish that you would give government a hint privately that they have embarked on too wide a
scale, and that the funds which they have provided cannot supply us and the Portuguese subsidy, and Sir John Moore's old
debts in Portugal and Spain.

P. S. I shall send you my dispatch, and one to the Regency
to-morrow.

To the Rt. Hon. J. H. Frere.

Talavera de la Reyna, 31st July, 1809.

I have the honor to enclose the copy of a letter which I have
received from Don M. de Garay, upon which I request of you
to convey to him the following observations.

I shall be very much obliged to him if he will understand that
I have no authority, nay, that I have been directed not to correspond with any of the Spanish ministers; and I request that he
will in future convey to me through you the commands which

he may have for me. I am convinced that I shall then avoid the
injurious and uncandid misrepresentations of what passes,
which Don M. de Garay has more than once sent to me, apparently with a view of placing on the records of his government
statements of my actions and conduct which are entirely inconsistent with the truth, and to which statements I have no regular
means of replying.

As soon as my line of march into Spain was determined
upon, which you and Don M. de Garay are aware was not till
a very late period, I sent to procure means of transport and
other supplies at the places in which I considered it most likely
I should get them, namely, Plasencia, Ciudad Rodrigo, Gata,
Bejar, &c.; and as soon as I found that I had failed, I wrote to
Gen. O'Donoju, on the 16th July, a letter, of which you have,
and of which I know the government have, a copy, in which I
told him that, as I had not received the assistance I required,
I could undertake for no more than the first operation, which I
had settled with Gen. Cuesta in my interview with him on the
11th. It is therefore an unfounded assertion that the first
account that the government received of my intentions not to
undertake any new operations was when they heard that I had
left Gen. Cuesta alone to pursue the enemy.

The statement is not true, for, although I disapproved of
Gen. Cuesta's advance of the 24th and 25th, which I knew
would end as it did, I did support it with two divisions of infantry and a brigade of cavalry, which covered his retreat to the
Alberche on the 26th, and his passage of that river on the
27th: and supposing the assertion to have been true, and that
Gen. Cuesta was exposed to be attacked by the enemy when
alone, it was his fault and not mine; and I had given him fair
notice, not only by my letter of the 16th July, but frequently
afterwards, that I could do no more.

It is not a difficult matter for a gentleman in the situation of
Don M. de Garay to sit down in his cabinet and write his ideas
of the glory which would result from driving the French
through the Pyrenees; and I believe there is no man in Spain
who has risked so much, or who has sacrificed so much, to
effect that object as I have. But I wish that Don M. de Garay,

or the gentlemen of the Junta, before they blame me for not doing more, or impute to me beforehand the probable consequences of the blunders or the indiscretion of others, would either come or send here somebody to satisfy the wants of our half starved army, which, although they have been engaged for 2 days, and have defeated twice their numbers, in the service of Spain, have not bread to eat. It is positively a fact that, during the last 7 days, the British army have not received one third of their provisions; that at this moment there are nearly 4000 wounded soldiers dying in the hospital in this town from want of common assistance and necessaries, which any other country in the world would have given even to its enemies; and that I can get no assistance of any description from the country. I cannot prevail upon them even to bury the dead carcasses in the neighbourhood, the stench of which will destroy themselves as well as us.

I cannot avoid feeling these circumstances; and the Junta must see that, unless they and the country make a great exertion to support and supply the armies, to which the invariable attention and the exertion of every man and the labor of every beast in the country ought to be directed, the bravery of the soldiers, their losses and their success, will only make matters worse and increase our embarrassment and distress. I positively will not move, nay, more, I will disperse my army, till I am supplied with provisions and means of transport as I ought to be.

To Visc. Castlereagh.

Talavera de la Reyna, 1st Aug. 1809.

My public letters will give you some idea of our situation. It is one of some embarrassment, but of which I think I shall get the better, I hope, without fighting another desperate battle, which would really cripple us so much as to render all our efforts useless. I certainly should get the better of every thing, if I could

manage Gen. Cuesta; but his temper and disposition are so
bad, that that is impossible.

Venegas' movement will probably relieve our front. I think
it probable also that the French will not like to press through
the Puerto de Baños, having Beresford's army on their rear, and
a victorious army in their front; and, indeed, that point would
be quite secure, if I could prevail upon Gen. Cuesta to reinforce
his troops at Bejar, so as to secure that point as I had understood it to be.

We are miserably supplied with provisions, and I do not
know how to remedy this evil. The Spanish armies are now so
numerous that they eat up the whole country. They have no
magazines, nor have we, nor can we collect any; and there is a
scramble for every thing.

I think the battle of the 28th is likely to be of great use to the
Spaniards; but I don't think them yet in a state of discipline to
contend with the French; and I prefer infinitely to endeavor to
remove the enemy from this part of Spain by manœuvre to the
trial of another pitched battle. The French, in the last, threw
their whole force upon us, and although it did not succeed, and
will not succeed in future, we shall lose great numbers of men,
which we can but ill afford. I dare not attempt to relieve ourselves from the weight of the attack by bringing forward the
Spanish troops, owing to their miserable state of discipline, and
their want of officers properly qualified. These troops are
entirely incapable of performing any manœuvre, however simple. They would get into irretrievable confusion, and the result
would probably be the loss of every thing.

I have received your Lordship's letter of the 11th July, for
which I am much obliged to you. I hope that your expedition
will succeed. I guessed the point to which it was directed.

To Visc. Castlereagh.

Deleytosa, 8th Aug. 1809.

I apprised your Lordship on the 1st inst. of the advance of a French corps towards the Puerto de Baños, and of the probable embarrassment of the operations of the army, which its arrival at Plasencia would occasion; and these embarrassments having since existed to a degree so considerable as to oblige us to fall back, and to take up a defensive position on the Tagus, I am induced to trouble you more at length with an account of what has passed upon this subject.

When I entered Spain, I had a communication with Gen. Cuesta, through Sir R. Wilson and Col. Roche, respecting the occupation of the Puerto de Baños and the Puerto de Perales; the former of which it was at last settled should be held by a corps to be formed under the Marques de la Reyna, to consist of 2 battalions from Gen. Cuesta's army, and 2 from Bejar; and that the Puerto de Perales was to be taken care of by the Duque del Parque, by detachments from the garrison of Ciudad Rodrigo. I doubted the capacity of the garrison of Ciudad Rodrigo to make the detachment to the latter, but so little as to the effectual occupation of the former, that in writing to Marshal Beresford on the 17th July, on this subject, I desired him to look to the Puerto de Perales, but that I considered Baños secure, as appears by the extract of my letter, which I enclose.

On the 30th intelligence was received at Talavera that 12,000 rations had been ordered at Fuente Roble for the 28th, and 24,000 at Los Santos for the same day, for a French corps, which it was believed was on its march towards the Puerto de Baños. Gen. Cuesta expressed some anxiety respecting this post, and sent me a message, to propose that Sir R. Wilson should be sent there with his corps. Sir Robert was on that day at Talavera, but his corps was in the mountains towards Escalona; and as he had already made himself very useful in that quarter, and had been near Madrid, with which city he had

had a communication which I was desirous of keeping up, I proposed that a Spanish corps should be sent to Baños without loss of time. I could not prevail with Gen. Cuesta, although he certainly admitted the necessity of a reinforcement when he proposed that Sir R. Wilson should be sent to Baños; and he was equally sensible with myself of the benefit to be derived to the cause from sending Sir Robert back to Escalona. At this time we had no further intelligence of the enemy's advance, than that the rations were ordered; and I had hopes that the enemy might be deterred from advancing by the intelligence of our success on the 28th; and that the troops in the Puerto might make some defence; and that, under these circumstances, it was not desirable to divert Sir Robert from Escalona.

On the 31st, however, I renewed my application to Gen. Cuesta, to send there a Spanish division of sufficient strength, in a letter to Gen. O'Donoju, of which I enclose a copy, but without effect; and he did not detach Gen. Bassecourt till the morning of the 2d Aug., after we had heard that the enemy had entered Bejar; and it was obvious that the troops in the Puerto would make no defence.

On the 2d, we received accounts that the enemy had entered Plasencia in 2 columns. The Marques de la Reyna, whose 2 battalions consisted only of 600 men, with only 20 rounds of ammunition each man, retired from the Puerto and from Plasencia, without firing a shot; and went to the bridge of Almaraz, which he declared that he intended to remove. The battalions of Bejar dispersed without making any resistance. Gen. Cuesta called upon me on that day, and proposed that half of the army should move to the rear to oppose the enemy, while the other half should maintain the post at Talavera. My answer was, that if, by half the army, he meant half of each army, I could only answer, that I was ready either to go or to stay with the whole British army, but that I could not divide it. He then desired me to choose whether I would go or stay; and I preferred to go, from thinking that the British troops were most likely to do the business effectually, and without contest; and from being of opinion, that to open the communication through Plasencia was more important to us than to the

Spanish army, although very important to them. With this decision Gen. Cuesta appeared perfectly satisfied.

The movements of the enemy in our front since the 1st had induced me to be of opinion that, despairing of forcing us at Talavera, they intended to force a passage by Escalona, and thus to open a communication with the French corps coming from Plasencia. This suspicion was confirmed in the night of the 2d by letters received from Sir R. Wilson, of which I enclose copies; and before I quitted Talavera on the 3d, I waited upon Gen. O'Donoju, and conversed with him upon the whole of our situation, and pointed out to him the possibility that, in the case of the enemy coming through Escalona, Gen. Cuesta might find himself obliged to quit Talavera before I should be able to return to him; and I urged him to collect all the carts that could be got, in order to remove our hospital. At his desire, I put the purport of this conversation in writing, and sent him a letter to be laid before Gen. Cuesta, of which I enclose a copy.

The British army marched on the 3d to Oropesa, Gen. Basse-court's Spanish corps being at Centenillo; where I desired that it might half the next day, in order that I might be nearer it. About 5 o'clock in the evening I heard that the French had arrived from Plasencia at Navalmoral, whereby they were between us and the bridge of Almaraz. About an hour afterwards, I received from Gen. O'Donoju the letter and its enclosures, of which I enclose copies, announcing to me the intention of Gen. Cuesta to march from Talavera in the evening, and to leave there my hospital, excepting such men as could be moved by the means he already had, on the grounds of his apprehension that I was not strong enough for the corps coming from Plasencia; and that the enemy was moving upon his flank, and had returned to Sᵗᵃ Olalla, in his front.

I acknowledge that these reasons did not appear to me sufficient for giving up so important a post as Talavera, for exposing the combined armies to an attack in front and rear at the same time, and for abandoning my hospital, and I wrote the letter of which I enclose a copy. This unfortunately reached the General after he had marched; and he arrived at Oropesa shortly after daylight on the morning of the 4th.

The question what was to be done was then to be considered. The enemy, stated to be 30,000 strong, but at all events, consisting of the corps of Soult and Ney, either united, or not very distant from each other, and supposed by Joseph Buonaparte and Marshal Jourdan to be sufficiently strong to attack the British army stated to be 25,000 strong, were, on one side, in possession of the high road to the passage of the Tagus at Almaraz, the bridge at which place we knew had been removed, although the boats still necessarily remained in the river. On the other side, we had reason to expect the advance of Victor's corps to Talavera, as soon as Gen. Cuesta's march should be known; and after leaving 12,000 men to watch Venegas, and allowing from 10,000 to 11,000 killed and wounded in the late action, this corps would have amounted to 25,000. We could extricate ourselves from this difficult situation only by great celerity of movement (to which the troops were unequal, as they had not had their allowance of provisions for several days), and by success in 2 battles: if we were unsuccessful in either, we should have been without a retreat; and if Soult and Ney, avoiding an action, had retired before us, and had waited the arrival of Victor, we should have been exposed to a general action with 50,000 men equally without a retreat. We had reason to expect that as the Marques de la Reyna could not remove the boats from the river at Almaraz, Soult would have destroyed them. Our only retreat therefore was by the bridge of Arzobispo; and if we had moved on, the enemy, by breaking that bridge while the army should be engaged with Soult and Ney, would have deprived us of that only resource. We could not take up a position at Oropesa, as we thereby left open the road to the bridge of Arzobispo from Talavera by Calera; and after considering the whole subject maturely, I was of opinion, that it was advisable to retire to the bridge of Arzobispo, and to take up a defensive position upon the Tagus.

I was induced to adopt this last opinion because the French have now at least 50,000 men disposable to oppose to the combined armies, and a corps of 12,000 to watch Venegas; and I was likewise of opinion that the sooner the defensive line should be taken up, the more likely were the troops to be able to defend it. Accordingly I marched on the 4th, and crossed the Tagus by the bridge of Arzobispo; and have continued my route to this place, in which I am well situated to defend the passage of Almaraz, and the lower parts of the Tagus. Gen. Cuesta crossed the river on the night of the 5th, and he is still at the bridge of Arzobispo.

About 2000 of the wounded have been brought away from Talavera, the remaining 1500 are there; and I doubt whether, under any circumstances, it would have been possible or consistent with humanity to attempt to remove any more of them. From the treatment some of the soldiers wounded on the 27th, and who fell into the hands of the enemy, experienced from them, and from the manner in which I have always taken care of their wounded who have fallen into my hands, I expect that these men will be well treated; and I have only to lament that a new concurrence of events, over which, from circumstances, I had and could have no control, should have placed the army in a situation to be obliged to leave any of them behind.

To Visc. Castlereagh.

Truxillo, 21st Aug. 1809.

Gen. Cuesta moved his head quarters from the neighbourhood of the bridge of Arzobispo, on the night of the 7th inst., to Peraleda de Garbin, leaving an advanced guard consisting of 2 divisions of infantry, and the Duque de Alburquerque's division of cavalry, for the defence of the passage of the Tagus at this point. The French cavalry passed the Tagus at a ford immediately above the bridge, at half past one in the afternoon of the 8th, and surprised this advanced guard, which retired, leaving behind them all their cannon, as well as those in the batteries constructed for the defence of the bridge. Gen. Cuesta then moved his head quarters to the Mesa de Ibor on the evening of the 8th, having his advanced guard at Bohonal. He resigned the command of the army on the 12th, on account of the bad state of his health, and the command has devolved upon Gen. Eguia. The head quarters of the Spanish army are now at Deleytosa.

It appears that a detachment of Venegas' army had some success against the enemy in an attack made upon it in the neighbourhood of Aranjuez on the 5th inst.: Gen. Venegas was then at Ocaña, and he had determined to retire towards the Sierra Morena; and after the 5th, he had moved in that direction. He returned, however, towards Toledo, with an intention of attacking the enemy on the 12th inst.; but on the 11th, the enemy attacked him with Sebastiani's corps, and 2 divisions of Victor's, in the neighbourhood of Almonacid. The action appears to have lasted some hours; but the French having at last gained an advantage on Gen. Venegas' left, he was obliged to retire, and was about to resume his position in the mountains of the Sierra Morena.

On the 9th, 10th, and 11th, large detachments of the French troops, which had come from Plasencia, returned to that quarter; and on the 12th, they attacked and defeated Sir R. Wilson in the Puerto de Baños, on their return to Salamanca. It appears now, that the French force in this part of Spain is distributed as follows: Marshal Victor's corps is divided between Talavera and La Mancha; Sebastiani's is in La Mancha; Marshal Mortier's at Oropesa, Arzobispo, and Navalmoral; Marshal Soult's at Plasencia; and Marshal Ney's at Salamanca.

From this distribution of their forces, it is obvious that they do not intend, at present, to undertake any offensive operation: if any; it will be upon the right in La Mancha; at the same time that if the combined armies were in a situation to be enabled to undertake any thing, they would experience great difficulty in the operation, and might be exposed to the same misfortune as that which stopped them lately, and deprived them of the fruits of their victory at Talavera. But, from what follows, your Lordship will observe, that the British part of the army, at least, is incapable of undertaking any thing; and that the distress for want of provisions, and its effects, have at last obliged me to move towards the frontiers of Portugal, in order to refresh my troops.

In my former dispatches, I have informed your Lordship of

our distress for the want of provisions and means of transport. These wants, which were the first cause of the loss of many advantages after the 22d July, which were made known to the government, and were actually known by them on the 20th of last month, still exist in an aggravated degree, and have produced all the evil effects upon the health and efficiency of the army which might have been expected from them.

Since the 22d of last month, when the Spanish and British armies joined, the troops have not received 10 days' bread; on some days they have received nothing; and for many days together only meat, without salt: frequently flour instead of bread, and scarcely ever more than one third, or at most half, of a ration. The cavalry and the horses of the army have not received, in the same time, three regular deliveries of forage, particularly of barley, the only wholesome subsistence for a horse in this country; and the horses have been kept alive by what they could pick up for themselves, for which they have frequently been obliged to go from 12 to 20 miles' distance, particularly lately.

During a great part of this time, at least till the 4th or 5th of this month, I know that the Spanish army received their regular rations daily: after they lost the bridge of Arzobispo, I believe they were in want for some days; but since they have come through the passes of the mountains, I know, from the best authority, that of Gen. Eguia, that the Spanish cavalry have been supplied daily with at least half a ration of barley, and I believe the troops have received their regular allowance of bread.

The consequence of these privations upon the British army has been the loss of many horses of the cavalry and artillery. We lost 100 in the cavalry last week; and we now want 1000 horses to complete the 6 regiments of dragoons, besides about 700 that are sick, and will probably be fit for service only after a considerable period of rest and good food. The horses of the artillery are also much diminished in numbers, and are scarcely able to draw the guns.

The sickness of the army, from the same cause, has increased considerably; particularly among the officers, who have fared no better than the soldiers; and have had nothing but water to drink, and frequently nothing but meat without salt to eat, and seldom any bread, for the last month. Indeed, there are few, if any, officers or soldiers of the army who, although doing their duty, are not more or less affected by dysentery, and the whole lie out, and nothing can be got for them in this part of the country.

To these circumstances I must add, that I have not been able to procure means of transport of any description since my arrival in Spain. I was obliged to employ the largest proportion of the carts in the army, whether they carried money or ammunition, to convey the wounded soldiers to the hospital at Elvas; and the ammunition which was laid down at Mesa de Ibor and Deleytosa was delivered to the Spanish General. The few carts which remained in the army were required to move the sick we have at present, and I have been obliged to leave behind me the remainder of the reserve ammunition, which I have also given to the Spanish troops; and if I had waited longer, I should not have been able to move at all without leaving the sick behind. Under these circumstances, I determined to break up on the 20th from Jaraicejo, where I had had my head quarters since the 11th, with the advanced posts on the Tagus, near the bridge of Almaraz, and to fall back upon the frontiers of Portugal; where I hope I shall be supplied with every thing I want.

I have given your Lordship only an outline of the distresses of the army. You will find the details of them in my correspondence with the British ministers at Seville, copies of which, I conclude, they will send home to the Foreign office.

Your Lordship will observe, that from the dispersed situation of the French army, and the losses the enemy has sustained, the Spanish troops are not likely to suffer any inconvenience from our absence; but I assure your Lordship that if I had been certain that the enemy could and would attack the Spaniards on the day after my departure, I could not, with justice to the army, have remained any longer; and there is not a General officer in the army who has not repeatedly represented the lamentable and neglected situation in which we were placed, and the absolute necessity which existed that I should withdraw from Spain altogether.

To Visc. Castlereagh.

Merida, 25th Aug. 1809.

I received by Mr Hay, on the day before yesterday, your letter of the 4th Aug., and having for some time past turned my mind very seriously to the consideration of the points to which it relates, I am not unprepared to give you an opinion upon them.

The information which I have acquired in the last two months has opened my eyes respecting the state of the war in the Peninsula; and I shall just state a few facts which will enable the King's ministers to form their own opinions upon it.

I calculate the French force in the Peninsula now to consist of about 125,000 men: of this number, about 70,000 are in this part of Spain; St Cyr's corps, about 20,000 men, are engaged in the siege of Gerona; Suchet's, about 14,000, in Aragon; and the remainder are employed in different garrisons, such as Avila, &c., and in keeping up the communication with France: all of which, if necessary, are disposable for the field. These 125,000 men are exclusive of the garrisons of Pamplona, Barcelona, &c. &c. These troops, you will observe, are all in Spain; and against this force the Spaniards have, under Venegas and Eguia, late Cuesta's army, about 50,000 men; Romana, the Duque del Parque, and every thing to the northward, about 25,000; Blake may have gotten together again about 5000 or 6000; and I believe there is nothing in Aragon and Catalonia, excepting an armed population.

Thus, the Spaniards have not, at the end of 18 months nearly, after the commencement of the revolution, above 80,000 men, of which the composition and quality will be found still more defective than the numbers are deficient to carry on the contest with the French even in their present strength. To these numbers add all the troops we can bring into the field at present, which are about 25,000 men, and about 10,000 Portuguese, and you will see that the allies are, at this moment, inferior in point of numbers only to the enemy in the Peninsula. However, in this account of the troops of the allies,

I do not reckon many garrisons and towns occupied by both Spaniards and Portuguese; not do I reckon the French garrisons. I count only those men on both sides who can be brought into the field to fight.

In respect to the composition of these armies, we find the French well supplied with troops of the different descriptions and arms required; viz., infantry, artillery, and cavalry, heavy and light. Cuesta's army had about 7000 cavalry, Venegas' about 3000, and there may be about 2000 more cavalry distributed throughout Spain. The English have about 2500 cavalry left, and the Portuguese army may have 500 or 600. Probably, if all this cavalry were efficient, and could be divided as it ought to be, it might be sufficient, and might be found more numerous than that of the French in the Peninsula: but you will observe that all the cavalry is now in the south, and Romana's army (which it is most important to bring forward, as unless it is brought forward the allies can never make any impression on the French to the southward) has neither cavalry nor artillery, and cannot quit the mountains; neither has the Duque del Parque more than one regiment, or Blake more than the same number.

I come now to the description of the troops, and here I am sorry to say that our allies fail us still more than they do in numbers and composition. The Spanish cavalry are, I believe, nearly entirely without discipline. They are in general well clothed, armed, and accoutred, and remarkably well mounted, and their horses are in good condition; I mean those of Eguia's army, which I have seen. But I have never heard any body pretend that in any one instance they have behaved as soldiers ought to do in presence of an enemy. They make no scruple of running off, and after an action are to be found in every village and every shady bottom within 50 miles of the field of battle. The Spanish artillery are, as far as I have seen of them, entirely unexceptionable, and the Portuguese artillery excellent.

In respect to the great body of all armies, I mean the infantry, it is lamentable to see how bad that of the Spaniards is, and how unequal to a contest with the French. They are armed, I believe, well; they are badly accoutred, not having the means of saving their ammunition from the rain; not clothed in some instances at all, in others clothed in such a manner as to make them look like peasants, which ought of all things to be avoided; and their discipline appears to me to be confined to placing them in the ranks, three deep at very close order, and to the manual exercise.

It is impossible to calculate upon any operation with these troops. It is said that sometimes they behave well; though I acknowledge that I have never seen them behave otherwise than ill. Bassecourt's corps, which was supposed to be the best in Cuesta's army, and was engaged on our left in the mountains, at the battle of Talavera, was kept in check throughout the day by one French battalion: this corps has since run away from the bridge of Arzobispo, leaving its guns; and many of the men, according to the usual Spanish custom, throwing away their arms, accoutrements, and clothing. It is a curious circumstance respecting this affair at Arzobispo (in which Soult writes that the French took 30 pieces of cannon), that the Spaniards ran off in such a hurry, that they left their cannon loaded and unspiked; and that the French, although they drove the Spaniards from the bridge, did not think themselves strong enough to push after them; and Col. Waters, whom I sent in with a flag of truce on the 10th, relating to our wounded, found the cannon on the road, abandoned by the one party, and not taken possession of, and probably not known of, by the other.

This practice of running away, and throwing off arms, accoutrements, and clothing, is fatal to every thing, excepting a re-assembly of the men in a state of nature, who as regularly perform the same manœuvre the next time an occasion offers. Nearly 2000 ran off on the evening of the 27th from the battle of Talavera (not 100 yards from the place where I was standing), who were neither attacked, nor threatened with an attack, and who were frightened only by the noise of their own fire: they left their arms and accoutrements on the ground, their officers went with them; and they, and the fugitive cavalry, plundered the baggage of the British army which had been sent to the rear. Many others went whom I did not see.

Nothing can be worse than the officers of the Spanish army;

and it is extraordinary that when a nation has devoted itself to war, as this nation has, by the measures it has adopted in the last 2 years, so little progress has been made in any one branch of the military profession by any individual, and that the business of an army should be so little understood. They are really children in the art of war, and I cannot say that they do any thing as it ought to be done, with the exception of running away and assembling again in a state of nature.

I really believe that much of this deficiency of numbers, composition, discipline, and efficiency, is to be attributed to the existing government of Spain. They have attempted to govern the Kingdom in a state of revolution, by an adherence to old rules and systems, and with the aid of what is called enthusiasm; and this last is, in fact, no aid to accomplish any thing, and is only an excuse for the irregularity with which every thing is done, and for the want of discipline and subordination of the armies. People are very apt to believe that enthusiasm carried the French through their revolution, and was the parent of those exertions which have nearly conquered the world; but if the subject is nicely examined, it will be found that enthusiasm was the name only, but that force was the instrument which brought forward those great resources under the system of terror which first stopped the allies; and that a perseverance in the same system of applying every individual and every description of property to the service of the army, by force, has since conquered Europe.

After this statement, you will judge for yourselves, whether you will employ any, and what strength of army, in support of the cause in Spain. Circumstances with which you are acquainted have obliged me to separate myself from the Spanish army, and I can only tell you that I feel no inclination to join in co-operation with them again, upon my own responsibility; and that I shall see my way very clearly before me indeed, before I do so; and I do not recommend you to have any thing to do with them in their present state.

Before I quit this part of the subject, it may be satisfactory to you to know that I do not think matters would have been much better if you had sent your large expedition to Spain, instead of to the Scheldt. You could not have equipped it in Galicia, or any where in the north of Spain. If we had had 60,000 men, instead of 20,000, in all probability we should not have got to Talavera to fight the battle, for want of means and provisions. But if we had got to Talavera, we could not have gone farther, and the armies would probably have separated for want of means of subsistence, probably without a battle; but certainly afterwards. Besides, you will observe that your 40,000 men, supposing them to be equipped and means to exist of feeding them, would not compensate for the deficiency of numbers, of composition, and of efficiency in the Spanish armies; and that supposing they had been able to remove the French from Madrid, they could not have removed them from the Peninsula, even in the existing state of the French force.

I now come to another branch of the subject, which is Portugal itself. I have not got from Beresford his report upon the present, and the probable future, state of the Portuguese army; and therefore I should wish to be understood as writing, upon this part of the subject, liable to corrections from him.

My opinion is, and always has been, that the mode of applying the services of the English officers to the Portuguese army has been erroneous. I think that Beresford ought to have had the temporary assistance of the ablest officers the British service could afford; that these officers ought not to have been posted to regiments in the Portuguese army, but under the title of 'Adjutants' to the Field Marshal, or any other, they ought to have superintended discipline, military movements, and arrangements of all descriptions, wherever they might be: fewer officers would then have answered his purpose, and every one given to him would have been useful; whereas many (all in the inferior ranks) are, under existing arrangements, useless. Besides this, the selection of officers sent out to Portugal for this service has been unlucky, and the decision on the questions which I sent to England on the 7th June has been made without reference to circumstances, or to the feelings or opinions of the individuals on whom it was to operate; and just like every other decision I have ever seen from the same quarter, as if men were stocks and stones. To this, add that rank (Portuguese rank, I

mean) has been given in the most capricious manner. In some
instances, a man not in the army at all is made a Brigadier General; in others, another who was the senior of the Brigadier
General when both were in the army, is a Lieutenant Colonel;
then a junior Lieutenant Colonel is made a Brigadier General,
his senior a Colonel, and his senior a junior Colonel; and there
are instances of juniors being preferred to seniors in every rank;
in short, the Prince Regent of Portugal is a despotic prince, and
his commissions have been given to British officers and subjects
in the most arbitrary manner at the Horse Guards; and the
answer to all these complaints at the Horse Guards must be
uniform, nobody has any right to complain; the Prince Regent
has a right to give to any body any commission he pleases,
bearing any date he chooses to assign to it. The officers of this
army have to a man quitted the Portuguese service, as I said
they would, and there is not an officer who has joined it from
England who would not quit it if we would allow him; but here
we keep them: so much for that arrangement.

The subject upon which particularly I wished Beresford to
report, was the state of the Portuguese army in respect to its
numbers. The troops have lately deserted to an alarming degree;
and, in fact, none of the regiments are complete. The Portuguese army is recruited by conscription constitutionally, very
much in the same manner with the French army; but then it
must be recollected, that, for the last 50 years nearly, the troops
have never left their province, and scarcely ever their native
town; and their discipline, and the labors and exertion required
from them, were nothing. Things are much altered lately, and
notwithstanding that the pay has been increased, I fear that the
animal is not of the description to bear up against what is
required of him; and he deserts most terribly.

The military forces stationed in the provinces enabled the
civil government to carry into execution the conscription;
but, under present circumstances, the military force is, upon
principle, as well as necessity, removed to a distance. The civil
government has been so frequently overthrown in all parts
of Portugal that it can hardly be said to exist; and there is
another circumstance which I am afraid cramps its operations,

particularly those operations which are to put a restraint upon the people, and that is, that they are all armed, and they defy the civil magistrate and the government who order them to march as conscripts, whose authority is unsupported by a sufficient military force. I am, therefore, very apprehensive that Beresford will find it impossible to fill his ranks: however, as I said before, I should wish government to delay making their minds up on this part of the subject till I shall be enabled to send them Beresford's report, for which I have called.

The next point in this subject is, supposing the Portuguese army to be rendered efficient, what can be done with it and Portugal, if the French should obtain possession of the remainder of the Peninsula? My opinion is, that we ought to be able to hold Portugal, if the Portuguese army and militia are complete. The difficulty upon this sole question lies in the embarkation of the British army. There are so many entrances into Portugal, the whole country being frontier, that it would be very difficult to prevent the enemy from penetrating; and it is probable that we should be obliged to confine ourselves to the preservation of that which is most important, the capital.

It is difficult, if not impossible, to bring the contest for the capital to extremities, and afterwards to embark the British army. You will see what I mean, by a reference to the map. Lisbon is so high up the Tagus that no army that we could collect would be able at the same time to secure the navigation of the river by the occupation of both banks, and the possession of the capital. One of the objects must, I fear, be given up, and that which the Portuguese would give up would be the navigation of the Tagus; and, of course, our means of embarkation. However, I have not entirely made up my mind upon this interesting point. I have a great deal of information upon it, but I should wish to have more before I can decide upon it.

In the mean time, I think that government should look to sending back at least the coppered transports, as soon as the grand expedition shall have done with them; and as they receive positive intelligence that Napoleon is reinforcing his armies in Spain: for you may depend upon it, that he and his Marshals must be desirous of revenging upon us the different blows we have given them; and that when they come into the Peninsula, their first and great object will be to get the English out.

I think the first part of my letter will give you my opinion respecting one notion you entertained, viz., that the Spaniards might be induced to give the command of their armies to a British Commander in Chief. If such offer should be made to me, I shall decline to accept it till I shall receive His Majesty's pleasure; and I strongly recommend to you, unless you mean to incur the risk of the loss of your army, not to have any thing to do with Spanish warfare on any ground whatever in the existing state of things. In respect to Cadiz, the fact is this, that the jealousy of all the Spaniards, even of those most attached to us, respecting Cadiz, is so rooted, that even if the government should cede that point (and in their present difficulties I should not be surprised if they were to cede it) to induce me to remain in Spain, I should not think any garrison which this army could spare to be safe in the place.

If you should take Cadiz, you must lay down Portugal, and take up Spain; you must occupy Cadiz with a garrison of from 15,000 to 20,000 men, and you must send from England an army to be employed in the field with the Spaniards, and make Cadiz your retreat instead of Lisbon. You ought, along with Cadiz, to insist upon the command of the armies of Spain. I think you would certainly be able in that case to get away your troops, secure the Spanish ships, &c.

But you see from the facts in the commencement of this letter, how little prospect you have of bringing the contest to the conclusion for which we all wish.

I shall be very glad if you will send us the remount horses, and any regiment of dragoons that is to come, as soon as possible; the best thing to do then, probably, would be to draft the horses of one of the regiments to complete the others, and send that regiment home dismounted. It would be very desirable also to send us 600 or 700 sets of horse appointments.

THREE

THE CAMPAIGNS OF 1810

Following the battle of Talavera, to the fury of the Spaniards who found themselves under concerted attack and in January 1810 lost the whole of the vital region of Andalucía to the French, Wellington's army did not fire a shot for almost a year. Instead, rightly convinced that a major invasion of Portugal was on the way, the British commander husbanded his forces whilst working on his plans for the defence of the country. In brief, these last were three-fold: the construction of a series of impregnable defensive positions known as the Lines of Torres Vedras that were designed to render Lisbon proof against any assault; the assimilation of a much reconstructed and reorganised Portuguese regular army into the structure of his own forces; and the development of a militia and homeguard organisation that could cut the communications of any invader and deprive him of the resources of the country. As Wellington expected, it was not long before the plans were put to the test. Having first captured the Spanish strongholds of Astorga and Ciudad Rodrigo, on 24 July 1810 65,000 French troops crossed the frontier under Marshal Masséna and drove back the elite Light Division in a fierce action at the River Coa. It had been hoped that the progress of an invasion would be greatly slowed by the need to reduce the imposing border fortress of Almeida, but scarcely had bombardment of its defences begun when a freak explosion destroyed the main powder magazine and with it much of the centre of the city. With the defenders left with no option but to surrender, by mid-September the French were pushing westwards towards Coimbra through a countryside devastated by the imposition of a ruthless 'scorched-earth' policy. What Wellington planned to do at this point has been the subject of much debate, but all the evidence suggests that he hoped to check the invasion at the imposing defensive position afforded by the Serra do Buçaco, an immensely high and steep north–south ridge that completely blocked the French line of march. In this, however, he was frustrated. Whilst a frontal assault was beaten off with heavy losses on 27 September, Masséna discovered a way round Wellington's northern flank, and the British commander therefore ordered his troops to fall back on Lisbon. Such a move was popular neither with his army, nor the council of regency that had been established to govern Portugal, nor the British government, but Wellington held firm to his strategy, and by 8 October the whole of his forces were safely ensconced within the Lines of Torres Vedras. As expected, these brought Masséna to a standstill – they were so terrifying a prospect that they were sufficient to daunt even the most seasoned French commander – but the marshal did not then simply retreat. Scouring the countryside for any food that he could find, he rather established a fortified base at Santarem, and sat down to wait on events in the hope that help would arrive from the French forces in southern Spain or even Napoleon. Lasting, as it did, all through the winter, the stalemate that resulted cost the population of Portugal very dear with over 100,000 people dying of famine. In purely military terms, however, Wellington's strategy had been proven to be prescient in the extreme, whilst the defence of Portugal that he had mounted is still reckoned as a masterpiece in the art of defensive warfare and has a strong claim to be the greatest triumph of his career.

Memorandum for Lieut. Col. Fletcher, commanding Royal Engineers.*

Lisbon, 20th Oct. 1809.

In the existing relative state of the Allied and French armies in the Peninsula, it does not appear probable that the enemy have it in their power to make an attack upon Portugal. They must wait for their reinforcements; and as the arrival of these may be expected, it remains to be considered what plan of defence shall be adopted for this country.

The great object in Portugal is the possession of Lisbon and the Tagus, and all our measures must be directed to this object. There is another also connected with that first object, to which we must likewise attend, viz.; the embarkation of the British troops in case of reverse.

In whatever season the enemy may enter Portugal, he will probably make his attack by two distinct lines, the one north, the other south of the Tagus; and the system of defence to be adopted must be founded upon this general basis.

In the winter season the river Tagus will be full, and will be a barrier to the enemy's enterprises with his left attack, not very difficult to be secured. In the summer season, however, the Tagus being fordable in many places between Abrantes and Salvaterra, and even lower than Salvaterra, care must be taken that the enemy does not, by his attack directed from the south of the Tagus, and by the passage of that river, cut off from Lisbon the British army engaged in operations to the northward of the Tagus.

The object of the allies should be to oblige the enemy as much as possible to make his attack with concentrated corps. They should stand in every position which the country could afford,

---

*   'The plan was altered after this memorandum was written, as it was found that the plain of Castanbeira could not be occupied with advantage; the right was therefore thrown back on Alhandra. But this memorandum is the foundation on which the whole work was commenced and completed. It was written after a detailed reconnaissance of the ground, and a personal visit to every part of it.'

such a length of time as would enable the people of the country to evacuate the towns and villages, carrying with them or destroying all articles of provisions and carriages, not necessary for the allied army; each corps taking care to preserve its communication with the others, and its relative distance from the point of junction.

In whatever season the enemy's attack may be made, the whole allied army, after providing for the garrisons of Elvas, Almeida, Abrantes, and Valença, should be divided into three corps, to be posted as follows: one corps to be in Beira; another in Alentejo; and the third, consisting of the Lusitanian legion, 8 battalions of caçadores, and 2 of militia, in the mountains of Castello Branco.

In the winter, the corps in Beira should consist of two thirds of the whole numbers of the operating army. In the summer, the corps in Beira and Alentejo should be nearly of equal numbers.

I shall point out in another memorandum the plan of operations to be adopted by the corps north and south of the Tagus in the winter months.

In the summer, it is probable, as I have above stated, that the enemy will make his attack in two principal corps, and that he will also push one through the mountains of Castello Branco and Abrantes. His object will be, by means of his corps south of the Tagus, to turn the positions which might be taken up in his front on the north of that river; to cut off from Lisbon the corps opposed to him; and to destroy it by an attack in front and rear at the same time. This can be avoided only by the retreat of the right centre, and left of the allies, and their junction at a point at which, from the state of the river, they cannot be turned by the passage of the Tagus by the enemy's left.

The first point of defence which presents itself below that at which the Tagus ceases to be fordable is the river of Castanheira, and here the army should be posted as follows: – 10,000 men, including all the cavalry, in the plain between the Tagus and the hills; 5000 infantry on the left of the plain; and the remainder of the army, with the exception of the following detachments, on the height in front, and on the right of Cadafoēs.

In order to prevent the enemy from turning, by their left, the positions which the allies may take up for the defence of the high road to Lisbon by the Tagus, Torres Vedras should be occupied by a corps of 5000 men; the height in the rear of Sobral de Monte Agraço by 4000 men; and Arruda by 2000 men.

There should be a small corps on the height east by south of the height of Sobral, to prevent the enemy from marching from Sobral to Arruda; and there should be another small corps on the height of Ajuda, between Sobral and Bucellas.

In case the enemy should succeed in forcing the corps at Torres Vedras, or Sobral de Monte Agraço, or Arruda; if the first, it must fall back gradually to Cabeça de Montachique, occupying every defensible point on the road; if the second, it must fall back upon Bucellas, destroying the road after the height of Ajuda; if the third, it must fall back upon Alhandra, disputing the road particularly at a point one league in front of that town.

In case any one of these three positions should be forced, the army must fall back from its position as before pointed out, and must occupy one as follows:

5000 men, principally light infantry, on the hill behind Alhandra; the main body of the army on the Serra de Serves, with its right on that part of the Serra which is near the Cazal de Portella, and is immediately above the road which crosses the Serra from Bucellas to Alverca; and its left extending to the pass of Bucellas. The entrance of the pass of Bucellas to be occupied by the troops retired from Sobral de Monte Agraço, &c., and Cabeça de Montachique by the corps retired from Torres Vedras.

In order to strengthen these several positions, it is necessary that different works should be constructed immediately, and that arrangements and preparations should be made for the construction of others.

Accordingly, I beg Col. Fletcher, as soon as possible, to review these several positions.

1st. He will examine particularly the effect of damming up the mouth of the Castanheira river; how far it will render that river a barrier, and to what extent it will fill.

2d. He will calculate the labor required for that work, and the time it will take, as well as the means of destroying the bridge over the river, and of constructing such redoubts as might be necessary on the plain, and on the hill on the left of the road, effectually to defend the plain. He will state particularly what means should be prepared for these works. He will also consider of the means and time required, and the effect which might be produced by sloping the banks of the river.

3d. He will make the same calculations for the works to be executed on the hill in front, and on the right of Cadafoēs, particularly on the left of that hill, to shut the entry of the valley of Cadafoēs.

4th. He will examine and report upon the means of making a good road of communication from the plain across the hills into the valley of Cadafoēs, and to the left of the proposed position, and calculate the time and labor it will take.

5th. He will examine the road from Otta by Abregada, Labrugeira to Merciana, and thence to Torres Vedras; and also from Merciana to Sobral de Monte Agraço. He will also examine and report upon the road from Alemquer to Sobral de Monte Agraço.

6th. He will entrench a post at Torres Vedras for 5000 men. He will examine the road from Torres Vedras to Cabeça de Montachique; and fix upon the spots, which to break up, might stop or delay the enemy; and if there should be advantageous ground at such spots, he will entrench a position for 400 men to cover the retreat of the corps from Torres Vedras.

7th. He will examine the position at Cabeça de Montachique, and determine upon its line of defence, and upon the works to be constructed for its defence, by a corps of 5000 men; of which he will estimate the time and the labor.

8th. He will entrench a position for 4000 men on the two heights which command the road from Sobral de Monte Agraço to Bucellas.

9th. He will entrench a position for 400 men on the height of Ajuda, between Sobral and Bucellas, to cover the retreat of the corps from Sobral to Bucellas; and he will calculate the means and the time it will take to destroy the road at that spot.

10th. He will construct a redoubt for 200 men and 3 guns at the windmill on the height of Sobral de Monte Agraço, which guns will bear upon the road from Sobral to Arruda.

11th. He will ascertain the points at which, and the means by which, the road from Sobral to Arruda can be destroyed.

12th. He will ascertain the labor and time required to entrench a position which he will fix upon for 2000 men to defend the road coming out of Arruda towards Villa Franca and Alhandra, and he will fix upon the spot at which the road from Arruda to Alhandra can be destroyed with advantage.

13th. He will construct a redoubt on the hill which commands the road from Arruda, about one league in front of Alhandra.

14th. He will examine the æstuaries at Alhandra, and see whether, by damming them up at the mouths, he could increase the difficulties of a passage by that place; and he will ascertain the time and labor and means which this work will require.

15th. He will fix upon the spots, and ascertain the time and labor required to construct redoubts upon the hill of Alhandra on the right, to prevent the passage of the enemy by the high road; and on the left, and in the rear, to prevent by their fire the occupation of the mountains towards Alverca.

16th. He will determine upon the works to be constructed on the right of the position upon the Serra de Serves, as above pointed out, to prevent the enemy from forcing that point; and he will calculate the means and the time required to execute them. He will likewise examine the pass of Bucellas, and fix upon the works to be constructed for its defence, and calculate the means, time, and labor required for the execution.

17th. He will calculate the means, time, and labor required to construct a work upon the hill upon which the windmill stands, at the southern entrance at the pass of Bucellas.

18th. He will fix upon spots on which signal posts can be erected upon these hills, to communicate from one part of the position to the other.

19th. It is very desirable that we should have an accurate plan of the ground.

20th. Examine the island in the river opposite to Alhandra, and fix upon the spot, and calculate the means and time required to construct batteries upon it to play upon the approach to Alhandra.

21st. Examine the effect of damming up the river which runs by Loures, and calculate the time and means required to break up the bridge at Loures.

To the Earl of Liverpool.

Alverca, 11th July, 1810.

Since I wrote to your Lordship this day, I have received a report
that Ciudad Rodrigo surrendered to the enemy yesterday evening. There was a large practicable breach in the place, and the
enemy had made all the preparations for a storm; when, Marshal Ney having offered terms of capitulation, the garrison
surrendered.

The enemy took up their ground before this place on the
26th April; they invested it completely on the 11th June; broke
ground before it on the 15th June, and opened their fire upon
it on the 24th June: and, adverting to the nature and position
of the place, to the deficiency and defects of its works, to the
advantages which the enemy had in their attack upon it, and to
the numbers and formidable equipment by which it was
attacked, I consider the defence of Ciudad Rodrigo to have
been most honorable to the Governor, Don Andres Herrasti,
and its garrison; and to have been equally creditable to the
arms of Spain, with the celebrated defence of other places, by
which this nation has been illustrated during the existing contest for its independence.

I have been most anxiously desirous to relieve the place since
it has been attacked; and have been prevented from attempting
its relief only by the certainty which I had that the attempt
must fail; and that the immediate fall of the place and the irrev-
ocable loss of the cause of the allies would be the consequence
of the failure.

I had intelligence, of the truth of which I could entertain no
doubt, that the enemy had collected in the neighbourhood of
Ciudad Rodrigo, for the purpose of the siege, the whole of the
6th and of the 8th corps of the army in Spain; the former consisting of 31,611 effectives, including 4856 cavalry; the latter
consisting of 25,956 effectives, including 4716 cavalry, according to returns of those corps of a very late period which had
been intercepted, and communicated to me. There were besides

other troops employed in the communications with the rear, and with the right of the enemy's army. The country in which I must have carried on the operations to raise the siege, or even to relieve the place, would have been highly advantageous to the enemy, on account of his superiority in cavalry.

Under these circumstances, however much I have been interested in the fate of this place, not only on account of its military and political importance, but on account of its brave Governor, and garrison, and inhabitants, I have considered it my duty to refrain from an operation which it was probable would be attended by the most disastrous consequences. While the Marques de la Romana was here, I had arranged with him an operation, by which it was hoped that we might save the garrison; but the absolute impossibility of communicating with the Governor, for several days, has prevented its execution.

There was an affair between our piquets and those of the enemy this morning, in which the enemy lost 2 officers and 31 men, and 29 horses, prisoners. I have not received the detailed account of this affair; but I understand that we have had the misfortune to lose Lieut. Col. Talbot and 8 men of the 14th light dragoons killed, and 23 men wounded.

To the Rt. Hon. H. Wellesley.

Alverca, 27th July, 1810.

The enemy obliged us to evacuate Fort Concepcion on the 21st, which we destroyed; and on the morning of the 24th they attacked Gen. R. Craufurd's advanced guard close to Almeida, and obliged him to retire across the Coa with the loss of 4 officers killed, 25 wounded; and 28 men killed, and 218 wounded. Although it was desirable to keep open the communication with Almeida as long as possible, both to supply the place with provisions, which the poverty of the Portuguese government had obliged them to defer till the last moment, and to maintain our communication with the other side of the Coa, and obtain intelligence of the enemy's movements, yet I had wished to withdraw sufficiently soon; but unfortunately Gen. Craufurd did not begin to retire till the last moment. The enemy's numbers were about 4 times his in cavalry, and at least 3 times in infantry. We hear that their loss has been great. They made 3 attempts afterwards to storm the bridge of the Coa, in all of which they failed.

Having lost our communication with Almeida and the other side of the Coa, there was no use in contesting the passage of that river, in which we might be turned at almost all points: and I therefore yesterday withdrew our posts from the Coa. I consider it by no means clear that the enemy purpose to attack Almeida. I should rather think they do not, and that they wish to embarrass us in a forward position in the mountains.

Regnier crossed the Tagus about the 17th or 18th, and I understand that he is now on his march through Perales, towards Sabugal. Gen. Hill is at Atalaya; but I believe that I shall allow him to retire by the Zezere rather than by this valley, as the enemy is still too strong for us, and can turn us by our left as well as by our right.

I have received your letter of the 9th.

To the Earl of Liverpool.

Celorico, 29th Aug. 1810.

The enemy opened their fire upon Almeida late on Saturday night, or early on Sunday morning, the 26th inst.; and I am concerned to add that they obtained possession of the place in the course of the night of the 27th.

I will not conceal from your Lordship that this unfortunate event has disappointed me much; as, adverting to the manner in which the garrison was supplied with all the necessaries for the defence of the fort, to the respectable state of the works, and to the good spirit which I had understood from the Governor that the garrison maintained, I had hoped that this place would hold out to the last extremity, if I should not have had an opportunity of relieving it; and at all events would have detained the enemy till a late period in the season. I have no intelligence, upon which I can rely, of the cause of its surrender. Some prisoners taken yesterday state that the magazine of the fort, which, however, was bomb proof, blew up on Saturday night; that, in the course of Monday, the Governor had desired to capitulate on the terms that the fort should be given up, but that the garrison and inhabitants should be allowed to join this army, which terms had been refused; and that the fire had then recommenced, and he had held out as long as his ammunition lasted, and had surrendered at 2 in the morning of yesterday; and that offers had been made to the soldiers of the garrison to take them into the service of the Emperor, or to send them prisoners to France, and that they had all preferred the latter.

This account deserves credit, as coming from an enemy; and it is so far confirmed, that I had an opportunity of observing that there was a cessation from hostilities from 1 P.M. till 9 on Monday night, when the fire recommenced, and lasted till near 2, when it ceased again. An explosion had likewise been heard at our advanced posts; and I observed, on Monday, that the steeple of the church was destroyed, and many of the houses of the town unroofed. I hope that this account will be found correct in all material points; and it will give me great satisfaction to find that the loss of Almeida, and the transfer to the enemy of the stores and provisions which it contains, have not been occasioned by any fault of the Governor or of the garrison.

I had a telegraphic communication with the Governor, but unfortunately the weather did not allow of our using it on Sunday, or during a great part of Monday; and when the weather cleared on that day, it was obvious that the Governor was in communication with the enemy.

Adverting to the position in which I had collected the army so near the place, it is unfortunate that I had not an opportunity of knowing their situation, after the loss of their magazine. After I was certain of the fall of the place, I moved the infantry of the army again into the valley of the Mondego, keeping a division upon Guarda, and the outposts of the cavalry at Alverca.

The enemy attacked our piquets twice yesterday in the morning, but feebly, and they were repulsed. In the afternoon, however, they obliged Sir S. Cotton to draw in his posts to this side of Freixedas. Capt. Lygon,* of the 16th light dragoons, was wounded in the morning; and 2 men of the Royal dragoons were wounded in the afternoon. A piquet of this regiment made a gallant and successful charge upon a party of the enemy's infantry and cavalry, and took some prisoners.

The 2d corps, under Gen. Regnier, has made no movement of any importance since I had the honor of addressing your Lordship last. A patrole, however, belonging to this corps, fell in with a squadron of dragoons, consisting of one troop of the 13th British, and one troop of the 4th Portuguese, belonging to Lieut. Gen. Hill's corps, under the command of Capt. White of the 13th, on the 22d inst.; and the whole of them were taken, with the exception of the Captain and one man, who, I since understand, have been killed. I enclose the copy of Brig. Gen. Fane's report to Lieut. Gen. Hill of this affair,† which it appears was highly creditable to Capt. White and the allied troops engaged.

*   Major General the Hon. H. B. Lygon.

†   *Brig. Gen. H. Fane to Lieut. Gen. Hill.*

                              Escalhos de Cima, 22d Aug. 1810.

I have the honor to report to you that the troop of the 13th light dragoons and one of the 4th Portuguese dragoons, forming the squadron under the command of Capt. White, of the 13th, at Ladoeiro, this morning fell in with a patrole of the enemy's dragoons, consisting of one captain, 2 subalterns, and about 60 men. Capt. White fortunately succeeded in coming up with them, when he immediately charged and overturned them; and the result has been the capture of 2 lieutenants, 3 serjeants, 6 corporals, one trumpeter, and 50 privates, and about 50 horses. The Captain was also a prisoner, but escaped during the bustle on foot.

I am happy to say this has been performed without the loss of a man on our side: 6 of the enemy are wounded. Capt. White expresses his obligation to Major Vigoureux, of the 38th regt., who was a volunteer with him, and to the Alferes Pedro Raimundo de Oliveira, commanding the Portuguese troop (which he states to have done its duty extremely well, and to have shown much gallantry); and also to Lieut. Turner, of the 13th light dragoons, to whose activity and courage he reports himself to be

To Charles Stuart, Esq.

Gouvea, 9th Sept. 1810.

Marshal Beresford has stated to me a circumstance which appears to deserve some attention, upon which I am now about to trouble you. It appears that there was a fire at Lisbon nearly about the time that the accounts were received of the fall of Almeida, and that the two regiments of militia of the town of Lisbon were employed upon the occasion. Either during the continuance of the fire, or after it, both officers and soldiers went into the neighbouring coffee houses to refresh themselves, and the general conversation among them turned upon the fall of Almeida, upon Massena's and Alorna's proclamations, and the probability that the English would embark; and the general notion appeared to be that it would be proper for these two battalions to take possession of *as Torres*,* and prevent the English from carrying their intention into execution. These battalions were destined to garrison Setuval and Palmella; but, as their disposition appears to be warlike, I have ordered them up to the army, and I shall send into these garrisons other battalions not quite so well disposed to war. I have, besides, given directions that Col. Peacocke will occupy the only *Torres* which can be of any importance to us; and I hope soon to have it in my power to secure the command of all the communications with Lisbon, in such a manner as to set at defiance these patriotic citizens.

---

indebted for several of his prisoners. I trust the whole will be considered to have merited the approbation of the Commander in Chief.

No movement has been made, and nothing of any importance has occurred, in Estremadura, since I addressed your Lordship last. In the north, the enemy moved a small body of infantry and cavalry on the 20th to Alcañices; but Gen. Silveira moved towards them from Braganza, and they immediately retired. The last accounts I have from Cadiz are of the 16th inst.; and I understand that Gen. Graham is about to send 2000 men from Cadiz round to the Tagus. Nothing extraordinary had occurred in that quarter.

*   The forts.

In the mean time, however, the temper of mind of Lisbon
becomes a subject of importance; and, as the French appear
inclined to afford us leisure to adopt any arrangements we may
think proper on any subject, I think we cannot employ our time
better than in accustoming these gentry to the discipline to
which it is obvious they must submit as soon as matters become
at all critical. What I should propose, therefore, is that the government should now carry into execution the plan of police
which I proposed to them some time ago. If they consent to
adopt it, it may be adopted, if they choose it, on a suggestion
which I shall make to them; but they ought to publish a proclamation, directing that all the coffee houses should be shut up
at sun set; that the patroles which are organised should go
every hour, day and night; that all disorderly assemblages of
people should be immediately dispersed, &c. These measures
will accustom the mob of Lisbon to the discipline they must
undergo, and will keep matters quiet at the critical moment. I
can only declare this, that if I find the government hesitating
upon this subject, and alarmed by the mob of Lisbon, and
inclined to allow them to go to the lengths in which they will be
really formidable, I shall forthwith embark the army, whatever
may be the prospects of final success in our military operations.
In taking this step, I shall literally obey the instructions which I
have received; and the Portuguese nation will have the satisfaction of losing itself, and the Peninsula, notwithstanding the
best prospects of salvation, by the folly of the people and the
pusillanimity of the government. I shall be obliged to you if you
will confer upon this subject with the government, and communicate to them my ideas as above stated.

I shall be very much obliged to you if you will let me know
what progress has been made in the organisation of the ship-
ping concerns, and the arrangements for embarkation, what
quantity of forage they will have disposable, &c., &c., as we
may as well take advantage of the present calm to settle all that
matter conclusively. I must say that I attribute much of the
existing agitation in Lisbon to the conduct of the government,
and particularly of the new members of it: not from evil inclination and design, but from what is worse, probably, in men in

public situations in these times; bad heads. If these foolish fellows cannot be kept in order, we must get rid of them; and one mode of doing so is, that I shall insist upon Sousa's being sent away; and he might go upon an embassy to England to ask for money, or any thing else that might be suggested; and once there, we might keep him there. However, it would be preferable, first, to try the effect of your presence in the government.

Pray write to Lord Wellesley, and beg him not to allow the English De Sousa to talk to him upon the affairs of Portugal, with which he has nothing to do.

To Charles Stuart, Esq.

Gouvea, 11th Sept. 1810.

I have received your letter of the 8th, which has induced me to suspend the execution of an intention which I had formed of writing to the government on the 3d article of their *Noticia*, respecting the officers of the army who have entered the service of the enemy. The arrangements under this article are directly contrary to those which Beresford and I had settled and agreed to recommend, and which I recommended in my letter to the government of the 5th, and which Beresford has, I believe, announced in G. O. to the army. However, as I understand from your letter that you approved of this *Noticia*, as well as of the Proclamation, &c., I shall defer noticing the subject to the government.

I do not recollect a circumstance which made such an impression on the British army, and upon the English officers serving with the Portuguese army, as the account of the conduct of the officers of the 24th regt.; and after full consideration, the measure which I recommended, and the distinct statement of the principle on which it was recommended, appeared the only means of reconciling the minds of the officers of the British army to what had occurred, and to further service with the Portuguese; at the same time that it held out a standard of sentiment and principle for the officers of the Portuguese service on similar occasions. I wished to avail myself of this opportunity of showing them what the principles of men of honor, and the sentiments of officers and gentlemen, ought to induce them to do on similar occasions. I am sorry to say that this object is defeated by the publication of the notice of the government; and it would have been accomplished, if the government would have waited for the official communication of the circumstances on which they have decided, as I am convinced that you would have seen at once my object in the measure which I recommended, and would have supported it with all your influence. As it is now the arrangement, it must be left to take its course.

While writing upon this subject, I should wish to draw your attention to the inconvenience resulting from the precipitation of the government, as well as from the practice, notwithstanding what I before wrote to them, of publishing Marshal Beresford's accounts, as well as mine, of the same transactions. There is no person who deprecates mystery more than I do; and it is impossible for two people to understand each other better than Beresford and I. He is 2 miles from this, and I see him every day; and I believe that we take pretty nearly the same view of every transaction. But a different mode of expression, a difference in the degree of importance assigned to any transaction, the details of which are related by different individuals, who probably have taken the same view, make a material difference in the eyes of the very jealous public, both of the Peninsula and of England, who will judge of our actions.

In a late instance I see that the Portuguese papers have observed and canvassed some little difference which they suppose there was between Beresford's reports and mine, which observations will certainly be copied into the English newspapers, with all the additional observations which malevolence can suggest. I attribute the publication of these reports made by Beresford to the feverish state in which the government has been since Principal Sousa has become a member of it. Beresford very properly makes a daily report of events, but it must be observed that the view to be given in these reports cannot be so accurate as that which is given after the events have been well considered and further inquired into.

For instance, if I had written to you yesterday, I should have told you that the enemy had on Sunday night marched a large column upon Guarda. I now know that this was merely a reconnaissance, that but a few cavalry entered Guarda, and that the whole fell back upon Sabugal yesterday, owing to their patroles falling in with ours. There is no harm in government being informed of these events as they come to our knowledge; but where is the use of keeping the public in a state of fever by the publication of them? But it comes to this, if the Portuguese government publish any report of military transactions, excepting mine, I shall make them no report; and I shall be much obliged to you if you will intimate this to them. They now have the same report that I make to my own government.

It appears that you have had a good smart contest with the government respecting our plan of operations. They will end in forcing me to quit them, and then they will see how they will get on. They will then find that I alone keep things in their present state. Indeed, the temper of some of the officers of the British army gives me more concern than the folly of the Portuguese government. I have always been accustomed to have the confidence and support of the officers of the armies which I have commanded; but, for the first time, whether owing to the opposition in England, or whether the magnitude of the concern is too much for their minds and their nerves, or whether I am mistaken and they are right, I cannot tell; but there is a system of croaking in the army which is highly injurious to the public service, and which I must devise some means of putting an end to, or it will put an end to us. Officers have a right to form their own opinions upon events and transactions; but officers of high rank or situation ought to keep their opinions to themselves: if they do not approve of the system of operations of their commander, they ought to withdraw from the army. And this is the point to which I must bring some, if I should not find that their own good sense prevents them from going on as they have done lately. Believe me that, if any body else, knowing what I do, had commanded the army, they would now have been at Lisbon, if not in their ships.

As for advancing into Spain, the idea is ridiculous. I can only tell you, that of which I am the most apprehensive is that the enemy will raise the blockade of Cadiz. Unless Heaven shall perform a miracle, and give the Spaniards an army, arms, and equipments, we should be ruined by this measure, and then the cause is gone. Now, supposing that I am wrong in my plan of operations, and the principal officers of the British army still more wrong, and Principal Sousa and the Bishop right, and that I have it in my power to act offensively in Spain, how would it be when the French army in Andalusia would be brought against us? Would the Spanish force, which a part of that army keeps shut up in Cadiz, be equal to the whole of it in the field? Not unless, by a miracle, Heaven would add to their numbers!

The intelligence from Madrid is very interesting. I observe, however, that they have omitted a great part of the French force in their statement. Regnier's force is not mentioned at all. I enclose a most interesting dispatch which my brother has desired me to send you. Let me have it again.

To the Earl of Liverpool.

Lorva, 20th Sept. 1810.

The 2d corps, under the command of Gen. Regnier, was again brought to the northward, and arrived at Sabugal and Alfaiates on the 12th and 13th inst. On the 15th, the enemy moved a large force of cavalry, infantry, and artillery upon Guarda the third time, and passed the hill into the valley of the Mondego, and obliged our party of observation which had been stationed there under Capt. Cocks, of the 16th light dragoons, to retire upon the Serra. On the same day, a large column passed the hill of Alverca (which forms the left of the Guarda range) and

Maçal do Chaõ, and halted at Baraçal, likewise in the valley of the Mondego; and the 8th corps, under Gen. Junot, passed the Coa at Porto de Vide. Lieut. Gen. Sir S. Cotton withdrew the British cavalry through Celorico on the morning of the 16th, and the enemy entered that place on that day from the side of Alverca and Guarda; and the 8th corps entered Trancoso.

The enemy, instead of following the retreat of our troops from Celorico by the valley of the Mondego and the left bank of that river, immediately marched by Jejua to the bridge of Fornos, and the advanced guard was in Fornos on that night. They followed this movement on the succeeding days by passing all the troops of the 2d and 6th corps from Celorico over the bridge of Fornos, with the exception of the advanced guard of the 2d corps, which, on the 18th, protected the passage of the rear of the column and passed yesterday at a bridge lower down the river. A small party entered Viseu yesterday. The enemy's intention in these movements is apparently to obtain possession of Coimbra, with a view to the resources which that town and the neighbouring country will afford them. The movements, however, which I had previously made to enable me to withdraw the army without difficulty from a position in which I did not consider it advisable to risk an action, enabled me to secure Coimbra against the attack of any small corps; and the whole of that part of the army which has been under my immediate command, with the exception of 5 regiments of cavalry, has passed to the right of the Mondego, and in front of Coimbra, Brig. Gen. Pack's brigade of Portuguese infantry being at Sta Comba Daõ with the Royal dragoons, and Brig. Gen. Craufurd's division at Mortagoa. The cavalry will pass to-morrow.

When Regnier made the former movement to the northward, apparently with the intention on the part of the enemy of attacking this part of the army with his whole force, I had directed Lieut. Gen. Hill, and Major Gen. Leith, who commanded a small corps upon the Zezere, to prepare to join me; and as soon as I found from the enemy's movement of the 15th, that he was then about to carry his intention into execution, and that the plan was decided, I directed those officers to march.

Major Gen. Leith is this day at Foz d'Arouce, and will join the army to-morrow; the head of Lieut. Gen. Hill's corps is at Espinhal, and will join on the next day. I also expect that Col. Le Cor, who has been with a small body of troops in the mountains of Castello Branco, will join about the same time. I shall thus have collected in one body the whole of the disposable force in Portugal, and I hope to have it in my power to frustrate the enemy's design.

I imagine that Marshal Massena has been misinformed, and has experienced greater difficulties in making his movements than he expected. He has certainly selected one of the worst roads in Portugal for his march.

Since the affair of the 11th Aug., in Estremadura, which I heretofore reported to your Lordship, the Marques de la Romana has been successful in carrying off two of the enemy's small detachments, one in the neighbourhood of Cordova, and the other in proceeding as a relief to the enemy's garrison in Castillo de las Guardias; and the Marques's advanced posts were within 3 leagues of Seville. Marshal Mortier, however, collected his corps, and moved out of Seville in strength, and the Marques de la Romana was obliged to retire into Estremadura. On the 14th the Spanish cavalry was engaged with that of the enemy near Fuente de Cantos, the Portuguese brigade, under Brig. Gen. Madden, being at La Calzadilla. After the engagement had lasted a considerable portion of the day, the Spanish cavalry gave way in some confusion, and Brig. Gen. Madden having moved forward, fell upon the enemy in a most decided and effectual manner, overthrew and pursued them to their cannon, and killed and wounded many, and took some prisoners and saved the Spaniards. The Marques de la Romana, from whom I have received the account, mentions in high terms the conduct of Brig. Gen. Madden, and of the Portuguese troops under his command, which he says has excited the admiration of the whole army. The Marques de la Romana has retired upon Merida, and after fixing a good garrison in Badajoz, is about to take a position between the Tagus and the Guadiana.

I must take this opportunity of mentioning to your Lordship

the obligations I am under to the British cavalry commanded by Lieut. Gen. Sir S. Cotton. Since the end of July, they have alone done the duty of the outposts, and the enemy has never been out of sight of some of them; and on every occasion their superiority has been so great, that the enemy does not use his cavalry excepting when supported and protected by his infantry. The 1st hussars, under Col. Arentschildt, in particular, have had many opportunities of distinguishing themselves; and it is but justice to mention the zeal and intelligence with which the duty of the outposts has been performed by Capt. Krauchenberg and Cornet Cordemann, of the 1st hussars, and by Capt. the Hon. C. Cocks, of the 16th light dragoons. Nothing of importance has occurred in the north. My last letter from Cadiz is of the 9th.

To the Earl of Liverpool.

Coimbra, 30th Sept. 1810.

While the enemy was advancing from Celorico and Trancoso upon Viseu, the different divisions of militia and Ordenanza were employed upon their flanks and rear; and Col. Trant with his division attacked the escort of the military chest and reserve artillery near Tojal, on the 20th inst. He took 2 officers and 80 prisoners, but the enemy collected a force from the front and rear, which obliged him to retire again towards the Douro. I understand that the enemy's communication is completely cut off, and he possesses only the ground upon which his army stands.

My dispatch of the 20th inst. will have informed you of the measures which I had adopted and which were in progress to collect the army in this neighbourhood, and, if possible, to prevent the enemy from obtaining possession of this town. On the 21st the enemy's advanced guard pushed on to Sta Comba Daõ, at the junction of the rivers Criz and Daõ; and Brig. Gen. Pack retired across the former and joined Brig. Gen. Craufurd at Mortagoa, having destroyed the bridges over those 2 rivers. The enemy's advanced guard crossed the Criz, having repaired the bridge, on the 23d, and the whole of the 6th corps was collected on the other side of the river. I therefore withdrew the cavalry through the Serra do Busaco, with the exception of 3 squadrons, as the ground was unfavorable for the operation of that arm.

On the 25th, the whole of the 6th and of the 2d corps crossed the Criz in the neighbourhood of Sta Comba Daõ; and Brig. Gen. Pack's brigade and Brig. Gen. Craufurd's division retired to the position which I had fixed upon for the army on the top of the Serra do Busaco. These troops were followed in this movement by the whole of the corps of Ney and Regnier (the 6th and the 2d); but it was conducted by Brig. Gen. Craufurd with great regularity, and the troops took their position without sustaining any loss of importance. The 4th Portuguese caçadores, which had retired on the right of the other troops, and the piquets of the 3d division of infantry, which were posted at S. Antonio de Cantaro, under Major Smyth of the 45th regt., were engaged with the advance of Regnier's corps in the afternoon, and the former showed that steadiness and gallantry which others of the Portuguese troops have since manifested.

The Serra do Busaco is a high ridge which extends from the Mondego in a northerly direction about 8 miles. At the highest point of the ridge, about 2 miles from its termination, is the convent and garden of Busaco. The Serra do Busaco is connected by a mountainous tract of country with the Serra de Caramula, which extends in a north easterly direction beyond Viseu, and separates the valley of the Mondego from the valley of the Douro. On the left of the Mondego, nearly in a line with the Serra do Busaco, is another ridge of the same description, called the Serra da Murcella, covered by the river Alva, and connected by other mountainous parts with the Serra d'Estrella. All the roads to Coimbra from the eastward lead over the one or the other of these Serras. They are very difficult for the passage of an army, the approach to the top of the ridge on both sides being mountainous.

As the enemy's whole army was on the right of the Mondego, and it was evident that he intended to force our position, Lieut. Gen. Hill crossed that river by a short movement to his left, on the morning of the 26th, leaving Col. Le Cor with his brigade on the Serra da Murcella, to cover the right of the army, and Brig. Gen. Fane, with his division of Portuguese cavalry and the 13th light dragoons, in front of the Alva, to observe and check the movements of the enemy's cavalry on the Mondego. With this exception, the whole army was collected upon the Serra do Busaco, with the British cavalry observing the plain in the rear of its left, and the road leading from Mortagoa to Oporto, through the mountainous tract which connects the Serra do Busaco with the Serra de Caramula.

The 8th corps joined the enemy in our front on the 26th, but he did not make any serious attack on that day. The light troops on both sides were engaged throughout the line. At 6 in the morning of the 27th the enemy made two desperate attacks upon our position, the one on the right, the other on the left of the highest part of the Serra. The attack upon the right was made by two divisions of the 2d corps, on that part of the Serra occupied by the 3d division of infantry. One division of French infantry arrived at the top of the ridge, where it was attacked in the most gallant manner by the 88th regt., under the command of Lieut. Col. Wallace, the 45th, under the command of Lieut. Col. the Hon. R. Meade, and by the 8th Portuguese regt., under the command of Lieut. Col. Douglas, directed by Major Gen. Picton. These 3 corps advanced with the bayonet, and drove the enemy's division from the advantageous ground which they had obtained. The other division of the 2d corps attacked farther on the right, by the road leading by S. Antonio de Cantaro, also in front of Major Gen. Picton's division. These were repulsed, before they could reach the top of the ridge, by the 74th, under the command of Lieut. Col. the Hon. R. Trench, and the brigade of Portuguese infantry of the 9th and 21st regts. under the command of Col. Champelmond, directed by

Col. Mackinnon. Major Gen. Leith also moved to his left to the support of Major Gen. Picton, and aided in the defeat of the enemy by the 3d batt. of Royals, the 1st batt. of the 9th, and the 2d batt. of the 38th regts. In these attacks Major Gens. Leith and Picton, Cols. Mackinnon and Champelmond, of the Portuguese service, who was wounded, Lieut. Col. Wallace, Lieut. Col. the Hon. R. Meade, Lieut. Col. Sutton of the 9th Portuguese, Major Smyth of the 45th, who was afterwards killed, Lieut. Col. Douglas, and Major Birmingham, of the 8th Portuguese regt., distinguished themselves. Major Gen. Picton reports the good conduct of the 9th and 21st Portuguese regts., commanded by Lieut. Col. Sutton and Lieut. Col. A. Bacellar, and of the Portuguese artillery, under the command of Major Arentschildt. I have also to mention, in a particular manner, the conduct of Capt. Dansey of the 88th. Major Gen. Leith reports the good conduct of the Royals, 1st batt., and 9th, and 2d batt. of the 38th regts.; and I beg to assure your Lordship that I have never witnessed a more gallant attack than that made by the 88th, 45th, and 8th Portuguese regts., on the enemy's division which had reached the ridge of the Serra.

On the left the enemy attacked with 3 divisions of infantry of the 6th corps, on the part of the Serra occupied by the Light division of infantry commanded by Brig. Gen. Craufurd, and by the brigade of Portuguese infantry commanded by Brig. Gen. Pack. One division of infantry only made any progress to the top of the hill, and they were immediately charged with the bayonet by Brig. Gen. Craufurd, with the 43d, 52d, and 95th, and the 3d Portuguese caçadores, and driven down with immense loss. Brig. Gen. Colman's brigade of Portuguese infantry, which was in reserve, was moved up to the right of Brig. Gen. Craufurd's division, and a battalion of the 19th Portuguese regt., under the command of Lieut. Col. Mac Bean, made a gallant and successful charge upon a body of another division of the enemy, which was endeavoring to penetrate in that quarter. In this attack, Brig. Gen. Craufurd, Lieut. Cols. Beckwith, of the 95th, and Barclay, of the 52d, and the Commanding officers of the regiments, distinguished themselves.

Besides these attacks, the light troops of the two armies were

engaged throughout the 27th; and the 4th Portuguese caçadores, and the 1st and 15th regts., directed by Brig. Gen. Pack,
and commanded by Lieut. Col. Hill, Lieut. Col. Luis do Rego,
and Major Armstrong, showed great steadiness and gallantry.

The loss sustained by the enemy in his attack of the 27th has
been enormous. I understand that the Generals of division,
Merle, Loison, and Maucune are wounded, and Gen. Simon
was taken prisoner by the 52d regt.; and 3 Colonels, — officers,
and 250 men. The enemy left 2000 killed upon the field of battle, and I understand from the prisoners and deserters that the
loss in wounded is immense.

The enemy did not renew his attack, excepting by the fire of
his light troops on the 28th; but he moved a large body of
infantry and cavalry from the left of his centre to the rear, from
whence I saw his cavalry in march on the road from Mortagoa
over the mountains towards Oporto. Having thought it probable that he would endeavor to turn our left by that road, I had
directed Col. Trant, with his division of militia, to march to
Sardaõ, with the intention that he should occupy the mountains, but unfortunately he was sent round by Oporto, by the
General officer commanding in the north, in consequence of a
small detachment of the enemy being in possession of S. Pedro
do Sul; and, notwithstanding the efforts which he made to
arrive in time, he did not reach Sardaõ till the 28th at night,
after the enemy were in possession of the ground. As it was
probable that, in the course of the night of the 28th, the enemy
would throw the whole of his army upon the road, by which he
could avoid the Serra do Busaco and reach Coimbra by the
high road of Oporto, and thus the army would have been
exposed to be cut off from that town or to a general action in
less favorable ground, and as I had reinforcements in my rear, I
was induced to withdraw from the Serra do Busaco.

The enemy did break up in the mountains at 11 at night of
the 28th, and he made the march I expected. His advanced
guard was at Avelans, on the road from Oporto to Coimbra,
yesterday, and the whole army was seen in march through the
mountains. That under my command, however, was already in
the low country, between the Serra do Busaco and the sea; and

the whole of it, with the exception of the advanced guard, is this day on the left of the Mondego.

Although, from the unfortunate circumstance of the delay of Col. Trant's arrival at Sardaõ, I am apprehensive that I shall not succeed in effecting the object which I had in view in passing the Mondego and in occupying the Serra do Busaco, I do not repent my having done so. This movement has afforded me a favorable opportunity of showing the enemy the description of troops of which this army is composed; it has brought the Portuguese levies into action with the enemy for the first time in an advantageous situation; and they have proved that the trouble which has been taken with them has not been thrown away, and that they are worthy of contending in the same ranks with British troops in this interesting cause, which they afford the best hopes of saving. Throughout the contest on the Serra, and in all the previous marches, and those which we have since made, the whole army have conducted themselves in the most regular manner. Accordingly all the operations have been carried on with ease; the soldiers have suffered no privations, have undergone no unnecessary fatigue, there has been no loss of stores, and the army is in the highest spirits.

I have received throughout the service the greatest assistance from the General and Staff officers. Lieut. Gen. Sir B. Spencer has given the assistance his experience enables him to afford me; and I am particularly indebted to the Adj. Gen. and the Q. M. Gens., and the officers of their departments, and to Lieut. Col. Bathurst, and the officers of my personal staff; to Major Gen. Howorth and the artillery, and particularly to Lieut. Col. Fletcher, Capt. Chapman, and the officers of the Royal Engineers. I must likewise mention Mr Kennedy, and the officers of the Commissariat, which department has been carried on most successfully.

I should not do justice to the service, or to my own feelings, if I did not take this opportunity of drawing your Lordship's attention to the merits of Marshal Beresford. To him exclusively, under the Portuguese government, is due the merit of having raised, formed, disciplined, and equipped the Portuguese army, which has now shown itself capable of engaging and defeating the enemy. I have besides received from him all the assistance which his experience and abilities, and his knowledge of this country, have qualified him to afford me.

The enemy have made no movement in Estremadura, or in the northern provinces, since I addressed your Lordship last. My last accounts from Cadiz are of the 9th inst. I enclose a return of the killed and wounded of the allied armies in the course of the 25th, 26th, and 27th. I send this dispatch by my aide de camp, Capt. Burgh,* to whom I beg to refer your Lordship for any further details, and I recommend him to your Lordship's notice.

*Return of the killed, wounded, and missing of
the army on the 25th, 26th, and 27th Sept. 1810.*

	Officers.	Serjeants.	R. and F.	Horses.	Total loss of officers, non-commissioned officers, and R. & F.
Killed	11	6	180	5	197
Wounded	62	32	920	12	1014
Missing	1	3	54	10	58

The Portuguese loss is included in the above numbers.

To the Earl of Liverpool.

Ajuda, 13th Oct. 1810.

The army continued its retreat by the routes of Alcobaça and of Rio Maior; and Lieut. Gen. Hill's corps by that of Santarem, till it arrived with its right at Castanheira and Villa Franca, its centre at Sobral, and its left at Torres Vedras, on the 7th and 8th inst., without being pressed or molested by the enemy. The

* Lord Downes, K. C. B.

movement of that part of the army under my own immediate command was covered by the British cavalry under Sir S. Cotton; and that of the troops under Lieut. Gen. Hill, by the 13th dragoons and Portuguese cavalry, under Major Gen. Fane. The British cavalry had several occasions of distinguishing themselves, upon which I enclose Sir S. Cotton's reports, and I must add my sense of the obligations which I owe to this body. They were preceded on the march immediately by the advanced guard of infantry, under Brig. Gen. Craufurd.

On the 8th the rain commenced, which usually falls at this season of the year in Portugal, and has continued with great violence ever since. This has probably increased the enemy's difficulties, and delayed his progress. He has shown some troops in front of our right at Villa Franca, and a large division of cavalry, with some infantry, patrolled up to Sobral de Monte Agraço on the 11th, having driven in our piquets of cavalry and infantry.

A large division of infantry, which I understand to be the advanced guard of the 8th corps, moved upon Sobral yesterday evening, from whence Lieut. Gen. Sir B. Spencer withdrew the advance of his division, and the enemy continue in that town; the division under the command of Lieut. Gen. Sir B. Spencer being closed on this side of it, and at no great distance from the great redoubt of Sobral. They also this day attacked the piquets of Gen. Cole's division near Sobral, but without much effect. I have learnt with great satisfaction that the Portuguese troops (Col. Harvey's brigade, the 11th and 23d regts.) again distinguished themselves upon this occasion. Col. Harvey unfortunately was wounded, but I hope not seriously.

As soon as I shall have ascertained the line of the enemy's operations, I shall take up the line of defence of the army; and as I conceive that I have reason to hope for success, I propose to bring matters to extremities, and to contend for the possession and independence of Portugal in one of the strong positions in this part of the country. The Marques de la Romana marched to Campo Maior on the 8th inst., to join this army and share our fortune.

All is quiet in the north of Portugal. I understand that one of

Gen. Bacellar's detachments, under Col. Wilson, was in the position of Busaco on the 6th inst.; and it is reported that Col. Trant has entered Coimbra. As all the inhabitants, however, have quitted the country, and the weather has rendered the communication by sea impossible, I cannot procure accurate intelligence from that part of the country. My last accounts from Cadiz are of the 4th inst.

FOUR

THE CAMPAIGNS OF 1811

Wellington once said of Masséna that he was the most dangerous enemy he had to face in the Peninsula. This, perhaps, is
debatable, but what is certainly the case is that the marshal was
easily the toughest and most determined. Thus, despite the fact
that the area he occupied in front of the Lines of Torres Vedras
was utterly denuded of foodstocks, he clung on until March
1811 and that notwithstanding the fact that his starving men
were dying like flies. Even when he did fall back, meanwhile, it
was not without a succession of sharp rearguard actions, as
well as a last-ditch effort to make a stand at the Portuguese
frontier that resulted in a fierce battle on 3 April at Sabugal.
Nor was he finished even then: after re-equipping his battered
forces as best he could, on 3 May he moved forward in strength
from his base at Ciudad Rodrigo and attacked Wellington at
Fuentes de Oñoro in an attempt to relieve the beleaguered garrison of Almeida. The result was a hard fight that it is arguable
that Wellington somewhat mishandled, but eventually even
Masséna was left with no option but to withdraw, the only
consolation being that the French troops in Almeida managed
to break out and make a successful dash for safety. At this
point Wellington might have moved on to attack Ciudad Rodrigo, but he was prevented from doing so by a fresh crisis that
had broken out far to the south in Extremadura. Just as was
the case with Almeida and Ciudad Rodrigo, here too the border was watched by twin fortresses, namely Elvas and Ciudad
Rodrigo. Until March 1811 both these fortresses had been in
Allied hands, but in February of that year a powerful force
had marched north from French-held Andalucía, defeated the

Spanish army defending the area round Badajoz and then laid siege to the fortress itself. Hearing of the crisis, Wellington had immediately sent a large relief column under William Beresford to restore the situation, but on 5 March the fortress had surrendered after an unlucky cannonball had cut down its commander. In consequence, it was decided that Badajoz should be besieged as soon as possible, but the French were not going to let so important a prize slip between their fingers so easily, and so Marshal Soult, who had now become the French commander in Andalucía, gathered together as many troops as he could and forced Beresford, whose Anglo-Portuguese troops had just been joined by a substantial Spanish army, to do battle at Albuera. The result was one of the fiercest engagements of the Peninsular War, British casualties alone amounting to some forty per cent of those engaged. In the end Beresford carried the day, but he had come close to being outfought by Soult, and Wellington therefore felt that he had no option but to come south to take charge of operations against Badajoz himself. Badajoz, however, was perhaps the strongest fortress in the whole of Spain and progress was very slow, not least because Wellington was forced to employ outdated seventeenth-century weapons brought across the frontier from Elvas. In consequence, Marshal Soult was able to join with Marshal Marmont – a new commander who had just replaced Masséna in charge of the forces that had fought at Fuentes de Oñoro – to launch a fresh relief effort, and this rare example of co-operation on the part of two of the various generals who commanded the French forces in Spain was enough to persuade Wellington to abandon the siege and take up a defensive position inside Portugal. Coming to the conclusion that the frontal attack that was the only option would be suicidal, Soult and Marmont declined to press matters to a conclusion, but they could not maintain a large force in poverty-stricken Extremadura for any length of time, and therefore soon went their separate ways. Presented with the initiative once more, Wellington turned once again to Ciudad Rodrigo and attempted to starve it into surrender, only for Marmont to rush to its rescue and, not just that, but catch some of the blockading forces napping at El Bodón. Fought on

25 September 1811, this action could have resulted in a serious reverse for Wellington, but once again the fighting qualities of his soldiers saved the day, leaving Marmont no choice but to fall back on Ciudad Rodrigo. Minor skirmishes aside, thus ended the campaign of 1811. Whilst scarcely a rewarding experience, this had at least shown that the French armies' offensive spirit was beginning to diminish, whilst very late in the year a powerful modern siege train had arrived from Britain, thereby giving Wellington the opportunity to take on such fortresses as Badajoz with a much greater chance of success. In short, as was in fact to be the case, 1812 promised to be a year in which Allied fortunes would change for the better.

To the Earl of Liverpool.

Villa Secca, 14th March, 1811.

The enemy retired from the position which they had occupied at Santarem and the neighbourhood on the night of the 5th inst. I put the British army in motion to follow them on the morning of the 6th. Their first movements indicated an intention to collect a force at Thomar; and I therefore marched upon that town, on the 8th, a considerable body of troops, formed of a part of Marshal Sir W. Beresford's corps, under Major Gen. the Hon. W. Stewart, which had crossed the Tagus at Abrantes, and afterwards the Zezere, and of the 4th and 6th, and part of the 1st, divisions of infantry, and 2 brigades of British cavalry.

The enemy, however, continued his march towards the Mondego, having one corps, the 2d, on the road of Espinhal, Gen. Loison's division on the road of Ançião, and the remainder of the army towards Pombal. These last were followed, and never lost sight of, by the Light division, and the Royal dragoons and 1st hussars, who took from them about 200 prisoners.

On the 9th, the enemy having collected in front of Pombal the 6th corps, with the exception of Gen. Loison's division, the 8th corps, and the 9th corps, and Gen. Montbrun's division of cavalry, the hussars, which, with the Royal dragoons and Light division, were immediately in front of the enemy's lines, distinguished themselves in a charge which they made on this occasion, under the command of Col. Arentschildt. A detachment of the 16th light dragoons, under Lieut. Weyland, which had been in observation of the enemy near Leiria, made prisoners a detachment consisting of 30 dragoons on that morning, and had followed the enemy from Leiria, and arrived on the ground just in time to assist their friends, the hussars, in this charge.

I could not collect a sufficient body of troops to commence an operation upon the enemy till the 11th. On that day the 1st, 3d, 4th, 5th, and 6th, and the Light divisions of infantry, and Gen. Pack's brigade, and all the British cavalry, joined upon the ground immediately in front of the enemy, who had commenced their retreat from their position during the night. They were followed by the Light division, the hussars and Royals, and Brig. Gen. Pack's brigade, under the command of Major Gen. Sir W. Erskine and Major Gen. Slade, and made an attempt to hold the antient castle of Pombal, from which they were driven; but the 6th corps, and Gen. Montbrun's cavalry, which formed the rear guard, supported by the 8th corps, held the ground on the other side of the town, the troops not having arrived in time to complete the dispositions to attack them before it was dark. Upon this occasion Lieut. Col. Elder's battalion of Portuguese caçadores distinguished themselves.

The enemy retired in the night; and on the 12th the 6th corps, with Gen. Montbrun's cavalry, took up a strong position at the end of a defile, between Redinha and Pombal, with their right in a wood upon the Soure river, and their left extending towards the high ground above the river of Redinha. This town was in their rear. I attacked them in this position on the 12th, with the 3d and 4th divisions of infantry, and Brig. Gen. Pack's brigade, and the cavalry, the other troops being in reserve.

The post in the wood upon their right was first forced by Sir W. Erskine, with the Light division. We were then able to form the troops in the plain beyond the defile; and the 3d division, under Major Gen. Picton, were formed in 2 lines, in the skirts of the wood, upon the right; the 4th division, under

Major Gen. Cole, in 2 lines, in the centre, having Gen. Pack's brigade supporting their right, and communicating with the 3d division; and the Light division, in 2 lines, on the left. These troops were supported in the rear by the British cavalry; and the 1st, 5th, and 6th divisions were in reserve. The troops were formed with great accuracy and celerity; and Lieut. Gen. Sir B. Spencer led the line against the enemy's position on the heights, from which they were immediately driven, with the loss of many men killed and wounded, and some prisoners.

Major Gen. Sir W. Erskine particularly mentioned the conduct of the 52d regt., and Col. Elder's caçadores, in the attack of the wood; and I must add that I have never seen the French infantry driven from a wood in a more gallant style.

There was but one narrow bridge, and a ford close to it, over the Redinha river, over which our light troops passed with the enemy; but as the enemy commanded these passages with cannon, some time elapsed before we could pass over a sufficient body of troops, and make a fresh disposition to attack the heights on which they had again taken post. The 3d division crossed, however, and manœuvred again upon the enemy's left flank, while the light infantry and cavalry, supported by the Light division, drove them upon their main body at Condeixa.

The light infantry of Gen. Picton's division, under Col. Williams, and the 4th caçadores, under Col. do Rego, were principally concerned in this operation.

We found the whole army yesterday, with the exception of the 2d corps, which was still at Espinhal, in a very strong position, at Condeixa; and I observed that they were sending off their baggage by the road of Ponte da Murcella. From this circumstance I concluded that Col. Trant had not given up Coimbra, and that they had been so pressed in their retreat, that they had not been able to detach troops to force him from that place. I therefore marched the 3d division, under Major Gen. Picton, through the mountains upon the enemy's left, towards the only road open for their retreat, which had the immediate effect of dislodging them from the strong position of Condeixa; and the enemy encamped last night at Cazal Novo, in the mountains, about a league from Condeixa.

We immediately communicated with Coimbra, and made prisoners a detachment of the enemy's cavalry which were upon the road. We found the 6th and 8th corps formed in a very strong position near Cazal Novo, this morning, and the Light division attacked and drove in the outposts. But we could dislodge them from their positions only by movements on their flanks. Accordingly I moved the 4th division, under Major Gen. Cole, upon Panella, in order to secure the passage of the river Deixa and the communication with Espinhal, to which place Major Gen. Nightingall had been in observation of the movements of the enemy's corps since the 10th; and the 3d division, under Major Gen. Picton, moved immediately round the enemy's left; while the Light division, and Brig. Gen. Pack's brigade, under Major Gen. Sir W. Erskine, turned their right; and Major Gen. Alex. Campbell, with the 6th division, supported the light troops, by which they were attacked in front. These troops were supported by the cavalry, and by the 1st and 5th divisions, and Col. Ashworth's brigade in reserve. These movements obliged the enemy to abandon all the positions which they successively took in the mountains, and the *corps d'armée* composing the rear guard were flung back upon the main body, at Miranda do Corvo, upon the river Deixa, with considerable loss of killed, wounded, and prisoners.

In the operations of this day, the 43d, 52d, and 95th regts., and 3d caçadores, under the command of Cols. Drummond and Beckwith, and Major Patrickson, Lieut. Col. Ross, and Majors Gilmour and Stewart, and Lieut. Col. Elder, particularly distinguished themselves; as also the light infantry of Gen. Picton's division, under Lieut. Col. Williams, and the 4th caçadores, under Col. do Rego; and the troops of horse artillery under the command of Capts. Ross and Bull.

The result of these operations has been that we have saved Coimbra and Upper Beira from the enemy's ravages; we have opened the communications with the northern provinces; and we have obliged the enemy to take for their retreat the road by Ponte da Murcella, on which they may be annoyed by the militia acting in security upon their flank, while the allied army will press upon their rear. The whole country, however, affords many advantageous positions to a retreating army, of which the enemy have shown that they know how to avail themselves. They are retreating from the country, as they entered it, in one solid mass, covering their rear on every march by the operations of either one or two *corps d'armée* in the strong positions which the country affords; which *corps d'armée* are closely supported by the main body. Before they quitted their position they destroyed a part of their cannon and ammunition, and they have since blown up whatever the horses were unable to draw away. They have no provisions, excepting what they plunder on the spot, or, having plundered, what the soldiers carry on their backs, and live cattle.

I am concerned to be obliged to add to this account, that their conduct throughout this retreat has been marked by a barbarity seldom equalled, and never surpassed. Even in the towns of Torres Novas, Thomar, and Pernes, in which the head quarters of some of the corps had been for 4 months, and in which the inhabitants had been invited, by promises of good treatment, to remain, they were plundered, and many of their houses destroyed, on the night the enemy withdrew from their position, and they have since burnt every town and village through which they have passed. The convent of Alcobaça was burnt by order from the French head quarters. The Bishop's palace, and the whole town of Leiria, in which Gen. Drouet had had his head quarters, shared the same fate; and there is not an inhabitant of the country, of any class or description, who has had any dealing or communication with the French army, who has not had reason to repent of it and to complain of them. This is the mode in which the promises have been performed, and the assurances have been fulfilled, which were held out in the proclamation of the French Commander in Chief, in which he told the inhabitants of Portugal that he was not come to make war upon them, but with a powerful army of 110,000 men to drive the English into the sea. It is to be hoped that the example of what has occurred in this country will teach the people of this and of other nations what value they ought to place on such promises and assurances; and that there is no security for life, or for any thing which makes life valuable, excepting in decided resistance to the enemy.

I have the honor to enclose returns of killed and wounded in the several affairs with the enemy since they commenced their retreat.

I have received the most able and cordial assistance throughout these operations from Lieut. Gen. Sir B. Spencer, and Marshal Sir W. Beresford, whom I had requested to cross the Tagus, and who has been with me since the 11th inst.; from Major Gens. Sir W. Erskine, Picton, Cole, Campbell; Major Gen. Slade, and Major Gen. the Hon. C. Colville, and the General and other officers commanding brigades under their orders respectively. I am particularly indebted to the Q. M. G., Col. Murray, for the assistance I have received from him, and to the D. A. G., Col. the Hon. E. Pakenham; and the officers of the Adj. Gen. and Q. M. Gen.'s departments, as also those of my personal staff, have given me every assistance in their power.

I am sorry to inform your Lordship that Badajoz surrendered on the 11th inst. I have not yet received the particulars of this event, but I have no doubt of the fact. Since the enemy entered Estremadura, and has directed his efforts against that place, my attention has been drawn to the means of saving it; and Mr Wellesley will have transmitted to England the copies of the correspondence which I have had with the Spanish officers upon this subject.

Before the unfortunate battle of the 19th Feb. I had intended to reinforce the Spanish army with about 14,000 men from that under my command; and thus to force the enemy to raise the siege, as soon as I should have been joined by the reinforcement which I expected would arrive in the Tagus by the end of January. I could not detach with safety till that reinforcement should arrive.

The battle of the 19th Feb. destroyed the Spanish troops upon whose assistance and co-operation I relied; and then it would have been impossible to detach a body of troops sufficient to effect the purpose, even after the arrival of the reinforcements, till the enemy should be removed from the Tagus. I had therefore determined to attack the enemy in his positions as soon as the reinforcements should arrive, if the weather should be such as to render the roads at all passable.

The reinforcements arrived in the first days of March, but have not yet joined the army; and on the 5th, at night, the enemy withdrew from their positions.

On the 6th, Gen. Leite, the governor of Elvas, began to inform the governor of Badajoz, by signal or otherwise, that Massena had retired, and that he might expect assistance as soon as it was in my power to give it to him; and that he must hold out till the last extremity. I had made all the arrangements for detaching the force immediately upon the enemy's quitting the Tagus and Zezere, and some of the troops actually marched from Thomar on the morning of the 9th; and others, that part of Sir W. Beresford's corps which had not crossed the Tagus, were put in motion; and their head has arrived within three marches of Elvas.

I received at Thomar, on the morning of the 9th, accounts of a most favorable nature from Badajoz, from which I was induced to believe, not only that the place was in no danger, but that it was in fact untouched; that its fire was superior to that of the enemy, and that it was in no want of provisions or ammunition, had sustained no loss, excepting that of the governor, Menacho, and was able and likely to hold out for a month. Gen. Imaz, a person of equally good reputation, succeeded to the command; and the greatest confidence was reposed in him. On the same afternoon of the 9th I was with the British advanced guard at Pombal, and saw in front of that town the collection of the enemy's troops which I have above recited to your Lordship. It appeared to me then, that I must decide either to allow the enemy to retreat from Portugal unmolested, by the road he should prefer, and expose Coimbra and Upper Beira to be ravaged; or that I must draw to the army some of the troops, cavalry particularly, which I had allotted for the expedition to Badajoz, and which still remained at Thomar. I accordingly called to the army the 4th division of infantry and a brigade of heavy cavalry, under the conviction that Badajoz would hold out for the time during which it should be necessary to employ them. Experience has shown me that I could not have done without these troops; and it is also very clear, that if I had left them behind, they could not have saved Badajoz, which place the governor surrendered on the day after he received my assurances that he should be relieved and my entreaty that he would hold out to the last moment.

It is useless to add any reflection to these facts. The Spanish nation have lost Tortosa, Olivença, and Badajoz, in the course of two months, without sufficient cause; and in the same period, Marshal Soult, with a corps never supposed to be more than 20,000 men, has taken, besides the last two places, or destroyed above 22,000 Spanish troops.

To Marshal Sir W. C. Beresford, K. B.

Sᵗᵃ Marinha, 25th March, 1811.

I received last night your letters of the 19th and 21st, and I am very uneasy at your not having received my letter of the 18th, which I sent you again in duplicate on the 20th. Unfortunately the magistrate at Goes stopped the guide on the 20th from an excess of zeal, as his horse was shod in the French mode, although the guide was Portuguese. I still hope that you will save Campo Maior. If so, the first thing to do will be to drive Mortier across the Guadiana, and shut up Badajoz.

The possession which the French have got of Alburquerque and Valencia de Alcantara may render it necessary for you to alter the course of proceeding, the general outlines of which were chalked out in my letter of the 20th. You must get these places from Mortier again; and it will be necessary to cover the operation against them by a respectable force on the right of the Guadiana, close to Badajoz. When you have cleared Estremadura between the Tagus and the Guadiana, then will be the time to make your arrangements for crossing the latter, and closing in Badajoz on the left of that river.

The French have gone towards the Coa. Their left will cross at Sabugal, I should think, and their right about Pinhel and Almeida. We have been a little distressed for provisions, which has prevented us from pressing them so hard for these last days as I should have wished. We are getting right now, however.

Gen. Graham has returned to the Isla, after having fought the hardest action that has been fought yet. The Spaniards left him very much to his own exertions. The Spanish General is to be brought to a court martial. Graham took 2 General officers, 6 pieces of cannon, an eagle, and 500 prisoners. He lost 1100, principally wounded. The 2 Portuguese companies of the 20th behaved remarkably well; Bushe is wounded. I will send you the dispatches as soon as Sir Brent shall return them.

I am sorry to tell you that the Portuguese troops here are diminishing in numbers terribly. Pack's brigade has only 1700; the 21st regt. but little more than 500; Pakenham tells me either the 3d or 15th only 300; but I have not seen this return. They are fed, and indeed have been ever since they marched, by our Commissaries, except Pack's, Ashworth's, and Barbacena's cavalry.

To Marshal Sir W. C. Beresford, K. B.

Sabugal, 4th April, 1811.

Since I wrote to you last I have received your letters of the 28th and 29th; but I have had so much to do, that I have not been able to write to you. I wrote to you on the 25th, 27th, 30th, and 31st March, and 1st April, all of which letters I hope you will have received.

I don't understand by whose orders the shoes and money for you were stopped at Aldea Galega. I believe, however, that Mr Thompson is very unequal to the management of the great concern now in Alentejo. Mr Thompson, therefore, is ordered to Abrantes, and Mr Ogilvie will manage the whole concern in the Alentejo.

The French army were posted on the Coa, with their right at Ponte Sequeiros; their left, the 2d corps, here; Loison at Rovina, opposite Rapoula de Coa; and a considerable body, and the head quarters, at Alfaiates.

We moved on the 2d, and the British army was formed opposite to them; the divisions of militia, under Trant and

Wilson, were sent across the river at Cinco Villas, to alarm Almeida for its communication. Yesterday morning we moved the whole army (with the exception of the 6th division, which remained at Rapoula de Coa, opposite Loison) to the right, in order to turn this position, and force the passage of the river. The 2d corps could not have stood here for a moment; but unfortunately the Light division, which formed the right of the whole, necessarily passed first, and the leading brigade, Beckwith's, drove in the enemy's piquets, which were followed briskly by 4 companies of the 95th, and 3 of Elder's caçadores, and supported by the 43d regt. At this time there came on a rain storm, and it was as difficult to see as in the fogs on Busaco, and these troops pushed on too far, and became engaged with the main body of the enemy. The light infantry fell back upon their support, which, instead of halting, moved forward. The French then seeing how weak the body was which had passed, attempted to drive them down to the Coa, and did oblige the 43d to turn. They rallied again, however, and beat in the French; but were attacked by fresh troops and cavalry, and were obliged to retire; but formed again, and beat back the enemy. At this time the 52d joined the 43d, and both moved on upon the enemy, and to be charged and attacked again in the same manner, and beat back. They formed again, moved forward upon the enemy, and established themselves on the top of the hill in an enclosure, and here they beat off the enemy.

But Regnier was placing a body of infantry on their left flank, which must have destroyed them, only that at that moment the head of the 3d division, which had passed the Coa on the left of the Light division, came up, and opened their fire upon this column; and the 5th division, which passed this bridge and through this town, made their appearance. The enemy then retired, having lost in this affair a howitzer, and I should think not less than 1000 men.

Our loss is much less than one would have supposed possible, scarcely 200 men. The 43d have 73 killed and wounded. But really these attacks in columns against our lines are very contemptible.

The contest was latterly entirely for the howitzer, which was taken and retaken twice, and at last remained in our hands. Our cavalry, which ought to have crossed the Coa on the right of the Light division, crossed at the same ford, and therefore could be of no use to them. Besides they went too far to the right. In short, these combinations for engagements do not answer, unless one is upon the spot to direct every trifling movement. I was upon a hill on the left of the Coa, immediately above the town, till the 3d and 5th divisions crossed, whence I could see every movement on both sides, and could communicate with ease with every body; but that was not near enough. We took 6 officers, and between 200 and 300 prisoners, and Soult's and Loison's baggage.

After this affair the whole French army retired from the Coa upon Alfaiates, and this morning from thence; and if they are not out of Portugal, they are, at the utmost, in the frontier villages of Aldea da Ponte and Aldea Velha. I suspect that they will have destroyed Almeida either last night or this morning.

You will be concerned to hear that Waters is at last taken prisoner. He crossed the Coa alone, I believe, yesterday morning, and was looking at the enemy through a spying glass, when 4 hussars pounced upon him. Nobody has seen him since yesterday morning; and we have the account from the prisoners, who tell the story of an officer attached to the Staff, a Lieut. Colonel, *blond*, with a *petit chapeau*. They saw him with Regnier.

To counterbalance the effect of this bad news, I announce to you the birth of the King of Rome, on the 20th March. This event was announced to the *Armée de Portugal* on the 2d inst., by the firing of 101 pieces of cannon!!!

P. S. I have received Cole's report, &c., upon Campo Maior. Now that you are upon the spot you had better determine what shall be done with that place, and give orders upon it. A good place in that situation would be very useful. Can the place, or the citadel of Campo Maior, be put in such a state as to render it probable that either will hold out so long as to render it worth while to risk the loss of the men who must be left in it?

To the Earl of Liverpool.

Villar Formoso, 1st May, 1811.

Having received intelligence from Lieut. Gen. Sir B. Spencer, on the 27th April, 2 days after I addressed your Lordship last, that the enemy were increasing their force on the Agueda, I arrived here on the 28th.

The enemy had, on the 23d, attacked our piquets on the Azava, but were repulsed. Capt. Dobbs and Campbell, of the 52d, and Lieut. Eeles of the 95th regt., distinguished themselves upon this occasion, in which the allied troops defended their post against very superior numbers of the enemy. Lieut. Prichard, 1st batt. 52d regt., and 17 soldiers, were wounded. The enemy repeated their attack upon our piquets on the Azava on the 27th, and were again repulsed; and this day again they reconnaitred the banks of this river with 8 squadrons of cavalry, and 3 battalions of infantry. They did not make any attempt to pass the river, nor did they attack the piquets upon the bridge of Marialva.

They have collected a very large force at Ciudad Rodrigo. Marshal Massena, and the head quarters of the army, are at that place; and it is generally reported in the country that they propose to raise the blockade of Almeida. I don't intend to allow them to relieve this place, unless I should be convinced that they have such a superiority of force as to render the result of a contest for this point doubtful. From all the accounts which I have received, I believe that they have still in that place provisions for the garrison, which is stated to consist of 1500 men, for one fortnight.

The enemy may be stronger than they were when they were obliged to evacuate Portugal, and they may be reinforced by detachments of troops, particularly the Guard, under the command of Marshal Bessières; but still I feel confident that they have it not in their power to defeat the allied army in a general action; and I hope to be able to prevent them from relieving this place, unless they should bring the contest to that issue in a situation unfavorable to us. The river Agueda is not yet fordable for infantry, but is so for cavalry.

Sir W. Beresford has taken up the position which I had proposed for him in Estremadura; but I have not yet heard that he had re-established his bridge at Jurumenha.

I have no late intelligence from Cadiz or from the north of Spain.

It has been frequently reported that King Joseph was about to quit Madrid; and I have always considered these reports to be so little founded, excepting in the wishes of those who circulated them, that I have omitted to communicate them to your Lordship. However, at last, I have reason to believe that there is some foundation for a report which I have received, that King Joseph was to be at Valladolid, on his road to France, on the 27th April. The guerrillas are all active to intercept his progress; but he has with him a considerable escort, of 1000 French troops; and all the Spanish troops in his cause, called *Juramentados*.

The departure of the King, whatever political effect it may have in Spain, will relieve the French from the necessity of taking care of his person, and will increase their disposable force, particularly in the southern provinces. But if we should be able to obtain possession of Almeida, I hope to have it in my power to reinforce our troops in that quarter to such an extent as to render our operations, at least in Estremadura, free from risk, whatever may be the force which the enemy may be enabled by circumstances to assemble.

To the Earl of Liverpool.

Villar Formoso, 7th May, 1811.

I had the honor of receiving yesterday morning, by the messenger, your Lordship's letter of the 11th April, to which I proceed to reply without loss of time.

Your Lordship will have observed in my recent reports of the state of the Portuguese force, that their numbers are much reduced, and I don't know what measure to recommend which will have the effect of restoring them. All measures recommended to the existing government in Portugal are either rejected, or are neglected, or are so executed as to be of no value whatever; and the countenance which the Prince Regent of Portugal has given to the Governors of the Kingdom, who have uniformly manifested this spirit of opposition to every thing proposed for the increase of the resources of the government, and the amelioration of their military system, must tend to aggravate these evils.

The radical defect, both in Spain and Portugal, is want of money to carry on the ordinary operations of the government, much more to defray the expenses of such a war as that in which we are engaged. The increase of the subsidy by Great Britain will have no direct effect in increasing the pecuniary means of the Portuguese government, as the greatest part of the increase must necessarily be given in kind; and that which will be given will most probably be in lieu of what was irregularly plundered from the country heretofore.

On all these accounts I have urged the Portuguese government most earnestly to adopt every measure in their power to augment their own pecuniary resources, but hitherto without much effect. And yet until the amount of money at their command is increased, it will be impossible to apply an effectual remedy to the evils which have gradually decreased, and continue daily to decrease, the numbers of the army. However, I am decidedly of opinion that if the British government are determined to do no more in the Peninsula than to maintain themselves in Portugal, 30,000 effective British troops would be sufficient, to be aided by a reserve maintained in Great Britain or Ireland, and ready to sail at a moment's notice. But these troops ought to be effective; and I would beg to refer your Lordship to the first letter which I addressed to you upon the subject, on the 14th Nov. 1809.

In respect to the second question which your Lordship has referred for my consideration, viz., the use to be made of our existing force, in the present state of the Peninsula, for active operations, I will inform your Lordship what plan I intended to follow under the existing instructions; and, indeed, however they may be enlarged, something of the same kind must be done.

The first object of our attention must be to regain Badajoz. This is very important, not only in respect to Portugal, but to the subsistence of Cadiz, the greatest part of which is, I understand, drawn from the Condado de Niebla. If Badajoz were not regained, it could not be expected that the war could be maintained at all in the Condado de Niebla. The loss of Badajoz is also very important in reference to the safety of Portugal. The siege of Elvas might be opened immediately.

Circumstances have enabled us to attempt to reduce Almeida by blockade, at the same time that we attempt to obtain possession of Badajoz by siege. A few days must bring the blockade to an issue; but if I find that I can neither maintain it, nor bring the enemy to a general action on terms which I shall think advantageous, I shall have no scruple in giving it up, as I undertook it not as a part of a plan, but as the consequence of our preceding operations during Massena's retreat, upon finding by intercepted letters and other intelligence that the place was but ill supplied with provisions.

If we should obtain possession of Badajoz, circumstances may render one or other of two lines of offensive operations expedient: viz., one directed to the south for the relief of Cadiz, remaining on the defensive in Beira; the other, supposing Almeida to have fallen by blockade, to undertake the siege of Ciudad Rodrigo; or, if Almeida should not have fallen by the blockade, to undertake the siege of both places, and afterwards to push on our operations into the heart of Spain, and open the communication with Valencia. This latter plan, if practicable, would relieve Cadiz and the south of Spain as soon and as effectually as the first mentioned.

I consider myself authorised to undertake the first by the existing instructions: the instructions must be altered to enable me to undertake the second. Circumstances vary to such a degree in this extraordinary war every day, that it is impossible for me to say which plan would be best, at the moment at which I should have it in my power to execute either.

Just to give you a notion of the degree in which circumstances have altered within this last month, which ought to weigh in determining upon any of the operations which are now carrying on, or which must be carried on in future, I mention to you the detachment of a considerable body of Spanish troops under Gen. Blake from Cadiz; on the other hand, the removal of the King from Madrid, which will set at liberty a considerable force which always attended his person; the junction with Massena of all the French cavalry in Old Castille, Leon, &c., while the army in Galicia, which was kept in check by this cavalry, still remain inactive. Then all plans would be overturned by the defeat of one of the Spanish corps which must co-operate with us; or by the refusal of the Spanish government to co-operate with us according to any plan founded on the reasonable system of security, on which alone I can venture to act under your Lordship's instructions. All plans of offensive operation would also of course be destroyed by the arrival in Spain of fresh reinforcements to the enemy's armies.

From this statement your Lordship will see how difficult it is for me to lay down a plan of operations for the campaign. I have not yet received the consent of Castaños and Blake to the plan of co-operation which I proposed for the siege of Badajoz; and I have been obliged to write to Beresford to desire him to delay the siege till they shall positively promise to act as therein specified, or till I can go to him with a reinforcement from hence. All that I can say is, therefore, that I shall carry on offensive operations against the enemy as far as it may lie in my power, and as my instructions will allow me, on one or the other of the plans which I have above detailed to you, according to the best judgment which I may be able to form of the situation of affairs at the time. It will be necessary that you should continue to reinforce us, and that you should send out to us particularly good horses for the cavalry and artillery.

I earnestly recommend to you not to undertake any of the maritime operations on the coast of Spain upon which you have desired to have my opinion. Unless you should send a very large force, you would scarcely be able to effect a landing, and maintain the situation of which you might obtain possession. Then that large force would be unable to move, or to effect any object at all adequate to the expense or to the expectation which would be formed from its strength, owing to the want of those equipments and supplies in which an army landed from its ships must be deficient.

It is in vain to hope for any assistance, even in this way, much less military assistance, to such expeditions from the Spaniards. The first thing they would require uniformly would be money; then arms, ammunition, clothing of all descriptions, provisions, forage, horses, means of transport, and every thing which your expedition would have a right to require from them; and, after all, this extraordinary and perverse people would scarcely allow the commander of your expedition to have a voice in the decision on the plan of operations to be followed, when the whole should be ready to undertake one.

Depend upon it that Portugal should be the foundation of all your operations in the Peninsula, of whatever nature they may be; upon which point I have never altered my opinion. If they are to be offensive, and Spain is to be the theatre of them, your commanders must be in a situation to be entirely independent of all Spanish authorities; by which means alone they will be enabled to draw some resources from the country, and some assistance from the Spanish armies. While writing upon this subject I may as well reply to your Lordship's official dispatch of the 11th, No. 19.

Of course all operations of an offensive nature must cease if the battalions, mentioned in the memorandum enclosed in that dispatch, are sent home before they shall be relieved. The plan which I would propose would be:

1st; To draft the 7 battalions of the K. G. L. into the 3 others, and send home the officers and non-commissioned officers of the 7 Line battalions.

2dly; To form into 6 companies the 2d batts. of the 24th, 31st, 38th, 42d, 53d, 58th, and 66th, and to send home to recruit, or to form the recruits, the officers and non-commissioned officers of the 4 companies drafted.

3dly; To send home entirely the 2d batts. of the 24th, 53d, and 66th, as soon as they shall be relieved; although, by the bye, the last two are two of the best 2d batts. we have.

According to this plan we should reduce in some degree our expense in this country. We should keep here officers inured to the climate, and accustomed to the service; at the same time that we should send to England officers and non-commissioned officers to raise and train recruits. Indeed it would be desirable if I were authorised from time to time to incorporate the 10 companies of a regiment into 8 or 6 companies, according to their numbers, and to send home to recruit, or train recruits, the officers and non-commissioned officers of the drafted companies.

To the Earl of Liverpool.

Villar Formoso, 8th May, 1811.

The enemy's whole army, consisting of the 2d, 6th, and 8th corps, and all the cavalry which could be collected in Castille and Leon, including about 900 of the Imperial Guard, crossed the Agueda at Ciudad Rodrigo on the 2d inst. The battalions of the 9th corps had been joined to the regiments to which they belonged in the other 3 corps; excepting a division consisting of battalions belonging to regiments in the corps doing duty in Andalusia; which division likewise formed part of the army.

As my object in maintaining a position between the Coa and the Agueda, after the enemy had retired from the former, was to blockade Almeida, which place I had learned from intercepted letters, and other information, was ill supplied with provisions for its garrison, and as the enemy were infinitely superior to us in cavalry, I did not give any opposition to their march, and they passed the Azava on that evening, in the neighbourhood of Espeja, Carpio, and Gallegos. They continued their march on the 3d, in the morning, towards the Dos Casas, in 3 columns; 2 of them, consisting of the 2d and 8th corps, to the neighbourhood of Almeida and Fort Concepcion, and the 3d column, consisting of the whole of the cavalry, and the 6th and that part of the 9th corps which had not already been drafted into the other 3.

The allied army had been cantoned along the river Dos Casas, and on the sources of the Azava, the Light division at Gallegos and Espeja. This last fell back upon Fuentes de Oñoro, on the Dos Casas, with the British cavalry, in proportion as the enemy advanced, and the 1st, 3d, and 7th divisions were collected at that place; the 6th division, under Major Gen. Campbell, observed the bridge at Alameda; and Major Gen. Sir W. Erskine, with the 5th division, the passages of the Dos Casas at Fort Concepcion and Aldea del Obispo. Brig. Gen. Pack's brigade, with the Queen's regt. from the 6th division, kept the blockade of Almeida; and I had prevailed upon Don J. Sanchez to occupy Nave d'Aver with his corps of Spanish cavalry and infantry. The Light division were moved in the evening to join Major Gen. Campbell, upon finding that the enemy were in strength in that quarter; and they were brought back again to Fuentes de Oñoro on the morning of the 5th, when it was found that the 8th corps had joined the 6th on the enemy's left.

Shortly after the enemy had formed on the ground on the right of the Dos Casas, on the afternoon of the 3d, they attacked with a large force the village of Fuentes de Oñoro, which was defended in a most gallant manner by Lieut. Col. Williams, of the 5th batt. 60th regt., in command of the light infantry battalion belonging to Major Gen. Picton's division, supported by the light infantry battalion in Major Gen. Nightingall's brigade, commanded by Major Dick of the 42d regt., and the light infantry battalion in Major Gen. Howard's brigade, commanded by Major M'Donnell of the 92d, and the light infantry battalion of the King's German Legion, commanded by Major Aly, of the 5th batt. of the line, and by the 2d batt. 83d regt., under Major Carr.

The troops maintained their position: but having observed the repeated efforts which the enemy were making to obtain possession of the village, and being aware of the advantage which they would derive from the possession in their subsequent operations, I reinforced the village successively with the 71st regt. under Lieut. Col. the Hon. H. Cadogan, and the 79th under Lieut. Col. Cameron, and the 24th under Major Chamberlain. The former, at the head of the 71st regt., charged the enemy, and drove them from a part of the village of which they had obtained a momentary possession. Nearly at this time Lieut. Col. Williams was unfortunately wounded, but I hope not dangerously; and the command devolved upon Lieut. Col. Cameron of the 79th.

The contest continued till night, when our troops remained in possession of the whole. I then withdrew the light infantry battalions, and the 83d regt., leaving the 71st and 79th regts. only in the village, and the 2d batt. 24th regt. to support them.

On the 4th the enemy reconnaitred the position which we had occupied on the Dos Casas river; and during that night they moved the Duc d'Abrantes' corps from Alameda to the left of the position occupied by the 6th corps, opposite to Fuentes de Oñoro.

From the course of the reconnaissance on the 4th, I had imagined that the enemy would endeavor to obtain possession of Fuentes de Oñoro, and of the ground occupied by the troops behind that village, by crossing the Dos Casas at Pozo Velho; and in the evening I moved the 7th division, under Major Gen. Houstoun, to the right, in order, if possible, to protect that passage.

On the morning of the 5th the 8th corps appeared in 2 columns, with all the cavalry, on the opposite side of the valley of the Dos Casas and Pozo Velho; and as the 6th and 9th corps also made a movement to their left, the Light division, which had been brought back from the neighbourhood of Alameda, were sent with the cavalry, under Sir S. Cotton, to support Major Gen. Houstoun; while the 1st and 3d divisions made a movement to their right, along the ridge between the Turones and Dos Casas rivers, corresponding to that of the 6th and 9th corps, on the right of the Dos Casas.

The 8th corps attacked Major Gen. Houstoun's advanced guard, consisting of the 85th regt., under Major Macintosh, and the 2d Portuguese caçadores, under Lieut. Col. Nixon, and obliged them to retire; and they retired in good order, although with some loss. The 8th corps being thus established in Pozo Velho, the enemy's cavalry turned the right of the 7th division, between Pozo Velho and Nave d'Aver, from which last place Don J. Sanchez had been obliged to retire; and the cavalry charged.

The charge of the advanced guard of the enemy's cavalry

was met by two or three squadrons of the different regiments of British dragoons, and the enemy were driven back; and Col. La Motte, of the 13th *chasseurs* and some prisoners, taken. The main body were checked and obliged to retire by the fire of Major Gen. Houstoun's division; and I particularly observed the Chasseurs Britanniques, under Lieut. Col. Eustace, as behaving in the most steady manner; and Major Gen. Houstoun mentions in high terms the conduct of a detachment of the Duke of Brunswick's light infantry. Notwithstanding that this charge was repulsed, I determined to concentrate our force towards the left, and to move the 7th and Light divisions and the cavalry from Pozo Velho towards Fuentes de Oñoro, and the other two divisions.

I had occupied Pozo Velho and that neighbourhood, in hopes that I should be able to maintain the communication across the Coa by Sabugal, as well as provide for the blockade, which objects it was now obvious were incompatible with each other; and I therefore abandoned that which was the least important, and placed the Light division in reserve in the rear of the left of the 1st division, and the 7th division on some commanding ground beyond the Turones, which protected the right flank and rear of the 1st division, and covered the communication with the Coa, and prevented that of the enemy with Almeida by the roads between the Turones and that river.

The movement of the troops upon this occasion was well conducted, although under very critical circumstances, by Major Gen. Houstoun, Brig. Gen. Craufurd, and Lieut. Gen. Sir S. Cotton. The 7th division was covered in its passage of the Turones by the Light division, under Brig. Gen. Craufurd; and this last, in its march to join the 1st division, by the British cavalry.

Our position thus extended on the high ground from the Turones to the Dos Casas. The 7th division, on the left of the Turones, covered the rear of the right; the 1st division, in 2 lines, were on the right; Col. Ashworth's brigade, in 2 lines, in the centre; and the 3d division, in 2 lines, on the left; the Light division and British artillery in reserve; and the village of Fuentes in front of the left. Don Julian's infantry joined the 7th division in Freneda; and I sent him with his cavalry to endeavor to intercept the enemy's communication with Ciudad Rodrigo.

The enemy's efforts on the right part of our position, after it was occupied as I have above described, were confined to a cannonade, and to some charges with his cavalry, upon the advanced posts. The piquets of the 1st division, under Lieut. Col. Hill of the 3d regt. of Guards, repulsed one of these; but as they were falling back they did not see the direction of another in sufficient time to form to oppose it, and Lieut. Col. Hill was taken prisoner, and many men were wounded, and some taken, before a detachment of the British cavalry could move up to their support. The 2d batt. 42d regt., under Lord Blantyre, also repulsed a charge of the cavalry directed against them.

They likewise attempted to push a body of light infantry upon the ravine of the Turones, to the right of the 1st division, which were repulsed by the light infantry of the Guards, under Lieut. Col. Guise, aided by 5 companies of the 95th under Capt. O'Hare. Major Gen. Nightingall was wounded in the course of the cannonade, but I hope not severely.

The enemy's principal effort was throughout this day again directed against Fuentes de Oñoro; and, notwithstanding that the whole of the 6th corps were at different periods of the day employed to attack this village, they could never gain more than a temporary possession of it. It was defended by the 24th, 71st, and 79th regts., under the command of Lieut. Col. Cameron; and these troops were supported by the light infantry battalions of the 3d division, commanded by Major Woodgate; the light infantry battalions of the 1st division, commanded by Major Dick, Major M'Donnell, and Major Aly; the 6th Portuguese caçadores, commanded by Major Pinto; by the light companies in Col. Champelmond's Portuguese brigade, under Col. Sutton; and those in Col. Ashworth's Portuguese brigade, under Lieut. Col. Pynn, and by the piquets of the 3d division, under the command of Col. the Hon. R. Trench. Lieut. Col. Cameron was severely wounded in the afternoon, and the command in the village devolved upon Lieut. Col. the Hon. H. Cadogan.

The troops in Fuentes were besides supported, when pressed by the enemy, by the 74th regt., under Major Russell Manners, and the 1st batt. 88th regt., under Lieut. Col. Wallace, belonging to Col. Mackinnon's brigade; and on one of these occasions the 88th, with the 71st and 79th, under the command of Col. Mackinnon, charged the enemy, and drove them through the village; and Col. Mackinnon has reported particularly the conduct of Lieut. Col. Wallace, Brigade Major Wilde, and Lieut. and Adj. Stewart. The contest again lasted in this quarter till night, when our troops still held their post; and from that time the enemy have made no fresh attempt on any part of our position.

The enemy manifested an intention to attack Major Gen. Sir W. Erskine's post at Aldea del Obispo on the same morning, with a part of the 2d corps; but the Major General sent the 2d batt. Lusitanian Legion across the ford of the Dos Casas, which obliged them to retire.

In the course of last night the enemy commenced retiring from their position on the Dos Casas; and this morning, at daylight, the whole was in motion. I cannot yet decide whether this movement is preparatory to some fresh attempt to raise the blockade of Almeida, or is one of decided retreat; but I have every reason to hope that they will not succeed in the first, and that they will be obliged to have recourse to the last. Their superiority in cavalry is very great, owing to the weak state of our horses, from recent fatigue and scarcity of forage, and the reduction of numbers in the Portuguese brigade of cavalry with this part of the army, in exchange for a British brigade sent into Estremadura with Marshal Sir W. Beresford, owing to the failure of the measures reported to have been adopted to supply horses and men with food on the service.

The result of a general action, brought on by an attack upon the enemy by us, might, under those circumstances, have been doubtful; and if the enemy had chosen to avoid it, or if they had met it, they would have taken advantage of the collection of our troops to fight this action, and throw relief into Almeida. From the great superiority of force to which we have been opposed upon this occasion, your Lordship will judge of the conduct of the officers and troops. The actions were partial, but very severe, and our loss has been great. The enemy's loss has also been very great, and they left 400 killed in the village of Fuentes, and we have many prisoners. I particularly request your attention to the conduct of Lieut. Col. Williams, and Lieut. Col. Cameron, and Lieut. Col. the Hon. H. Cadogan; and to that of Col. Mackinnon and Lieut. Col. Kelly, 24th regt.; of the several officers commanding battalions of the line and of light infantry, which supported the troops in Fuentes de Oñoro; likewise to that of Major Macintosh of the 85th, and of Lieut. Col. Nixon, of the 2d caçadores, and of Lieut. Col. Eustace, of the Chasseurs Britanniques, and of Lord Blantyre.

Throughout these operations I have received the greatest assistance from Lieut. Gen. Sir B. Spencer, and all the General officers of the army; and from the Adj. Gen. and Q. M. Gen., and the officers of their several departments, and those of my personal Staff.

By intelligence from Sir W. Beresford I learn that he has invested Badajoz, on the left of the Guadiana, and is moving stores there for the attack of the place.

I have the honor to inform you that the intelligence which I transmitted in my last dispatch has since been confirmed, and that King Joseph passed Valladolid, on his way to Paris, on the 27th April. It is not denied by the French officers that he is gone to Paris.

Return of the killed, wounded, and missing in the battle at Fuentes de Oñoro, on the 3d and 5th May, 1811.

	Officers.	Non-commissioned officers & drummers.	R. and F.	Horses.	Total loss of officers, non-commissioned officers, and R. & F.
Killed	11	16	208	49	235
Wounded	81	72	1081	101	1234
Missing	7	10	300	5	317

The Portuguese killed, wounded, and missing, are included in the above numbers.

To the Earl of Liverpool.

Villar Formoso, 15th May, 1811.

You will receive by this post the account of the blowing up of Almeida; and, although I believe that we have taken or destroyed the greatest part of the garrison, I have never been so much distressed by any military event as by the escape of even a man of them.

The enemy having retired across the Azava during the night of the 9th, I went forward in the morning to observe their subsequent movements. About 1 o'clock of the day of the 10th, having seen their whole army in march to cross the Agueda, I sent orders for the right of the army to resume their cantonments on the Dos Casas; the advanced guard and cavalry upon the Azava and Upper Agueda; the 5th division (Sir W. Erskine) to send a regiment to Barba de Puerco; and the 6th division (Major Gen. Campbell) to resume the blockade of Almeida.

Sir W. Erskine was dining with Sir B. Spencer at head quarters, and received his orders about 4 o'clock; and he says he sent them off forthwith to the 4th regt., which were stationed, under former orders, on the Dos Casas, half way between Aldea del Obispo and Barba de Puerco. Gen. Campbell called upon me about 5½ or 6 o'clock, and told me that, before dark, his division would have resumed their positions for the blockade.

At about 12½ the place was blown up; and the garrison had about 14 miles to march to Barba de Puerco, and nearly the same distance to the only fords on the Agueda, the whole of which were occupied by our dragoons.

Gen. Pack and Gen. Campbell both expected that the garrison would attempt to escape, and were both at Malpartida, about 4 miles from Almeida, on the road towards the Agueda and Barba de Puerco. Gen. Pack joined the piquets, and followed the enemy with 10 men, and kept up a fire upon them, as a guide to the other troops, which he supposed were following. Gen. Campbell did follow with 8 companies of the 36th regt. The 8th Portuguese regt., under Lieut. Col. Douglas, which were at Junça, on the south-west side of Almeida, marched when the explosion was heard, and arrived at Barba de Puerco before the French; but finding nobody there excepting a piquet of cavalry, they passed the Dos Casas again, and thus missed them.

The Queen's regt., which were within a mile of Almeida, on the road to Malpartida, were not aware that the place was blown up, and did not march at all; and the 4th regt., which it is said did not receive their orders before midnight, and had only 2½ miles to march, missed their road, and did not arrive at Barba de Puerco till after the French, and with Gen. Campbell and Gen. Pack; and the flank battalions of the 5th division which Sir W. Erskine had detached from Aldea del Obispo (so long after he had heard the explosion, that he had sent an officer to Almeida, between 5 and 6 miles, to ascertain what it was, and this officer had returned), arrived nearly at the same time.

The other corps of the 6th division had marched different distances in pursuit of the enemy; but, excepting the 36th and the 8th Portuguese, none had crossed the Turones.

Thus your Lordship will see that, if the 4th regt. had received the orders, issued at 1, before it was dark at 8 o'clock at night; or if they had not missed their road, the garrison must have laid down their arms; and the same would have occurred if Lieut. Col. Douglas had remained at Barba de Puerco; and possibly the same would have occurred had the pursuit been judiciously managed.

Possibly I have to reproach myself for not having been on the spot; but really, when the enemy's whole army had crossed the Agueda, with the exception of one brigade of cavalry, in front of Ciudad Rodrigo, I did not think it probable that the attempt to escape would be made; and having employed 2 divisions and a brigade, to prevent the escape of 1400 men, who I did not think it likely would attempt to escape, the necessity of my attending personally to this operation, after I had been the whole day on the Azava, did not occur to me. However, it is that alone in the whole operation in which I have to reproach myself, as every thing was done that could be done in the way of order and instruction. I certainly feel, every day, more and more the difficulty of the situation in which I am placed. I am obliged to be everywhere, and if absent from any operation, something goes wrong. It is to be hoped that the General and other officers of the army will at last acquire that experience which will teach them that success can be attained only by attention to the most minute details; and by tracing every part of every operation from its origin to its conclusion, point by point, and ascertaining that the whole is understood by those who are to execute it.

To the Rt. Hon. H. Wellesley.

Elvas, 22d May, 1811.

We have had warm work here; however, I hope that the French have suffered more than we have. I mean, if Soult goes far enough from me, to renew the operations of the siege of Badajoz; but he will soon have a large reinforcement from Castille, and another such battle would ruin us.

The Spanish troops, I understand, behaved admirably; they stood like stocks, both parties at times firing on them, but they were quite immoveable; and this is the great cause of all our losses. After they had lost their position, the natural thing to do would have been to attack it with the nearest Spanish troops, but they could not be moved; the British troops were the next, and they were brought up, and must always in these cases be brought up; and they suffered accordingly. The battle of Talavera was an example of the same defect in the Spanish troops; they could not be moved, however advantageous this movement might have been; and I suspect that the battle of Barrosa was something of the same kind. It is scarcely to be believed that any officer, who could depend upon the discipline of his troops in their movements, would have remained the quiet spectator of such an action at such a moment.

From these circumstances, you will believe that I am not very easy about the result of another action, if we should be obliged to fight one. What a pity it is that the Spaniards will not set to work seriously to discipline their troops! We do what we please now with the Portuguese troops; we manœuvre them under fire equally with our own, and have some dependence on them; but these Spaniards can do nothing, but stand still, and we consider ourselves fortunate if they don't run away.

Beresford tells me that it would be a great point gained if Blake were to return to the Regency, as he is not very accommodating, although he adhered strictly to the letter of every thing I laid down for his guidance.

P. S. Show every thing to Graham.

To the Earl of Liverpool.

Elvas, 23d May, 1811.

I have received your letter of the 8th.

When Hill comes he must return to his command; and I must confine Beresford to the management of the detail of the Portuguese army, which has suffered from his employment in this campaign, as well as from other circumstances. I should like to have Gen. Graham; but I rather think that your Lordship's letters don't go so far as to allow me to call him to this country, till the force at Cadiz shall be reduced to 2000 men.

You see from my dispatches how affairs are here. Soult had south of the Sierra Morena an army of about 53,000 effectives on the 25th March, including what is called the Catholic army, which is Dessolles' reserve, and was sent to him from the army of the centre, of this number 7000 are cavalry. Drouet is marching to him with 17 battalions, which, however, are weak, and can scarcely make 3000 men, and some cavalry, of which I don't exactly know the number. From this force must be deducted the losses since the 25th March, which cannot be less than 10,000 men, including the battle of the 16th May, and the garrison of Badajoz about 2500; and Soult will remain, when Drouet arrives, with about 50,000 effective men. From this statement you will see that, supposing that I can get through the siege of Badajoz, it will be impossible to do more to the southward, till I shall have closed the door upon Beira, by obtaining possession of Ciudad Rodrigo: indeed I am thinking of bringing another division from Castille, in order to make sure of Badajoz, in consequence of Beresford's large losses; but I can scarcely venture to do that, and certainly cannot do more, without exposing to risk the frontier of Beira.

Fortunately for me, the French armies have no communication, and one army no knowledge of the position or of the circumstances in which the other is placed; both depend upon orders from Paris, whereas I have a knowledge of all that passes on all sides. From this knowledge I think I may draw more troops from Beira for my operations against Badajoz; but I cannot venture farther south till I shall get Ciudad Rodrigo, without exposing all to ruin. I beg, therefore, that people in England will have patience about Cadiz, and allow us to do our work gradually.

I should feel no anxiety about the result of any of our operations, if the Spaniards were as well disciplined as the soldiers of that nation are brave, and if they were at all moveable; but this is, I fear, beyond all hope; all our losses have been caused by this defect. At Talavera the enemy would have been destroyed, if we could have moved the Spanish army; at Albuera, the natural thing would have been to support the Spaniards on the right with the Spaniards who were next to them; but any movement of that body would have created inextricable confusion; and it was necessary to support the right with British, and thus the great loss fell upon our troops; in the same way, I suspect, the difficulty and danger of moving the Spanish troops was the cause that Gen. La Peña did not support Gen. Graham at Barrosa.

I am glad to hear such good accounts of affairs in the north. God send that they may prove true, and that we may overthrow this disgusting tyranny: however, of this I am very certain, that whether true or not at present, something of the kind must occur before long, and, if we can only hold out, we shall yet see the world relieved.

To Col. Gordon, Commissary in Chief.

Quinta de Granicha, 12th June, 1811.

I have received your letter of the 17th May, and I am much obliged to you for the desire you express to render your department useful to us in this country.

The Portuguese commissariat, and all the departments attached to that army, are in a miserably inefficient state from two causes: the want of authority to enforce obedience to order and regulation; the want of money to defray the necessary expenses.

The departments attached to the army are not liable to the military law; we therefore have no power to punish those guilty of any offence; and, as for expecting punishment from complaint to the government or to the civil tribunals, it would be just as reasonable to expect the coming of the Messiah, or the return of King Sebastian.

These unfortunate governments in the Peninsula had been reduced to such a state of decrepitude, that I believe there was no authority existing within Spain or Portugal before the French invaded these countries. The French invasion did not improve this state of things; and since what is called in Spain the revolution, and in Portugal the restoration, no crime that I know of has been punished in either, excepting that of being a French partisan. Those malversations in office; those neglects of duty; the disobedience of orders; the inattention to regulation, which tend to defeat all plans for military operation, and ruin a state that is involved in war, more certainly than the plots of all the French partisans, are passed unnoticed; and notwithstanding the numerous complaints which Marshal Beresford and I have made, I don't know that one individual has yet been punished, or even dismissed from his office.

The cause of this evil is the mistaken principle on which the government have proceeded. They have imagined that the best foundation for their power was a low, vulgar popularity, of which the evidence is the shouts of the mob of Lisbon, and the regular attendance at their levees, and the bows and scrapes, of people in office, who ought to have other modes of spending their time; and to obtain this bubble the government of Portugal, as well as the successive governments in Spain, have neglected to perform those essential duties of all governments, viz., to force those they are placed over to do their duty, by which, before this time, these countries would have been out of danger.

The other evil is connected very materially with the first. The government will not regulate their finances, because it will interfere with some man's job. They will not lay on new taxes, because in all countries those who lay on taxes are not favorites with the mob. They have a general income tax called 10 *per cent.*, and in some cases 20 *per cent.*, which they have regulated in such a manner as that no individual, I believe, has paid a hundredth part of what he ought to have paid. Then, from want of money, they can pay nobody, and of course have not even the influence which they ought to have over the subordinate departments. The hire of mules and carts, the food for the animals and drivers, are never paid; and of course the animals die, and the people desert the service.

The Commissaries have no money to purchase any thing in the country. I will not allow the soldiers to pillage. The government have no money to pay for the transport of provisions from the magazines on the coast to the army, and are bankrupt in credit, and are unwilling to execute their own law to force means of transport; and the result is that the troops get nothing, and every department and branch of the service is paralysed.

The remedy which has been proposed from England has been that we should take the commissariat upon ourselves. I have already done as much as I could in this way; that is, under an arrangement which provides for the expense being subtracted from the subsidy. I have arranged that the Commissary Gen. shall provide for those parts of the army serving with the

British divisions. I know that we cannot do more without failure.

In addition to embarrassments of all descriptions surrounding us on all sides, I have to contend with an ancient enmity between these two nations, which is more like that of cat and dog than any thing else, of which no sense of common danger, or common interest, or any thing, can get the better, even in individuals.

Our transport, which is the great lever of the commissariat, is done principally, if not entirely, by Spanish muleteers; and, to oblige Mr Kennedy, they would probably once or twice carry provisions to a Portuguese regiment, but they would prefer to quit us, and attend the French, to being obliged to perform this duty constantly.

When a Portuguese brigade is in a British division, the muleteers don't inquire, and don't know, for whom they carry the supplies; and the Commissary with the division issues to the Portuguese Commissary what is required for the Portuguese troops, taking his receipt for the quantities, and a charge is made against the subsidy for the actual cost, including a certain sum for transport from the magazines.

There are but few Portuguese troops not serving in our divisions; but there is the militia, there are the forts, and other establishments, to be provided for, into which we could not enter without involving ourselves in inextricable details and an enormous expense.

The remedy for the existing evils is simple, and has been repeatedly recommended by me as far back as Nov. 1809, at the period of the Austrian peace. It consists in the following measures:

1st; To make the disposable income of the State more nearly equal to the expenditure, by reforms, improvements in collection, and some increase of taxation. Something has lately been done in this way, and I understand with very considerable success: but, notwithstanding my repeated remonstrances, and telling the government over and over again that money (that is, specie) could not be got for their expenses in England, and that they must look to the produce of their own exertions alone for that necessary, it is only lately that they have done any thing.

2dly; To make all officers and departments connected with the army liable to the military law of the country.

3dly; To alter the military law of the country so as to render it more conformable to the circumstances of the present day.

4thly; To appoint a Commissary Gen., with a sufficient number of deputies and assistants, to perform the duty of the army, instead of what is called a Junta, consisting of merchants of Lisbon and their clerks, who have no responsibility, and know nothing of provisioning an army, excepting the profitable jobs they themselves derive from it, and to regulate the duties of the Commissary Gen.'s office, in the manner the details of which have been proposed to them.

5thly; To regulate the medical department, and render it liable to military law. You will scarcely believe that the office of Physician General is a sinecure, held for life, with a right to appoint a deputy, likewise a sinecure held for life, and at the same time a right to interfere in the medical department, and to prevent any body else from doing any good.

6thly; To regulate the department of the arsenal, and render its officers liable to the military law. This is a department connected not only with army and military stores, but with the clothing and appointments of the army; and this also is managed by a Junta, responsible to nobody, and who do nothing.

It may be observed that all these improvements would do very well, but still that a British Commissary or two might be of use. So they might if they were worth having; but if they are worth having, I can't spare them; and if they are not, they will do no good to the Portuguese concerns. In fact, there is no want of ability in the country or of good will. The wants consist in what we can't give them, unless more disposition is shown to attend to our counsel, and the local governments determine to alter their system, and really to do their duty by their country.

To the Earl of Liverpool.

Quinta de Granicha, 13th June, 1811.

In consequence of a report from the Chief Engineer, Lieut. Col.
Fletcher, that the fire from San Cristoval might occasion the
loss of many lives in the operations on the left of the Guadiana,
and the breach in that outwork having been apparently much
improved by the fire throughout the 6th, I directed that an
attempt might be made to carry San Cristoval by storm that
night. Major Gen. Houstoun, who conducted the operations of
the siege on the right of the Guadiana, accordingly ordered a
detachment under Major Macintosh, of the 85th regt., to make
the attempt. The men advanced under a very heavy fire of musketry and hand grenades from the outworks, and of shot and
shells from the town, with the utmost intrepidity, and in the
best order, to the bottom of the breach; the advanced guard
being led by Ensign Dyas, of the 51st regt., who volunteered to
perform this duty: but they found that the enemy had cleared
the rubbish from the bottom of the escarp; and, notwithstanding that they were provided with ladders, it was impossible to
mount it. They retired with some loss.

The fire upon San Cristoval, as well as upon the place, continued on the 7th, 8th, and 9th, on which day the breach in the
wall of San Cristoval appeared practicable, and I directed that
a second attempt should be made on that night to obtain possession of that outwork. Major Gen. Houstoun ordered another
detachment for this service, under the command of Major
M'Geechy, of the 17th Portuguese regt., who, with the officers
destined to command the different parties composing the
detachment, had been employed throughout the 8th and 9th in
reconnaitring the breach and the different approaches to it.
They advanced at about 9 at night, in the best order, though
opposed by the same means, and with the same determination
as had been opposed to the detachment which had made the
attempt on the 6th. Ensign Dyas again led the service, and the
storming party arrived at the foot of the breach; but they found

it impossible to mount it, the enemy having again cleared the rubbish from the bottom of the escarp. The detachment suffered considerably, and Major M'Geechy, the Commanding officer, was unfortunately killed, and others of the officers fell; but the troops continued to maintain their station till Major Gen. Houstoun ordered them to retire.

When the reinforcements had arrived from the frontiers of Castille, after the battle of Albuera, I undertook the siege of Badajoz, entertaining a belief that the means of which I had the command would reduce the place before the end of the second week in June, at which time I expected that the reinforcement for the enemy's southern army, detached from Castille, would join Marshal Soult. I was unfortunately mistaken in my estimate of the quality of these means.

The ordnance belonging to the garrison of Elvas is very ancient and incomplete; unprovided with the improvements adopted by modern science to facilitate and render more certain the use of cannon; and although classed generally as 24 pounders, the guns were found to be of a calibre larger than the shot in the garrison of that weight. The fire from this ordnance was therefore very uncertain, and the carriages proved to be worse even than we supposed they were; and both guns and carriages were rendered useless so frequently by the effect of our own fire as to create delay, in consequence of the necessity which existed for exchanging both in the advanced batteries. Those who are accustomed to observe the effect of the fire of artillery will be astonished to learn that fire was kept up from the 2d to the 10th inst. from fourteen 24 pounders, upon the wall of the castle of Badajoz, constructed of rammed earth and loose stones, of which the foot was seen at the distance of from 400 to 600 yards, and that it had not at last effected a practicable breach. It was impossible to estimate the length of time which would elapse before a practicable breach could have been effected in this wall; and, even if one had been effected, it was the opinion of the engineers and others, as well as my own, that although the breach could have been stormed, we could not have formed our troops to attack the enemy's intrenchment within, unless we had possession of Fort San Cristoval.

We had failed in two attempts to obtain possession of Fort San Cristoval, and it was obvious to me that we could not obtain possession of that outwork without performing a work which would have required the labor of several days to accomplish it.

On the morning of the 10th inst. I received the enclosed intercepted dispatch, from the Duc de Dalmatie to the Duc de Raguse, which pointed out clearly the enemy's design to collect in Estremadura their whole force; and I had reason to believe that Bonet's corps, which had marched from Toledo on the 28th and 29th May, and was expected at Cordova on the 5th and 6th inst., would have joined the southern army by the 10th; and it was generally expected in the country that the southern army would have moved by that time.

The movement of this army alone would have created a necessity for raising the siege; but on the same morning I received accounts from the frontiers of Castille, which left no doubt of the destination of the 'Armée de Portugal' to the southward, and gave ground for belief that they would arrive at Merida on the 15th inst. I therefore ordered that the siege should be raised. I am concerned to add that this measure was rendered expedient, not only by the military considerations to which I have above referred, but by others relative to the security of Elvas.

If the siege had been continued only for 2 days longer there would have remained in Elvas only 10,000 24 pound shot; a quantity by no means sufficient for its defence, if the course of events should enable the enemy to attack that place; and I learn that there are none at Lisbon, and if there were any, the government, under present circumstances, have not the power of procuring means of transport to send it up.

Since the troops under Sir W. Beresford have been in this part of the country, Gen. Hamilton's division of Portuguese troops, consisting of 3 brigades, had been supplied with provisions generally from the stores of Elvas, as well as the troops of the garrison; and the stores of Elvas had been very inadequately, if at all, upheld to answer these demands. The consequence is that there are not at this moment in the fort supplies for the garrison for one fortnight.

All the means of transport which could be collected in this neighbourhood were employed in aid of the operations of the siege, from which they could not be relieved till the siege should be raised, and the ordnance and stores returned to Elvas.

The application of these means of transport, to bring a supply to Elvas from the British magazines at Abrantes (which is the resource from which at last it must be drawn), and the eventual safety of that place, depended upon the early discontinuance of the operations against Badajoz; and this, independent of the circumstances above referred to, and the military considerations resulting from them, was a principal motive with me for raising the siege on the 10th inst. From this circumstance your Lordship will see additional reason to lament the state of inefficiency of all the Portuguese departments attached to the army. It affords an additional proof of the embarrassments which meet me at every turn, from wants and deficiencies for which the Portuguese government ought to provide, but which invariably at last fall, at the most critical moments, upon the resources which have been provided, with great difficulty and labor, and at great expense, by the departments of the British army.

I have every reason to be satisfied with the conduct of all the officers and troops employed at the siege of Badajoz, whose labors and exertions deserved a very different result. Major Gen. Picton directed the operations on the left of the Guadiana, and Major Gen. Houstoun on the right; and I am much indebted to those officers, as well as to Major Gen. Hamilton, and the other General and Staff officers, and the officers and troops under their command respectively. Lieut. Col. Fletcher, of the Royal engineers, was the directing engineer, and immediately superintended the operations on the left of the Guadiana, and Capt. Squire those on the right of that river; and these officers, and the corps of Royal engineers, have, by their conduct on this occasion, augmented their claims to my approbation. Lieut. Col. Framingham commanded the artillery, having under his orders Major Dickson, attached to the Portuguese service, who, during the absence of Lieut. Col. Framingham with the troops which were employed to cover the operations, conducted all the details of this important department. I had every reason to be satisfied with these officers, and most particularly with Major Dickson, from whose activity, zeal, and intelligence, the British service has derived great advantage in the different operations against Badajoz. Capt. Cleves, of the Hanoverian artillery, conducted that department on the right of the Guadiana with great success.

The service of the batteries was performed by detachments from the 1st, 2d, and 3d regts. of Portuguese artillery, who conducted themselves remarkably well. They were aided by Capt. Rainsford's company of the Royal artillery, who were indefatigable; some of them having never quitted the batteries.

I am much indebted to Gen. Leite, the governor of the province of Alentejo and of Elvas, for the assistance which he again afforded me in this operation.

I enclose a return of the killed and wounded throughout the siege, from which your Lordship will observe that, excepting in the attempts to obtain possession of San Cristoval, our loss has not been severe. We still maintain the blockade of Badajoz; and I know from an intercepted letter, that the enemy had in the place, on the 28th May, only 3 weeks' provisions.

I have not yet heard that the enemy have moved from their position at Llerena, and I imagine that the arrival of the 9th corps has been delayed longer than was expected; and it is probable that Soult will be unwilling to move till he hears of the movements of the 'Armée de Portugal'. They broke up from the Tormes on the 3d, and their advanced guard arrived at Ciudad Rodrigo on the evening of the 5th. They moved forward again on the 6th, and Lieut. Gen. Sir B. Spencer withdrew the advanced guard of the troops under his command, first to Nave d'Aver, and thence to Alfaiates; having his main body on the high ground behind Soito; and on the following morning he retired behind the Coa at Sabugal. The enemy patrolled on the 6th into Fuentes de Oñoro and into Nave d'Aver.

I enclose Sir B. Spencer's report of these operations, from which it appears that the Royal dragoons, under Col. Clifton, and a squadron of the 14th, the whole directed by Major Gen. Slade, distinguished themselves.

I imagine that the enemy's march in this direction was intended as a reconnaissance, and to cover the march of a convoy to Ciudad Rodrigo, as on the following day, the 7th, the whole moved from thence to Morasverdes, in the direction of the Puerto de Baños; near which pass Gen. Regnier had been with 2 divisions of the 'Armée de Portugal' since the 5th. On the 8th, in the evening, one division of Gen. Regnier's troops had come through Baños; and I expect that those divisions will have arrived at Plasencia on the 9th, and the whole army on the 10th.

I had directed Lieut. Gen. Sir B. Spencer to make a movement corresponding with those of the enemy, if they should move to the southward; and the greatest part of his corps is now at Castello Branco and Villa Velha; and a part of it on this side of the Tagus, at Niza.

The Commissary Gen. has thrown a sufficient quantity of provisions into all the places on the frontier, and measures are in progress to improve the defence of them all.

P. S. Since writing this dispatch I have received accounts that Gen. Drouet's troops joined on the enemy's right at Berlanga and Azuaga yesterday, and a report that their cavalry were in movement towards Los Santos this morning. The British cavalry and the 2d and 4th divisions were about to march from Villa Franca and Almendralejo towards Albuera; and I have ordered there Gen. Hamilton's division; and I shall proceed there this night myself, if I should find this report confirmed.

To the Earl of Liverpool.

Quinta de S. João, 11th July, 1811.

The enemy continued in the positions reported in my dispatch of the 4th inst., till the 7th, when they moved a large body of cavalry, and about 2 battalions of infantry, from Montijo, towards the Gevora; and from thence upon Villar del Rey, La Roca, and Alburquerque. The object of this movement was apparently to cut off our detachments employed in observing the enemy on that side, in which, however, they did not succeed; Major Cocks having retired with all his detachments upon San Vicente, still keeping communications open with Arronches and Portalegre. The enemy's troops retired from Alburquerque on the 8th, and Major Cocks again entered that town with his parties on the same day.

The '*Armée de Portugal*' are again in the same positions on the right of the Guadiana which they occupied when I addressed your Lordship on the 4th inst. It appears by a letter of the 1st inst., from Marshal Marmont to the Prince de Neufchâtel, that Soult has returned into Andalusia, leaving with Marshal Marmont the 5th corps and the greater part of his cavalry. Marmont appears to entertain the intention of posting his army on the Tagus at Almaraz, where he has a bridge, and maintain an intermediate post between his army and Badajoz, probably Truxillo, where I understand that the enemy are at work upon the ancient castle.

Excepting from this intercepted letter, I have had no reason to believe that the enemy had sent back so large a body of troops into Andalusia. But it is almost impracticable to procure intelligence of the enemy's movements in this part of the country; notwithstanding that I believe the inhabitants are as well disposed towards the Spanish government as those of any other part of Spain.

If the battalions of the 9th corps, belonging to the regiments in the 5th corps, have made good the losses sustained by the latter in the battle of Albuera, I should conceive, from the returns I have, that the 5th corps consists of 12,000 effective infantry; which, added to the army of Portugal, would leave under the command of Marmont from 36,000 to 40,000 infantry, and between 5000 and 6000 cavalry, besides artillery. The allied army under my command consists of 42,000 effective infantry, and 4000 cavalry, of which 3000 are British cavalry, and this strength will in a short time be considerably increased.

Gen. Blake made an attempt to obtain possession of Niebla on the night of the 30th June; in which place the enemy had a garrison of about 300 infantry. I am sorry to say, that this attempt failed; and he remained before the place till the 2d inst., and then retired towards the Guadiana. On the 6th 2 divisions of infantry, and the cavalry of the 5th army, under the Conde de Penne Villemur, were crossing the Guadiana on a bridge constructed for them at San Lucar by Col. Austin. The artillery was embarked at Ayamonte, and Gen. Ballesteros, with the advanced guard, remained upon the river Piedra; but I think it probable that Gen. Ballesteros would have been obliged to retire, as a division of the enemy's troops which had moved from Seville had arrived at Almendro on the 6th, and had turned off from thence upon Cartaya. It appeared to be Gen. Blake's intention to embark his troops for Cadiz; but neither Gen. Castaños nor I have heard from him since he marched from Jurumenha, on the 18th June.

In the north, Gen. Bessières has returned again to Valladolid from Benavente; and in the end of the month of June the enemy assembled at, and in the neighbourhood of, Valladolid, a considerable body of troops. Gen. Bonet, however, still remained in the neighbourhood of Leon and Benavente with the troops under his command; and I have received from Gen. Silveira a report of the defeat of the French in an attack made upon a Spanish detachment from the army in Galicia, in front of Astorga, on the 25th June. The guerrillas likewise continue their operations, and besides the alarm given to Valladolid on the 15th, reported in my last dispatch, Don Julian gave a similar alarm to Salamanca on the 29th June; but a considerable party of guerrillas belonging to different chiefs, which had taken a convoy at Peñaranda, were afterwards surprised there on the 30th June, and dispersed; about 200 having been killed, wounded, and made prisoners.

I wish that I could report to your Lordship that some more beneficial advantage had resulted from the collection of the enemy's troops in Estremadura to raise the siege of Badajoz, and better calculated to reconcile us to the disappointment upon that occasion. But I am apprehensive that, till the Spanish government shall reform their military system; till the officers shall be instructed and the troops disciplined; till regular resources shall be found, and faithfully applied to the support of their armies on an expedition; and till the armies shall be equipped as they ought for the service required from them, the history of every attempt on our part to alter the nature of the war, on any general combined plan, will be the same as the last.

The enemy will collect to oppose us a larger body of troops than the allied British and Portuguese army can bring into the field, and will oblige us to take the defensive; and they will experience no danger, or even inconvenience, from their weakness in all other parts of the Peninsula, in consequence of their collecting their whole force to oppose us, because the Spanish armies are neither disciplined nor provided or equipped in such a manner as that they can perform any operation, even of the most trifling nature, if there should be any opposition on the part of the enemy. The only chance, therefore, is to watch for opportunities of undertaking important operations of short duration, with the means at our own disposal, till the Spanish armies shall be in a better state.

To Lieut. Gen. Graham.

Portalegre, 27th July, 1811.

I had the pleasure of receiving your letter of the 24th last night; and I write to let you know that there is no reason why you should hurry yourself from Lisbon.

Upon a comparison of the strength which we can bring upon one point with that which the enemy can collect in Castille, I think I have a chance of succeeding in taking Ciudad Rodrigo, and the preparations are in progress for that enterprise. I can certainly undertake nothing else at present which would at all improve the situation of the allies in the Peninsula; and, adverting to the facility with which the French march corps from one side of the Peninsula to the other, and to the little detriment to their interests which results from the abandonment of a province or Kingdom to collect a large force against us, I must consider it not improbable that I shall be obliged to abandon the enterprise. The preparation for it, however, will take up a considerable time, and you will see that there is no occasion for your hurrying yourself. We have reports, as usual, that Ciudad Rodrigo is but ill supplied with provisions, for which I believe there is no more foundation than for these reports in general. It may be advisable, therefore, that we should approach the place a little earlier than I at first intended; and with this view, and because the whole of Marmont's army have crossed the Tagus, I am sending more troops across, and I have it in contemplation to make a general movement to our left.

Soult certainly intends to avail himself of the large force he now has in the south to make an effort against the position of the allies at Cadiz, or to obtain possession of Carthagena. I don't think it quite clear which plan he will follow. He has certainly sent to Granada the division of the 4th corps which was lately in Estremadura, and, it is said, some troops under Latour Maubourg; but I believe these last are cavalry only, which would not be of much use in an attack upon the Isla de Leon. These reinforcements may have been sent to enable Leval (who I believe now commands the 4th corps) to keep Freyre in check, as this last General had lately made some progress, and had got as far as Guadix. I am inclined to believe he will attack Cadiz, as I have not heard that any of the heavy ordnance moved out of Badajoz has been sent from Seville towards Granada, and I suspect that it is going down the Guadalquivir unobserved by those who are employed to procure intelligence for the Spanish government.

I have written to my brother about the state of the works on the Isla de Leon; but, from all I see and hear, I am very apprehensive that the affairs of Spain are nearly irretrievable. There is no money, and there are no means of getting any, and there are no disciplined troops. Even if we should strike a fortunate blow, I fear that we should do them no good.

Till Soult's design upon Carthagena is manifest, nothing can be more absurd than to send Blake's corps into Murcia, where they have already 20,000 men opposed to 5000 French, which may have been increased to 12,000 by the first reinforcement from Estremadura, and probably to 14,000 by the last. My opinion is, that Blake's corps should be employed either in the

Sierra de Ronda or in the Condado de Niebla, as this may be depended upon (although the Spaniards will not admit it), that they may increase the corps in Murcia to any extent they please; but they will not be able to drive the French out of Granada. The strength of their corps in Murcia, therefore, ought to be fixed with a view to a defensive war in a very strong country, and should be increased in proportion as the enemy, by the increase of his force, and his other measures in that quarter, should manifest a design to attack Carthagena.

A force stationed in Niebla, or the Sierra de Ronda, would always have a secure retreat. From either situation they would threaten Seville, which is the foundation of the enemy's existence in the south of Spain. In Niebla they would be in direct communication with us, and they might be equipped in such a manner as to render it quite impossible for Soult to move all his troops, with impunity, upon us; and from Niebla or La Ronda the troops might be brought to Cadiz, with facility, if wanted. But this plan will not be adopted, because it does not afford ground for any body to boast for a few days that the enemy will be overthrown, and that the southern provinces of Spain will be relieved.

To the Earl of Liverpool.

Fuente Guinaldo, 27th Aug. 1811.

I have received your Lordship's letter of the 8th Aug.

*   *   *   *   *   *

       *   *   *   *   *

*   *   *   *   *   *

Any severe loss or serious check to our cavalry might have an influence on the result of the war; and adverting to the enemy's superiority of numbers, particularly in that arm, I have always been unwilling on this account, as well as for other reasons, to risk large bodies at the same moment.

*   *   *   *   *   *

By reference to the states which I send you by this post, your

Lordship will see how we stand in respect to British cavalry. As for the Portuguese cavalry, I am afraid that, owing to starvation, they are worse than useless, and we must not reckon upon more than the British. I am very confident that, even with the numbers which I have now with me, no accident can happen to us; but we have not enough to take the field on a decidedly offensive plan.

In my letter of the 18th July I reckoned the French cavalry actually with the '*Armée de Portugal*' about 3500 men. Recent reports state that the army of the north have 2500 cavalry. These are already double the numbers which we can produce, on this frontier, of British cavalry. But I believe there is also, in Castille, a brigade of light cavalry belonging to Marmont's army; at least he mentions it in a letter which we have intercepted. When, in my letter of the 18th July, I mentioned 3500 as the number of cavalry with the army of the south, I meant the cavalry which had come into Estremadura, and had joined with that of the '*Armée de Portugal*'. According to the returns which I have of Soult's army of the south, he has 7774 cavalry, of which he brought only the number above mentioned, as I believe, into Estremadura. From this statement, your Lordship will see how unlikely it is that you can make us equal to the French in cavalry for a decidedly offensive operation.

It has never been possible for us to assemble our whole army on this frontier, more particularly since the fall of Badajoz and the destruction of the Spanish army of Estremadura. We are nearly twice as far from Lisbon at this spot as Badajoz is. The Tagus is fordable nearly every where from Abrantes to below Santarem; and if I were to leave the Alentejo without a respectable body of troops, the enemy might and would move the 5th corps through that province, and they would be at Lisbon as soon as I should hear that they had passed the Guadiana. It is as necessary to leave cavalry with that corps in Alentejo as it is to leave infantry; and accordingly your Lordship will see that some of the British cavalry remain there. These, however, are not the most efficient regiments.

There is another point also to be considered in the assembling of these large bodies of cavalry, and that is, their food. It

is impossible to describe the difficulty with which food is procured for them. The cavalry collected with this army are now
50 or 60 miles distant, in order to get food, and I trust to be
able to assemble them when I shall want them. If I should bring
them together too soon, or keep them together too long, the
horses would starve.

At the same time I am of opinion that we cannot have too
much British cavalry. We can certainly do nothing without
them in a general action out of our mountains; and, from all
that I can learn, the expense of feeding the horses is not greater
than it is in England, as the hay or grass they eat is seldom paid
for, and the straw, when they get it, is not nearly so expensive
as the hay is in England. An augmentation of cavalry, therefore,
should the season be favorable, and the country which is the
scene of our operations produce forage, will give us great
advantages; and even if we should be obliged to keep part of
our cavalry in the rear, from the want of forage, it will enable
us to relieve those in front occasionally, and thus always to
have a body of cavalry in good condition. I am therefore very
glad that you have sent Le Marchant's brigade.

I am almost certain that I shall not be able to attack Ciudad
Rodrigo, and I think it is doubtful whether I shall be able to
maintain the blockade of that place. However, I shall not give
up my intention until I am certain that the enemy are too strong
for me in an action in the field. The place, although weak in
itself, and though the ground on which it stands is badly occupied (the French have improved it in some degree), is in the best
chosen position of any frontier fortress that I have ever seen. It
is impossible to do any thing against it, either in the way of
siege or blockade, excepting by crossing the Agueda, and of all
the ravines that I have ever seen this is the most difficult to
cross, excepting close to the fort; and in winter it cannot be
crossed at all, excepting at the bridges, of which the only practicable one for carriages is under the guns of the fort. We must
fight the battle, therefore, to maintain this blockade, with our
backs to this river, over which we should have to retire in case
of check; and this would be an awkward position, in which I
ought not to involve the army, unless the numbers are so nearly

equal as to render success probable. You will observe that these circumstances all favored the French when they attacked the place from Spain. However, there is one thing very clear, that if we cannot maintain this blockade, the enemy must bring 50,000 men to oblige us to raise it; and they can undertake nothing else this year, for they must still continue to watch this place, and we shall so far save the cause. In the mean time, if they offer me a favorable opportunity of bringing any of them to action, I shall do it.

I hear reports of peace from all parts of Spain, and it is a subject of common conversation and general joy among the French officers. I know that some of them have received accounts from Paris, stating that peace was likely to take place. We have certainly altered the nature of the war in Spain; it has become, to a certain degree, offensive on our part. The enemy are obliged to concentrate large corps to defend their own acquisitions; they are obliged to collect magazines to support their armies (Marmont says he can do nothing without magazines, which is quite a new era in the modern French military system); and I think it probable, from all that I hear, that they are either already reduced, or they must soon come, to the resources of France for the payment of those expenses which must be defrayed in money. As soon as this shall be the case, and as soon as the war will not produce resources to carry itself on, your Lordship may be certain that Buonaparte will be disposed to put an end to it, and will submit to any thing rather than draw from France the resources which must be supplied in order to keep together his armies. I think it not unlikely, therefore, that peace is speculated upon in France.

We have a great many officers and men sick, but none or very few seriously so. It is astonishing how easily the officers and soldiers of our army are affected by sickness, and the little care they take of themselves. In some situations also the effects of the climate are terrible. Very recently the officer commanding a brigade of artillery encamped them in one of the most unwholesome situations, and every man of them is sick. However, the weather will soon become cool in this part of the country, and I hope there will be an end of the sickness.

P. S. I enclose the morning state of the 25th, with a note on the back, showing the state of the army in cavalry and infantry in Castille and in Alentejo.

To the Earl of Liverpool.

Quadrazaes, 29th Sept. 1811.

The enemy commenced their movements towards Ciudad Rodrigo with the convoys of provisions from the Sierra de Bejar, and from Salamanca on the 21st inst., and on the following day I collected the British army in positions, from which I could either advance or retire without difficulty, and which would enable me to see all that was going on, and the strength of the enemy's army.

The 3d division, and that part of Major Gen. Alten's brigade of cavalry which was not detached, occupied the range of heights which are on the left of the Agueda: having their advanced guard, under Lieut. Col. Williams, of the 60th, on the heights of Pastores, within 3 miles of Ciudad Rodrigo; the 4th division was at Fuente Guinaldo, where I had strengthened a position with some works; the Light division on the right of the Agueda, having their right resting upon the mountains which separate Castille and Estremadura. Lieut. Gen. Graham commanded the troops on the left of the army, which were posted on the Lower Azava; the 6th division, and Major Gen. Anson's brigade of cavalry, being at Espeja, and occupying Carpio, Marialva, &c. Don Carlos de España observed the Lower Agueda with Don J. Sanchez's cavalry and infantry.

Lieut. Gen. Sir S. Cotton, with Major Gen. Slade's and Major Gen. De Grey's brigades of cavalry, were on the Upper Azava, in the centre, between the right and left of the army, with Gen. Pack's brigade at Campillo; and the 5th division was in observation of the Pass of Perales, in the rear of the right, the French General Foy having remained and collected a body of troops in Upper Estremadura, consisting of part of his own division of the '*Armée de Portugal*', and a division of the army of the centre; and the 7th division was in reserve at Alamedilla.

The enemy first appeared in the plain near Ciudad Rodrigo, on the 23d, and retired again in a short time; but on the 24th, in the morning, they advanced again in considerable force, and entered the plain by the roads of Santi-espiritus and Tenebron; and before evening they had collected there all their cavalry, to the amount of about 6000 men, and 4 divisions of infantry, of which one division was of the Imperial Guard; and the remainder of the armies were encamped on the Guadapero, immediately beyond the hills which surround the plain of Ciudad Rodrigo.

On the morning of the 25th the enemy sent a reconnaissance of cavalry towards the Lower Azava, consisting of about 14 squadrons of the cavalry of the Imperial Guard. They drove in our posts on the right of the Azava, but having passed that river, the Lanciers de Berg were charged by 2 squadrons of the 16th, and one of the 14th light dragoons, and driven back; they attempted to rally and to return, but were fired upon by the light infantry of the 61st regt., which had been posted in the wood on their flank, by Lieut. Gen. Graham; and Major Gen. Anson pursued them across the Azava, and afterwards resumed his posts on the right of that river. Lieut. Gen. Graham was highly pleased with the conduct of Major Gen. Anson's brigade; and Major Gen. Anson particularly mentions Lieut. Col. Hervey, and Capt. Brotherton, of the 14th, and Capt. Hay and Major Cocks, of the 16th.

But the enemy's attention was principally directed during this day to the position of the 3d division, in the hills between Fuente Guinaldo and Pastores. About 8 in the morning, they moved a column, consisting of between 30 and 40 squadrons of cavalry, and 14 battalions of infantry, and 12 pieces of cannon, from Ciudad Rodrigo, in such a direction, that it was doubtful whether they would attempt to ascend the hills by La Encina, or by the direct road of El Bodon, towards Fuente Guinaldo; and I was not certain by which road they would make their attack, till they actually commenced it upon the last.

As soon as I saw the direction of their march, I had reinforced the 2d batt. 5th regt., which occupied the post on the

hill over which the road passes to Guinaldo, by the 77th regt.,
and the 21st Portuguese regt., under the command of Major
Gen. the Hon. C. Colville, and Major Gen. Alten's brigade of
cavalry, of which only 3 squadrons remained which had not
been detached, drawn from El Bodon; and I ordered there a
brigade of the 4th division from Fuente Guinaldo, and afterwards from El Bodon the remainder of the troops of the 3d
division, with the exception of those at Pastores, which were
too distant.

In the mean time, however, the small body of troops in this
post sustained the attack of the enemy's cavalry and artillery.
One regiment of French dragoons succeeded in taking 2 pieces
of cannon which had been posted on a rising ground on the
right of our troops; but they were charged by the 2d batt. 5th
regt., under the command of Major Ridge, and the guns were
immediately retaken.

While this operation was going on on the flank, an attack
was made on the front by another regiment, which was repulsed
in a similar manner by the 77th regt.; and the 3 squadrons of
Major Gen. Alten's brigade charged repeatedly different bodies
of the enemy which ascended the hill on the left of the 2 regiments of British infantry, the Portuguese regiment being posted
in the rear of their right.

At length, the division of the enemy's infantry which had
marched with the cavalry from Ciudad Rodrigo, were brought
up to the attack on the road of Fuente Guinaldo; and seeing
that they would arrive and be engaged before the troops could
arrive either from Guinaldo or El Bodon, I determined to withdraw our post, and to retire with the whole of Fuente Guinaldo.
The 2d batt. 5th regt., and the 77th regt., were formed into one
square, and the 21st Portuguese regt. into another, supported
by Major Gen. Alten's small body of cavalry and the Portuguese artillery.

The enemy's cavalry immediately rushed forward, and
obliged our cavalry to retire to the support of the Portuguese
regiment; and the 5th and 77th regts. were charged on three
faces of the square by the French cavalry, but they halted and
repulsed the attack with the utmost steadiness and gallantry.

We then continued the retreat, and joined the remainder of the 3d division, also formed in squares, on their march to Fuente Guinaldo, and the whole retired together in the utmost order, and the enemy never made another attempt to charge any of them; but were satisfied with firing upon them with their artillery, and with following them.

Lieut. Col. Williams with his light infantry, and Lieut. Col. the Hon. R. Trench with the 74th regt., retired from Pastores across the Agueda; and thence marched by Robleda, where they took some prisoners, and recrossed the Agueda, and joined at Guinaldo in the evening.

I placed the 3d and 4th divisions, and Gen. Pack's brigade of infantry, and Major Gen. Alten's, Major Gen. De Grey's, and Major Gen. Slade's brigades of cavalry in the position at Fuente Guinaldo on the evening of the 25th, and ordered Major Gen. R. Craufurd to retire with the Light division across the Agueda, the 7th division to form at Albergueria, and Lieut. Gen. Graham to collect the troops under his command at Nave d'Aver, keeping only posts of observation on the Azava; and the troops were thus formed in an *échelon*, of which the centre was in the position at Guinaldo; and the right upon the Pass of Perales; and the left at Nave d'Aver; Don Carlos de España was placed on the left of the Coa; and Don J. Sanchez was detached with the cavalry to the enemy's rear.

The enemy brought up a second division of infantry from Ciudad Rodrigo in the afternoon of the 25th; and in the course of that night, and of the 26th, they collected their whole army in front of our position at Guinaldo; and not deeming it expedient to stand their attack in that position, I retired about 3 leagues, and on the 27th formed the army as follows: viz., the 5th division on the right, at Aldea Velha; the 4th, and light dragoons, and Major Gen. Alten's cavalry, at the convent of Sacaparte, in front of Alfaiates; the 3d and 7th divisions in second line, behind Alfaiates; and Lieut. Gen. Graham's corps on the left at Bismula, having their advanced guard beyond the Villar Maior river; and Lieut. Gen. Sir S. Cotton's cavalry near Alfaiates, on the left of the 4th division, and having Gen. Pack's and Gen. M'Mahon's brigades at Rebolosa, on their left. The piquets of the cavalry were in front of Aldea da Ponte, beyond the Villar Maior river; and those of Gen. Alten's brigade beyond the same river, towards Furcalhos.

It had been the enemy's intention to turn the left of the position of Guinaldo by moving a column into the valley of the Upper Azava, and thence ascending the heights in the rear of the position by Castillejos; and from this column they detached a division of infantry and 14 squadrons of cavalry to follow our retreat by Albergueria, and another body of the same strength followed us by Furcalhos. The former attacked the piquets of the cavalry at Aldea da Ponte, and drove them in; and they pushed on nearly as far as Alfaiates. I then made Gen. Pakenham attack them with his brigade of the 4th division, supported by Lieut. Gen. the Hon. G. L. Cole, and the 4th division, and by Sir S. Cotton's cavalry; and the enemy were driven through Aldea da Ponte, back upon Albergueria, and the piquets of the cavalry resumed their station.

But the enemy having been reinforced by the troops which marched from Furcalhos, again advanced about sunset and drove in the piquets of the cavalry from Aldea da Ponte, and took possession of the village.

Lieut. Gen. Cole again attacked them with a part of Gen. Pakenham's brigade, and drove them through the village; but night having come on, and as Gen. Pakenham was not certain what was passing on his flanks, or of the numbers of the enemy, and he knew that the army were to fall back still farther, he evacuated the village, which the enemy occupied, and held during the night.

On the 28th, I formed the army on the heights behind Soito; having the Serra de Meras on their right, and the left at Rendo, on the Coa; about a league in rear of the position which they had occupied on the 27th. The enemy also retired from Aldea da Ponte, and had their advanced posts at Albergueria; and as it appears that they are about to retire from this part of the country, and as we have already had some bad weather, and may expect more at the period of the equinoctial gales, I propose to canton the troops in the nearest villages to the position which they occupied yesterday.

I can't conclude this report of the occurrences of the last week, without expressing to your Lordship my admiration of the conduct of the troops engaged in the affairs of the 25th inst. The conduct of the 2d batt. 5th regt., commanded by Major Ridge, in particular, affords a memorable example of what the steadiness and discipline of the troops, and their confidence in their officers, can effect in the most difficult and trying situations. The conduct of the 77th regt., under the command of Lieut. Col. Bromhead, was equally good; and I have never seen a more determined attack than was made by the whole of the enemy's cavalry, with every advantage of the assistance of a superior artillery, and repulsed by these 2 weak battalions. I must not omit also to report the good conduct, on the same occasion, of the 21st Portuguese regt., under the command of Col. Bacellar, and of Major Arentschildt's artillery. The Portuguese infantry were not actually charged, but were repeatedly threatened, and they showed the utmost steadiness and discipline, both in the mode in which they prepared to receive the enemy, and in all the movements of a retreat made over 6 miles of plain in front of a superior cavalry and artillery. The Portuguese artillerymen were cut down at their guns, which were for a moment in the enemy's possession.

The infantry upon this occasion were under the command of Major Gen. the Hon. C. Colville; Lieut. Gen. Picton having remained with the troops at El Bodon; and the conduct of Major Gen. Colville was beyond all praise.

Your Lordship will have observed by the details of the action which I have given you, how much reason I had to be satisfied with the conduct of the 1st hussars and 11th light dragoons of Major Gen. Alten's brigade. There were not more than 3 squadrons of the 2 regiments on the ground, this brigade having for some time furnished the cavalry for the outposts of the army, and they charged the enemy's cavalry repeatedly; and notwithstanding the superiority of the latter, the post would have been maintained if I had not preferred abandoning it to risking the loss of these brave men by continuing the unequal contest under additional disadvantages, in consequence of the immediate entry of 14 battalions of infantry into the action, before the support which I had ordered up could arrive. Major Gen. Alten, and Lieut. Cols. Cumming and Arentschildt, and the officers of these regiments, particularly distinguished themselves upon this occasion. I have also to mention that the Adj. Gen., Major Gen. the Hon. C. Stewart, being upon the field, gave his assistance as an officer of cavalry with his usual gallantry.

In the affair of the 27th, at Aldea da Ponte, Brig. Gen. Pakenham and the troops of the 4th division, under the orders of Lieut. Gen. the Hon. G. L. Cole, likewise conducted themselves remarkably well.

H. S. H. the Hereditary Prince of Orange accompanied me during the operations which I have detailed to your Lordship, and was for the first time in fire; and he conducted himself with a spirit and intelligence which afford a hope that he will become an ornament to his profession.

The enemy having collected for the object of relieving Ciudad Rodrigo the army of the north, which were withdrawn from the attack they had commenced on Gen. Abadia in Galicia, in which are included 22 battalions of the Imperial Guard, and Gen. Souham's division of infantry, composed of troops recently arrived in Spain from the army of Naples, and now drawn from the frontier of Navarre, where they had been employed in operations against Mina, together with 5 divisions and all the cavalry of the army called '*de Portugal*', composing altogether an army of not less than 60,000 men, of which 6000 were cavalry, with 125 pieces of artillery, I could not pretend to maintain the blockade of Ciudad Rodrigo, nor could any effort which I could make prevent or materially impede the collection of the supplies or the march of the convoy for the relief of that place. I did all that I could expect to effect without incurring the risk of great loss for no object; and as the reports as usual were so various in regard to the enemy's real strength, it was necessary that I should see their army in order that the people of this country might be convinced that to raise the blockade was a measure of necessity, and that the momentary relief of Galicia, and of Mina, were the only objects which it was in my power immediately to effect.

I have had no reports from the north since I addressed your Lordship last, nor from the south of Spain.

Gen. Girard had collected at Merida a small body of troops, I believe with the intention of making an incursion into Portugal, under the notion that I had withdrawn Lieut. Gen. Hill's corps from the Alentejo, for the purpose of maintaining the blockade of Ciudad Rodrigo; but I imagine that he will break up this collection again, as soon as he shall hear that Gen. Hill is at Portalegre.

P. S. I enclose a return of the killed and wounded on the 25th and 27th inst.

Return of the killed, wounded, and missing, in an affair with the enemy on the heights of El Bodon on the 25th, and near Aldea da Ponte on the 27th Sept. 1811.

	Officers.	Non-commissioned officers & drummers.	R. and F.	Horses.	Total loss of officers, non-commissioned officers, and R. & F.
Killed	1	1	40	40	42
Wounded	16	13	156	63	185
Missing	—	1	33	9	34

FIVE

THE CAMPAIGNS OF 1812

The stalemate that had characterised the campaigns of 1811 did not last for very long, and was in fact broken only days into the new year of 1812. In essence, Wellington had been penned up on the Portuguese frontier by the ability of the French commanders to bring superior forces against him and prevent him from capturing Ciudad Rodrigo and Badajoz. Following the battle of El Bodón, however, this ability was lost. With Napoleon massing his forces for his impending attack on Russia, he had no reinforcements to spare for the Peninsula. Yet pride prevented him from ordering his generals to go on to the defensive, and the result was that in the autumn of 1811 many of the troops that had been containing Wellington were drawn away to take part in operations against Spanish armies fighting elsewhere in the Peninsula. Presented with a golden opportunity, Wellington did not lose a moment. Closing in on Ciudad Rodrigo in bitter winter weather, on 19 January 1812 he took it after a siege of just eleven days, and on 6 April this feat was followed by the storm of Badajoz. At this point faced by a choice of marching into Andalucía to confront Soult, or moving back north to attack Marmont, the British commander opted for the latter, and by mid-June 1812, his troops were therefore bearing down on Salamanca. For a moment the campaign that followed seemed that it would once again end in frustration: although the Anglo-Portuguese army successfully liberated Salamanca, though not without first having to deal with a small garrison that had been left behind in the citadel the French had constructed to overawe the city, and advanced to the River Duero, Marmont then launched a counter-attack

that forced Wellington to fall back to Salamanca and even
threatened to put him back on the Portuguese frontier. On
22 July, however, Marmont overextended himself in an effort
to get past Salamanca and threaten Wellington's communications with Portugal. This proved a dangerous mistake. Pouncing
on the French army, the Anglo-Portuguese army defeated it in
detail and by the end of the day their opponents were fleeing
from the field in complete disorder. This victory was followed
on 12 August by the liberation of Madrid, but Wellington now
faced a difficult problem in that, with the French forces falling
back from much of western and southern Spain in response to
his triumphs, he faced the possibility that his army would be
attacked by vastly superior forces. With the Spanish armies
unable to provide much support, the British commander real-
ised that his position was potentially critical, and for the only
time in his career he faltered in his conduct of operations. Thus,
a move against the French forces in northern Spain was badly
botched and ended in an improvised attempt to take the castle
of Burgos. This last proved too tough a target even for Wellington's soldiers, but, even had it fallen, it is difficult to see
what advantage it could have afforded the British commander.
Overwhelming numbers of French troops were now moving
against the Anglo-Portuguese armies from both the north and
east, and Wellington therefore had to order his forces to retreat
to Ciudad Rodrigo, this proving a difficult experience that
cost his men some 5000 casualties, not the least of the problems being that the whole withdrawal was conducted in the
midst of some of the worst weather that an Iberian winter
could offer. As in 1811, then, the campaign of 1812 appeared
to have ended in failure, and yet the situation was very different from what it had been a year before. If the French had been
able to regain control of Madrid and most of Old Castile,
they had been cleared from Asturias, Santander, León, Extremadura and Andalucía, whilst the British government had
been much heartened by Wellington's successes and was sending out large numbers of reinforcements (something that the
French commanders in Spain could no longer hope for for
themselves: Napoleon's *grande armée* having been destroyed in

the campaign of 1812, the emperor needed every man that he could muster in Germany). And, as if all this was not enough, in much of northern Spain, the irregular forces that had been harassing the invaders for much of the war had emerged as combatants of a far more dangerous nature than ever before. As before, then, it seemed unlikely that the situation would remain unchanged for very long.

To the Earl of Liverpool.

Freneda, 1st Jan. 1812.

The division of the '*Armée de Portugal*', cantoned about the sources of the Tormes, broke up with precipitation on the 26th Dec., and marched in the direction of Avila; and it is reported that the division cantoned at Avila were making preparations to march likewise; but they had not marched on the 29th. I have not yet heard that the '*Armée de Portugal*' have passed Talavera. They have their posts still at Navalmoral.

I have received reports that the cavalry of the Guard had returned to France, and that the infantry of the Guard had likewise moved from Valladolid in a northerly direction. I conclude that all these movements have for their object to support Suchet's operations in Valencia; or even to co-operate with him, by keeping in check the guerrillas from whom he has received so much injury. I propose, therefore, to make an attack upon Ciudad Rodrigo, in which, if I should not succeed, I shall at least bring back some of the troops of the army of the north and the '*Armée de Portugal*'; and shall so far relieve the guerrillas and the Spanish armies in Valencia.

I have had no accounts upon which I can rely, of the state of affairs at Valencia since the 20th Nov.; but I hear from Madrid that Suchet was still before the place on the 10th of last month.

Lieut. Gen. Hill moved on the 24th and 25th Dec., but I have not yet heard of his arrival at Merida.

Since I addressed your Lordship on the 25th Dec., I have

received the dispatches from Cadiz which had not then reached
me. It appears that Col. Skerrett had, at the requisition of Gen.
Ballesteros, embarked at Algeziras on the 29th Nov., and had
gone to Gibraltar to aid Gen. Ballesteros in an attack upon the
enemy. He had however returned to Tarifa on the 2d Dec., having learned from an intercepted letter that the enemy's object
was certainly to endeavor to obtain possession of that post.
They had made no attack upon it on the 13th Dec.; and Gen.
Castaños, who had letters from Cadiz of the 20th, informs me
that Gen. Ballesteros was at Los dos Barrios, according to the
last account.

To the Earl of Liverpool.

Gallegos, 20th Jan. 1812.

I informed your Lordship, in my dispatch of the 9th, that I had
attacked Ciudad Rodrigo, and in that of the 15th, of the progress of the operations to that period, and I have now the
pleasure to acquaint your Lordship that we took the place by
storm yesterday evening after dark.

We continued, from the 15th to the 19th, to complete the
second parallel, and the communications with that work, and
we had made some progress by sap towards the crest of the
glacis. On the night of the 15th we likewise advanced from
the left of the first parallel down the slope of the hill towards
the convent of San Francisco, to a situation from which the
walls of the *fausse braie* and of the town were seen, on which a
battery for 7 guns was constructed, and these commenced their
fire on the morning of the 18th. In the mean time, the batteries
in the first parallel continued their fire; and, yesterday evening,
their fire had not only considerably injured the defences of the
place, but had made breaches in the *fausse braie* wall, and in
the body of the place, which were considered practicable; while
the battery on the slope of the hill, which had been commenced
on the night of the 15th, and had opened on the 18th, had been

equally efficient still farther to the left, and opposite to the suburb of San Francisco.

I therefore determined to storm the place, notwithstanding that the approaches had not been brought to the crest of the glacis, and the counterscarp of the ditch was still entire.

The attack was accordingly made yesterday evening, in 5 separate columns, consisting of the troops of the 3d and Light divisions, and of Brig. Gen. Pack's brigade. The 2 right columns, conducted by Lieut. Col. O'Toole of the 2d caçadores, and Major Ridge of the 5th regt., were destined to protect the advance of Major Gen. Mackinnon's brigade, forming the 3d, to the top of the breach in the *fausse braie* wall; and all these, being composed of troops of the 3d division, were under the direction of Lieut. Gen. Picton.

The 4th column, consisting of the 43d and 52d regts., and part of the 95th regt., being of the Light division, under the direction of Major Gen. Craufurd, attacked the breaches on the left in front of the suburb of San Francisco, and covered the left of the attack of the principal breach by the troops of the 3d division; and Brig. Gen. Pack was destined, with his brigade, forming the 5th column, to make a false attack upon the southern face of the fort.

Besides these 5 columns, the 94th regt., belonging to the 3d division, descended into the ditch in 2 columns, on the right of Major Gen. Mackinnon's brigade, with a view to protect the descent of that body into the ditch and its attack of the breach in the *fausse braie*, against the obstacles which it was supposed the enemy would construct to oppose their progress.

All these attacks succeeded; and Brig. Gen. Pack even surpassed my expectations, having converted his false attack into a real one; and his advanced guard, under the command of Major Lynch, having followed the enemy's troops from the advanced works into the *fausse braie*, where they made prisoners all opposed to them.

Major Ridge, of the 2d batt. 5th regt., having escaladed the *fausse braie* wall, stormed the principal breach in the body of the place, together with the 94th regt., commanded by Lieut. Col. Campbell, which had moved along the ditch at the same time, and had stormed the breach in the *fausse braie*, both in front of Major Gen. Mackinnon's brigade. Thus, these regiments not only effectually covered the advance from the trenches of Major Gen. Mackinnon's brigade by their first movements and operations, but they preceded them in the attack.

Major Gen. Craufurd, and Major Gen. Vandeleur, and the troops of the Light division, on the left, were likewise very forward on that side; and, in less than half an hour from the time the attack commenced, our troops were in possession, and formed on the ramparts, of the place, each body contiguous to the other. The enemy then submitted, having sustained a considerable loss in the contest.

Our loss was also, I am concerned to add, severe, particularly in officers of high rank and estimation in this army. Major Gen. Mackinnon was unfortunately blown up by the accidental explosion of one of the enemy's expense magazines, close to the breach, after he had gallantly and successfully led the troops under his command to the attack. Major Gen. Craufurd likewise received a severe wound while he was leading on the Light division to the storm, and I am apprehensive that I shall be deprived for some time of his assistance. Major Gen. Vandeleur was likewise wounded in the same manner, but not so severely, and he was able to continue in the field.

I have to add to this list Lieut. Col. Colborne of the 52d regt., and Major G. Napier, who led the storming party of the Light division, and was wounded on the top of the breach.

I have great pleasure in reporting to your Lordship the uniform good conduct, and spirit of enterprise, and patience, and perseverance in the performance of great labor, by which the General officers, officers, and troops of the 1st, 3d, 4th, and Light divisions, and Brig. Gen. Pack's brigade, by whom the siege was carried on, have been distinguished during the late operations.

Lieut. Gen. Graham assisted me in superintending the conduct of the details of the siege, besides performing the duties of the General officer commanding the 1st division; and I am much indebted to the suggestions and assistance I received from him for the success of this enterprise.

The conduct of all parts of the 3d division, in the operations which they performed with so much gallantry and exactness on the evening of the 19th in the dark, afford the strongest proof of the abilities of Lieut. Gen. Picton and Major Gen. Mackinnon, by whom they were directed and led; but I beg particularly to draw your Lordship's attention to the conduct of Lieut. Col. O'Toole of the 2d caçadores, of Major Ridge of the 2d batt. 5th foot, of Lieut. Col. Campbell of the 94th regt., of Major Manners of the 74th, and of Major Grey of the 2d batt. 5th foot, who has been twice wounded during this siege.

It is but justice also to the 3d division to report that the men who performed the sap belonged to the 45th, 74th, and 88th regts., under the command of Capt. Macleod of the Royal Engineers, and Capt. Thompson of the 74th, Lieut. Beresford of the 88th, and Lieut. Metcalfe of the 45th; and they distinguished themselves not less in the storm of the place than they had in the performance of their laborious duty during the siege.

I have already reported, in my letter of the 9th inst., my sense of the conduct of Major Gen. Craufurd, and of Lieut. Col. Colborne, and of the troops of the Light division, in the storm of the redoubt of San Francisco, on the evening of the 8th inst. The conduct of these troops was equally distinguished throughout the siege; and in the storm, nothing could exceed the gallantry with which these brave officers and troops advanced and accomplished the difficult operation allotted to them, notwithstanding that all their leaders had fallen.

I particularly request your Lordship's attention to the conduct of Major Gen. Craufurd, Major Gen. Vandeleur, Lieut. Col. Barnard of the 95th, Lieut. Col. Colborne, Major Gibbs, and Major Napier of the 52d, and Lieut. Col. Macleod of the 43d. The conduct of Capt. Duffy of the 43d, and that of Lieut. Gurwood of the 52d regt., who was wounded, have likewise been particularly reported to me. Lieut. Col. Elder and the 3d caçadores were likewise distinguished upon this occasion.

The 1st Portuguese regt., under Lieut. Col. Hill, and the 16th, under Col. Campbell, being Brig. Gen. Pack's brigade, were likewise distinguished in the storm under the command of the Brig. General, who particularly mentions Major Lynch.

In my dispatch of the 15th, I reported to your Lordship the

attack of the convent of Sta Cruz by the troops of the 1st division, under the direction of Lieut. Gen. Graham, and that of the convent of San Francisco, on the 14th inst., under the direction of Major Gen. the Hon. C. Colville. The first mentioned enterprise was performed by Capt. Laroche de Starkerfels, of the 1st line batt. K. G. L.; the last by Lieut. Col. Harcourt, with the 40th regt. This regiment remained from that time in the suburb of San Francisco, and materially assisted our attack on that side of the place.

Although it did not fall to the lot of the troops of the 1st and 4th divisions to bring these operations to a successful close, they distinguished themselves throughout their progress by the patience and perseverance with which they performed the labor of the siege. The brigade of Guards, under Major Gen. H. Campbell, were particularly distinguished in this respect.

I likewise request your Lordship's attention to the conduct of Lieut. Col. Fletcher, the chief Engineer, and of Brigade Major Jones, and the officers and men of the Royal Engineers. The ability with which these operations were carried on exceeds all praise; and I beg leave to recommend these officers to your Lordship most particularly.

Major Dickson of the Royal artillery, attached to the Portuguese artillery, has for some time had the direction of the heavy train attached to this army, and has conducted the intricate details of the late operation, as he did those of the two sieges of Badajoz in the last summer, much to my satisfaction. The rapid execution produced by the well directed fire kept up from our batteries affords the best proof of the merits of the officers and men of the Royal artillery, and of the Portuguese artillery, employed on this occasion; but I must particularly mention Brigade Major May, and Capts. Holcombe, Power, Dynely, and Dundas, of the Royal artillery, and Capts. Da Cunha and Da Costa, and Lieut. Silva, of the 1st regt. of Portuguese artillery.

I have likewise particularly to report to your Lordship the conduct of Major Sturgeon of the Royal Staff corps. He constructed and placed for us the bridge over the Agueda, without which the enterprise could not have been attempted; he afterwards materially assisted Lieut. Gen. Graham and myself in our reconnaissance of the place on which the plan of the attack was founded; and he finally conducted the 2d batt. 5th regt., as well as the 2d caçadores, to their points of attack.

The A. G., and the D. Q. M. G., and the officers of their several departments, gave me every assistance throughout this service, as well as those of my personal Staff; and I have great pleasure in adding that notwithstanding the season of the year, and the increased difficulties of procuring supplies for the troops, the whole army have been well supplied, and every branch of the service provided for during the late operations, by the indefatigable exertions of Commissary Gen. Bissett, and the officers belonging to his department.

Mariscal de Campo, Don Carlos de España, and Don Julian Sanchez, observed the enemy's movements beyond the Tormes during the operations of the siege; and I am much obliged to them, and to the people of Castille in general, for the assistance I received from them. The latter have invariably shown their detestation of the French tyranny, and their desire to contribute, by every means in their power, to remove it.

I shall hereafter transmit to your Lordship a detailed account of what we have found in the place; but I believe that there are 153 pieces of ordnance, including the heavy train belonging to the French army, and great quantities of ammunition and stores. We have the Governor, Gen. Barrié, about 78 officers, and 1700 men, prisoners.

I transmit this dispatch by my aide de camp, Major the Hon. A. Gordon, who will give your Lordship any further details you may require; and I beg leave to recommend him to your protection.

To the Duke of Richmond.

Gallegos, 29th Jan. 1812.

I have not written to you lately, as I have had nothing to tell you deserving your attention.

My troops have been remarkably unhealthy during the

summer and autumn, and, although numerous, were so inferior in numbers to those the enemy had in my front, that I could do nothing more than keep them in check, and prevent them, at least, from undertaking any thing against the Spaniards. At length, in the end of December, convinced, I believe, by the reports in our own newspapers, that we were too sickly to undertake any thing, they broke up from Castille and the western parts of Estremadura, and marched off towards Valencia and Aragon, the former to assist Suchet, and the latter to endeavor to check the guerrillas. I immediately pushed forward the preparations for the siege of Ciudad Rodrigo; invested the place and broke ground on the 8th, and we took it by assault, as you will have seen, on the 19th Jan. Marmont returned upon hearing of our first movements, and collected about 50,000 men on the Tormes about the 23d and 24th of the month, but he has advanced only a reconnaitring party from thence; and it appears that he will not attempt to prevent us from putting the place again in a state of defence. It is already provisioned; and has been for some days in such a state as that it could not have been carried by a *coup de main*.

I have likewise restored the works of Almeida, so that I shall have this frontier as good as it ever was; and I hope to be able to get the whole army together, when I shall have a better chance with these gentlemen.

We proceeded at Ciudad Rodrigo on quite a new principle in sieges. The whole object of our fire was to lay open the walls. We had not one mortar; nor a howitzer, excepting to prevent the enemy from clearing the breaches, and for that purpose we had only two; and we fired upon the flanks and defences only when we wished to get the better of them, with a view to protect those who were to storm. This shows the kind of place we had to attack, and how important it is to cover the works of a place well by a glacis. The French, however, who are supposed to know every thing, could not take this place in less than 40 days after it was completely invested, or than 25 days after breaking ground.

March came here about a month ago, remarkably well; but he has had two slight attacks of fever since he arrived, from one of which he is now recovering. He is very liable to catch cold, and with the cold he always has fever. This must be a consequence of his disorder in the summer; but I hope that he will be quite well before the hot weather shall set in. If he should not be so, I shall certainly send him home.

Pray remember me most kindly to the Duchess and all your family.

To the Earl of Liverpool.

Camp before Badajoz, 20th March, 1812.

According to the intention which I announced to your Lordship in my dispatch of the 13th inst., I broke up the cantonments of the army on the 15th and 16th inst., and invested Badajoz, on the left of the river Guadiana, on the 16th inst., with the 3d, 4th, and Light divisions of infantry, and with a brigade of Lieut. Gen. Hamilton's division on the right. These troops are under the command of Marshal Sir W. Beresford and Lieut. Gen. Picton. We broke ground on the following day, and have established a parallel within 200 yards of the outwork called La Picurina, which embraces the whole of the south-east angle of the fort. The work has continued ever since with great celerity, notwithstanding the very bad weather which we have had since the 17th.

The enemy made a sortie yesterday from the gate called La Trinidad, on the right of our attack, with about 2000 men. They were almost immediately driven in, without effecting any object, with considerable loss, by Major Gen. Bowes, who commanded the guard in the trenches. We lost, upon this occasion, a very promising officer, Capt. Cuthbert, aide de camp to Lieut. Gen. Picton, killed; and Lieut. Col. Fletcher was slightly wounded, but I hope that he will soon be able to resume his duties. I have not got the returns, but I believe that our loss since the commencement of these operations amounts to 120 men killed and wounded.

On the same day that Badajoz was invested, Lieut. Gen. Sir T. Graham crossed the Guadiana with the 1st, 6th, and 7th divisions of infantry, and Gen. Slade's and Gen. Le Marchant's brigades of cavalry, and directed his march upon Valverde and Sᵗᵃ Marta, and thence towards Llerena; while Lieut. Gen. Sir R. Hill, with the 2d and Lieut. Gen. Hamilton's divisions, and Major Gen. Long's cavalry, marched from his cantonments near Alburquerque upon Merida, and thence upon Almendralejo. These movements induced Gen. Drouet to retire from Villa Franca upon Hornachos, in order, I conclude, to be in communication with Gen. Darricau's division, which was about La Serena.

I have heard from Sir T. Graham and from Sir R. Hill to the 19th inst. The former was at Los Santos and Zafra, with Gen. Slade's cavalry at Villa Franca, and the latter at Almendralejo. Lieut. Gen. Hill took 3 officers and a few hussars prisoners in Merida.

I have reports from the neighbourhood of Ciudad Rodrigo of the 17th inst., and from Salamanca of the 16th inst. The enemy had sent a small detachment to Bejar, principally with a view to plunder; but there was no appearance of any immediate movement.

The 6th division had moved from Talavera through the Puerto del Pico on the 8th and 9th inst., and the 4th division from Toledo on the same days, through the Guadarrama, and the 1st division only remained on the Tagus, near Talavera. The march of these divisions was directed, as I understand, upon Valladolid; and I conclude either that the reports are founded which have been in circulation, that the Guards had been withdrawn from Spain, or that the enemy intend to endeavor to divert my attention from the attack of Badajoz, by making some movement upon Galicia, or upon the north of Portugal. The rain, however, which has annoyed us here, it may be expected, will have filled the rivers in the north; and I made arrangements, before I left Castille, to provide for any plans of that kind which the enemy might adopt. Having lost their train, they cannot attack Ciudad Rodrigo or Almeida, at least till they shall have replaced it.

I have not heard of any movements in the south. Marshall Soult was at the lines opposite Cadiz according to the last accounts.

To the Earl of Liverpool.

Camp before Badajoz, 20th March, 1812.

I received this morning your letter of the 5th March, marked 'secret and confidential,' enclosing your correspondence with Lord W. Bentinck. I shall write to his Lordship, and to Sir E. Pellew, as soon as I can get a little leisure; in the mean time, I think it proper to apprise your Lordship that the attack of Tarragona or of Barcelona appears to me, of all the objects on the Eastern coast, to be the most desirable. I think it probable, however, that neither (most probably not the latter) will succeed. A siege requires time, and the French will move heaven and earth to save these places; and they can bring troops from France as well as from Aragon and Valencia, in addition to what they have in Catalonia. Besides, 10,000 men are not quite sufficient to attack Barcelona, where there must be 5000 in garrison. Lord William may expect some assistance from Gen. Lacy, but the foundation of his strength must be his British troops.

I don't know how I can give him any assistance from Cadiz. Your Lordship will recollect that from Cadiz we now occupy Carthagena and Tarifa, and that there are included in the division at Cadiz and those places 1400 Portuguese troops, and about 2000 foreigners in the regiment 'de Watteville' and the battalion of foreign detachments. In fact there is no British regiment now at Cadiz to be detached, excepting the 1st regt. of foot guards, which I have not allowed to be sent into Carthagena or Tarifa.

I would besides beg leave to draw your Lordship's attention to the result of the operation I have now in hand. If it should succeed and matters turn out as I wish, we may relieve the Andalusias. But if I should succeed in that object, I shall bring the whole of the enemy's force upon me; and I can't expect that, for some time at least, I shall receive any assistance from the Spaniards, or that they can make any material diversion in my favor. Will it not therefore be necessary to draw to this army the division at Cadiz?

If I should not relieve the Andalusias, I beg to have your positive orders respecting the degree to which I shall reduce the garrison of Cadiz, and what regiments I shall send to Lord W. Bentinck. I beg once more to repeat that it is entirely a matter of indifference to me, and always has been so, as far as I am personally concerned, whether the body of troops under my command be large or small. I shall perform service in proportion to the means placed at my disposal, in comparison with those of the enemy, and adverting to your Lordship's instructions.

We are getting on here, notwithstanding that the weather is excessively bad. The constitutions of the troops have been so much shaken with Walcheren, &c. &c., that I am always apprehensive of the consequences of exposing them to the weather. However, I have them in tents now, and I hope that the rain will not last.

To the Earl of Liverpool.

Camp before Badajoz, 27th March, 1812.

The operations of the siege of Badajoz have continued since I addressed you on the 20th inst., notwithstanding the badness of the weather, till the 25th inst. On that day we opened our fire from 28 pieces of ordnance, in 6 batteries in the first parallel, 2 of which were intended to fire upon the outwork called La Picurina, and the other 4 to enfilade or destroy the defences of the fort on the side attacked. I directed Major Gen. Kempt, who commanded in the trenches on that afternoon, to attack La Picurina by storm, after it was dark that night, which service he effected in the most judicious and gallant manner.

The attack was made by 500 men of the 3d division, formed into 3 detachments, the right under the command of Major Shaw, of the 74th, the centre under Capt. the Hon. H. Powys, of the 83d, and the left under Major Rudd, of the 77th. The communication between the outwork and the body of the place was entered on its right and left by the right and left detachments, each consisting of 200 men; half of each which detachments protected the attack from sallies from the fort, while the others attacked the work in its gorge. It was first entered, however, by the centre detachment of 100 men, under the command of Capt. the Hon. H. Powys, of the 83d regt., who escaladed the work at the salient angle, at a point at which the palisades had been injured by our fire. The detachment which attacked the work by the gorge had the most serious difficulties to contend with, as it was closed by not less than 3 rows of palisades, defended by musketry, and a place of arms for the garrison, musket proof, and loopholed throughout. When the attack upon the salient angle, however, succeeded, the whole got into the work.

The enemy's garrison in the outwork consisted of 250 men, with 7 pieces of artillery, under the command of Col. Gaspard Thierry, of the Etat Major of the army of the south. But very few if any escaped: the Colonel, 3 other officers, and 86 men have been taken prisoners, and the remainder were either killed by the fire of our troops or drowned in the inundation of the river Rivillas. The enemy made a sortie from the ravelin called San Roque, either with a view to recover La Picurina, or to protect the retreat of the garrison, but they were immediately driven in by the detachment stationed in the communication to protect the attack.

Major Gen. Kempt mentions in high terms in his report the cool and persevering gallantry of the officers and troops; of which indeed the strength of the work which they carried affords the best proof. He particularly mentions Lieut. Col. Hardinge, of the Staff of the Portuguese army, who attended him on this occasion, Capt. Burnet, his aide de camp, and Brig. Major Wilde, who was unfortunately killed by a cannon shot, after the work was in our possession. Likewise Capt. Holloway, Lieuts. Gipps and Stanway, of the Royal Engineers, who conducted the several detachments to the points of attack; and Majors Shaw and Rudd, and Capt. the Hon. H. Powys, who commanded the several detachments: these 3 officers were wounded, the latter on the parapet of the work, which he had been the first to mount by the ladders. I have to add to this account the high sense I entertain of the judicious manner and the gallantry with which Major Gen. Kempt carried into execution the service which I had entrusted to him. We thus established ourselves in La Picurina on the night of the 25th, and opened the second parallel within 300 yards of the body of the place, in which batteries were commenced last night.

It is impossible that I can do justice to the zeal, activity, and indefatigable labor of the officers and soldiers, with which these operations have been carried on in the most unfavorable weather. The Guadiana swelled so considerably that, notwithstanding all precautions, our bridge of pontoons was carried away on the 22d inst., and the flying bridges were so much injured as almost to become useless. But still the operations have been carried on without interruption.

I cannot, however, avoid taking this opportunity of calling the attention of your Lordship and of His Majesty's government to the neglect of the Portuguese authorities to furnish the means of transport necessary for the success of this or any other operation. My own anxiety, and the detail into which I am obliged to enter in order to find resources to overcome difficulties which occur at every moment, I put out of the question, although I believe no officer at the head of an army was ever so hampered, and it is desirable that the attention of one in that situation should be turned to other objects. But the serious inconveniences to which the troops are exposed, and the difficulties and risks which attend the execution of all services, for want of means of transport, become of such a magnitude, that no officer can venture to be responsible for them. If there was any want of means of transport in the country I should not complain, but I know there is no want; and I attribute the deficiency entirely to the defect of the Portuguese law upon the subject, and to the unwillingness of the magistrates to carry it into execution. In every country the supply of carriages for the service of the army is an obligation upon the owners of carriages; and I have repeatedly urged the Portuguese government to frame a law upon the subject, with sufficient penalties to insure obedience to it, and that the army should have means of transport. Instead of doing that, the object of the law lately made by the government would appear to be to prevent the army from getting carriages, and the consequence is that every service becomes a matter of difficulty and risk; and as the carriages of the poor alone are forced into the service by the magistrates, they suffer all the hardships which result from the law.

I had intended to commence the operations against Badajoz between the 6th and 8th March, and all the arrangements were made accordingly; but because the large and rich town of Evora, which has suffered in no manner by the war, would supply no carriages, I could not commence till the 17th, and thus the troops have been exposed to, and have been obliged to carry on the works of the siege during the rains of the equinox, which I had intended to avoid. At this moment the powder for the siege, and much of the shot, and many of the engineers' stores, are not arrived at Elvas, and we are obliged to consume the stores of that garrison. I am destroying the equipments of the army in transporting the stores from Elvas to the ground of the siege, because no assistance is given by the country, or assistance that is quite inadequate to the demand and wants of the service.

I hope that His Majesty's government will exert their influence with the Prince Regent of Portugal, to order the Local Government not only to frame a law which shall have for its object the equipment of the armies in such a manner as to enable them to defend the country, but to carry that law into execution, so that the people of the country shall understand that they must comply with its provisions.

Since I addressed your Lordship on the 20th, Gen. Drouet has had his troops on the line between Medellin on the Guadiana, and Zalamea de la Serena and Llerena, apparently with the view of keeping the communication open between the army of the south and the divisions of the 'Armée de Portugal' stationed on the Tagus. Lieut. Gen. Sir T. Graham made a movement to Llerena on the 25th at night, but the enemy, consisting of 3 battalions of infantry and 2 regiments of cavalry, which were there, having heard of his march, retired into the mountains during the night. Lieut. Gen. Sir R. Hill has likewise sent a detachment to La Guareña, and proposed to march himself this morning upon Medellin, in order to co-operate with Lieut. Gen. Sir T. Graham in obliging the enemy to remove to a greater distance, and to endeavor to destroy some of their detached corps.

The divisions of the 'Armée de Portugal' which were in Castille, and those which have lately marched thither, have not yet moved, and the object of their movement is still doubtful. It is understood to be to attempt a *coup de main* upon Ciudad Rodrigo, or to blockade the place. But I consider the success of the former impracticable, and that the latter is equally so at present, as the rain, which has been general, has filled all the rivers in that part of the country.

I am sorry to say that the Spanish authorities have neglected to transport to Ciudad Rodrigo the provisions which I had given them from the British magazine at S. João da Pesqueira, and a part of these provisions only will arrive at that place on the 30th of this month. The place has now, therefore, in it only one month's provisions for the garrison, which I had been able to give them from the stores of the army before I quitted Castille. I have transmitted to Mr Wellesley, for the information of the Spanish government, the copies of the correspondence which I have had with Don Carlos de España on this subject, in which His Majesty's government will see the measures which I had adopted to secure this important place, and the state in which it is at present.

I have not heard from any authority that the troops have yet moved in the south, but it is reported that those at Seville had marched upon Cordova, to which point I understand that those at Granada had been brought.

To the Earl of Liverpool.

Camp before Badajoz, 7th April, 1812.

My dispatch of the 3d inst. will have apprised your Lordship of the state of the operations against Badajoz to that date; which were brought to a close on the night of the 6th, by the capture of the place by storm.

The fire continued during the 4th and 5th against the face of the bastion of La Trinidad, and the flank of the bastion of Sta Maria; and on the 4th, in the morning, we opened another battery of 6 guns in the second parallel against the shoulder of the ravelin of San Roque, and the wall in its gorge.

Practicable breaches were effected in the bastions above mentioned on the evening of the 5th; but as I had observed that the enemy had entrenched the bastion of La Trinidad, and the most formidable preparations were making for the defence, as well of the breach in that bastions, as of that in the bastion of Sta Maria, I determined to delay the attack for another day, and to turn all the guns in the batteries in the second parallel on the curtain of La Trinidad; in hopes that by effecting a third breach, the troops would be enabled to turn the enemy's works for the defence of the other two; the attack of which would besides be connected by the troops destined to attack the breach in the curtain. This breach was effected in the evening of the 6th, and the fire of the face of the bastion of Sta Maria and of the flank of the bastion of La Trinidad being overcome, I determined to attack the place that night.

I had kept in reserve in the neighbourhood of this camp the 5th division under Lieut. Gen. Leith, which had left Castille only in the middle of March, and had but lately arrived in this part of the country; and I brought them up on that evening. The plan for the attack was, that Lieut. Gen. Picton should attack the castle of Badajoz by escalade with the 3d division; and a detachment from the guard in the trenches furnished that evening by the 4th division, under Major Wilson of the 48th regt., should attack the ravelin of San Roque upon his left, while the 4th division under Major Gen. the Hon. C. Colville, and the Light division under Lieut. Col. Barnard, should attack the breaches in the bastions of La Trinidad and Sta Maria, and in the curtain by which they are connected. The 5th division were to occupy the ground which the 4th and Light divisions had occupied during the siege; and Lieut. Gen. Leith was to make a false attack upon the outwork called the Pardaleras; and another on the works of the fort towards the Guadiana, with the left brigade of the division under Major Gen. Walker, which he was to turn into a real attack, if circumstances should prove favorable; and Brig. Gen. Power, who invested the place with his Portuguese brigade on the right of the Guadiana, was directed to make false attacks on the tête-de-pont, the Fort San Christoval, and the new redoubt called Mon Cœur.

The attack was accordingly made at 10 at night: Lieut. Gen. Picton preceding by a few minutes the attacks by the remainder of the troops. Major Gen. Kempt led this attack, which went out from the right of the first parallel. He was unfortunately wounded in crossing the river Rivillas below the inundation; but notwithstanding this circumstance, and the obstinate resistance of the enemy, the castle was carried by escalade; and the 3d division established in it at about 11½ o'clock. While this was going on, Major Wilson of the 48th carried the ravelin of San Roque by the gorge, with a detachment of 200 men of the guard in the trenches; and with the assistance of Major Squire, of the Engineers, established himself within that work.

The 4th and Light divisions moved to the attack from the camp along the left of the river Rivillas, and of the inundation. They were not perceived by the enemy till they reached the covered-way; and the advanced guards of the two divisions descended without difficulty into the ditch, protected by the fire of the parties stationed on the glacis for that purpose; and they advanced to the assault of the breaches, led by their gallant officers, with the utmost intrepidity. But such was the nature of the obstacles prepared by the enemy at the top and behind the breaches, and so determined their resistance, that our troops could not establish themselves within the place. Many brave officers and soldiers were killed or wounded by explosions at the top of the breaches; others who succeeded to them were obliged to give way, having found it impossible to penetrate the obstacles which the enemy had prepared to impede their progress. These attempts were repeated till after 12 at night; when, finding that success was not to be attained, and that Lieut. Gen. Picton was established in the castle, I ordered that the 4th and Light divisions might retire to the ground on which they had been first assembled for the attack.

In the mean time, Lieut. Gen. Leith had pushed forward

Major Gen. Walker's brigade on the left, supported by the 38th regt. under Lieut. Col. Nugent, and the 15th Portuguese regt. under Col. Do Rego, and he had made a false attack upon the Pardaleras with the 8th caçadores under Major Hill. Major Gen. Walker forced the barrier on the road of Olivença, and entered the covered-way on the left of the bastion of San Vicente, close to the Guadiana. He there descended into the ditch, and escaladed the face of the bastion of San Vicente. Lieut. Gen. Leith supported this attack by the 38th regt., and 15th Portuguese regt.; and our troops being thus established in the castle, which commands all the works of the town, and in the town; and the 4th and Light divisions being formed again for the attack of the breaches, all resistance ceased; and at daylight in the morning, the Governor, Gen. Philippon, who had retired to Fort San Christoval, surrendered, together with Gen. Vieland, and all the Staff, and the whole garrison. I have not got accurate returns of the strength of the garrison, or of the number of prisoners: but Gen. Philippon has informed me that it consisted of 5000 men at the commencement of the siege, of which 1200 were killed or wounded during the operations; besides those lost in the assault of the place. There were 5 French battalions, besides 2 of the regiment of Hesse Darmstadt, and the artillery, engineers, &c.; and I understand there are 4000 prisoners.

It is impossible that any expressions of mine can convey to your Lordship the sense which I entertain of the gallantry of the officers and troops upon this occasion. The list of killed and wounded will show that the General officers, the Staff attached to them, the Commanding, and other officers of the regiments, put themselves at the head of the attacks which they severally directed, and set the example of gallantry which was so well followed by their men.

Marshal Sir W. Beresford assisted me in conducting the details of this siege; and I am much indebted to him for the cordial assistance which I received from him, as well during its progress, as in the last operation which brought it to a termination.

The duties in the trenches were conducted successively by

Major Gen. the Hon. C. Colville, Major Gen. Bowes, and Major Gen. Kempt, under the superintendence of Lieut. Gen. Picton. I have had occasion to mention all these officers during the course of the operations; and they all distinguished themselves, and were all wounded in the assault. I am particularly obliged to Lieut. Gen. Picton for the manner in which he arranged the attack of the castle, and also for that in which he supported the attack, and established his troops in that important post.

Lieut. Gen. Leith's arrangements for the false attack upon the Pardaleras, and that under Major Gen. Walker, were likewise most judicious; and he availed himself of the circumstances of the moment, to push forward and support the attack under Major Gen. Walker, in a manner highly creditable to him. The gallantry and conduct of Major Gen. Walker, who was also wounded, and that of the officers and troops under his command, were conspicuous.

The arrangements made by Major Gen. the Hon. C. Colville for the attack by the 4th division, were very judicious; and he led them to the attack in the most gallant manner. In consequence of the absence, on account of sickness, of Major Gen. Vandeleur, and of Col. Beckwith, Lieut. Col. Barnard commanded the Light division in the assault, and distinguished himself not less by the manner in which he made the arrangements for that operation, than by his personal gallantry in its execution.

I have also to mention Brig. Gen. Harvey of the Portuguese service, commanding a brigade in the 4th division, and Brig. Gen. Champelmond, commanding the Portuguese brigade in the 3d division, as highly distinguished. Brig. Gen. Harvey was wounded in the storm.

Your Lordship will see in the list of killed and wounded a list of the Commanding officers of regiments. In Lieut. Col. Macleod of the 43d regt., who was killed in the breach, His Majesty has sustained the loss of an officer who was an ornament to his profession, and was capable of rendering the most important services to the country. I must likewise mention Lieut. Col. Gibbs of the 52d, who was wounded, and Major O'Hare of the 95th, unfortunately killed in the breach; Lieut. Col. Elder of the 3d, and Major Algeo of the 1st caçadores.

Lieut. Col. Harcourt of the 40th, likewise wounded, was highly distinguished; and Lieut. Cols. Blakeney of the Royal Fusiliers, Knight of the 27th, Erskine of the 48th, and Capt. Leaky, who commanded the 23d Fusiliers, Lieut. Col. Ellis having been wounded during the previous operation of the siege.

In the 5th division I must mention Major Hill of the 8th caçadores, who directed the false attack upon the fort Pardaleras. It was impossible for any men to behave better than these did.

I must likewise mention Lieut. Col. Brooke, of the 4th regt., and Lieut. Col. the Hon. G. Carleton of the 44th, and Lieut. Col. Gray of the 30th, who was unfortunately killed. The 2d batt. 38th regt. under Lieut. Col. Nugent, and the 15th Portuguese regt. under Col. Luiz do Rego, likewise performed their part in a very exemplary manner.

The officers and troops in the 3d division have distinguished themselves as usual in these operations. Lieut. Gen. Picton has reported to me particularly the conduct of Lieut. Col. Williams of the 60th; Lieut. Col. Ridge of the 5th, who was unfortunately killed in the assault of the castle; Lieut. Col. Forbes of the 45th, Lieut. Col. Fitzgerald of the 60th, Lieut. Col. the Hon. R. Le P. Trench, and Lieut. Col. Manners of the 74th; Major Carr of the 83d, and Major the Hon. H. Pakenham, A. A. G. to the 3d division. He has likewise particularly reported the good conduct of Col. Campbell of the 94th, commanding Major Gen. the Hon. C. Colville's brigade, during his absence in command of the 4th division, whose conduct I have so repeatedly had occasion to report to your Lordship.

The officers and men of the corps of engineers and artillery were equally distinguished during the operations of the siege and in its close.

Lieut. Col. Fletcher continued to direct the works (notwithstanding that he was wounded in the sortie made by the enemy on the 19th March), which were carried on by Major Squire and Major Burgoyne, under his directions. The former established the detachments under Major Wilson, in the ravelin of San Roque, on the night of the storm; the latter attended the attack of the 3d division on the castle. I have likewise to report the good conduct of Major Jones, Capt. Nicholas, and Capt. Williams, of the Royal Engineers.

Major Dickson conducted the details of the artillery service during the siege, as well as upon former occasions, under the general superintendence of Col. Framingham, who, since the absence of Major Gen. Borthwick, has commanded the artillery with the army.

I cannot sufficiently applaud the officers and soldiers of the Royal and Portuguese artillery during the siege; particularly Lieut. Col. Robe, who opened the breaching batteries; Major May, Capt. Gardiner, Major Holcombe, and Lieut. Bourchier of the Royal artillery; Capt. de Rettberg of the German, and Major Tulloh of the Portuguese artillery.

Adverting to the extent of the details of the ordnance department during this siege, to the difficulties of the weather, &c., with which Major Dickson had to contend, I must mention him most particularly to your Lordship.

The officers of the Adj. Gen. and Q. M. Gen.'s departments rendered me every assistance on this occasion, as well as those of my personal Staff; and I have to add that I have received reports from the General officers commanding divisions, of the assistance they received from the officers of those departments attached to them, the greatest number of whom, and of their personal Staff, are wounded.

In a former dispatch I reported to your Lordship the difficulties with which I had to contend, in consequence of the failure of the civil authorities of the province of Alentejo to perform their duty and supply the army with means of transport. These difficulties have continued to exist; but I must do Major Gen. Victoria, the Governor of Elvas, the justice to report that he, and the troops under his command, have made every exertion, and have done every thing in their power to contribute to our success.

Marshal Soult left Seville on the 1st inst., with all the troops which he could collect in Andalusia; and he was in communication with the troops which had retired from Estremadura, under Gen. Drouet, on the 3d, and he arrived at Llerena on the 4th. I had intended to collect the army on the Albuera rivulet, in proportion as Marshal Soult should advance; and I had requested Lieut. Gen. Sir T. Graham to retire gradually upon Albuera, while Lieut. Gen. Sir R. Hill should do the same on Talavera, from Don Benito and the upper parts of the Guadiana. I don't think it certain that Marshal Soult has made any decided movement from Llerena since the 4th, although he has patrolled forward with small detachments of cavalry, and the advanced guard of his infantry have been at Usagre. None of the 'Armée de Portugal' have moved to join him.

According to the last reports which I have received of the 4th inst., from the frontier of Castille, it appears that Marshal Marmont had established a body of troops between the Agueda and the Coa, and he had reconnaitred Almeida on the 3d. Brig. Gen. Trant's division of militia had arrived upon the Coa, and Brig. Gen. Wilson's division was following with the cavalry, and Lieut. Gen. the Conde de Amarante was on his march, with a part of the corps under his command, towards the Douro.

It would be very desirable that I should have it in my power to strike a blow against Marshal Soult before he could be reinforced; but the Spanish authorities having omitted to take the necessary steps to provision Ciudad Rodrigo, it is absolutely necessary that I should return to the frontiers of Castille within a short period of time. It is not very probable that Marshal Soult will risk an action in the province of Estremadura, which it would not be difficult for him to avoid, and it is very necessary that he should return to Andalusia, as Gen. Ballesteros was in movement upon Seville on the 29th of last month, and the Conde de Penne Villemur moving on the same place from the Lower Guadiana.

It will be quite impossible for me to go into Andalusia till I shall have secured Ciudad Rodrigo. I therefore propose to remain in the positions now occupied by the troops for some days; indeed a little time is required to take care of our wounded; and if Marshal Soult should remain in Estremadura I shall attack him; if he should retire into Andalusia, I must return to Castille.

I have the honor to enclose returns of the killed and wounded from the 31st March, and in the assault of Badajoz, and a return of the ordnance, small arms, and ammunition found in the place. I shall send the returns of provisions in the place by the next dispatch. This dispatch will be delivered to your Lordship by my aide de camp Capt. Canning, whom I beg leave to recommend to your protection.

He has likewise the colors of the garrison, and the colors of the Hesse Darmstadt regiment, to be laid at the feet of H. R. H. the Prince Regent. The French battalions in the garrison had no eagles.

Return of the killed, wounded, and missing of the army, at the siege and capture of Badajoz, from the 18th March to 7th April, 1812, inclusive.

	Officers.	Serjeants.	R. and F.	Total loss of officers, non-commissioned officers, and R. & F.
Killed	72	51	912	1035
Wounded	306	216	3265	3787
Missing	—	1	62	63

The Portuguese loss is included in the above numbers.

To the Earl of Liverpool.

Salamanca, 18th June, 1812.

The army crossed the Agueda on the 13th inst., and marched forward in three columns, the troops under Don Carlos de España forming a fourth; and the whole arrived upon the Valmusa rivulet, about six miles from hence, on the 16th. The enemy showed some cavalry and a small body of infantry in front of the town on that day, and manifested a design to hold the heights on the south side of the Tormes. But their cavalry were immediately driven in by ours, and the enemy evacuated

Salamanca on the night of the 16th, leaving a garrison of about 800 men in the fortifications which they have erected·on the ruins of the colleges and convents which they have demolished. By the fire from these they protect the passage of the Tormes by the bridge, and our troops crossed that river yesterday morning, by 2 fords which are in this neighbourhood.

The forts were immediately invested by the 6th division, under the command of Major Gen. H. Clinton, and having been accurately reconnaitred, it was found necessary to break ground before them. This was done last night, and I hope that we shall commence our fire to-morrow morning from 8 pieces of cannon, at the distance of 300 yards from the principal of the enemy's works, the possession of which will, I hope, give us the possession of the others. Major Gen. Clinton conducts these operations.

It is impossible to describe the joy of the people of the town upon our entrance. They have now been suffering for more than three years; during which time the French, among other acts of violence and oppression, have destroyed 13 of 25 convents, and 22 of 25 colleges, which existed in this celebrated seat of learning.

The enemy retired by the road to Toro, and their rear guard was about 15 miles from hence last night. They retired again this morning by the same road; and I understand that they intend to collect their army on the Duero, between Toro and Zamora. Our advanced guard is advanced on the road to Toro, and the main body of the army in this neighbourhood.

I enclose a return of the 'Armée de Portugal', of the 1st April, which has been intercepted, from which it appears that there are at present under arms 2074 officers and 51,492 troops in this body, of which 43,396 are infantry, and 3204 cavalry. Of the 4244 men returned detached, there are about 1500 infantry and about 1000 cavalry in this neighbourhood, who will of course be called in to join the army.

I enclose the morning state of this army of yesterday, in which I have marked thus * those troops which are in this part of the country, the others being in Estremadura, under the command of Lieut. Gen. Hill. To these numbers must be added about 3000 Spanish infantry, under Don Carlos de España, and about 500 Spanish cavalry, under Don J. Sanchez, who are with the army.

This state includes only the cavalry and infantry of the army; but your Lordship will observe that the enemy are superior to us in numbers in those arms; and it appears from the return, that the enemy have 92 pieces of cannon.

I have adopted every measure in my power to prevent the enemy from collecting their forces against us. I have urged the Conde de Amarante to move upon the enemy's flank from Braganza, along the Douro, with 4 battalions of militia and 3 regiments of Portuguese cavalry, under Gen. D'Urban, and to cut off the enemy's communication between Zamora and Benavente and Astorga. Gen. Castaños has promised me to attack Astorga with the army of Galicia; and I have urged Gen. Mendizabal and the chiefs of the guerrillas in all the northern parts of Spain to make an effort to prevent Marshal Marmont from collecting his whole force against this army. But I am apprehensive that I can place no reliance on the effect to be produced by these troops. The guerrillas, although active and willing, and although their operations in general occasion the utmost annoyance to the enemy, are so little disciplined that they can do nothing against the French troops, unless the latter are very inferior in numbers; and if the French take post in house or church, of which they only barricade the entrance, both regular troops and guerrillas are so ill equipped, as military bodies, that the French can remain in security till relieved by a larger body.

Then Gen. Castaños, although I believe he is equipped with a few guns for the attack of Astorga, has no pecuniary resources to enable him to collect and keep together the army of Galicia. And if the enemy should abandon Astorga to its fate, and should withdraw Gen. Bonet from the Asturias, I am very apprehensive that the advantages of my march into Castille will be confined to regaining the principality of Asturias for Gen. Castaños, and to the little advantages which the guerrillas will derive from the evacuation of different parts of the country by the enemy's posts.

Your Lordship will observe from my letter of the 26th ult., that I did not calculate that the enemy's '*Armée de Portugal*' was so strong when I determined upon this expedition, and I had certainly reason to believe that Marshal Marmont would not evacuate the Asturias. I shall not give up the plan, however, unless I should see that success is not to be looked for, as I am convinced that the most advantageous consequences will result from success in this quarter, or even from my remaining in an advanced position in Castille.

From intercepted letters between the King and Marshals Soult and Marmont, which, however, I have not been able entirely to decipher, I judge that the King's plan, referred to in my dispatch of the 10th inst., is to collect a corps in the valley of the Tagus, consisting of a part of the army of the South, and a division of the army of the Centre, in order to create a diversion in favor of Marshal Marmont. I had requested the Empecinado to alarm the King for the safety of his situation at Madrid; and I hope that Marshal Soult will find ample employment for his troops in the south in the blockade of Cadiz, the continued operations of Gen. Ballesteros, and those in Estremadura of Lieut. Gen. Hill, whose attention I have called to the probable march of this corps of the army of the South through part of Estremadura.

The King is very desirous of restoring the bridge of Almaraz, which can only be for the object of collecting a corps upon the Tagus, but hitherto he has sent there only two small boats, for the purpose of communicating with the post at Mirabete.

I enclose a letter from Lieut. Gen. Sir R. Hill, and its enclosures, being two from Major Gen. Slade, giving an account of an affair which he had with the enemy on the 11th inst., in which, owing to the eagerness and impetuosity of the soldiers, considerable loss was sustained.

Your Lordship is aware that misfortunes of this kind have happened more than once in this country from the same cause, and I have frequently been present on occasions when the same conduct in the cavalry was likely to be attended by the same unfortunate results. Notwithstanding that this misfortune has occurred upon this occasion to a brigade consisting of two of the best and most experienced regiments we have, I have concurred with Lieut. Gen. Sir R. Hill in thinking that it is necessary to make a formal inquiry into the causes which occasioned the disorder, and the consequent losses in the attack made by Major Gen. Slade on the enemy on the 11th inst. Gen. Slade's action was occasioned by his advancing to Llera, to cover a movement by the Conde de Penne Villemur on Llerena, in order to collect the harvest of Estremadura; and I learn that the enemy have since retired to Cordova.

I have reports from the south, stating that Gen. Ballesteros had had an action with the enemy near Bornos, on the 1st inst., of which I have not received the detail, or any regular confirmation, notwithstanding that there is no doubt of the fact. The result has been stated differently by the two parties, and it is reported by the enemy that Ballesteros is badly wounded. But they have certainly reinforced their troops in that direction since the action, from which circumstance it may be inferred that the success, if on their side at all, was not very decisive.

To the Earl of Liverpool.

Salamanca, 25th June, 1812.

Marshal Marmont collected his army on the Duero between the 16th and 19th inst., with the exception of Gen. Bonet's division, which I believe is still in the Asturias, and some small garrisons, and he moved forward from Fuente el Sauco on the 20th. I formed the allied army, with the exception of the troops engaged in the operations against the forts at Salamanca, on the heights extending from the neighbourhood of Villares to Morisco; and the advanced posts of the cavalry and infantry retired upon the army in good order, and without material loss. The enemy remained in our front on that night, and during the 21st; and during that night they established a post on our right flank, the possession of which by them deprived us of an advantage which might eventually be of importance; I therefore requested Lieut. Gen. Sir T. Graham to attack them in that post on the 22d with the troops on the right, which he did with those of the 7th division, which were the reserve of the right, under the command of Major Gen. Hope and Major Gen. de Bernewitz. The enemy were driven from the ground immediately, with some loss. Our troops conducted themselves remarkably well in this affair, which took place in the view of every man of both armies. The enemy retired during that night; and on the following evening, they posted themselves with their right on the heights near Cabeza Vellosa, and their left on the Tormes, at Huerta; their centre at Aldea Rubia.

The object of the enemy in this movement being to endeavor to communicate with the garrisons in the forts of Salamanca, by the left of the Tormes, I changed the front of the army, and placed the right at Sta Marta, where there is a ford over the Tormes; and the advanced posts at Aldea Lengua; and I extended the troops so as to cover Salamanca completely, while I had it in my power to concentrate the army at any point at a short notice.

I sent Major Gen. Bock's brigade of heavy dragoons across the Tormes, in order to observe the passages of that river. The enemy crossed the Tormes at Huerta, about 2 o'clock on the morning of the 24th, in considerable numbers of cavalry, infantry, and artillery; and there was every appearance of a general movement in that direction. The conduct of Major Gen. Bock's dragoons was conspicuously good upon this occasion. They did every thing in their power to make known the enemy's movement; and opposed their advance vigorously under many disadvantages, in order to afford time for the dispositions necessary to be made. As soon as I was certain that the enemy had crossed the Tormes, I requested Lieut. Gen. Sir T. Graham to cross that river with the 1st and 7th divisions, and I sent over Major Gen. Le Marchant's brigade of cavalry; and I concentrated the remainder of the army between Morisco and Cabrerizos, keeping the advanced posts still at Aldea Lengua. At about noon, the enemy advanced as far as Calvarrasa de Abaxo; but observing the disposition made for their reception, they retired again in the afternoon across the Tormes to Huerta; and they have since remained in the position which they occupied on the 23d.

Between the 20th and 22d, I had a favorable opportunity of attacking the enemy, of which, however, I did not think it proper to avail myself, for the following reasons:

1st; It was probable he had advanced with an intention to attack us, and, in the position which we occupied, I considered it advantageous to be attacked; and that the action would be attended by less loss on our side.

2dly; The operations against the forts of Salamanca took up the attention of some of our troops; and although I believe the superiority of numbers in the field was on our side, it was not so great as to render an action decisive of the result of the campaign, in which we should sustain great loss.

3dly; In case of failure, the passage of the Tormes would have been difficult, the enemy continuing in the possession of the forts, and commanding the bridge of Salamanca.

The siege of the forts of Salamanca has not advanced with the rapidity which I expected when I addressed your Lordship last. Although, from the pains taken and the expense incurred in their construction, and the accounts which I had received of them, I was prepared to meet with some difficulties, and provided an equipment accordingly; the difficulties are of a more formidable nature than they were represented; and the forts, 3 in number, each defending the other, are very strong, although not of a regular construction, and the equipment which I had provided for their attack was not sufficient; and I have been obliged to send for more, which has created some delay in the operations.

We have breaches open in the Convent of San Vicente, which is the principal convent; but these cannot be attacked in security till we shall have possession of Fort Los Cayetanos. Major Gen. Clinton made an attempt to carry that work by storm on the night of the 23d inst., the gorge having been considerably damaged by the fire of our artillery. This attempt unfortunately failed; and I am concerned to add, that Major Gen. Bowes was killed. He was so eager for the success of the enterprise, that he had gone forward with the storming party, which consisted of a part of his brigade, and was wounded; and after his first wound was dressed, he returned again to the attack, and received a second wound, which killed him. Our loss in officers and men was likewise considerable.

I expect that every thing that is necessary to get the better of these forts will arrive to-morrow, and that I shall soon have the happiness of reporting that they are in our possession.

We have discovered the cipher in which King Joseph wrote his orders to Gen. Drouet in regard to his operations against Lieut. Gen. Sir R. Hill, which were to move upon the allied troops in Estremadura. Your Lordship will observe from my dispatch of the 10th inst., that I had left Lieut. Gen. Sir R. Hill in strength, and I have desired him to collect his troops in the position of Albuera, which is the best in the country; and to act according to circumstances, and to the movements of the enemy. By a letter from Lieut. Gen. Sir R. Hill of the 22d, I learn that Gen. Drouet had been considerably reinforced from Andalusia since the defeat of Gen. Ballesteros at Bornos, in the beginning of the month, and had advanced as far as Almendralejo and Villa Franca; and Lieut. Gen. Sir R. Hill had concentrated his troops at Albuera. He had not decided whether he should attack Drouet or not, and he delayed the decision only because he was not quite certain of Drouet's strength.

Gen. Ballesteros had sustained a severe loss in his action at Bornos on the 1st June; and I understand that he retired to the neighbourhood of Gibraltar.

In the north, Gen. Santocildes, under the direction of Gen. Castaños, has invested Astorga with the Galician army, and is about to attack that place; in which operation I imagine that he cannot be interrupted, as the whole of the enemy's army, excepting Gen. Bonet's division in Asturias, is employed against that under my command.

The guerrillas are in unmolested possession of all parts of the country; and the enemy's weak and scattered garrisons are cut off from all communication with each other, or with the country.

To the Earl of Liverpool.

Fuente la Peña, 30th June, 1812.

The ammunition to enable us to carry on the attack of the forts having arrived at Salamanca in the afternoon of the 26th, the fire was immediately recommenced upon the gorge of the redoubt of Los Cayetanos, in which a practicable breach was effected at about 10 o'clock in the morning of the 27th; and we had succeeded nearly about the same time in setting fire to the buildings in the large fort of San Vicente, by the fire from which the approach to Los Cayetanos by its gorge was defended.

Being in Salamanca at this moment, I gave directions that the forts of Los Cayetanos and La Merced should be stormed; but some little delay occurred in consequence of the commanding officer of these forts in the first instance, and afterwards the commanding officer of San Vicente, having expressed a desire to capitulate after the lapse of a certain number of hours.

As it was obvious that these propositions were made in order to gain time till the fire in San Vicente should be extinguished, I refused to listen to any terms, unless the forts should be instantly surrendered; and having found that the commanding officer of Los Cayetanos, who was the first to offer to surrender, was entirely dependent upon the Governor of San Vicente, and could not venture to carry into execution the capitulation which he had offered to make, I gave directions that his fort and that of La Merced might be stormed forthwith.

These operations were effected in the most gallant manner by a detachment of the 6th division, under the command of Lieut. Col. Davis of the 36th regt., under the direction of Major Gen. Clinton.

The troops entered the fort of Los Cayetanos by the gorge, and escaladed that of La Merced; and I am happy to add that our loss was but trifling.

The Governor of San Vicente then sent out a flag of truce to ratify the surrender of that fort on the terms I had offered him, viz., the garrison to march out with the honors of war; to be prisoners of war; and the officers to retain their personal military baggage, and the soldiers their knapsacks: and notwithstanding that the 9th regt. of caçadores had actually stormed one of the outworks of San Vicente, and were in possession of it, I deemed it expedient to accept the fort by capitulation on those terms, and to stop the attack. I have already informed your Lordship that Major Gen. Clinton commanded the attack against these forts, which was carried on with great vigor and ability; and he mentions in strong terms of commendation the conduct of the General officers, officers, and troops employed under his command; particularly Col. Hinde of the 32d regt., Lieut. Col. Davis of the 36th regt., Capt. Owen of the 61st regt., Brigade Major Hobart, and Ensign Newton of the 32d regt., who distinguished himself in the attack of the night of the 23d inst., and volunteered to lead the advanced party in the attack of the 27th. He likewise mentions in strong terms Lieut. Col. May, who commanded the artillery under the direction of Col. Framingham, and the officers and soldiers of the Royal and Portuguese artillery under his command, and Lieut. Col. Burgoyne, Lieut. Reid and the officers of the Engineers, and Major Thompson of the 74th regt., who acted as an engineer during these operations.

The enemy had been employed for nearly 3 years in constructing these works, but with increased activity for the last 8 or 9 months. A large expense had been incurred; and these works, sufficiently garrisoned by about 800 men, and armed with 30 pieces of artillery, were of a nature to render it quite impossible to take them, excepting by a regular attack; and it is obvious that the enemy relied upon their strength, and upon their being sufficiently garrisoned and armed; as they had left in San Vicente large depôts of clothing, and military stores of every description. I was mistaken in my estimate of the extent of the means which would be necessary to subdue these forts; and I was obliged to send to the rear for a fresh supply of ammunition. This necessity occasioned a delay of 6 days.

The enemy withdrew their garrison from Alba de Tormes as soon as they heard of the fall of the forts of Salamanca; and I have ordered that the works at both places may be destroyed.

The operations against the forts of Salamanca were carried on in sight of Marshal Marmont's army, which remained in its position with the right at Cabeza Vellosa, and the left at Huerta, till the night of the 27th inst., when they broke up, and retired in three columns towards the river Duero; one of them directing its march upon Toro, and the others upon Tordesillas. The allied army broke up the following day, and are this day encamped upon the Guareña.

We have various reports of reinforcements on their march to join the enemy, but none on which I can rely. I know from intercepted letters, that Marshal Marmont expects to be joined by a division of the army of the North, reported to have been at Burgos on the 24th; and it is reported that Gen. Bonet had withdrawn from the Asturias by San Andres, and was on his march likewise for the same purpose. It is also reported that Gen. Bonet had received a check in the Asturias, and had sustained the loss of a considerable number of men. If this last report be true, it will account for his withdrawing from the Asturias; in which province I have reason to believe, from the intercepted letters, that he had been ordered to maintain himself; and that these orders had proceeded from Paris.

By accounts from Estremadura of the 26th inst., it appears that the enemy still continued in the position which they had occupied in Estremadura; and Lieut. Gen. Sir R. Hill was in front of Albuera. It is obvious that they don't intend to attack him, and I have recommended to him to attack them, if he should deem his force sufficiently strong, and of a sufficiently good description to give a fair chance of success, rather than allow them to keep him in check, and to remain in possession of a large part of the province of Estremadura.

I have not yet heard that Gen. Santocildes has commenced his attack upon Astorga. Gen. Cabrera is at Benavente with his division; and I understand there are Spanish troops in Leon. The Conde de Amarante has his infantry at Carvajales, and Brig. Gen. D'Urban had crossed the Duero below Zamora, in order to aid in intercepting the enemy's communication with Toro, before he heard of the fall of Salamanca. I have now desired him, however, to return across the Duero.

I have received no late intelligence from the south.

P. S. I enclose a return of the killed, wounded, and missing of the army since my last dispatch.

Return of the killed, wounded, and missing in the siege of the Forts of San Vicente, Los Cayetanos, and La Merced, and in the position on the heights of Villares, from the 16th to the 27th June, 1812, inclusive.

	Officers.	Serjeants.	R. and F.	Horses.	Total loss of officers, non-commissioned officers, and R. & F.
Killed	6	5	104	28	115
Wounded	28	44	340	—	412
Missing	2	—	11	5	13

To Earl Bathurst.

Rueda, 7th July, 1812.

The army broke up from the encampment on the Guareña on the morning of the 1st inst., and the enemy having retired from Alaejos, encamped on the Trabancos, with the advanced guard at La Nava del Rey. Having heard that the enemy had destroyed the bridge of Tordesillas, and knowing, from intercepted letters, that Marshal Marmont intended to take a position near this town, our advanced guard crossed the Zapardiel, and moved upon Rueda on the morning of the 2d, supported by the left of the army, while the right and centre moved towards Medina del Campo. The enemy, however, had not destroyed the bridge over the Duero, as reported; and the main body of the army had retired upon Tordesillas, leaving the rear guard at Rueda.

Lieut. Gen. Sir S. Cotton immediately attacked the rear

guard with Major Gen. Anson's and Major Gen. V. Alten's brigades of cavalry, and drove them in upon the main body at Tordesillas. As the right and centre of the army were at a considerable distance, I could not bring up a sufficient body of troops in time to attack the enemy during their passage of the Duero; and they effected that operation without material loss, and took their position on that river with their right on the heights opposite Pollos, their centre at Tordesillas, and their left at Simancas on the Pisuerga.

I moved our left to Pollos on the 3d, and obtained possession of the ford over the Duero at that place. But as the ford was scarcely practicable for infantry, and the enemy's corps was strongly posted with a considerable quantity of cannon on the heights which command the plain, on which the troops must have formed after crossing the ford; and as I could not establish the army on the right of the Duero till I should have adequate means of passing the river, I did not think it proper to push our troops farther. We have since been employed in endeavors to discover the fords of the Duero, which are in general but imperfectly known; and are waiting till they become practicable for infantry. By that time I hope that the army of Galicia, under Gen. Santocildes, will have been able to advance, the siege of Astorga having been brought to a conclusion. The fire against that place opened on the 2d inst., but I have not heard with what effect; and I have recommended to Gen. Santocildes to leave a small body of troops to continue the siege, and to move forward with the remainder.

Lieut. Gen. the Conde de Amarante remains at Carvajales, and Brig. Gen. D'Urban is with his cavalry in rear of the enemy's right flank at Castromonte. The guerrilla Marquiñez is at Palencia.

Gen. Bonet was at Aguilar de Campo in the end of last month, and orders have been sent to him to join the army. As many copies of these orders have been intercepted, it is doubtful whether he has received them; and I have not heard of his moving. There are no accounts of the movement of the troops of the army of the North.

By the last accounts from Lieut. Gen. Sir R. Hill, of the 1st inst., he was about to move to attack Gen. Drouet, whose force he considered inferior to that under his command.

To Earl Bathurst.

Cabrerizos, near Salamanca, 21st July, 1812.

In the course of the 15th and 16th the enemy moved all their troops to the right of their position on the Duero, and their army was concentrated between Toro and San Roman. A considerable body passed the Duero at Toro, on the evening of the 16th; and I moved the allied army to their left on that night, with an intention to concentrate on the Guareña.

It was totally out of my power to prevent the enemy from passing the Duero at any point at which he might think it expedient, as he had in his possession all the bridges over that river, and many of the fords; but he recrossed that river at Toro in the night of the 16th, moved his whole army to Tordesillas, where he again crossed the Duero on the morning of the 17th, and assembled his army on that day at La Nava del Rey; having marched not less than 10 leagues in the course of the 17th.

The 4th and Light divisions of infantry, and Major Gen. Anson's brigades of cavalry, had marched to Castrejon on the night of the 16th, with a view to the assembly of the army on the Guareña, and were at Castrejon under the orders of Lieut. Gen. Sir S. Cotton on the 17th, not having been ordered to proceed farther, in consequence of my knowledge that the enemy had not passed the Duero at Toro, and there was not time to call them in between the hour at which I received the intelligence of the whole of the enemy's army being at La Nava and daylight of the morning of the 18th. I therefore took measures to provide for their retreat and junction, by moving the 5th division to Torrecilla de la Orden; and Major Gen. Le Marchant's, Major Gen. Alten's, and Major Gen. Bock's brigades of cavalry to Alaejos.

The enemy attacked the troops at Castrejon at the dawn of day of the 18th, and Sir S. Cotton maintained the post without suffering any loss till the cavalry had joined him. Nearly about the same time the enemy turned, by Alaejos, the left flank of our position at Castrejon.

The troops retired in admirable order to Torrecilla de la Orden, having the enemy's whole army on their flank, or in their rear, and thence to the Guareña, which river they passed under the same circumstances, and effected their junction with the army. The Guareña, which runs into the Duero, is formed by 4 streams, which unite about a league below Cañizal, and the enemy took a strong position on the heights on the right of that river; and I placed the 5th, 4th, and Light divisions on the opposite heights, and had directed the remainder of the army to cross the Upper Guareña at Vallesa, in consequence of the appearance of the enemy's intention to turn our right.

Shortly after his arrival, however, the enemy crossed the Guareña at Castrillo, below the junction of the streams; and manifested an intention to press upon our left, and to enter the valley of Cañizal. Major Gen. Alten's brigade of cavalry, supported by the 3d dragoons, were already engaged with the enemy's cavalry, and had taken, among other prisoners, the French General de Carrié; and I desired Lieut. Gen. the Hon. G. L. Cole to attack with Major Gen. W. Anson's and Brig. Gen. Harvey's brigades of infantry, the latter under the command of Col. Stubbs, the enemy's infantry, which were supporting their cavalry. He immediately attacked and defeated them with the 27th and 40th regts., which advanced to the charge with bayonets, Col. Stubbs' Portuguese brigade supporting; and the enemy gave way; many were killed and wounded; and Major Gen. Alten's brigade of cavalry having pursued the fugitives, 240 prisoners were taken.

In these affairs, Lieut. Gen. the Hon. G. L. Cole, Major Gen. V. Alten, Major Gen. W. Anson, Lieut. Cols. Arentschildt of the 1st hussars, and Hervey of the 14th light dragoons; Lieut. Col. Maclean of the 27th, and Major Archdall of the 40th; Col. Stubbs, Lieut. Col. Anderson, commanding the 11th, and Major de Azeredo, commanding the 23d Portuguese regts., distinguished themselves. The enemy did not make any further attempt on our left, but having reinforced their troops on that side, and withdrawn those which had moved to their left, I brought back ours from Vallesa.

On the 19th, in the afternoon, the enemy withdrew all the

troops from their right, and marched to their left by Tarazona, apparently with an intention of turning our right. I crossed the Upper Guareña at Vallesa and El Olmo, with the whole of the allied army, in the course of that evening and night; and every preparation was made for the action which was expected on the plain of Vallesa on the morning of the 20th. But shortly after daylight the enemy made another movement, in several columns, to his left along the heights of the Guareña, which river he crossed below Cantalapiedra, and encamped last night at Babila-fuente and Villoruela; and the allied army made a corresponding movement to its right to Cantalpino, and encamped last night at Cabeza Vellosa, the 6th division and Major Gen. Alten's brigade of cavalry being upon the Tormes at Aldea Lengua. During these movements, there have been occasional cannonades, but without loss on our side.

I have this morning moved the left of the army to the Tormes, where the whole are now concentrated; and I observe that the enemy have also moved towards the same river near Huerta. The enemy's object hitherto has been to cut off my communication with Salamanca and Ciudad Rodrigo, the want of which he knows well would distress us very materially. The wheat harvest has not yet been reaped in Castille, and even if we had money, we could not now procure any thing from the country, unless we should follow the example of the enemy, and lay waste whole districts, in order to procure a scanty subsistence of unripe wheat for the troops.

It would answer no purpose to attempt to retaliate upon the enemy, even if it were practicable. The French armies in Spain have never had any secure communication beyond the ground which they occupy; and provided the enemy opposed to them is not too strong for them, they are indifferent in respect to the quarter from which their operations are directed, or on which side they carry them on.

The 'Armée de Portugal' has been surrounded for the last 6 weeks, and scarcely ever a letter reaches its commander; but the system of organised rapine and plunder, and the extraordinary discipline so long established in the French armies, enable it to subsist at the expense of the total ruin of the country in which it has been placed; and I am not certain that Marshal Marmont has not now at his command a greater quantity of provisions and supplies of every description than we have. Any movement upon his flank, therefore, would only tend to augment the embarrassments of our own situation, while it would have no effect whatever upon that of the enemy; even if such a movement could have been made with advantage as an operation purely military: this, however, was not the case, and when the French attempted to turn our right, I had the choice only of marching towards Salamanca, or of attacking the enemy in a position highly advantageous to him, which, for several reasons, I did not think expedient.

I have invariably been of opinion, that unless forced to fight a battle, it is better that one should not be fought by the allied army, unless under such favorable circumstances as that there would be reason to hope that the allied army would be able to maintain the field, while those of the enemy should not. Your Lordship will have seen by the returns of the 2 armies that we have no superiority of numbers, even over that single army immediately opposed to us; indeed, I believe that the French army is of the two the strongest; and it is certainly equipped with a profusion of artillery double ours in numbers, and of larger calibres. It cannot be attacked therefore in a chosen position, without considerable loss on our side.

To this circumstance, add that I am quite certain that Marshal Marmont's army is to be joined by the King's which will be 10,000 or 12,000 men, with a large proportion of cavalry, and that troops are still expected from the army of the North, and some are ordered from that of the South; and it will be seen that I ought to consider it almost impossible to remain in Castille after an action, the circumstances of which should not have been so advantageous as to have left the allied army in a situation of comparative strength, while that of the enemy should have been much weakened. I have therefore determined to cross the Tormes, if the enemy should; to cover Salamanca as long as I can; and above all, not to give up our communication with Ciudad Rodrigo; and not to fight an action, unless under very advantageous circumstances, or it should become absolutely necessary.

Since I wrote to your Lordship on the 14th, I have learnt that Gen. Drouet had not crossed the Guadiana, nor had he moved in that direction. Lieut. Gen. Sir R. Hill therefore still remains at Llerena.

The siege of Astorga continues. Gen. Santocildes had detached a division of 4000 infantry, under Gen. Cabrera, to Benavente. Gen. D'Urban, with the Portuguese cavalry, joined on the left of the allied army, on the 17th inst.

The enemy abandoned and destroyed the fort of Mirabete on the Tagus on the 11th inst., and the garrison marched to Madrid to form part of the army of the Centre. They were reduced to 5 days' provisions. From all that I have seen and heard, I am quite certain that the King is making every effort to collect a body of troops to oppose us.

P. S. I enclose a return of the killed and wounded on the 18th inst.

Return of the killed, wounded, and missing of the army near Castrejon, on the 18th July, 1812.

	Killed.	Wounded.	Missing.
British	61	297	27
Portuguese	34	96	27
Total ...	95	393	54

To Earl Bathurst.

Flores de Avila, 24th July, 1812.

My aide de camp, Capt. Lord Clinton, will present to your Lordship this account of a victory which the allied troops under my command gained in a general action, fought near Salamanca on the evening of the 22d inst., which I have been under the necessity of delaying to send till now, having been engaged ever since the action in the pursuit of the enemy's flying troops.

In my letter of the 21st, I informed your Lordship that both armies were near the Tormes; and the enemy crossed that river with the greatest part of his troops, in the afternoon, by the fords between Alba de Tormes and Huerta, and moved by their left towards the roads leading to Ciudad Rodrigo. The allied army, with the exception of the 3d division, and Gen. D'Urban's cavalry, likewise crossed the Tormes in the evening by the bridge of Salamanca and the fords in the neighbourhood; and I placed the troops in a position, of which the right was upon one of the two heights called Dos Arapiles, and the left on the Tormes, below the ford of Sta Marta. The 3d division, and Brig. Gen. D'Urban's cavalry, were left at Cabrerizos, on the right of the Tormes, as the enemy had still a large corps on the heights above Babila-fuente, on the same side of the river; and I considered it not improbable that, finding our army prepared for them in the morning on the left of the Tormes, they would alter their plan, and manœuvre by the other bank.

In the course of the night of the 21st, I received intelligence, of the truth of which I could not doubt, that Gen. Chauvel had arrived at Pollos on the 20th with the cavalry and horse artillery of the army of the North, to join Marshal Marmont; and I was quite certain that these troops would join him on the 22d or 23d at latest.

There was no time to be lost therefore; and I determined that, if circumstances should not permit me to attack him on the 22d, I would move towards Ciudad Rodrigo without further loss of time, as the difference of the numbers of cavalry might have made a march of manœuvre, such as we have had for the last 4 or 5 days, very difficult, and its result doubtful.

During the night of the 21st, the enemy had taken possession of the village of Calvarassa de Arriba, and of the heights near it called N. S. de la Peña, our cavalry being in possession of Calvarassa de Abaxo; and shortly after daylight, detachments from both armies attempted to obtain possession of the more distant from our right of the two hills called Dos Arapiles. The enemy,

however, succeeded; their detachments being the strongest, and
having been concealed in the woods nearer the hill than we were;
by which success they strengthened materially their own position, and had in their power increased means of annoying ours.

In the morning the light troops of the 7th division, and the
4th caçadores belonging to Gen. Pack's brigade, were engaged
with the enemy on the height called N. S. de la Peña, on which
height they maintained themselves with the enemy throughout
the day. The possession by the enemy, however, of the more
distant of the Arapiles rendered it necessary for me to extend
the right of the army *en potence* to the height behind the village
of Arapiles, and to occupy that village with light infantry; and
here I placed the 4th division, under the command of Lieut.
Gen. the Hon. L. Cole: and although, from the variety of the
enemy's movements, it was difficult to form a satisfactory judgment of his intentions, I considered that upon the whole his
objects were upon the left of the Tormes. I therefore ordered
Major Gen. the Hon. E. Pakenham, who commanded the 3d
division in the absence of Lieut. Gen. Picton, on account of ill
health, to move across the Tormes with the troops under his
command, including Brig. Gen. D'Urban's cavalry, and to place
himself behind Aldea Tejada; Brig. Gen. Bradford's brigade of
Portuguese infantry, and Don Carlos de España's infantry, having been moved up likewise to the neighbourhood of Las
Torres, between the 3d and 4th divisions.

After a variety of evolutions and movements, the enemy
appears to have determined upon his plan about 2 in the afternoon; and, under cover of a very heavy cannonade, which,
however, did us but very little damage, he extended his left, and
moved forward his troops, apparently with an intention to
embrace, by the position of his troops, and by his fire, our post
on that of the two Arapiles which we possessed, and from
thence to attack and break our line, or, at all events, to render
difficult any movement of ours to our right. The extension of
his line to his left, however, and its advance upon our right,
notwithstanding that his troops still occupied very strong
ground, and his position was well defended by cannon, gave
me an opportunity of attacking him, for which I had long been

anxious. I reinforced our right with the 5th division, under
Lieut. Gen. Leith, which I placed behind the village of Arapiles,
on the right of the 4th division, and with the 6th and 7th divisions in reserve; and as soon as these troops had taken their
station, I ordered Major Gen. the Hon. E. Pakenham to move
forward with the 3d division and Gen. D'Urban's cavalry, and
2 squadrons of the 14th light dragoons, under Lieut. Col.
Hervey, in 4 columns, to turn the enemy's left on the heights;
while Brig. Gen. Bradford's brigade, the 5th division, under Lieut.
Gen. Leith, the 4th division, under Lieut. Gen. the Hon. L. Cole,
and the cavalry under Lieut. Gen. Sir S. Cotton, should attack
them in front, supported in reserve by the 6th division, under
Major Gen. Clinton, the 7th, under Major Gen. Hope, and
Don Carlos de España's Spanish division; and Brig. Gen. Pack
should support the left of the 4th division, by attacking that of
the Dos Arapiles which the enemy held. The 1st and Light divisions occupied the ground on the left, and were in reserve.

The attack upon the enemy's left was made in the manner
above described, and completely succeeded. Major Gen. the
Hon. E. Pakenham formed the 3d division across the enemy's
flank, and overthrew every thing opposed to him. These troops
were supported in the most gallant style by the Portuguese cavalry, under Brig. Gen. D'Urban, and Lieut. Col. Hervey's
squadrons of the 14th, who successfully defeated every attempt
made by the enemy on the flank of the 3d division. Brig. Gen.
Bradford's brigade, the 5th and 4th divisions, and the cavalry
under Lieut. Gen. Sir S. Cotton, attacked the enemy in front,
and drove his troops before them from one height to another,
bringing forward their right, so as to acquire strength upon the
enemy's flank in proportion to the advance. Brig. Gen. Pack
made a very gallant attack upon the Arapiles, in which, however, he did not succeed, excepting in diverting the attention of
the enemy's corps placed upon it from the troops under the
command of Lieut. Gen. Cole in his advance. The cavalry
under Lieut. Gen. Sir S. Cotton made a most gallant and successful charge against a body of the enemy's infantry, which
they overthrew and cut to pieces. In this charge Major Gen. Le

Marchant was killed at the head of his brigade; and I have to regret the loss of a most able officer.

After the crest of the height was carried, one division of the enemy's infantry made a stand against the 4th division, which, after a severe contest, was obliged to give way, in consequence of the enemy having thrown some troops on the left of the 4th division, after the failure of Brig. Gen. Pack's attack upon the Arapiles, and Lieut. Gen. the Hon. L. Cole having been wounded. Marshal Sir W. Beresford, who happened to be on the spot, directed Brig. Gen. Spry's brigade of the 5th division, which was in the second line, to change its front, and to bring its fire on the flank of the enemy's division; and I am sorry to add that, while engaged in this service, he received a wound which I am apprehensive will deprive me of the benefit of his counsel and assistance for some time. Nearly about the same time Lieut. Gen. Leith received a wound which unfortunately obliged him to quit the field. I ordered up the 6th division, under Major Gen. Clinton, to relieve the 4th, and the battle was soon restored to its former success.

The enemy's right, however, reinforced by the troops which had fled from his left, and by those which had now retired from the Arapiles, still continued to resist; and I ordered the 1st and Light divisions, and Col. Stubbs' Portuguese brigade of the 4th division, which was reformed, and Major Gen. W. Anson's brigade, likewise of the 4th division, to turn the right, while the 6th division, supported by the 3d and 5th, attacked the front. It was dark before this point was carried by the 6th division; and the enemy fled through the woods towards the Tormes. I pursued them with the 1st and Light divisions, and Major Gen. W. Anson's brigade of the 4th division, and some squadrons of cavalry under Lieut. Gen. Sir S. Cotton, as long as we could find any of them together, directing our march upon Huerta and the fords of the Tormes, by which the enemy had passed on their advance; but the darkness of the night was highly advantageous to the enemy, many of whom escaped under its cover who must otherwise have been in our hands. I am sorry to report that, owing to this same cause, Lieut. Gen. Sir S. Cotton was unfortunately wounded by one of our own sentries after we had halted.

We renewed the pursuit at break of day in the morning with the same troops, and Major Gen. Bock's and Major Gen. Anson's brigades of cavalry, which joined during the night; and, having crossed the Tormes, we came up with the enemy's rear of cavalry and infantry near La Serna. They were immediately attacked by the 2 brigades of dragoons, and the cavalry fled, leaving the infantry to their fate. I have never witnessed a more gallant charge than was made on the enemy's infantry by the heavy brigade of the King's German Legion, under Major Gen. Bock, which was completely successful; and the whole body of infantry, consisting of 3 battalions of the enemy's 1st division, were made prisoners. The pursuit was afterwards continued as far as Peñaranda last night, and our troops were still following the flying enemy. Their head quarters were in this town, not less than 10 leagues from the field of battle, for a few hours last night; and they are now considerably advanced on the road towards Valladolid, by Arevalo. They were joined yesterday on their retreat by the cavalry and artillery of the army of the North, which have arrived at too late a period, it is to be hoped, to be of much use to them.

It is impossible to form a conjecture of the amount of the enemy's loss in this action; but, from all reports, it is very considerable. We have taken from them 11 pieces of cannon,* several ammunition waggons, 2 eagles, and 6 colors; and 1 General, 3 Colonels, 3 Lieut. Colonels, 130 officers of inferior rank, and between 6000 and 7000 soldiers are prisoners;† and our detachments are sending in more at every moment. The number of dead on the field is very large.

I am informed that Marshal Marmont is badly wounded,

---

*   The official returns only account for 11 pieces of cannon, but it is believed that 20 have fallen into our hands.
†   The prisoners are supposed to amount to 7000; but it has not been possible to ascertain their number exactly, from the advance of the army immediately after the action was over.

and has lost one of his arms; and that 4 General officers have been killed, and several wounded.

Such an advantage could not have been acquired without material loss on our side; but it certainly has not been of a magnitude to distress the army, or to cripple its operations.

I have great pleasure in reporting to your Lordship that, throughout this trying day, of which I have related the events, I had every reason to be satisfied with the conduct of the General officers and troops. The relation which I have written of its events will give a general idea of the share which each individual had in them; and I cannot say too much in praise of the conduct of every individual in his station.

I am much indebted to Marshal Sir W. Beresford for his friendly counsel and assistance, both previous to and during the action; to Lieut. Gens. Sir S. Cotton, Leith, and Cole, and Major Gens. Clinton, and the Hon. E. Pakenham, for the manner in which they led the divisions of cavalry and infantry under their command respectively; to Major Gen. Hulse, commanding a brigade in the 6th division; Major Gen. G. Anson, commanding a brigade of cavalry; Col. Hinde; Col. the Hon. W. Ponsonby, commanding Major Gen. Le Marchant's brigade after the fall of that officer; to Major Gen. W. Anson, commanding a brigade in the 4th division; Major Gen. Pringle, commanding a brigade in the 5th division, and the division after Lieut. Gen. Leith was wounded; Brig. Gen. Bradford; Brig. Gen. Spry; Col. Stubbs; and Brig. Gen. Power, of the Portuguese service; likewise to Lieut. Col. Campbell of the 94th, commanding a brigade in the 3d division; Lieut. Col. Williams of the 60th foot; Lieut. Col. Wallace of the 88th, commanding a brigade in the 3d division; Lieut. Col. Ellis of the 23d, commanding Major Gen. the Hon. E. Pakenham's brigade in the 4th division, during his absence in the command of the 3d division; Lieut. Col. the Hon. C. Greville of the 38th regt., commanding Major Gen. Hay's Brigade in the 5th division, during his absence on leave; Brig. Gen. Pack; Brig. Gen. the Conde de Rezende of the Portuguese service; Col. Douglas of the 8th Portuguese regt.; Lieut. Col. the Conde de Ficalho of the same regiment; and Lieut. Col. Bingham of the 53d regt.; likewise to Brig. Gen. D'Urban and

Lieut. Col. Hervey of the 14th light dragoons; Col. Lord E. Somerset, commanding the 4th dragoons; and Lieut. Col. the Hon. F. Ponsonby, commanding the 12th light dragoons. I must also mention Lieut. Col. Woodford, commanding the light battalion of the brigade of Guards, who, supported by 2 companies of the Fusiliers, under the command of Capt. Crowder, maintained the village of Arapiles against all the efforts of the enemy, previous to the attack upon their position by our troops.

In a case in which the conduct of all has been conspicuously good, I regret that the necessary limits of a dispatch prevent me from drawing your Lordship's notice to the conduct of a larger number of individuals; but I can assure your Lordship that there was no officer or corps engaged in this action who did not perform his duty by his Sovereign and his country.

The Royal and German Artillery, under Lieut. Col. Framingham, distinguished themselves by the accuracy of their fire wherever it was possible to use them; and they advanced to the attack of the enemy's position with the same gallantry as the other troops.

I am particularly indebted to Lieut. Col. De Lancey, the D. Q. M. G., the head of the department present, in the absence of the Q. M. G., and to the officers of that department and of the Staff corps, for the assistance I received from them, particularly Lieut. Col. the Hon. L. Dundas and Lieut. Col. Sturgeon of the latter, and Major Scovell of the former; and to Lieut. Col. Waters, at present at the head of the Adj. Gen.'s department at head quarters; and to the officers of that department, as well at head quarters as with the several divisions of the army; and Lieut. Col. Lord FitzRoy Somerset, and the officers of my personal Staff. Among the latter I particularly request your Lordship to draw the attention of H. R. H. the Prince Regent to H. S. H. the Hereditary Prince of Orange, whose conduct in the field, as well as upon every other occasion, entitles him to my highest commendation, and has acquired for him the respect and regard of the whole army.

I have had every reason to be satisfied with the conduct of the Mariscal de Campo Don Carlos de España, and of Brig. Don Julian Sanchez, and with that of the troops under their command respectively; and with that of the Mariscal de Campo Don M. de Alava, and of Brig. Don José O'Lawlor, employed with this army by the Spanish government, from whom, and from the Spanish authorities and people in general, I received every assistance I could expect.

It is but justice likewise to draw your Lordship's attention upon this occasion to the merits of the officers of the civil departments of the army. Notwithstanding the increased distance of our operations from our magazines, and that the country is completely exhausted, we have hitherto wanted nothing, owing to the diligence and attention of the Commissary Gen., Mr Bissett, and the officers of the department under his direction. I have likewise to mention that, by the attention and ability of Dr M'Grigor, and of the officers of the department under his charge, our wounded, as well as those of the enemy, left in our hands, have been well taken care of; and I hope that many of these valuable men will be saved to the service.

Capt. Lord Clinton will have the honor of laying at the feet of H. R. H. the Prince Regent the eagles and colors taken from the enemy in this action. I enclose a return of the killed and wounded.

By letters received from Lieut. Col. Sir H. Douglas, I learn that Gen. Santocildes had left 8000 men to carry on the siege of Astorga, and had joined Gen. Cabrera's division at Benavente with about 3000; and that the whole 7000 were on their march along the Esla towards the Duero.

Return of killed, wounded, and missing, of the allied army, in the battle near Salamanca, on the 22d July, 1812.

	Officers.	Serjeants.	R and F.	Horses.	Total.	British.	Portuguese.	Spanish.
Killed	41	28	625	114	694	388	304	2
Wounded	252	178	3840	133	4270	2714	1552	4
Missing	1	1	254	44	256	74	182	–

To Earl Bathurst.

Flores de Avila, 24th July, 1812.

I hope that you will be pleased with our battle, of which the dispatch contains as accurate an account as I can give you. There was no mistake; every thing went on as it ought; and there never was an army so beaten in so short a time. If we had had another hour or two of daylight, not a man would have passed the Tormes; and as it was, they would all have been taken, if Don Carlos de España had left the garrison in Alba de Tormes as I wished and desired; or, having taken it away, as I believe before he was aware of my wishes, he had informed me that it was not there. If he had, I should have marched in the night upon Alba, where I should have caught them all, instead of upon the fords of the Tormes. But this is a little misfortune, which does not diminish the honor acquired by the troops in the action, nor, I hope, the advantage to be derived from it by the country; as I don't believe there are many soldiers who were in that action who are likely to face us again till they shall be very largely reinforced indeed.

I am very anxious that a mark of His Royal Highness' favor should be conferred upon Sir S. Cotton. I believe he would be much gratified at receiving the Red Riband. No cavalry could act better than ours did in the action; and I must say for Sir Stapleton, that I don't know where we should find an officer that would command our cavalry in this country half so well as he does.

I request your Lordship to send us out remount horses for the cavalry and the artillery. These daily marches, skirmishes, battles, &c., consume an immense number of them; and we can get none here to suit our purpose for either artillery or cavalry. Marmont has now had a reinforcement of not less than 2000 cavalry since I came to Salamanca in June. I hope that we have deprived him of a few hundreds of them; and that, at all events, his late reinforcement does not make him now more than 500 or 600 more than he was when he last crossed the Duero. But the loss has fallen principally upon the French infantry; and our cavalry must be kept up, or we cannot stay in the plains. I should wish also to be able to equip some more artillery, and of a larger calibre; as it is not agreeable to be cannonaded for hours together, and not be able to answer even with one gun.

I see that the King is very anxious to collect every thing against us. I think the French could not now remain in Andalusia, probably not south of the Duero, if the Anglo-Sicilian army had appeared upon the eastern coast.

Marmont has lost his arm,* Gens. Foy, Clausel, Bonet, and Ferey, are wounded; Gen. Thomière is killed. These are five of 8 Generals of division. There are, besides, a great number of Generals of brigade killed or wounded. Gen. Curto is missing, and I believe is prisoner. How they get on their troops at such a rate, I can't conceive; but they left this about 2 this morning, and they will arrive in Valladolid to-morrow. I will answer your letter of the — , which I have received, by the next post.

To Lieut. Gen. Sir T. Graham, K. B.

Flores de Avila, 25th July, 1812.

I can't allow the dispatches to go off without writing you a few lines respecting our action of the 22d. You will see our previous movements detailed in my dispatch of the 21st, and that of yesterday.

I took up the ground which you were to have taken during the siege of Salamanca, only the left was thrown back on the heights, it being unnecessary, under the circumstances, to cover the ford of Sta Marta. We had a race for the large Arapiles, which is the more distant of the two detached heights which you will recollect on the right of your position: this race the French won, and they were too strong to be dislodged without a general action.

I knew that the French were to be joined by the cavalry of the army of the North on the 22d or 23d, and that the army of

---

*   This proved to be incorrect.

the Centre was likely to be in motion. Marmont ought to have given me a *pont d'or*, and he would have made a handsome operation of it. But instead of that, after manœuvring all the morning in the usual French style, nobody knew with what object, he at last pressed upon my right in such a manner, at the same time without engaging, that he would have either carried our Arapiles, or he would have confined us entirely to our position. This was not to be endured, and we fell upon him, turning his left flank; and I never saw an army receive such a beating.

I had desired the Spaniards to continue to occupy the castle of Alba de Tormes. Don Carlos de España had evacuated it, I believe, before he knew my wishes; and he was afraid to let me know that he had done so; and I did not know it till I found no enemy at the fords of the Tormes. When I lost sight of them in the dark, I marched upon Huerta and Encinas, and they went by Alba. If I had known there had been no garrison in Alba, I should have marched there, and should probably have had the whole.

Marmont, Clausel, Foy, Ferey, and Bonet, are wounded badly. Ferey, it is supposed, will die. Thomière is killed. Many Generals of brigade killed or wounded.

I am in hopes that our loss has not been great. In 2 divisions, the 3d and 5th, it is about 1200 men, including Portuguese. There are more in the 4th and 6th; but there are many men who left the ranks with wounded officers and soldiers, who are eating and drinking, and engaged in *regocijos* with the inhabitants of Salamanca; I have sent, however, to have them all turned out of the town.

I need not express how much I regret the disorder in your eyes since this action. I hope that you receive benefit from the advice of the oculists in London.

P. S. Beresford's wound is not dangerous. Leith's arm is broken, and his wound painful. Cole's wound is through the body, and it is apprehended will be tedious. Cotton's is through the fleshy part, and the two bones of his arm: it may be a bad wound, if there should be hæmorrhage.

To Earl Bathurst.

Olmedo, 28th July, 1812.

The army have continued their march in pursuit of the enemy since I addressed you on the 24th inst., and we have continued to take many prisoners.

A part of the enemy's army crossed the Duero yesterday, near Puente de Duero, and the remainder, their left wing, were in march towards the bridge of Tudela this morning at 9 o'clock, when I last heard from our advanced posts.

The main body of the allied army is this day on the Adaja and Zapardiel rivers, in this neighbourhood, the light cavalry being in front in pursuit of the enemy.

I have requested Gen. Santocildes, who is upon the Esla with 8000 men of the army of Galicia, to move forward to the heights of San Roman on this side of Toro, and to communicate with our left by the fords of Castro Nuño.

It appears that the King left Madrid on the 21st, with the army of the Centre, supposed to consist of from 10,000 to 12,000 infantry, and from 2000 to 3000 cavalry; and he directed his march by the Escurial upon Alba de Tormes. He arrived at Blasco Sancho, between Avila and Arevalo, on the 25th, where he heard of the defeat of Marshal Marmont; and he retired in the evening; and between that time and the evening of the 26th he marched through Villa Castin to Espinar. A non-commissioned officer's patrole of the 14th Light dragoons and 1st hussars, from Arevalo, took in Blasco Sancho, on the evening of the 25th, shortly after the King had left the place, 2 officers and 27 men of the King's cavalry, who had been left there to follow his rear guard. I have reason to believe that the King had no regular account of the action of the 22d till he passed the Puerto de Guadarrama yesterday; but he then returned, and was directing his march upon Segovia. I have not yet heard how far he had advanced. All accounts concur in regard to the great loss sustained by the '*Armée de Portugal*';

but I think it probable that they will endeavor to join the King on the Upper Duero, if the King should continue on this side of the mountains, unless I should previously have it in my power to strike a blow against his corps.

By accounts from Lieut. Gen. Sir R. Hill to the 24th inst., it appears that the enemy had in some degree reinforced the troops in Estremadura. The Lieut. General had removed to Zafra, as being the coolest and most healthy situation in Estremadura, and preparatory to the detachment which I ordered him to make to the right of the Tagus, in case the enemy should detach in that direction. It is reported that Gen. Ballesteros had marched on another expedition towards Malaga, and that he was opposed by a division of the army of the South, under Gen. Leval.

I have not received detailed accounts of Commodore Sir H. Popham's operations on the coast since the capture of Lequeitio, but I understand that he has taken Castro Urdiales; and there is no doubt that those operations have drawn the enemy's attention to that quarter, and that Gen. Caffarelli has been able to detach only cavalry to the assistance of the '*Armée de Portugal*'. From the advantage derived from these operations, your Lordship will form a judgment of that which would have been derived, under existing circumstances, from the expedition which had been concerted and agreed upon to the Eastern coast of the Peninsula, with the troops from Sicily, combined with the Spanish troops in Majorca and at Alicante.

I enclose a statement which I have made out from a return in my possession of the strength of the army of Aragon in the month of April, from which your Lordship will see that, after allowing for the divisions detached to the army of the North, under Gen. Palombini, which was destined to join Marshal Marmont, there will still remain a very formidable army under Marshal Suchet, which it is desirable should not be added to the other troops acting against this army.

To Earl Bathurst.

Cuellar, 4th Aug. 1812.

The French army of the Centre, after having passed through the Guadarrama pass, and after its head had arrived at the Venta de San Rafael, returned to Segovia, where King Joseph arrived on the 27th July at night. The object of this movement was apparently to divert the allied troops from the pursuit of the '*Armée de Portugal*', and to enable the latter to maintain themselves upon the Duero, in which, however, the enemy did not succeed. Their rear guard remained in some strength on the left of the Duero during the 28th and 29th; but the Light and 1st divisions, and the cavalry, having crossed the Eresma and Cegar rivers on the latter day, the enemy's rear guard retired during the night across the Duero, and thence followed the movements of the main body towards Villavañez, abandoning Valladolid, and leaving there 17 pieces of cannon, a large quantity of shot and shells, and other stores, and the hospital, with about 800 sick and wounded.

The guerrilla chief, Marquiñez, took 300 prisoners in the neighbourhood of Valladolid on the 30th. Our advanced guard crossed the Duero, and our parties entered Valladolid on the same day; and I had the satisfaction of being received by the people in that city with the same enthusiastic joy as I had been in all other parts of the country.

The '*Armée de Portugal*' having thus crossed and quitted the Duero, it was necessary to attend to the movements of the army of the Centre, and to prevent a junction between the two on the Upper Duero, which it was reported was intended. While therefore the advanced guard and left continued the pursuit of the '*Armée de Portugal*', I moved the right along the Cegar to Cuellar, where I arrived on the 1st inst.

The King retired from Segovia on the evening of the 1st, and marched through the Guadarrama; and he left at Segovia an advanced guard, principally of cavalry, under Gen. Espert, having destroyed the cannon and ammunition which were in the castle; having carried off the church plate and other valuable property, and having levied a considerable contribution on the inhabitants of the town. I have not yet heard whether a detachment which I sent to Segovia yesterday, under Brig. Gen. D'Urban, had entered that town. The '*Armée de Portugal*' have continued their retreat towards Burgos.

The siege of Astorga is not yet brought to a conclusion; but upon finding that the King had returned from La Venta de San Rafael on the 27th July, I requested Gen. Santocildes to come nearer to this army, and to cross the Duero with that part of his corps which had approached that river, and he is now at La Nava del Rey; but he is about to return to the right of that river, and he will place himself near the fords of Pollos and Herreros, and communicate with our left.

The enemy have continued to increase their force in Estremadura, and had moved about the 27th or 28th towards the Guadiana, and threatened a force which I had requested Lieut. Gen. Sir R. Hill to place at Merida, with a view to its march to the right of the Tagus, in case the enemy's long-threatened detachment should move in this direction. But Lieut. Gen. Sir R. Hill having moved from Zafra to Villa Franca, the enemy retired again into La Serena.

I enclose Lieut. Gen. Sir R. Hill's report of a very handsome affair with the enemy's cavalry on the 24th July, by the division of cavalry under the command of Lieut. Gen Sir W. Erskine.

By accounts from Cadiz of the 24th July, I learn that Gen. Ballesteros having moved towards Malaga, some apprehensions were entertained that he was cut off from San Roque and Gibraltar, by the rapid movements of Gen. Villatte's division from the blockade of Cadiz to the neighbourhood of Los Barrios; and it appears that Gen. Leval, with another division, was between Gen. Ballesteros and Malaga.

There had been no accounts from Gibraltar of a later date than the 21st, at which time it appears to me that it was not practicable for Gen. Ballesteros to retire to Gibraltar; but I trust that, finding that to be impracticable, he will at once have taken his line of retreat upon the kingdom of Murcia.

To Earl Bathurst.

Madrid, 13th Aug. 1812.

Having found that the army under Marshal Marmont continued their retreat upon Burgos, in a state not likely to be able to take the field again for some time; and knowing that I could not quit the river Duero in pursuit of them at the present moment, without incurring great inconvenience, and exposing the rear and communications of the army to the operations of the army of the Centre, under the King, I determined to move upon that army, and to endeavor to bring the King to a general action, or to force him to quit Madrid.

Accordingly I moved from Cuellar on the 6th inst., leaving there the 6th division, and the regiments which had lately joined the army from England and Gibraltar, and which were in a state of health not to be able to bear the march, and Major Gen. Anson's brigade of cavalry on the Duero, to observe the movements of the 'Armée de Portugal.' These troops were put in communication with Gen. Santocildes' division of the army of Galicia, likewise on the Duero, near the fords of Pollos and Herreros; and the parties of guerrillas under Marquiñez, Principe, and Saornil, were attached to Major Gen. Anson and Gen. Santocildes, and objects fixed for their attention. We arrived at Segovia on the 7th, and at San Ildefonso on the 8th, where I halted one day, to allow the right of the army more time to come up.

No opposition was made to the passage of the troops through the mountains; and Brig. Gen. D'Urban, with the Portuguese cavalry, the 1st light battalion of the K. G. L., and Capt. Macdonald's troop of horse artillery, had been through the Guadarrama pass since the 9th. He moved forward on the morning of the 11th, from the neighbourhood of Galapagar, and, supported by the heavy cavalry of the K. G. L. from Torre Lodones, he drove in the French cavalry, about 2000 in number, and placed himself at Majadahonda, with the Portuguese cavalry, and Capt. Macdonald's troop, and the cavalry and light infantry of the K. G. L. at Las Rozas, about three quarters of a mile distant.

The enemy's cavalry which had been driven off in the morning, and had moved towards Navalcarnero, returned about 5 in the afternoon; and Brig. Gen. D'Urban having formed the Portuguese cavalry in front of Majadahonda, supported by the horse artillery, ordered the cavalry to charge the enemy's leading squadrons, which appeared too far advanced to be supported by their main body. The Portuguese cavalry advanced to the attack, but unfortunately turned about before they reached the enemy; and they fled through the village of Majadahonda, and back upon the German dragoons, leaving behind them unprotected and unsupported the guns of Capt. Macdonald's troop, which had been moved forward to co-operate with the cavalry. By the activity of the officers and soldiers of Capt. Macdonald's troop, the guns were, however, moved off; but owing to the unfavorable nature of the ground over which they were moved, the carriage of one was broken, and 2 others were overturned, and these 3 guns fell into the enemy's hands.

The Portuguese dragoons having fled through Majadahonda, were rallied and re-formed, when the heavy dragoons of the K. G. L., which were formed between that village and Las Rozas, and the German cavalry, charged the enemy, although under many disadvantages, and stopped their further progress; but I am sorry to say that they suffered considerable loss, and that Col. de Jonquières, who commanded the brigade, was taken prisoner.

The left of the army was about 2½ miles distant, at the Puente del Retamar, on the Guadarrama river; and Col. Ponsonby's brigade of cavalry and a brigade of infantry of the 7th division having moved forward to the support of the troops in advance, the enemy retired upon Majadahonda as soon as they observed these troops, and night having come on they retired upon Alcorcon, leaving our guns at Majadahonda.

I have reason to believe, both from the manner in which the enemy came on to the attack of the Portuguese troops, and from other circumstances, that they had been informed that we had none but Portuguese dragoons in front, and that there were no troops in the neighbourhood to support them. The occurrences of the 22d July had induced me to hope that the Portuguese dragoons would have conducted themselves better, or I should not have placed them at the outposts of the army. But every day's experience shows that no reliance can be placed on cavalry which is not in a perfect state of discipline, and of which the men don't feel a perfect confidence in the officers. I shall therefore not place them again at the outposts, or in situations in which by their misconduct they can influence the safety of the other troops.

I am happy to report that the officers of the Portuguese cavalry behaved remarkably well, and showed a good example to their men, particularly the Visconde de Barbacena, who was taken prisoner. The conduct of the brave German cavalry was, I understand, excellent, as well as that of Capt. Macdonald's troop of horse artillery. The light infantry battalion were not engaged.

The army moved forward yesterday morning, and its left took possession of the city of Madrid, the King having retired with the army of the Centre by the roads of Toledo and Aranjuez, leaving a garrison in the Retiro.

It is impossible to describe the joy manifested by the inhabitants of Madrid upon our arrival, and I hope that the prevalence of the same sentiments of detestation of the French yoke, and of a strong desire to secure the independence of their country, which first induced them to set the example of resistance to the usurper, will induce them again to make exertions in the cause of their country, which, being more wisely directed, will be more efficacious than those formerly made.

The heavy guns, with the aid of which we took Salamanca, are in the rear of the army, and I hope that we shall not find it difficult to take the Retiro. But I believe that we must break ground before the place.

I have not yet heard that Astorga has fallen; but the garrison which the enemy left in Tordesillas, about 260 in number, surrendered to Gen. Santocildes on the 5th inst.

I have received no further reports of the situation of Gen. Ballesteros since the 21st July.

I have letters from Gen. J. O'Donell and Gen. Roche of the 26th July; and the army of Murcia, under the command of the former, was defeated by Gen. Harispe on the 21st July. It appears that the Spanish troops moved forward to attack Gen. Harispe's posts at Castalla and at Ybi. Those which attacked the former were repulsed with the loss of 2000 men and 2 pieces of cannon. Those which attacked the latter, under the command of Gen. Roche, conducted themselves remarkably well, and covered the retreat of the troops under Gen. O'Donell, and afterwards effected their own retreat in good order to Alicante.

I have not heard from Gen. Maitland since the 18th July.

There had been no movement of importance in Estremadura as late as the 9th inst.

Return of the killed, wounded, and missing, in the affair at Majadahonda, on the 11th Aug. 1812.

	King's German Legion and Royal Horse Artillery.				Portuguese.			
	Officers.	Serjeants.	R. and F.	Horses.	Officers.	Serjeants.	R. and F.	Horses.
Killed	1	1	18	12	3	—	30	11
Wounded	5	5	36	12	3	—	49	5
Missing	1	—	20	44	1	1	21	37

To Earl Bathurst.

Madrid, 18th Aug. 1812.

I have received your letter of the 23d July, in which you have enclosed statements of the bills drawn on the Treasury from this country between the 1st Jan. and the 4th July, upon which I beg to assure you that they afford no evidence of the quantity of specie which has gone through the military chest in that period.

The Commissary Gen. is very unwell; but I hope by the next post to let you know the exact amount which we have received in money.

The whole sum of £410,000, drawn by Commissary O'Meara, is for provisions and supplies for the troops at Cadiz; and the sum of £386,000, drawn by Mr Mackenzie at Oporto, is for the same. The whole of the drafts of Mr Duff is for money, more than half of which is spent at Cadiz &c.; Mr Pipon's drafts are generally for supplies of provisions purchased from the Americans, &c., and a very small proportion for money; but you shall know exactly how this matter stands.

In the mean time, whatever may be the sums for which we have drawn, we are in the greatest distress, which is certainly at present occasioned in some degree by our distance from Lisbon, and the difficulty of carrying the money to the army. I have been able to pay the troops only half of their pay for the month of April, the Staff only for February; and I did that by applying to our own service the money sent by my brother for Spanish services.

I am sorry to say that I have reports that the sick and wounded officers at Salamanca have been obliged to sell their clothes to get money.

The want of money in the army is become a most serious evil; and we may trace to this want many of the acts of plunder and indiscipline by which we are disgraced every day. We must be regularly supplied, or we cannot go on.

More has been done by government lately than had been done for many months, I may almost say years, before; but I think that government have been wrong in employing the Bank to make their purchase of bullion to supply this army. My opinion has invariably been, that if a small sum, even £100,000, were sent out every month, it would enable us to manage the exchanges, and to obtain our money at a cheaper rate. I can never believe that inconvenience would be felt in England by the export in coin of £100,000 every month; but the fact is, that government go to the Bank to procure the coin, instead of employing their agents to purchase it as the dealers in coin do; and the Directors of the Bank, having upon their shoulders the supply of the coin for the interior circulation, as well as the supply of the wants of government for the service abroad, act like all other men; they supply that demand which is made with most noise and clamour, and our distant whispers are unattended to. Thus, when the China fleet arrived lately with a sum of money, the Bank took the whole that I believe appeared on the manifest for the interior circulation, and did not give us even a shilling; and we get the gleanings.

I am quite convinced that if government were to employ an agent to purchase £100,000 every month, the circulation in England would not feel the drain, and we should be very much relieved, and the exchanges would be much improved. We must, however, prevent Lord W. Bentinck from coming to Gibraltar and carrying off four millions of dollars at 6s. 8d. each, while we give from 5s. 4d. to 5s. 8d.

You will see how we stand by the report in my dispatch. I think that the French mean to carry off the garrisons from Zamora and Toro, which I hope they will effect, as otherwise I must go and take them. If I don't, nobody else will, as is obvious from what has been passing for the last 2 months at Astorga. My wish is now to canton the army for 2 or 3 weeks, till the rains in September, and then to march into Andalusia with part of it, and Hill's corps, so as to be certain that Soult will go out.

Any other but a modern French army would now leave the province, as they have absolutely no communication of any kind with France, or with any other French army; and they are pressed on all sides by troops not to be despised, and they can evidently do nothing. But I suspect that Soult will not stir till I force him out by a direct movement upon him; and I think of making that movement as soon as I can take the troops to the south without incurring the risk of injuring their health. In the mean time I must have possession of the whole course of the Duero, and I may then venture to leave in this part of the country a large detachment of our army, and the Galician army, which I hope I shall get Beresford to command. I am not so certain of this, however, as he is still confined by his wound.

I don't expect much from the exertions of the Spaniards, notwithstanding all that we have done for them. They cry *viva*, and are very fond of us, and hate the French; but they are, in general, the most incapable of useful exertion of all the nations that I have known; the most vain, and at the same time the most ignorant, particularly of military affairs, and above all of military affairs in their own country. I can do nothing till Gen. Castaños shall arrive, and I don't know where he is. I am afraid that the utmost we can hope for is, to teach them how to avoid being beat. If we can effect that object, I hope we might do the rest. My opinion is, that the government and Cortes should come to Ciudad Rodrigo, or the frontiers of Galicia, which I think of proposing to them; but I must wait till I see Castaños.

To the Rt. Hon. Sir H. Wellesley, K. B.

Madrid, 23d Aug. 1812.

Since I wrote to you on the 18th respecting the appointment of Señor [Lozano de Torres] to be Intendant of Salamanca, I find that official notification of that gentleman's appointment has been received, which, however, I hope will be cancelled as soon as you shall have received my letter. Alava and O'Lawlor (particularly the latter) know the reason which I have to complain of this person, and both have made representations against the appointment.

So much depends upon the regular supply of our armies, that I hope the Spanish government will take care to avoid making themselves so far responsible for this important object, as to dismiss from the office of Intendant of Castille a man who has hitherto given the greatest satisfaction; and to place in it one entirely inefficient, one who before was a very efficient cause of our withdrawing from the Spanish territory, and whom I was obliged to turn out of my house.

I don't at all like the way in which we are going on, particularly in relation to appointments to offices and great situations, in which branch of the government alone it is, I am afraid, in the power of the existing Regency to do much good.

They have sent an inefficient person, a [Marquess del Palacio] to command in Estremadura, displacing Monsalud, with whom we have all hitherto gone on well. Another equally inefficient, and without character, Gen. [Gallegos], has been sent to supersede Don Carlos in Old Castille; and I learn that they have appointed a Gen. [Orcasitas] to command in New Castille, in which situation is included that of Governor of Madrid, which is at present by far the most important post in the country, with duties to be performed which require activity and intelligence; and yet the person selected to fill this office is, I understand, an idiot, of between 70 and 80 years of age. I assure you that I don't at all like the way in which we are going on, and persons here are much dissatisfied with the neglect of them by the government.

A month has now elapsed since the battle of Salamanca, and I have not even heard of Gen. Castaños.

Excepting in this town, where there was no regular authority when I entered it, and when I forced them to proclaim the constitution, and proceed to the elections immediately, these ceremonies have been, as usual, unaccountably delayed; and at Valladolid, Santocildes contrived to delay them till the French came in, and there the constitution has never been proclaimed at all, and the town is still governed by the French authorities.

I am afraid also that, owing to the usual delays, the French found there their artillery and stores, and, what is particularly to be lamented, their muskets, of which they were much in want, as, even of those who were not wounded in the battle, the greater number threw away their arms afterwards, or during the retreat.

What can be done for this lost nation? As for raising men or supplies, or taking any one measure to enable them to carry on the war, that is out of the question. Indeed, there is nobody to excite them to exertion, or to take advantage of the enthusiasm of the people, or of their enmity against the French. Even the guerrillas are getting quietly into the large towns, and amusing themselves, or collecting plunder of a better and more valuable description; and nobody looks forward to the exertions to be made, whether to improve or to secure our advantage.

This is a faithful picture of the state of affairs; and though I still hope to be able to maintain our position in Castille, and even to improve our advantages, I shudder when I reflect upon the enormity of the task which I have undertaken, with inadequate powers myself to do any thing, and without assistance of any kind from the Spaniards, or I may say, from any individual of the Spanish nation.

I enclose the copy of a letter from Sir H. Douglas of the 18th, and the copy of intelligence from Salamanca of the 20th, which will show you how Spanish military affairs are going on.

I hope the French will carry off the garrisons of Zamora and Astorga, as well as that of Toro. Any thing is better than that I should have to attack and carry those places; but I am repairing my heavy train for that object, and my troops are in march in that direction; and I must go if the French should maintain their garrisons. But whether I go, or the French should withdraw these garrisons, what will the world say? What will the Spanish nation in particular say of the Spanish officers and army upon such occurrences as the failure to take such a place as Astorga, after nearly 3 months' siege, and of allowing the garrison of Zamora to be relieved and carried off by a defeated army? At the same time I am so well aware of the inefficiency of the Spanish officers and troops when alone, that I recommended the measures which will enable the enemy to relieve Zamora: that is, foreseeing that the French would endeavor to relieve or carry off the garrison of Astorga as soon as they should hear that I had marched towards Madrid, I recommended that Santocildes should take care to be first upon the Esla; but if I had conceived 8000 Spanish to be equal to 4000 men of any other nation, I should have recommended him to maintain the blockade of Zamora, and to cover the siege of Astorga.

Pray request Gen. O'Donell to peruse the account of the transactions at the head quarters of the army of Galicia, given by Sir H. Douglas. Can any army carry on operations against the French under such circumstances? I have a great regard for

Gen. [Castanos]; but I should like to know what military part
he plays in this drama. If he is a Commander in Chief, why
does he not put himself at the head of his troops? The army of
Galicia is the only one in Spain, and the 8000 men under Santocildes the active part of that army. Why is not the Commander
in Chief with that part? These are questions which must occur
to every reflecting mind; but there is no inquiry in Spain on
subjects of this description.

I am apprehensive that all this will turn out but ill for the
Spanish cause. If, for any cause, I should be overpowered, or
should be obliged to retire, what will the world say? What
will the people of England say? What will those in Spain say?
That we had made a great effort, attended by some glorious
circumstances; and that from Jan. 1812, we had gained more
advantages for the cause, and had acquired more extent of territory by our operations, than had ever been gained by any
army in the same period of time, against so powerful an enemy;
but that, being unaided by the Spanish officers and troops, not
from disinclination, but from inability on account of the gross
ignorance of the former, and the want of discipline of the latter,
and from the inefficiency of all the persons selected by the government for great employment, we were at last overpowered,
and compelled to withdraw within our own frontier.

What will be Lord Castlereagh's reply to the next proposition for peace? Not that we will not treat if the government of
Joseph is to be the guaranteed government, but he will be too
happy to avail himself of any opportunity of withdrawing with
honor from a contest in which it will be manifest that, owing to
the inability of those employed to carry it on on the part of the
Spaniards, there is no prospect of military success. Thus this
great cause will be lost, and this nation will be enslaved for the
want of men at their head capable of conducting them.

Pray represent these matters to the government and the leading men in the Cortes, and draw their attention seriously to the
situation of their affairs.

I have a letter from Gen. Maitland of the 17th. He was at
Monforte, Roche at Alcoy, O'Donell at Yecla; and Suchet at
San Felipe, it is supposed about to cross the Jucar. Maitland

says that Soult is certainly about to retire, and he says through Valencia. I don't know how he has discovered either one or the other fact. I have later intelligence from Andalusia, and I don't believe Soult will retire till I go there.

I have not heard of the King for 2 or 3 days. He was near Belmonte when I heard last.

To Earl Bathurst.

Madrid, 30th Aug. 1812.

According to accounts which I have received from Gen. J. O'Donell, commanding the Spanish army of Murcia, of the 25th and 27th inst., I learn that the King had decidedly marched into Valencia. His troops passed the castle of Chinchilla (the garrison of which fired upon them), and they arrived at Bonete on the 24th. The cavalry under Gen. O'Donell, 1500 in number, were at Albacete on the 25th, and the General himself, still at Hellin on the 27th, and his infantry, 4000 in number, were in that neighbourhood.

It appears, that upon hearing of the King's approach to the kingdom of Valencia to join Suchet, Lieut. Gen. Maitland had determined to retire eventually upon Alicante, with the Sicilian division under his command, and the Spanish troops under Gens. Whittingham and Roche. He had advanced as far as Elda; but he retired to Monforte, from whence he writes on the 20th; Gen. Whittingham's division being still at Elda, and the Spanish cavalry advanced to Castalla. I have directed the General to maintain himself at Alicante; and I have ordered that he may be supplied with provisions.

Gen. Maitland's determination to retire upon Alicante, and his stating that he has a sufficient number of men to maintain himself there without the assistance of Gen. O'Donell's corps, and the reports which Gen. O'Donell had received of the intention of Soult to join the King's army in Valencia, through Murcia and Granada, and the prevalence of the yellow fever in

Murcia, had induced Gen. O'Donell to move to the northward, and I have suggested to him to put himself in communication with the allied army in this quarter.

Since I wrote to your Lordship on the 25th inst., I have received reports that the garrison of Astorga had surrendered by capitulation on the 19th, to the number of 1200 men. Gen. Foy arrived at La Bañeza for their relief on the 21st, with the detachment which I informed you was in march for that purpose; and his parties found the place abandoned by the Spanish troops, the French garrison having been carried away as prisoners; and I expect that he arrived at Zamora on the 25th or 26th.

As soon as the King's march into Valencia was decided, I ordered the 1st and 5th divisions, Gen. Pack's and Gen. Bradford's brigades, and Col. Ponsonby's brigade of cavalry, to assemble at Arevalo, to which place the 6th division had been marched also by Gen. Clinton by mistake; and I propose to join these troops, and to proceed to establish a secure communication between this army and the army of Galicia; and to drive off the parties of the '*Armée de Portugal*' which have come forward to the Duero since I have been obliged to attend to the state of affairs in this quarter.

The reports still continue to prevail of the intention of Soult to evacuate Andalusia, and I enclose a paper which is a translation of the order issued to the army of the South on the 15th inst., the Emperor's birth-day, from which there is reason to believe that such a design is entertained; and Gen. O'Donell tells me in his letter of the 27th from Hellin, that he has reason to believe that the march will be by Granada and Murcia. Lieut. Gen. Sir R. Hill had no intelligence that the march was commenced on the 23d inst., when I last heard from him; but there was every appearance of it; and it is reported that Gen. La Cruz's troops were in possession of San Lucar la Mayor, and even of San Lucar at the mouth of the Guadalquivir. If these reports should be well founded, the siege of Cadiz is certainly abandoned.

I propose to return to this part of the country, as soon as I shall have settled matters to my satisfaction on the right of the Duero; and I hope I shall be here, and shall be joined by the troops under Sir R. Hill, before Soult can have made much progress to form his junction with the King.

With a view to Sir R. Hill's march, we are employed in repairing the bridge at Almaraz.

To Earl Bathurst.

Valladolid, 7th Sept. 1812.

I quitted Madrid on the 1st inst., in order to direct the movements of the troops ordered to be collected at Arevalo, as reported in my dispatch of the 30th Aug.; to which I subsequently added the 7th division of infantry, and Major Gen. Bock's brigade of dragoons.

We moved from Arevalo the 4th, and passed the Duero on the 6th, at the fords of Herrera and El Abrojo.

After Gen. Foy had found that the garrison of Astorga had surrendered by capitulation, he returned to the Esla, and marched upon Carvajales with a view to surprise and cut off the corps of Portuguese militia which had been employed under Lieut. Gen. the Conde de Amarante in the blockade of Zamora. The Lieut. General, however, made good his retreat without loss to the frontiers of Portugal; and Gen. Foy carried off the garrison of Zamora on the 29th Aug., and marched for Tordesillas.

I can't avoid drawing your Lordship's attention to the conduct of the Conde de Amarante, and of the militia under his command, in these operations. The zeal of the militia of the province of Tras os Montes in voluntarily serving beyond the frontier of the Kingdom, deserves the highest commendation.

The whole of the remains of the '*Armée de Portugal*' having been thus collected between this place and Tordesillas, we found their advanced guard yesterday strongly posted on the heights of La Cisterniga, and I knew that there was a considerable body of troops in and about this town. As it was late in the day before our troops had crossed the Duero, we did not move forward till this morning. The enemy retired from La Cisterniga during the night; and they abandoned the town on our approach to it in the morning, and crossed the Pisuerga, and blew up the bridge. They were closely followed by Lieut. Col. the Hon. F. Ponsonby with a detachment of the 12th light dragoons through the town; but as some time had elapsed before the infantry could come up, the enemy could not be prevented from destroying the bridge. They then retired along the right of the Pisuerga to Dueñas, where their rear will probably halt this night.

When Gen. Foy moved towards Astorga, the army of Galicia retired; and since his march to the Duero, they have again advanced to the Esla. I have requested Gen. Castaños, who is now with the Galician army, to move forward and put himself in immediate communication with me; and I propose to push the '*Armée de Portugal*' as far as I can, preparatory to the operations which I may expect to the southward.

I have received several reports that Marshal Soult had raised the blockade of Cadiz, and had entirely evacuated Seville about the 25th or 26th Aug.; but by some unaccountable accident, I have received no letter from Lieut. Gen. Sir R. Hill since the 25th, nor any from Cadiz of a later date than the 17th. I give credit, however, to the reports to which I have above referred; and I shall return to the south as soon as I shall be made acquainted with Soult's progress.

The Empecinado has informed me that Gen. Villa Campa had taken prisoners the troops which had been the garrison, and had evacuated Cuenca after the surrender of the Retiro. These troops amounted to 1000 men, with 2 guns, and belonged to Suchet's army.

My last accounts from Lieut. Gen. Maitland are of the 24th. He was then in Alicante. Major Gen. Ross had returned to Carthagena with his detachment.

To Lieut. Gen. the Hon. Sir E. Paget, K. B.

Villa Toro, 20th Sept. 1812.

I have received your letters of the 8th and 12th, and I am delighted to find that you are come out. I direct this letter to Ciudad Rodrigo, to which place I think it probable that you will come from Castello Branco, as it is scarcely possible that it can meet you at the latter. You will do well to come to head quarters by the military route of Salamanca, Arevalo, Valladolid, &c. Arevalo is a little out of the way; but I have kept our communication by that point, because it answers for communication with Madrid and with Hill, who is, I hope, at Oropesa.

When I found that the King had decidedly passed the mountains into Valencia, I determined to make use of the time which would elapse before I could go to the south (which I then thought it possible I should be obliged to do) in settling our affairs upon the Duero, and in establishing a good communication between us and the Spanish army of Galicia.

The probability that Soult would evacuate Andalusia, of which I was aware before I quitted Madrid, or the certainty that he had raised the siege of Cadiz, and abandoned Seville, which I obtained at a subsequent period, was not calculated to induce me to alter this determination. I was certain that, whenever Soult should connect himself with Suchet and the King, we should be pressed a little on the Tagus, and that it was desirable to remove to a distance all embarrassments existing on this side, and to strengthen ourselves as much as possible in this quarter, preparatory to the events which might be expected on the Tagus.

We passed the Duero on the 6th, and drove the French from Valladolid: on the 7th we pushed them on, but not very vigorously, till the 16th, on which day we were joined by about 12,000 men of the army of Galicia. We then drove the enemy before us to Burgos: on the 17th they retired through the

town at night, and have since continued their march to
Riobena.*

The castle of Burgos commands all the bridges over the
Arlanzon so completely, that we were not able to cross that
river till yesterday morning. We immediately drove in all the
enemy's posts; and last night took by storm a horn work lately
constructed upon a hill within 300 yards of the castle, which
has a considerable command over many of the works of the
castle. Although we succeeded, the operation was not very well
carried on, and I am afraid that our loss is not less than
300 men. After all, I am a little apprehensive that I have not
means to take this castle, which the French have strengthened
to the utmost of their power. I shall be able to judge better
however in a day or two. Although I have here only 4 divisions
of infantry and 3 brigades of cavalry, I think that with the
Spaniards we are strong enough for any thing the French have
or can now bring against us on this side. If I could get this castle, I think I might take some of the force southward, and I
must still endeavor to do so, even though I should not succeed
in taking the castle.

I have accounts from Madrid to the 17th. They had not any
late accounts of Soult which could be much relied upon; nor
does it appear that he had quitted Granada. He had intended to
move into Valencia through Murcia; but as the yellow fever
prevails in Murcia, I think he will pass by Caravaca to Albacete, from whence he will communicate with the King in
Valencia. I have one account stating that he was on the 9th
within 9 leagues of Caravaca; but, on the other hand, I have
letters from Gen. Elio from San Clemente to the 15th, who
does not mention Soult, of whom he must have heard, if he had
been on the 9th so far forward as is stated. I have now given
you an outline of our situation as far as I am acquainted with it.

Besides Hill's corps I have 3 weak divisions and 2 weak brigades of cavalry, at and near Madrid. But we shall have, I

---

*   Thus written in the draft of this letter, and also in the great map of Lopez;
       but Rubena in the Diccionario Geografico-estadistico of Miñano, and the
       Guia de Caminos of the Madrid Post office.

should think, not less than 12,000 Spaniards, besides innumerable guerrillas; indeed we have plenty of that commodity every where; and Ballesteros has 12,000 or 15,000 men, which will be on Soult's left, where are likewise 4000 or 5000 men on their march from Cadiz; and there is an army under Gen. Maitland at Alicante. Upon the whole therefore I don't despair of the continuance of our success through the campaign, particularly if the cavalry expected from England should land at an early period.

To Earl Bathurst.

Villa Toro, 27th Sept. 1812.

The operations against the castle of Burgos have been continued, since I addressed you on the 20th; and on the night of the 22d, I directed that an attempt might be made to take by storm the exterior line of the enemy's works, one of the batteries destined to support our position within them having been in such a state of preparation as to afford hopes that it would be ready to open on the morning of the 23d. The attack was to have been made by detachments of Portuguese troops belonging to the 6th division which occupied the town of Burgos, and invested the castle on the S. W. side on the enemy's left, while a detachment of the 1st division under Major Lawrie of the 79th should scale the wall in front. Unfortunately, the Portuguese troops were so strongly opposed that they could not make any progress on the enemy's flank; and the escalade could not take place.

I am sorry to say that our loss was severe. Major Lawrie was killed, and Capt. Frazer, who commanded a detachment from the brigade of Guards, was wounded. Both these officers, and indeed all those employed on this occasion, exerted themselves to the utmost; but the attack on the enemy's flank having failed, the success of the escalade was impracticable. We have since established ourselves close to the exterior wall, and have carried a gallery towards it; and I hope that a mine under it will be completed in the course of to-morrow. In the mean time our batteries are completed, and ready to open upon the enemy's interior lines, as soon as we shall have established our troops within the exterior lines.

The enemy's army are about Pancorbo, and at Miranda on the Ebro, with their advanced posts at Briviesca. They have made no movement to interrupt our operations.

Marshal Soult left Granada on the 15th, and marched towards the kingdom of Valencia, it is said by Caravaca. Gen. Ballesteros entered Granada on the 17th.

I imagine that Lieut. Gen. Sir R. Hill is by this time at Toledo; but I have not heard from him since he passed the Tagus.

Gen. Elio, who now commands the troops lately commanded by Gen. J. O'Donell, took Consuegra by capitulation on the 22d.

*Return of the killed, wounded, and missing at
the siege of the castle of Burgos, from the 20th
to the 26th Sept. 1812, inclusive.*

	Officers.	Serjeants.	R. and F.	Total loss of officers, non-commissioned officers, and R. & F.
Killed	7	2	50	59
Wounded	12	13	264	289
Missing	—	—	—	—

To Earl Bathurst.

Villa Toro, 5th Oct. 1812.

One of the mines which had been prepared under the exterior line of the castle of Burgos was exploded at midnight of the 29th, and effected a breach in the wall, which some of the party, destined to attack it, were enabled to storm; but owing to the darkness of the night, the detachment who were to support the advanced party missed their way, and the advance were driven off the breach again before they could be effectually supported. The breach effected by the mine was not of a description to be stormed except at the moment of the explosion, and it was necessary to improve it by fire, before the attempt could be repeated. But all our endeavors to construct batteries in the best situation to fire upon the wall failed, in consequence of the great superiority of the enemy's fire. One of the only 3 battering guns we had and 2 carriages were destroyed, and another gun was much injured. In the mean time another mine had been placed under the wall, which was ready yesterday, and a fire was opened yesterday morning from a battery constructed under cover of the horn work.

The fire from this battery improved the breach first made; and the explosion of the mine, at 5 o'clock yesterday evening, effected a second breach. Both were immediately stormed by the 2d batt., of the 24th regt., under the command of Capt. Hedderwick, which I had ordered into the trenches for that purpose; and our troops were established within the exterior line of the works of the castle of Burgos. The conduct of the 24th regt. was highly praiseworthy; and Capt. Hedderwick and Lieuts. Holmes and Fraser, who led the two storming parties, particularly distinguished themselves. I am happy to add, the operation was effected without suffering a very severe loss.

The enemy are still upon the Ebro, and have not made any attempt to interrupt our operations. It is reported they have extended to their left as far as Logroño.

My last reports from the frontiers of Valencia are of the 25th. It is stated that King Joseph was at Almanza, with 15,000 men, to join Marshal Soult, who was on his march through Murcia from Granada. My last letter from Lieut. Gen. Maitland is of the 21st ult. He was about to relinquish the command on account of ill health, and give it over to Major Gen. Mackenzie.

Lieut. Gen. Sir R. Hill is on the Tagus, between Aranjuez and Toledo. I have not yet heard what steps Major Gen. Cooke has taken in obedience to the orders which I gave him to send

a part of the troops composing the garrison of Cadiz to join
Lieut. Gen. Sir R. Hill.

By the last accounts I have of Gen. Ballesteros he was at
Granada, but he has been ordered to Alcaraz.

I enclose a return of killed and wounded since the 27th ult.

Return of the killed, wounded, and missing,
at the siege of the castle of Burgos, from the
27th Sept. to the 5th Oct. inclusive.

	Officers.	Serjeants.	R. and F.	Total loss of officers, non-commissioned officers, and R. & F.
Killed	—	5	71	76
Wounded	11	10	302	323
Missing	—	—	4	4

To Earl Bathurst.

Villa Toro, 11th Oct. 1812.

The enemy have made two *sorties* on the head of the sap
between the exterior and interior lines of the castle of Burgos,
in both of which they materially injured our works, and we
suffered some loss. In the last, at 3 in the morning of the 8th,
we had the misfortune to lose Major the Hon. C. Cocks of the
79th, who was field officer of the trenches, and was killed in
the act of rallying the troops who had been driven in. I have
frequently had occasion to draw your Lordship's attention to
the conduct of Major Cocks, and in one instance very recently
in the attack on the horn work of the castle of Burgos, and I
consider his loss as one of the greatest importance to this army
and to His Majesty's service.

Notwithstanding the efforts of the enemy, our troops are established within about 100 yards of the enemy's interior line, which we have it in our power to assault; and we have effected a good breach in another part of the same line, and our troops are established close to the breach.

I am sorry to say, however, that the consumption of musket ammunition by the troops has been so large, particularly in the late *sorties* made by the enemy, that notwithstanding that some has been made, and that a supply of powder and musket ammunition has been received from Commodore Sir H. Popham, I can't venture to allow the consumption of ammunition which must take place in the storm of the enemy's works, till I shall be certain of receiving a further supply. I have ordered to Santander the transports which have musket ammunition on board at Coruña, and an officer of the ordnance has been waiting at Santander since the beginning of the month, to receive what is required. I have heard that the vessels sailed from Coruña on the 3d inst., but I have not yet heard of their arrival at Santander. I likewise sent to the magazines of the army in the rear, on the 24th Sept.; but I have not yet heard of the approach of the ammunition. I am obliged to defer any further attack upon the enemy till I shall be certain of a supply. In the mean time we are carrying on our works under ground; and I hope that I shall have another mine in readiness in a day or two; and we are endeavoring to burn the enemy's magazines by the fire of hot shot.

The enemy have not made any movement to interrupt our operations. They are still upon the Ebro, and I understand have received another reinforcement from France.

By the accounts which I have from Lieut. Gen. Sir R. Hill, of the 7th inst., it appears that Marshal Soult joined the King on the frontier of Valencia and Murcia, on the 29th Sept. A detachment of Marshal Soult's army occupied Albacete on the 3d inst., and a small detachment of cavalry was as far forward as Minaya on the 6th inst.; but I don't consider the movement to be as yet decided.

I have not yet heard of Gen. Ballesteros having passed the Sierra Morena, or at all of his movements since the 17th Sept., when he entered Granada; nor have I heard from Major Gen.

Cooke since he received my directions for the movement of the troops under his command.

I have reports, however, that the troops marched from Seville on the 28th Sept.

I enclose a return of the killed and wounded since the 6th inst.

Return of the killed, wounded, and missing,
at the siege of the castle of Burgos, from the
6th to the 10th Oct. 1812, inclusive.

	Officers.	Serjeants.	R. and F.	Total loss of officers, non-commissioned officers, and R. & F.
Killed	7	4	116	127
Wounded	16	8	268	292
Missing	–	–	18	18

To Earl Bathurst.

Cabezon, 26th Oct. 1812.

I have been so much occupied by the movements and operations of the army since the 18th inst., that I have not been able to write to your Lordship. The operations of the siege of the castle of Burgos continued nearly in the state in which they were when I addressed your Lordship on the 11th inst. until the 18th. Having at that time received a supply of musket ammunition from Santander, and having, while waiting for that necessary article, completed a mine under the church of San Roman, which stood in an outwork of the second line, I determined that the breach which we had effected in the second line should be stormed that evening, at the moment this mine should explode; and that at the same time the line should be attacked by escalade.

The mine succeeded, and Lieut. Col. Brown lodged a party

of the 9th caçadores and a detachment of Spanish troops of the regiment of *Asturias* in the outwork. A detachment of the K. G. L. under Major Wurmb carried the breach, and a detachment of the Guards succeeded in escalading the line; but the enemy brought such a fire upon these 2 last detachments from the third line and the body of the castle itself, and they were attacked by numbers so superior, before they could receive the support allotted to them, that they were obliged to retire, suffering considerable loss. Major Wurmb was unfortunately killed.

It is impossible to represent in adequate terms my sense of the conduct of the Guards and German Legion upon this occasion; and I am quite satisfied, that if it had been possible to maintain the posts which they had gained with so much gallantry, those troops would have maintained them. Some of the men stormed even the third line, and one was killed in one of the embrasures of that line; and I had the satisfaction of seeing, that if I could breach the wall of the castle, we should carry the place.

Sir H. Popham had succeeded in an experiment which he had tried for the removal of guns from Santander for the siege of Santoña; and knowing our wants of ordnance and stores, and that our battering guns and carriages had been destroyed by the enemy's fire, he sent two 24 pounders and stores from Santander, and I intended, as soon as they should arrive, to endeavor to breach the wall of the castle.

In the mean time, another mine was commenced under the second line from the church of San Roman, of which we remained in possession.

The enemy had on the 13th moved forward a considerable body of infantry and 6 squadrons of cavalry from Briviesca, to reconnaitre our outpost at Monasterio. They attacked the piquet at the bridge in front of the town, but were repulsed by the fire of a detachment of the infantry of the Brunswick Legion. In this affair Lieut. Col. the Hon. F. Ponsonby, who commanded at Monasterio, was wounded, but not severely; and I hope I shall soon again have the benefit of his assistance.

I had long had reports of the enemy's intention to advance for the relief of the castle of Burgos with the '*Armée de*

Portugal,' reinforced by troops recently arrived from France, and with that part of the army of the North which was disposable; and they did advance in considerable force against the post of Monasterio, on the evening of the 18th. Lieut. Lyznewsky, of the Brunswick Legion, who commanded a piquet in Sᵗᵃ Olalla, disobeyed his orders in remaining in that village upon the approach of the enemy; and he was taken with his piquet. The enemy consequently obtained possession of the heights which command the town of Monasterio, and our outpost was obliged to retire, on the morning of the 19th, to the Burgos side of the town.

I assembled the troops, excepting those necessary for carrying on the operations of the siege, as soon as it appeared, by the enemy's movement of the 18th, that they entertained serious intentions of endeavoring to raise it; and placed the allied army on the heights, having their right at Ibeas, on the Arlanzon, the centre at Riobena and Mijaradas, and the left at Soto Palacios. The enemy's army likewise assembled in the neighbourhood of Monasterio.

They moved forward on the evening of the 20th with about 10,000 men, to drive in our outposts from Quintana-palla and Olmos. The former withdrew by order; but the latter was maintained with great spirit by the Chasseurs Britanniques. Seeing a fair opportunity of striking a blow upon the enemy, I requested Lieut. Gen. Sir E. Paget to move with the 1st and 5th divisions upon the enemy's right flank; which movement having been well executed, drove them back upon Monasterio; and our posts were replaced in Quintana-palla.

On the morning of the 21st, I received a letter from Sir R. Hill of the 17th, in which he acquainted me with the enemy's intention to move towards the Tagus, which was already fordable by individuals in many places, and was likely to become so by an army.

The castle of Chinchilla had surrendered on the 9th inst., and Gen. Ballesteros, although he had entered Granada on the 17th Sept., had not assumed the position in La Mancha which he had been ordered to assume by the Spanish government, at my suggestion.

The enemy's force in Valencia was supposed to amount to not less than 70,000 men, a very large proportion of which, it was expected, would be disposable for service out of that kingdom.

I had desired Lieut. Gen. Sir R. Hill to retire from his position on the Tagus, if he should find that he could not maintain himself in it with advantage, and it was necessary that I should be near him, in order that the corps under my command might not be insulated in consequence of the movements which he should find himself under the necessity of making. I therefore raised the siege of Burgos on the night of the 21st, and moved the whole army back towards the Duero.

I felt severely the sacrifice I was obliged to make. Your Lordship is well aware that I never was very sanguine in my expectations of success in the siege of Burgos, notwithstanding that I considered that success was attainable, even with the means in my power, within a reasonably limited period. If the attack on the first line, made on the 22d or the 29th, had succeeded, I believe we should have taken the place, notwithstanding the ability with which the Governor conducted the defence, and the gallantry with which it was executed by the garrison. Our means were very limited; but it appeared to me that if we should succeed, the advantage to the cause would be great, and the final success of the campaign would have been certain.

I had every reason to be satisfied with the conduct of the officers and troops during the siege of Burgos, particularly with the brigade of Guards. During the latter part of the siege, the weather was very unfavorable, and the troops suffered much from the rain. The officers at the head of the Artillery and Engineer departments, Lieut. Col. Robe, and Lieut. Col. Burgoyne, and Lieut. Col. Dickson, who commands the reserve artillery, rendered me every assistance, and the failure of success is not to be attributed to them. By their activity we carried off every thing in the course of one night, excepting the 3 18 pounders destroyed by the enemy's fire, and the 8 pieces of cannon which we had taken from the enemy on the night of the 19th ult., in the storm of the horn work, not having cattle to move them.

The enemy were not aware of our movements, and did not

follow us till late on the 22d, when 10,000 men encamped on this side of Burgos.

The British army encamped at Celada del Camino and Hornillos, with the light cavalry at Estepar and Buniel. We continued our march the following day; the right of the army to Torquemada, the left to Cordovilla, at which places we crossed the Pisuerga.

The enemy followed our movement with their whole army. Our rear guard consisted of the two light battalions of the King's German Legion, under Col. Halkett, and of Major Gen. Anson's brigade of cavalry; and Major Gen. Bock's brigade was halted at the Venta del Pozo, to give them support; the whole under the command of Lieut. Gen. Sir S. Cotton. Don J. Sanchez marched on the left of the Arlanzon; and the party of guerrillas heretofore commanded by the late Marquiñez, in the hills on the left of our rear guard.

Major Gen. Anson's brigade charged twice, with great success, in front of Celada del Camino, and the enemy were detained above 3 hours by the troops under Lieut. Gen. Sir S. Cotton, in the passage of the Hormaza, in front of that village.

The rear guard continued to fall back in the best order, till the guerrillas on the left having been driven in, they rode towards the flank of the rear guard of Major Gen. Anson's brigade, and 4 or 5 squadrons of the enemy mixed with them. These were mistaken for Spaniards, and they fell upon the flank and rear of our troops. We sustained some loss; and Lieut. Col. Pelly, of the 16th dragoons, having had his horse shot, was taken prisoner.

The delay occasioned by this misfortune enabled the enemy to bring up a very superior body of cavalry, which was charged by Major Gen. Bock's and Major Gen. Anson's brigades, near the Venta del Pozo, but unsuccessfully; and our rear guard was hard pressed. The enemy made 3 charges on the 2 light battalions of the King's German Legion, formed in squares, but were always repulsed with considerable loss by the steadiness of these 2 battalions. They suffered no loss, and I can't sufficiently applaud their conduct, and that of Col. Halkett, who commanded them.

The exertions and conduct of Lieut. Gen. Sir S. Cotton, and of the officers and Staff attached to him, throughout this day, were highly meritorious; and although the charge made by the cavalry was not successful, I had the satisfaction of observing great steadiness in their movements. Major Bull's troop of horse artillery, under Major Downman and Capt. Ramsay, distinguished themselves.

The army continued its march on the 24th, and took up its ground on the Carrion, with its right at Dueñas, and left at Villa-muriel; and the 1st batt. 1st Guards joined us from Coruña. I halted there on the 25th, and the enemy attacked our left at Villa-muriel. They were repulsed, however, by the 5th division of infantry, under the command of Major Gen. Oswald, in the absence of Lieut. Gen. Leith, on account of indisposition.

I had directed the 3d batt. of the Royals to march to Palencia, to protect the destruction of the bridges over the Carrion at that place; but it appears that the enemy assembled in such force at that point, that Lieut. Col. Campbell thought it necessary to retire upon Villa-muriel, and the enemy passed the Carrion at Palencia. This rendered it necessary to change our front, and I directed Major Gen. Oswald to throw back our left, and the Spanish troops upon the heights, and to maintain the Carrion with the right of the 5th division. The bridge of Villa-muriel was destroyed, but the enemy discovered a ford, and passed over a considerable body of cavalry and infantry. I made Major Gen. Pringle and Brig. Gen. Barnes attack these troops, under the orders of Major Gen. Oswald; in which attack the Spanish troops co-operated, and they were driven across the river with considerable loss. The fire upon the left had been very severe throughout the day, from which we suffered a good deal; and Major Gen. Don M. de Alava was unfortunately wounded while urging on the Spanish infantry in the pursuit of the enemy.

I broke up this morning from the Carrion, and marched upon Cabezon del Campo, where I have crossed the Pisuerga.

The enemy appear to be moving in this direction from Dueñas. I propose to halt here to-morrow.

Return of the killed, wounded, and missing,
at the siege of the castle of Burgos, from the
18th to the 21st Oct. inclusive.

	Officers.	Serjeants.	R. and F.	Total loss of officers, non-commissioned officers, and R. & F.
Killed	4	3	89	96
Wounded	10	4	160	174
Missing	–	–	4	4

To Earl Bathurst.

Cabezon, 28th Oct. 1812.

Since I wrote to you on the 26th, I have had an opportunity of seeing the enemy's whole army, as they placed themselves opposite to us on the Pisuerga yesterday. They are certainly in very great strength. The '*Armée de Portugal*' have received a reinforcement of 10,000 men (including cavalry) from France; and I have reason to believe that there are 2 divisions of infantry now with this army, belonging to the army of the North. The cavalry of the army of the North is certainly with the '*Armée de Portugal*', and they have at least 5000 good cavalry.

I don't think that I am sufficiently strong to contend with this army thus reinforced. I have here only 4 weak divisions of British and Portuguese troops, and 3 very weak brigades of cavalry.

There are with this army 12,000 Spanish troops of the army of Galicia, including about 600 cavalry, and the cavalry under Don J. Sanchez.

I was sorry to observe, however, in the affair of the 25th, that although the Spanish soldiers showed no want of spirit or of disposition to engage with the enemy, they were totally unable to move upon them with the regularity and order of a disciplined body, by which alone success can be hoped for in any contest with the French. We must depend upon ourselves, therefore; and the difference of numbers, from what I saw yesterday, is much against us.

Under these circumstances, I have thought it proper to desire Lieut. Gen. Sir R. Hill to retire from his position on the Tagus, and to join me, if possible, on the Adaja. It is absolutely necessary that I should cross the Duero; and if the enemy should follow me with his whole force, which is probable, I cannot expect to be able to maintain myself, and I shall be obliged to retire towards the Tormes. In this case Lieut. Gen. Sir R. Hill would be exposed to the evil which I raised the siege of Burgos to avoid, thinking it possible he might be obliged to retire, and be attacked by a superior army in front, and by another in his rear. This misfortune would be more certain if any accident should unfortunately happen to the troops under my command.

By accounts from Lieut. Gen. Sir R. Hill to the 26th inst., I find that the enemy had approached the Tagus with their left, and had moved their right upon Cuenca. He does not state the force they have with them, but I should imagine not less than 50,000 men; and, as far as I can judge, there are not less than 40,000 now opposed to this army. Both armies are infinitely superior to ours in cavalry and artillery, as well as in total numbers. Lieut. Gen. Sir R. Hill has with him about as many Spanish troops as there are with this army, but I believe they are equally unused to order and discipline.

Under these circumstances, I acknowledge that I have no expectations that I shall be able to maintain myself very forward in Castille, if the enemy should be able to keep this large body collected.

Your Lordship will recollect that I have always been of opinion that, as far as the allied British and Portuguese army was concerned, the discontinuance of the blockade of Cadiz and the evacuation of Andalusia would be misfortunes, however important as political events. The reason is, that in consequence of those events, these armies are opposed to larger bodies of the enemy than they were before, at the same time that they don't receive proportionate assistance from the Spanish troops, owing to the state in which these troops are found.

If Gen. Ballesteros had moved into La Mancha, as he was desired, I don't believe the enemy could have ventured upon the march towards the Tagus, nor do I believe they would have attempted to interrupt the siege of Burgos; an operation which I have reason to believe was ordered by the King from Valencia, and is connected with his movement towards the Tagus. If they had moved towards the Tagus, they must have detached to observe and check Ballesteros, and their force against Sir R. Hill would have been diminished, and I might have drawn reinforcements from him. It is fortunate that I was induced to raise the siege of Burgos, and to retire to the Duero, upon learning the state of affairs on the Tagus, as it is obvious that my force is far inferior in numbers and composition to that of the enemy; and the result of a battle, fought to save the siege, might have been very doubtful.

No event of importance has occurred since I addressed your Lordship on the 26th. The enemy formed their cavalry in the plain on our front yesterday; they have cannonaded different parts of our line, without doing us any injury, excepting that Lieut. Col. Robe, of the Royal artillery, was wounded severely, but not dangerously, yesterday.

To the Rt. Hon. Sir H. Wellesley, K. B.

Rueda, 1st Nov. 1812.

I have the honor to enclose copies of my last dispatches to the Sec. of State; and I beg you to lay such parts of them as you may think proper before the Spanish government, for their information. I beg you also to take that opportunity of expressing to them the grateful sense I entertain for the cordiality with which his Excellency Gen. Castaños and the officers under him have co-operated with me.

The Spanish troops have invariably manifested a disposition to engage with the enemy; and in an affair of the cavalry on the 19th ult., the Spanish cavalry under the Conde de Fiquelmont were very successful, and destroyed many of the enemy, and took many horses and prisoners. The infantry likewise, in the affair of Villa-muriel, on the 25th, manifested a disposition to engage with the enemy.

The truth, however, ought to be known to the government; and I must say that the army of Galicia is not in the state of discipline in which they ought to be before they are brought to a contest with the enemy; or which could gain for them either the confidence of their allies or of themselves. In the affair at Villa-muriel, they could neither advance nor retreat in order. Their movements were made *à la débandade*; and if I had not ordered a movement on the enemy's flank by the British troops, not only the enemy would not have been driven across the Carrion, but they would have carried the heights above Villa-muriel, on which the Spanish troops were posted. It may be depended upon, that order and discipline alone can insure any solid success against the enemy with whom we are engaged.

I had an opportunity of seeing the enemy's whole army on the 27th Oct. on their march across the plains to Cigales, and it appeared to me to consist of 40,000 infantry and 5000 cavalry, with an immense train of artillery. To oppose these troops, I have not more than 20,000 British and Portuguese troops; and there were 12,000 men, including 600 cavalry, in the army of Galicia. It is obvious, however, that, in their present state of discipline, I cannot reckon upon these troops in a field of battle. I should have been obliged to continue my retreat therefore; and my communication with Lieut. Gen. Sir R. Hill, and his retreat, would have been cut off.

Under these circumstances, I thought it proper to order that General to retire from Madrid upon Arevalo, there to join with me, sending the troops under Gen. Elio, Gens. Bassecourt and Villa Campa, and Gen. Freyre, to join Gen. Ballesteros.

I beg you to explain to the Spanish government, that Lieut. Gen. Sir R. Hill, and the allies on the Tagus, are as much inferior in force to the enemy opposed to them as I am to the enemy opposed to me, the enemy having brought all their forces to bear upon the centre of Spain, with the exception, I conclude, of a part of Suchet's army left in Valencia. I imagined that they would adopt this plan when I wrote to you from Valladolid on the 9th Sept.; and it is very unfortunate that Gen. Ballesteros did not take the position at Alcaraz which he was ordered to take by the Minister at War, in consequence of my suggestion. If he had, the enemy could not have moved against Gen. Hill; and I might have drawn a reinforcement from his army to this, still keeping possession of Madrid.

Under present circumstances, I think it not improbable that I may not be able to retain much of Castille; but it may be depended upon, that I will do every thing in my power.

To Earl Bathurst.

Rueda, 3d Nov. 1812.

I take the opportunity of the return of the messenger (Myers) to Coruña, to inform you that the army have continued in the position in which I placed them on the 30th Oct., and the enemy have made no attempt to pass the Duero.

The bridge of Tordesillas is repaired, and they are employed in the repair of that of Toro. Their troops are extended along the Duero, from the latter place to Valladolid.

In the mean time, the troops under Lieut. Gen. Sir R. Hill will arrive this day and to-morrow on the Adaja. The General received my orders to break up from his position on the Jarama on the 29th, and he intended to carry them into execution on the morning of the 30th. He had intended to destroy the Puente Larga, but the mine failed; and the enemy having collected a large body of troops between the bridge and Aranjuez, they immediately attacked our post on the bridge, but were repulsed, with considerable loss, by the 2d batt. of the 47th regt. and a detachment of the 95th, under the command of Col. Skerrett. I have not received the returns of our loss on this occasion; but I understand it is about 40 men. No officer was touched. Lieut. Gen. Sir R. Hill speaks in high terms of the conduct of the troops.

These circumstances delayed the march from the right of Lieut. Gen. Sir R. Hill's position till the evening of the 30th; and he has since continued it, without being at all molested by the enemy.

The building called La China in the Retiro, and all the guns, stores, &c., which that work contained, which had not been carried away, were destroyed before the troops were withdrawn from Madrid.

The Spanish divisions of Don Carlos de España, and the Conde de Penne Villemur, are with Lieut. Gen. Sir R. Hill.

I had recommended that the detachments of the 2d and 3d armies, under Gens. Elio, Villa Campa, Bassecourt, and Freyre, should cross the Tagus at Toledo, or Talavera, or Arzobispo, and should join Gen. Ballesteros; but I am not certain that this recommendation has been attended to. I have not yet heard that Gen. Ballesteros has entered La Mancha.

A small body of the enemy's troops were at Val de Moro on the 31st, and entered Madrid at 10 o'clock on the morning of the 1st inst.

By a letter from Gen. Mackenzie to Lieut. Gen. Sir R. Hill, dated at Alicante on the 23d Oct., it appears that the enemy had kept but a small force in the kingdom of Valencia, under Gen. Harispe, which was extended from Caudete to Alcira upon the Jucar; the works of the city of Valencia being dismantled and destroyed, and the city itself abandoned by the French troops and their adherents.

From the tenor of Gen. Mackenzie's letter, I judge that he proposes to attack the force under Gen. Harispe; and he has already pushed forward his posts to Alcoy and Concentayna.

I have no accounts upon which I can rely that Marshal Suchet has accompanied the King's march into the centre of Spain with any large portion of his army; but it is so reported, and the letter above referred to, from Gen. Mackenzie, tends to confirm the report. The advanced posts of Lieut. Gen. Sir R.

Hill have seen the regiment of Cuirassiers which belong to the army of Aragon.

I have accounts from the North, stating that Longa has taken a convoy, escorted by 300 men, near Vitoria.

I learn likewise that the post at Santoña is much distressed for provisions; and I hope that Sir H. Popham may have been able to make his attack upon that place.

These events will probably oblige Gen. Caffarelli to withdraw his troops from our front.

To Earl Bathurst.

Ciudad Rodrigo, 19th Nov. 1812.

The troops under the command of Lieut. Gen. Sir R. Hill crossed the Tormes at Alba on the 8th inst., and those under my command took the position on the heights of San Cristoval de la Cuesta on the same day; Brig. Gen. Pack's brigade occupying Aldea Lengua, and Brig. Gen. Bradford's Cabrerizos, on our right, and the British cavalry covering our front. I had desired Lieut. Gen. Sir R. Hill to occupy the town and castle of Alba with Major Gen. Howard's brigade of the 2d division, leaving Lieut. Gen. Hamilton's Portuguese division on the left of the Tormes to support those troops, while the 2d division was posted in the neighbourhood of the fords of Encinas and Huerta, and the 3d and 4th divisions remained at Calvarrasa de Arriba in reserve.

On the 9th, the enemy drove in the piquets of Major Gen. Long's brigade of cavalry in front of Alba; and Major Gen. Long was obliged to withdraw his troops through Alba on the morning of the 10th. In the course of the day, the enemy's whole army approached our positions on the Tormes; and they attacked the troops in Alba with 20 pieces of cannon and a considerable body of infantry. They made no impression on them, however, and withdrew the cannon and the greatest part of the troops in the night, and this attack was never renewed.

I enclose Lieut. Gen. Hamilton's report to Sir R. Hill of the transactions at Alba, which were highly creditable to the troops employed. From the 10th to the 14th, the time was passed in various reconnaissances, as well of the fords of the Tormes, as of the position which the troops under my command occupied, on the right of that river in front of Salamanca; and, on the 14th, the enemy crossed that river in force at the fords near Encinas, about 2 leagues above Alba.

I immediately broke up from San Cristoval, and ordered the troops towards the Arapiles; and as soon as I had ascertained the direction of the enemy's march from the fords, I moved with the 2d division of infantry, and all the cavalry I could collect, to attack them, leaving Lieut. Gen. Sir R. Hill with the 4th and Lieut. Gen. Hamilton's divisions in front of Alba, to protect this movement, and the 3d division in reserve on the Arapiles, to secure the possession of that position.

The enemy, however, was already too strong, and too strongly posted at Mozarbes to be attacked; and I confined myself to a cannonade of their cavalry, under cover of which I reconnaitred their position.

In the evening I withdrew all the troops from the neighbourhood of Alba to the Arapiles, leaving a small Spanish garrison in the castle, with directions to evacuate it, if they should find that the enemy retired, and having destroyed the bridge. In the course of the night and following morning I moved the greatest part of the troops through Salamanca, and placed Lieut. Gen. Sir E. Paget with the 1st division of infantry on the right at Aldea Tejada, in order to secure that passage for the troops over the Zurguen, in case the movements of the enemy on our right flank should render it necessary for me to make choice either of giving up my communication with Ciudad Rodrigo or Salamanca.

On the morning of the 15th, I found the enemy fortifying their position at Mozarbes, which they had taken up the night before, at the same time that they were moving bodies of cavalry and infantry towards their own left, and to our communications with Ciudad Rodrigo. It was obvious that it was the enemy's intention to act upon our communications; and as they were too strong, and too strongly posted, for me to think of attacking them, I determined to move upon Ciudad Rodrigo. I therefore put the army in march in 3 columns, and crossed the Zurguen, and then passed the enemy's left flank, and encamped that night on the Valmuza. We continued our march successively on the 16th, 17th, 18th, and this day, when part of the army crossed the Agueda, and the whole will cross that river to-morrow, and canton between the Agueda and Coa.

The enemy followed our movement on the 16th with a large body, probably the whole of the cavalry, and a considerable body of infantry; but they did not attempt to press upon our rear. They took advantage of the ground to cannonade our rear guard, consisting of the Light division, under Major Gen. Alten, on the 17th, on its passage of the Huebra at San Muñoz, and occasioned some loss.

The troops have suffered considerably from the severity of the weather, which, since the 13th, has been worse than I have ever known at this season of the year. The soldiers, as usual, straggled from their regiments in search of plunder, and I am apprehensive that some may have fallen into the enemy's hands.

I am sorry to add, that we have had the misfortune to lose Lieut. Gen. Sir E. Paget, who was taken prisoner on the 17th. He commanded the centre column, and the fall of rain having greatly injured the roads, and swelled the rivulets, there was an interval between the 5th and 7th divisions of infantry. Sir Edward rode alone to the rear to discover the cause of this interval, and as the road passed through a wood, either a detachment of the enemy's cavalry had got upon the road, or he missed the road, and fell into their hands in the wood. I understand that Sir Edward was not wounded, but I cannot sufficiently regret the loss of his assistance at this moment.

In my dispatch of the 7th inst., I communicated to your Lordship my opinion of the strength of the enemy as far as I could judge of it from the reports I had received, and from what I had seen. I have since learnt that Gen. Caffarelli, with the army of the North, certainly remained joined with the 'Armée de Portugal'. King Joseph left Madrid on the 4th inst., and arrived at Peñaranda on the 8th, leaving at Madrid the civil authorities of his government, and a small garrison. These authorities and troops evacuated Madrid on the 7th, and marched for Castille; and Col. Don J. Palecca took possession of that city.

Your Lordship will have seen Gen. Ballesteros' letter of the 24th Oct. to the Regency, from which you will observe that he disobeyed the orders of the government given to him at my suggestion, to march his troops into La Mancha, and hang upon the enemy's left flank, because the Regency and Cortes had offered me the chief command of the Spanish armies. Gen. Virues, who succeeded to the command upon Gen. Ballesteros being removed, had not advanced farther than Jaen, when I last heard from that quarter on the 8th inst.

The whole of the enemy's disposable force in Spain was therefore upon the Tormes in the middle of this month, and they were certainly not less than 80,000 men, but more probably 90,000. Of these, 10,000 were cavalry; and as the '*Armée de Portugal*' alone had 100 pieces of cannon, it is probable that they had not less in all than 200 pieces.

I had 52,000 British and Portuguese troops, of which 4000 were British cavalry, on the Tormes, and from 12,000 to 16,000 Spaniards; and, although I should have felt no hesitation in trying the issue of a general action on ground which I should have selected, I did not deem it expedient to risk the cause on the result of an attack of the enemy in a position which they had selected and strengthened.

I entertained hopes that I should have been able to prevent the enemy from crossing the Tormes, in which case they must have attacked me in the position of San Cristoval, or must have retired, leaving us in possession of the line of the Tormes. I considered either to be likely to be attended by so many advantages to the cause, that I deemed it expedient to delay my march from the Tormes till the enemy should be actually established on the left of that river; and if the weather had been more favorable, we should have made the movement without inconvenience or loss.

It is difficult to form a judgment of the enemy's intentions at present. They have not pushed any troops beyond the Yeltes, and very few beyond the Huebra. But it is obvious, and a general sense is said to prevail among the French officers, that until they can get the better of the allied army, it is useless to attempt the conquest and settlement of Spain; and as far as I can form a judgment from one of Marshal Soult's letters to the King in cipher, which was intercepted, and fell into my hands some time ago, it was his opinion, and he urged, that Portugal should be made the seat of the war.

The result of the campaign, however, though not so favorable as I at one moment expected, or as it would have been if I could have succeeded in the attack of the castle of Burgos, or if Gen. Ballesteros had made the movement into La Mancha which was suggested, is still so favorable, that this operation appears out of the question.

The strong places of Ciudad Rodrigo and Badajoz being in our possession, and Almeida being re-established, it is not easy for the enemy to penetrate by either of the great entrances into Portugal; and although the two former of these places (particularly the first mentioned) are neither in the state of defence nor garrisoned as I should wish to see them, having deprived the enemy of their ordnance, arsenals, and magazines in Andalusia, at Madrid, at Salamanca, and Valladolid, it does not appear possible that these places should be attacked.

I conclude, therefore, that for the present they will canton their army in Old Castille, and in the valley of the Tagus, and will wait for the arrival of fresh reinforcements and means from France.

To the Earl of Liverpool.

Ciudad Rodrigo, 23d Nov. 1812.

I received by the last post your letter of the 27th Oct. When one army is so inferior in numbers to another as ours is to the French army now assembled in Castille, its operations must depend in a great degree upon those of its opponent. It is impossible therefore for me at this period to point out what line I shall follow. The enemy having abandoned Madrid, and having given up all their communications with the north, solely with a view to collect a still larger force against us, there is no diversion which would answer at present to effect an alteration in our relative numbers, even if I could depend upon the Spaniards to do any thing. But I am quite in despair about them. The only man among them who ever did any thing (Ballesteros) is gone; and I am apprehensive that it will be quite impossible to employ him again. But even he never did more than give employment for a short period to one or at most two divisions of the enemy's army. Then there is another circumstance which must be attended to, and that is the situation of our own army. It has been actively employed since the beginning of last January, and requires rest. The horses of the cavalry and artillery in particular require both that and good food and care during the winter; and the discipline of the infantry requires to be attended to, as is usual in all armies after so long a campaign, and one of so much activity.

I believe that the enemy require repose as much if not more than we do; and that their immense numbers are rather embarrassing to them in a country already exhausted. But I am not quite certain that they do not propose to penetrate into Portugal this winter. I hope the enterprise will end fatally to them; but our troops will suffer a good deal if they are to have a winter campaign, and if the weather should continue as severe as it has been since the 15th of this month.

I believe that I have underrated rather than overrated the enemy's force. They say themselves at Salamanca that they have 90,000 infantry and 14,000 cavalry; and their demand for provisions from the country is 140,000 rations daily. I think they have 90,000 men altogether, including from 10,000 to 12,000 cavalry. The morning state will show what we have.

It is not easy to form a judgment in Spain of the strength of the enemy's armies. The disposition of the Spaniards to exaggerate their own advantages induces the best intentioned among them to deceive; and no individual will ever allow that the French have more men than he has seen himself. The numbers of the army now in Castille have been stated to me at

15,000, and at almost every number from 15,000 to 90,000. I have never found myself mistaken in my estimate of the numbers of the enemy, when I relied upon the returns, making a reasonable abatement for losses during the period elapsed since their date. The only occasion on which I have been seriously mistaken was at Burgos, when I relied upon the reports of the country; and was induced to believe that Sir H. Popham's operations would continue to give employment to Caffarelli. But I afterwards found that the 'Armée de Portugal' had been very largely reinforced in cavalry as well as in infantry, to a larger amount even than I stated in my dispatch to Lord Bathurst, as it was 31 battalions instead of 23, as I stated, and the 130th regt. There were besides two divisions of infantry, and from 1000 to 1400 cavalry of the army of the North; and most certainly when I saw the whole drawn out near Cigales, they were not less than 45,000 men, of which 5000 were cavalry. Soult has 6 divisions of infantry, and 16 regiments of cavalry. The gross numbers of his army last April were 65,000. He has since sustained no great loss excepting the garrison of Badajoz, 5000 men. But I strike off from his gross strength, for losses, sickness, and men on his strength who were employed principally in the siege of Cadiz, 25,000 or 30,000, including the garrison of Badajoz; and I believe his army consists of 35,000 men, of which from 4000 to 5000 are cavalry. The army of the King, when it quitted Madrid in August, was from 20,000 to 22,000 men, including *Juramentados*, and an Italian division belonging to Suchet's army, under Gen. Palombini, and the 16th regt., likewise belonging to Suchet. Supposing the King to have lost by desertion, or to have sent away, all the *Juramentados*, and that the troops belonging to Suchet's army were left in Valencia, there will still remain the French troops of the King's guard, 5000 men, about 3500 more French and German infantry (I know the numbers of the regiments), which belong to the army of the Centre, and from 2000 to 3000 good French cavalry. I believe all this put together will amount to 90,000 men.

What are our prospects against this army? At present none certainly. In the spring, as soon as the green forage shall appear, I shall be able to take the field with a very large British and

Portuguese force, probably larger than we have yet produced, and more efficient I hope in cavalry and artillery. I have sent the army of Galicia home; and I hope advantage will be taken of the winter to do something with them; but unless some changes are effected I shall certainly be disappointed. There are besides, applicable to the *guerre* in Castille, the Spanish army lately under the command of Ballesteros, and the troops under the command of Elio.

If I should find that the French remain quiet during the winter, I propose to go to Cadiz for a short time, to endeavor to put matters upon a better footing, at least as far as regards the armies of Galicia, and that lately under the command of Ballesteros, which must be brought forward in co-operation with us. It will likewise be necessary to apprise the government of the inconvenience and danger of the system on which they have been acting in the provinces which have been freed from the enemy; and of the inefficiency of all the persons selected for public trusts; and of the inconvenience of loading the resources of the provinces with the maintenance of such people. It is useless to trouble your Lordship with a detail of these facts; but I can only say that, if I cannot by the exercise of fair influence in concert with my brother produce some alteration, it is quite hopeless to continue the contest in the Peninsula with the view of obliging the French to evacuate it by force of arms. After this detail of facts, your Lordship will see that it is very useless to trouble you with my opinion of what ought to be done after the French shall leave the Peninsula, more particularly as I have already communicated that opinion to Lord Bathurst.

From what I see in the newspapers I am much afraid that the public will be disappointed at the result of the last campaign, notwithstanding that it is in fact the most successful campaign in all its circumstances, and has produced for the cause more important results, than any campaign in which a British army has been engaged for the last century. We have taken by siege Ciudad Rodrigo, Badajoz, and Salamanca; and the Retiro surrendered. In the mean time the allies have taken Astorga, Guadalaxara, and Consuegra, besides other places taken by Duran and Sir H. Popham. In the months elapsed since January this army has sent to England little short of 20,000 prisoners, and they have taken and destroyed or have themselves the use of the enemy's arsenals in Ciudad Rodrigo, Badajoz, Salamanca, Valladolid, Madrid, Astorga, Seville, the lines before Cadiz, &c.; and upon the whole we have taken and destroyed, or we now possess, little short of 3000 pieces of cannon. The siege of Cadiz has been raised, and all the countries south of the Tagus have been cleared of the enemy.

We should have retained still greater advantages, I think, and should have remained in possession of Castille and Madrid during the winter, if I could have taken Burgos, as I ought early in October, or if Ballesteros had moved upon Alcaraz as he was ordered, instead of intriguing for his own aggrandisement.

The fault of which I was guilty in the expedition to Burgos was, not that I undertook the operation with inadequate means, but that I took there the most inexperienced instead of the best troops. I left at Madrid the 3d, 4th, and Light divisions, who had been with myself always before; and I brought with me that were good the 1st division, and they were inexperienced. In fact the troops ought to have carried the exterior line by escalade on the first trial on the 22d Sept.; and if they had, we had means sufficient to take the place. They did not take the line because [Major Laurie], the field officer who commanded, did that which is too common in our army. He paid no attention to his orders, notwithstanding the pains I took in writing them, and in reading and explaining them to him twice over. He made none of the dispositions ordered; and instead of regulating the attack as he ought, he rushed on as if he had been the leader of a forlorn hope, and fell, together with many of those who went with him. He had my instructions in his pocket; and as the French got possession of his body, and were made acquainted with the plan, the attack could never be repeated. When he fell, nobody having received orders what to do, nobody could give any to the troops. I was in the trenches, however, and ordered them to withdraw. Our time and ammunition were then expended, and our guns destroyed, in taking this line; than which at former sieges we had taken many stronger by assault.

I see that a disposition already exists to blame the government for the failure of the siege of Burgos. The government had nothing to say to the siege. It was entirely my own act. In regard to means, there were ample means both at Madrid and at Santander for the siege of the strongest fortress. That which was wanting at both places was means of transporting ordnance and military stores to the place where it was desirable to use them. The people of England, so happy as they are in every respect, so rich in resources of every description, having the use of such excellent roads, &c., will not readily believe that important results here frequently depend upon 50 or 60 mules more or less, or a few bundles of straw to feed them; but the fact is so, notwithstanding their incredulity. I could not find means of moving even one gun from Madrid. [Admiral Sir Home Popham] is a gentleman who piques himself upon his overcoming all difficulties. He knows the length of time it took to find transport even for about 100 barrels of powder, and a few hundred thousand rounds of musket ammunition, which he sent us. As for the 2 guns which he endeavored to send, I was obliged to send our own cattle to draw them; and we felt great inconvenience from the want of those cattle in the subsequent movements of the army.

To E. Cooke, Esq.

Freneda, 25th Nov., 1812.

I have received your letter of the 21st October; and in case your friend should come in communication with me, I will attend to what you desire respecting the junction of the cards. You will certainly be disappointed in your expectations of the result of the campaign here; and I am afraid others will be so likewise. Yet I acknowledge that what has at last happened ought to have been expected, and was expected and foretold by me when I thought it probable that Soult would raise the siege of Cadiz, and would evacuate Andalusia.

I entertained hopes that things might have taken a different turn if I could have succeeded at Burgos, and if Ballesteros had come forward as he ought in the end of September. But I believe those hopes are like many others regarding the war in Spain, and ought more properly to be termed wishes. However, this cause bewitches everybody; and nobody that I have seen can form and act upon a cool judgment in almost any case.

I ought to have succeeded at Burgos early in October, and then how should I have stood? I might have driven the Army of Portugal, whose reinforcements were not then organised, beyond the Ebro, and I might have left there or at Burgos an army of 20,000 English and Portuguese (by the by, the worst of that description I have yet had, having nearly all the German troops among them), and from 12,000 to 16,000 Spaniards, against what turned out to be 45,000 French. If I could have stayed with them myself, this might have done; but there is nobody else on whom I could have imposed the charge, or who would have liked to undertake it.

I reckon that the King and Soult brought out of Valencia about 45,000 men, of which from 5000 to 7000 cavalry. Hill had on the Tagus about 30,000 of the best we have, and about 10,000 Spaniards of sorts. My plan was to bring Ballesteros upon the left flank and rear of Soult's march out of Valencia, by placing him at Alcaraz, in the Sierra, where he would have been safe, at the same time that nobody could move on the great road from Valencia to attack Hill upon the Tagus.

If this game had been well played, it would have answered my purpose. Soult and the King could not have remained in Valencia, and they must have crossed the Ebro, where I should have assembled all the allies, and should have worked upon their right flank.

Had I any reason to expect that it would be well played? Certainly not. I have never yet known the Spaniards do anything, much less do anything well. Ballesteros has sometimes drawn the attention of a division or two for a moment, but that is all. Everything else you see and read is false and rotten. A few rascals called guerrillas attack one quarter of their numbers, and sometimes succeed, and sometimes not; but as for any regular operation, I have not known of such a thing, and successful, in the whole course of the war.

Under all these circumstances, probably I ought not to have remained so long at Burgos, and ought to have withdrawn Hill at an earlier period from Madrid, and to have taken earlier measures to retire to the Agueda. The way in which matters stood are as follows: I was deceived respecting the numbers in my front in the North. I had no reason to believe that the enemy were so strong till I saw them. Fortunately they did not attack me: if they had, I must have been destroyed.

I raised the siege of Burgos and retired, not because there was any pressure upon me, but because I did not think Hill secure; and I knew that if he was obliged to retire, I should be lost.

When I saw the enemy in my front, it was clear that I was less able to contend with them than Hill was those in his front, and that the danger threatened him, the apprehension of which as coming from his quarter had induced me to move from Burgos. I therefore ordered him to move; and I fairly *bullied* the French into remaining quiet upon the Douro for seven days in order to give him time to make his march. Afterwards our situation on the Tormes depended in some degree on the weather. If the rain which fell on the 15th had fallen on the 13th, the French must have attacked me at St Christoval, or we must have remained in the cantonments on the Tormes; and after all I don't know that we have sustained any great loss or inconvenience by remaining as long as we could in our positions at Madrid and the Tormes.

In short, I played a game which might succeed (the only one which could succeed), and pushed it to the last; and the parts having failed, as I admit was to be expected, I have at last made a handsome retreat to the Agueda, with some labour and inconvenience, but without material loss. I believe I have done right.

SIX

THE CAMPAIGNS OF 1813

Following the retreat to Ciudad Rodrigo, there followed another lull in the operations of the Anglo-Portuguese army. Thousands of men were sick; many of the reinforcements that had been sent out from Britain had yet to arrive; and Wellington, who had just been appointed commander-in-chief of the Spanish armies by the national assembly that had been established in the temporary capital of Cádiz, was anxious to integrate the Spanish forces into his operations, this being something that necessitated a short visit to Cádiz. Even had all this not been the case, Wellington preferred to wait until spring growth had rendered the countryside green enough to provide fresh forage for his cavalry. Thus, it was not until 21 May 1813 that the Anglo-Portuguese army marched across the frontier and recommenced its operations. Even then it did so without the support of most of the Spanish forces, these having been held back by a chronic lack of transport and footwear, the impossibility of restoring order to the areas that had been evacuated by the French in 1812, and the determination of certain elements in the political and military elite to do all that they could to limit Wellington's authority. Yet, for all that, the Spaniards still played an important role in the campaign. As we have seen, the famous guerrilla war that had harassed the French ever since 1808 had reached heights that were more dramatic than ever before, and Napoleon became so exercised by this problem that he sent peremptory orders to his commanders in Spain to put an end to it immediately. No reinforcements being made available for them to undertake this task, their only option was to divert troops who might otherwise have been containing Wellington. Much as was the case in 1812, then, the Anglo-Portuguese army advanced against an opponent that was badly disorganised and unable to match its strength. Indeed, further incommoded by Wellington's decision not to attack them directly but rather to lead his troops on a series of outflanking operations that forced the French to keep on the move, the invaders did not even make a stand at all until they had crossed the River Ebro and reached the city of Vitoria. Even here they bungled such opportunity as they had of putting up a good fight, and it was in large part only through the mistakes of some of Wellington's subordinate commanders, not to mention the irresistible lure represented by the French baggage train, that they were able to salvage anything from the disaster that followed. Even as it was, however, the French field armies were out of action for a month, Wellington therefore being enabled to close up to the Pyrenees and besiege the fortresses of San Sebastián and Pamplona. The latter, it was decided, should be reduced by blockade alone, but San Sebastián was made the target of regular siege operations. However, being both well fortified and inconveniently situated, the fortress proved a difficult target and on 25 July the garrison beat off a full-scale assault with heavy losses. On that same day fighting erupted in the Pyrenees. Following the defeat at Vitoria, Napoleon had placed all the troops facing Wellington under the command of the highly experienced Marshal Soult, and, having succeeded in reorganising his forces in a remarkably short space of time, on 25 July the marshal launched a major offensive in a bid to relieve Pamplona. Known as the battle of the Pyrenees, the result was a series of clashes spread over several days that eventually saw the French bundled back across the frontier into France. San Sebastián having finally been stormed on 31 August, though not before another French counteroffensive had been staved off by Spanish troops at the battle of San Marcial, on 7 October Wellington sent his forces across the frontier into France. At first the advance did not penetrate very far, and Soult was therefore able to set up a defensive line along a series of mountains a little way back from the frontier, but on 10 November these positions were forced in their turn in the battle of the River Nivelle, Wellington then advancing on the French fortress of Bayonne. There followed the last battle of the campaign. With the position of the Anglo-Portuguese army rendered rather difficult by the fact that it was split in two by the River Nive, on 9 December Soult launched a series of counter-attacks designed to defeat Wellington in detail. In four days of heavy fighting the latter was frequently hard-pressed, but eventually the French were thrown back, leaving the Anglo-Portuguese forces in control of the same positions as they had occupied at the start of the fighting. It was a fitting end to the campaign: in seven months of hard fighting, Wellington's troops had proved themselves to be superior to their opponents in almost every way, and in the process liberated most of Spain, the only area of the country that now remained under the control of the French being northern Catalonia.

To Earl Bathurst.

Freneda, 11th May, 1813.

I have received your letter of the 20th April, and I am very much obliged to you for the care you take of our money concerns. It is certainly true that large sums have been exported from this country to America in payment for corn imported; but this corn is besides that imported in consequence of our orders, and paid for by our bills negotiated in America. One of my reasons for agreeing to the purchase of corn in Brazil and Egypt was to put a stop to the purchases of the imported American corn, if the American government should have allowed of the intercourse after the declaration of war.

I enclose a copy of the instructions which I have given to Sir J. Murray, and Generals Copons, Elio, and the Duque del Parque. Sir J. Murray has informed me that he proposes to carry into execution the plan recommended in the first instance, viz., the attack upon Tarragona; and, by a letter from him of the 30th, I understand that he is well satisfied with what is proposed for him and the troops on that side. I likewise enclose an extract of a letter from him of the 24th, which shows the nature of Suchet's position, and how impracticable it would be to make any thing of it in any other manner. These papers will make you acquainted with the plan of operations for the troops on the other side of the Peninsula, which are necessarily disconnected with those of the troops on this side, at least for a time.

I propose on this side to commence our operations by turning the enemy's position on the Duero, by passing the left of our army over that river within the Portuguese frontier. I should cross the right in the same manner, only that I have been obliged to throw the right very forward during the winter, in order to cover and connect our cantonments; and I could not well draw them back for this movement without exposing a good deal of country and incurring the risk of a counter movement on the part of the enemy. I therefore propose to strengthen our right and to move with it myself across the Tormes, and establish a bridge on the Duero below Zamora. The two wings of the army will thus be connected, and the enemy's position on the Duero will be turned. The Spanish army of Galicia will be on the Esla on the left of our army at the same time that our army will be on that river.

Having turned the enemy's position on the Duero, and established our communication across it, our next operation must depend upon circumstances. I don't know whether I am now stronger than the enemy, even including the army of Galicia; but of this I am very certain, that I shall not be stronger throughout the campaign, or more efficient, than I now am; and the enemy will not be weaker. I cannot have a better opportunity for trying the fate of a battle, which, if the enemy should be unsuccessful, must oblige him to withdraw entirely.

We have been sadly delayed by the bridge, without which it is obvious we can do nothing. The equipment is quite new, and has marched only from Abrantes; but there has already been much breakage, and I understand that the carriages are shamefully bad. The truth is, that English tradesmen, particularly contractors, are become so dishonest, that no reliance can be placed on any work, particularly in iron, done by contract. I have the same complaint of some carts made for the Commissariat; 18 out of 25 of which broke on a good road without loads in 80 miles. I shall have sad work with this bridge throughout the campaign, and yet we can do nothing without it.

I shall send the Prince of Orange home, as you desire, unless you should comply with his wish to join the Prussian army, and allow him to go home for that purpose.

To Earl Bathurst.

Carvajales, 31st May, 1813.

The troops arrived at Salamanca on the 26th inst., and we found the enemy still in the town with one division of infantry, and 3 squadrons of cavalry, and some cannon of the army of the South, under the command of Gen. Villatte. The enemy evacuated the town on our approach, but they waited longer than they ought on the high ground in the neighbourhood, and afforded an opportunity for the cavalry, under Gen. Fane and Gen. V. Alten, the former of which crossed the Tormes at the ford of Sta Marta, and the latter at the bridge, to do them a good deal of injury in their retreat. Many were killed and wounded, and we took about 200 prisoners, 7 tumbrels of ammunition, some baggage, provisions, &c. The enemy retired by the road of Babila-fuente, and near Huerta were joined by a body of infantry and cavalry on their march from Alba. I then ordered our troops to discontinue their pursuit, our infantry not being up.

Major Gen. Long, and Don P. Morillo, in command of the Spanish division, attacked Alba, from which place the enemy retired. In the course of the 27th and 28th, I established the troops which had marched from the Agueda and Upper Estremadura, between the Tormes and Duero, under the command of Lieut. Gen. Sir R. Hill, with the view to their early communication and junction with the main body of the army, on the right of the Duero, and in the mean time, to their retaining possession of the Tormes, and of the communication with Ciudad Rodrigo; and I set off myself on the 29th to join the troops here, and arrived that day at Miranda de Douro; and here on the 30th I found the troops on the Esla, under the orders of Sir T. Graham, as I had intended, with their left at Tabara, and in communication with the Galician army, and their right at this place, and all the arrangements made for passing the Esla. The greater part passed that river this morning, the cavalry by fords, and the infantry by a bridge, which it was necessary to throw over the river, as it was so deep that some men, even of the cavalry, were lost in the passage. The English hussars, who crossed first, took an officer and 30 prisoners near Val de Perdices.

The enemy have evacuated Zamora, and our patrols have been in that town. The troops which were there have fallen back upon Toro, where I understand they have one division of infantry and a brigade of cavalry.

It appears that the enemy have joined at La Nava del Rey the troops which retired from Salamanca, Avila, &c. with those which were at Arevalo and Medina del Campo; and I imagine that as this part of the army will advance, they will retire across the Duero. The enemy's troops were still at Madrid and on the Tagus on the 22d inst. I conclude that they will have evacuated that part of the country on hearing of our movement.

I have received a report to which I give credit, though it is not official, that the Spanish garrison have evacuated Castro Urdiales, and have embarked in His Majesty's ships.

I have received no accounts from Alicante since I addressed your Lordship last.

Zamora, 1st June, 1813.

P. S. This dispatch having been detained, I have to inform your Lordship that I moved the head quarters here this day.

The enemy have evacuated Toro, into which place our troops have entered. The head quarters will be there to-morrow.

To Earl Bathurst.

Ampudia, 6th June, 1813.

The troops have continued to advance since I wrote to your Lordship on the 31st of last month, and were on the 1st at Zamora, and on the 2d they arrived at Toro.

The English hussars, being in the advanced guard, fell in, between Toro and Morales, with a considerable body of the enemy's cavalry, which were immediately attacked by the 10th, supported by the 18th and 15th. The enemy were overthrown, and pursued for many miles; and 210 prisoners, with many horses, and 2 officers, fell into our hands.

I enclose Col. Grant's report of this gallant affair, which reflects great credit upon Major Robarts and the 10th hussars, and upon Col. Grant, under whose directions they acted. On the same evening, Don Julian Sanchez surprised the enemy's post at Castro-nuño, and took 2 officers and 30 cavalry prisoners; and he drove their posts from the ford of Pollos.

The enemy had destroyed the bridges of Zamora and Toro; and the difficulties in the passage of the Esla had retarded the movement of our rear, while the enemy had concentrated their force to a considerable amount between Torre-lobaton and Tordesillas. I therefore halted on the 3d at Toro, in order to bring the Light division and the troops under the command of Lieut. Gen. Sir R. Hill across the Duero by the bridge of that town, and to close up our rear, and to bring the Galician army to join our left; and we moved again on the 4th.

The enemy had commenced collecting their troops towards the Duero when they found that we passed Ciudad Rodrigo; and they crossed the Duero at Tordesillas on the 1st and 2d. The troops at Madrid, and the detachments on the Tagus, broke up on the 27th, and crossed the Duero at the Puente de Duero on the 3d; and Valladolid was entirely evacuated on the 4th. The enemy left considerable magazines of grain at Arevalo, and some ammunition at Valladolid and Zamora. The enemy have passed the Carrion, and are apparently on their retreat towards Burgos.

I have received a report, to which I give credit, that the enemy, having brought 5 guns to Castro Urdiales from Santoña by sea, effected a breach in the town wall on the 11th May, which they stormed and carried, the garrison having retired to the castle. They attempted to storm the castle, but were repulsed with considerable loss; and the garrison were carried off on the morning of the 12th by H. M.'s sloops *Lyra, Royalist,* and *Sparrow,* and were landed at Beromeo.

I have received no accounts from Alicante since I addressed your Lordship last.

To Lieut. Col. Bourke.

Melgar on the Pisuerga, 10th June, 1813.

There are at Coruña certain ships loaded with biscuit and flour, and certain others loaded with a heavy train of artillery and ammunition, and some musket ammunition; and I shall be very much obliged to you if you will request any officer of the navy who may be at Coruña when you receive this letter to take under his convoy all the vessels loaded as above mentioned, and to proceed with them to Santander. If he should find Santander occupied by the enemy, I beg him to remain off the port till the operations of this army have obliged the enemy to abandon it. If the enemy should not be in Santander, I beg him to enter the port; but to be in readiness to quit it again, if the enemy should approach the place, until I shall communicate with him.

If Mr White should have any money in his hands which he can spare, I beg he will send it by the same opportunity.

I have directed that 100,000 dollars should be sent round from Lisbon for the use of the Spanish army; and I learn from Adm. Martin that a ship was ready at the end of May to take this money to Coruña. I beg that, when this sum shall arrive, it may be delivered to the order of Gen. Giron at Coruña.

To Earl Bathurst.

Villadiego, 13th June, 1813.

The army passed the Carrion on the 7th, the enemy having retired across the Pisuerga; and on the 8th, 9th, and 10th we brought forward our left and passed that river.

The celerity of our march up to this period, and the probable difficulties in, and the necessity of providing for the subsistence of the army in our farther progress, induced me to make short movements on the 11th, and to halt the left on the 12th; but on the latter day I moved forward the right under Lieut. Gen. Sir R. Hill, consisting of the 2d British, Gen. Morillo's Spanish, and the Conde de Amarante's Portuguese divisions of infantry; and the Light division under Major Gen. Baron C. Alten; and Major Gen. Fane's, Major Gen. Long's, Major Gen. V. Alten's, Brig. Gen. Ponsonby's, and Col. Grant's (Hussar) brigades of cavalry, towards Burgos, with a view to reconnaitre the enemy's position and numbers near that town, and to force them to a decision whether to abandon the castle to its fate, or to protect it with all their force.

I found the enemy posted with a considerable force, commanded, as I understand, by Gen. Reille, on the heights on the left of the Hormaza, with their right above the village of Hormaza, and their left in front of Estepar. We turned their right with the hussars and Gen. Ponsonby's brigade of cavalry and the Light division from Isar, while Gen. V. Alten's brigade of cavalry and Col. the Hon. R. W. O'Callaghan's brigade of the 2d division moved up the heights from Hormaza, and the remainder of the troops under the command of Lieut. Gen. Sir R. Hill threatened the heights of Estepar.

These movements dislodged the enemy from their position immediately. The cavalry of our left and centre were entirely in the rear of the enemy, who were obliged to retire across the Arlanzon by the high road towards Burgos. Although pressed by our cavalry, and suffering considerable loss by the fire of Major Gardiner's troop of horse artillery, and obliged to make their movements at an accelerated pace, that they might not give time to our infantry to come up, they made it in admirable order; but they lost one gun and some prisoners, taken by a squadron of the 14th light dragoons, commanded by Capt. Milles, and a detachment of the 3d dragoons which charged their rear.

The enemy took post on the left of the Arlanzon and Urbel rivers, which were much swollen with rain, and in the course of the night retired their whole army through Burgos, having abandoned and destroyed as far as they were able, in the short space of time during which they were there, the works of the castle which they had constructed and improved at so large an expense; and they are now on their retreat towards the Ebro by the high road of Briviesca and Miranda. In the mean time the whole of the army of the allies has made a movement to the left this day; and the Spanish corps of Galicia under Gen. Giron, and the left of the British and Portuguese army under Lieut. Gen. Sir T. Graham, will, I hope, pass the Ebro to-morrow at the bridges of Rocamunde and San Martin.

In the course of the 9th, 10th, and 11th, Don Julian Sanchez was very active on the left of the enemy, and took several prisoners.

The Conde de la Bisbal with the army of reserve of Andalusia will arrive at Medina del Campo on the 14th.

I have received a letter from Gen. Elio of the 1st inst., in which he informs me that the 3d Spanish army had joined the 2d, that these armies had taken the positions before occupied by the 2d army and the Anglo-Sicilian troops under Sir J. Murray, and that Gen. Sir J. Murray had embarked in obedience to the orders which he had received with the troops under his command; had sailed from Alicante with a fair wind, and was out of sight on the 1st inst.

I have had the castle of Burgos examined this day, and I am happy to inform your Lordship that I have reason to believe that it is possible to put it in a state of repair at a reasonable expense. It is a post of the greatest importance to the country, particularly during the winter; and if I should find it practicable, I will have it put in a state of defence.

To Earl Bathurst.

Subijana, on the Bayas, 19th June, 1813.

The left of the army crossed the Ebro on the 14th, by the bridges of San Martin and Rocamunde, and the remainder on the 15th, by those bridges and that of Puente de Arenas. We continued our march on the following days towards Vitoria.

The enemy assembled on the 16th and 17th a considerable corps at Espejo, not far from the Puente Larra, composed of some of the troops which had been for some time in the Biscayan provinces in pursuit of Longa and Mina, and others detached from the main body of the army, which were still at Pancorbo. They had likewise a division of infantry and some cavalry at Frias since the 16th, for the purpose of observing our movements on the left of the Ebro. Both these detachments marched yesterday morning: that from Frias, upon San Millan, where it was found by the Light division of the Allied army, under Major Gen. C. Alten; and that from Espejo, on Osma, where it met the 6th and 5th divisions, under Lieut. Gen. Sir T. Graham. Major Gen. C. Alten drove the enemy from San Millan, and afterwards cut off the rear brigade of the division, of which he took 300 prisoners; killed and wounded many, and the brigade was dispersed in the mountains.

The corps from Espejo was considerably stronger than the Allied corps under Sir T. Graham, which had arrived nearly at the same time at Osma. The enemy moved on to the attack, but were soon obliged to retire; and they were followed to Espejo, from whence they retired through the hills to this place. It was late in the day before the other troops came up to the advanced position which those under Lieut. Gen. Sir T. Graham had taken; and I halted the 4th division, which relieved the 5th, near Espejo.

The army moved forward this day to this river. I found the enemy's rear guard in a strong position, on the left of the river, having his right covered by Subijana, and his left by the heights in front of Pobes. We turned the enemy's left with the Light division, while the 4th division, under Lieut. Gen. Sir L. Cole, attacked them in front; and the rear guard was driven back upon the main body of the army, which was in march from Pancorbo to Vitoria, having broken up from thence last night. I am informed that the enemy have dismantled Pancorbo. Col. Longa's division joined the army on the 16th, on its arrival at Medina de Pomar.

The Conde de la Bisbal will arrive at Burgos on the 24th or 25th.

I have not received any intelligence from the eastern coast since I addressed your Lordship last.

Return of the killed, wounded, and missing,
from the 12th to the 19th June, 1813.

	Officers.	Serjeants.	R. and F.	Horses.	Total loss of officers, non-commissioned officers, and R. & F.
Killed	—	4	23	18	27
Wounded	9	7	137	26	153
Missing	—	—	—	7	—

To Earl Bathurst.

Salvatierra, 22d June, 1813.

The enemy, commanded by King Joseph, having Marshal Jourdan as the Major General of the army, took up a position, on the night of the 19th inst., in front of Vitoria; the left of which rested upon the heights which end at La Puebla de Arganzon, and extended from thence across the valley of the Zadorra, in front of the village of Ariñez. They occupied with the right of the centre a height which commanded the valley to the Zadorra. The right of their army was stationed near Vitoria, and was destined to defend the passages of the river Zadorra, in the neighbourhood of that city. They had a reserve in rear of their left, at the village of Gomecha. The nature of the country through which the army had passed since it had reached the Ebro, had necessarily extended our columns; and we halted on the 20th, in order to close them up, and moved the left to Murguia, where it was most likely it would be required. I reconnaitred the enemy's position on that day, with a view to the attack to be made on the following morning, if they should still remain in it. We accordingly attacked the enemy yesterday, and I am happy to inform your Lordship, that the Allied army under my command gained a complete victory, having driven them from all their positions; having taken from them 151 pieces of cannon, waggons of ammunition, all their baggage, provisions, cattle, treasure, &c., and a considerable number of prisoners.

The operations of the day commenced by Lieut. Gen. Sir R. Hill obtaining possession of the heights of La Puebla, on which the enemy's left rested, which heights they had not occupied in great strength. He detached for this service one brigade of the Spanish division under Gen. Morillo; the other brigade being employed in keeping the communication between his main body on the high road from Miranda to Vitoria, and the troops detached to the heights. The enemy, however, soon discovered the importance of these heights, and reinforced their troops there to such an extent, that Lieut. Gen. Sir R. Hill was obliged to detach, 1st, the 71st regt. and the light infantry battalion of Gen. Walker's brigade, under the command of Lieut. Col. the Hon. H. Cadogan, and successively other troops to the same point; and the Allies not only gained, but maintained possession of these important heights throughout their operations, notwithstanding all the efforts of the enemy to retake them.

The contest here was, however, very severe, and the loss sustained considerable. Gen. Morillo was wounded, but remained in the field; and I am concerned to have to report, that Lieut. Col. the Hon. H. Cadogan has died of a wound which he received. In him His Majesty has lost an officer of great merit and tried gallantry, who had already acquired the respect and regard of the whole profession, and of whom it might have been expected that, if he had lived, he would have rendered the most important services to his country. Under cover of the possession of these heights, Sir R. Hill successively passed the Zadorra, at La Puebla, and the defile formed by the heights and the river Zadorra, and attacked and gained possession of the village of Subijana de Alava, in front of the enemy's line, which the enemy made repeated attempts to regain.

The difficult nature of the country prevented the communication between our different columns moving to the attack from their stations on the river Bayas at as early an hour as I had expected; and it was late before I knew that the column, composed of the 3d and 7th divisions, under the command of the Earl of Dalhousie, had arrived at the station appointed for them. The 4th and Light divisions, however, passed the Zadorra immediately after Sir R. Hill had possession of Subijana de Alava; the former at the bridge of Nanclares, and the latter at the bridge of Tres-puentes; and almost as soon as these had crossed, the column under the Earl of Dalhousie arrived at Mendoza; and the 3d division, under Lieut. Gen. Sir T. Picton, crossed at the bridge higher up, followed by the 7th division, under the Earl of Dalhousie. These four divisions, forming the centre of the army, were destined to attack the height on which the right of the enemy's centre was placed, while Lieut. Gen. Sir R. Hill should move forward from Subijana de Alava to attack the left. The enemy, however, having weakened his line to strengthen his detachment on the hills, abandoned his position in the valley as soon as he saw our disposition to attack it, and commenced his retreat in good order towards Vitoria.

Our troops continued to advance in admirable order, notwithstanding the difficulty of the ground. In the mean time, Lieut. Gen. Sir T. Graham, who commanded the left of the army, consisting of the 1st and 5th divisions, and Gens. Pack's and Bradford's brigades of infantry, and Gens. Bock's and Anson's of cavalry, and who had been moved on the 20th to Murguia, moved forward from thence on Vitoria, by the high road from that town to Bilbao. He had, besides, with him the Spanish division under Col. Longa; and Gen. Giron, who had been detached to the left, under a different view of the state of affairs, and had afterwards been recalled, and had arrived on the 20th at Orduña, marched that morning from thence, so as to be in the field in readiness to support Lieut. Gen. Sir T. Graham, if his support had been required.

The enemy had a division of infantry with some cavalry advanced on the great road from Vitoria to Bilbao, resting their right on some strong heights covering the village of Gamarra Mayor. Both Gamarra and Abechuco were strongly occupied as *têtes de pont* to the bridges over the Zadorra at these places. Brig. Gen. Pack with his Portuguese brigade, and Col. Longa with his Spanish division, were directed to turn and gain the heights, supported by Major Gen. Anson's brigade of light dragoons, and the 5th division of infantry under the command of Major Gen. Oswald, who was desired to take the command of all these troops.

Lieut. Gen. Sir T. Graham reports, that in the execution of this service the Portuguese and Spanish troops behaved admirably. The 4th battalion of caçadores, and the 8th caçadores, particularly distinguished themselves. Col. Longa being on the left, took possession of Gamarra Menor.

As soon as the heights were in our possession, the village of Gamarra Mayor was most gallantly stormed and carried by Major Gen. Robinson's brigade of the 5th division, which advanced in columns of battalions, under a very heavy fire of artillery and musketry, without firing a shot, assisted by 2 guns of Major Lawson's brigade of artillery. The enemy suffered severely, and lost 3 pieces of cannon.

The Lieut. General then proceeded to attack the village of Abechuco with the 1st division, by forming a strong battery against it, consisting of Capt. Dubourdieu's brigade, and Capt. Ramsay's troop of horse artillery; and under cover of this fire, Col. Halkett's brigade advanced to the attack of the village, which was carried; the light battalions having charged and taken 3 guns and a howitzer on the bridge. This attack was supported by Gen. Bradford's brigade of Portuguese infantry. During the operation at Abechuco the enemy made the greatest efforts to repossess themselves of the village of Gamarra Mayor, which were gallantly repulsed by the 5th division, under the command of Major Gen. Oswald. The enemy had, however, on the heights on the left of the Zadorra, 2 divisions of infantry in reserve; and it was impossible to cross by the bridges till the troops which had moved upon the enemy's centre and left had driven them through Vitoria. The whole then co-operated in the pursuit, which was continued by all till after it was dark.

The movement of the troops under Lieut. Gen. Sir T. Graham, and their possession of Gamarra and Abechuco, intercepted the enemy's retreat by the high road to France. They were then obliged to turn to the road towards Pamplona; but they were unable to hold any position for a sufficient length of time to allow their baggage and artillery to be drawn off. The whole, therefore, of the latter which had not already been taken by the troops in their attack of the successive positions taken up by the enemy in their retreat from their first position at Ariñez and on the Zadorra, and all their ammunition and baggage, and every thing they had, were taken close to Vitoria. I have reason to believe that the enemy carried off with them one gun and one howitzer only.

The army under King Joseph consisted of the whole of the armies of the South and of the Centre, and of 4 divisions and all the cavalry of the army of Portugal, and some troops of the army of the North. Gen. Foy's division of the army of Portugal was in the neighbourhood of Bilbao; and Gen. Clausel, who commanded the army of the North, was near Logroño with one division of the army of Portugal commanded by Gen. Taupin, and Gen. Van-der-Maesen's division of the army of the North. The 6th division of the allied army under Major Gen. the Hon. E. Pakenham was likewise absent, having been detained at Medina de Pomar for 3 days, to cover the march of our magazines and stores.

I cannot extol too highly the good conduct of all the General officers, officers, and soldiers of the army in this action. Lieut. Gen. Sir R. Hill speaks highly of the conduct of Gen. Morillo and the Spanish troops under his command, and of that of Lieut. Gen. the Hon. W. Stewart, and the Conde de Amarante, who commanded divisions of infantry under his directions.

He likewise mentions the conduct of Col. the Hon. R. W. O'Callaghan, who maintained the village of Subijana de Alava against all the efforts of the enemy to regain possession of it, and that of Lieut. Col. Rooke of the Adj. Gen.'s department, and Lieut. Col. the Hon. A. Abencromby of the Q. M. G.'s department. It was impossible for the movements of any troops to be conducted with more spirit and regularity than those of their respective divisions, by Lieut. Gens. the Earl of Dalhousie, Sir T. Picton, Sir L. Cole, and Major Gen. Baron C. Alten. The troops advanced in *échelons* of regiments in 2, and occasionally 3 lines; and the Portuguese troops in the 3d and 4th divisions, under the command of Brig. Gen. Power and Col. Stubbs, led the march with steadiness and gallantry never surpassed on any occasion.

Major Gen. the Hon. C. Colville's brigade of the 3d division was seriously attacked in its advance by a very superior force well formed, which it drove in, supported by Gen. Inglis's brigade of the 7th division, commanded by Col. Grant of the 82d. These officers and the troops under their command distinguished themselves.

Major Gen. Vandeleur's brigade of the Light division was, during the advance upon Vitoria, detached to the support of the 7th division; and Lieut. Gen. the Earl of Dalhousie has reported most favorably of its conduct. Lieut. Gen. Sir T. Graham particularly reports his sense of the assistance he received from Col. De Lancey, the D. Q. M. G., and from Lieut. Col. Bouverie, of the Adj. Gen.'s department, and from the officers of his personal staff; and from Lieut. Col. the Hon. A. Upton, A. Q. M. G., and Major Hope, A. A. G., with the 1st division; and Major Gen. Oswald reports the same of Lieut. Col. Berkeley of the Adj. Gen's department, and Lieut. Col. Gomm of the Q. M. G.'s department.

I am particularly indebted to Lieut. Gen. Sir T. Graham, and to Lieut. Gen. Sir R. Hill, for the manner in which they have respectively conducted the service entrusted to them since the commencement of the operations which have ended in the battle of the 21st; and for their conduct in that battle; as likewise to Marshal Sir W. Beresford for the friendly advice and assistance which I have received from him upon all occasions during the late operations.

I must not omit to mention likewise the conduct of Gen. Giron, who commands the Galician army, who made a forced march from Orduña, and was actually on the ground in readiness to support Lieut. Gen. Sir T. Graham.

I have frequently been indebted, and have had occasion to call the attention of your Lordship to the conduct of the Quarter Master Gen., Sir G. Murray, who in the late operations, and in the battle of the 21st June, has again given the greatest assistance. I am likewise much indebted to Lord Aylmer, the D. A. G., and to the officers of the departments of the Adj. and Q. M. G. respectively; and also to Lord FitzRoy Somerset, and Lieut. Col. Campbell and those of my personal staff; and to Lieut. Col. Sir R. Fletcher, and the officers of the Royal Engineers.

Col. H. S. H. the Hereditary Prince of Orange was in the field as my aide de camp, and conducted himself with his usual gallantry and intelligence.

Mariscal de Campo Don L. Wimpffen, and the Inspector Gen. Don T. O'Donoju, and the officers of the Staff of the Spanish army, have invariably rendered me every assistance in their power in the course of these operations; and I avail myself of this opportunity of expressing my satisfaction with their conduct; as likewise with that of Mariscal de Campo Don M. Alava; and of the Brig. Gen. Don José O'Lawlor, who have been so long and usefully employed with me.

The artillery was most judiciously placed by Lieut. Col. Dickson, and was well served; and the army is particularly indebted to that corps. The nature of the ground did not allow of the cavalry being generally engaged; but the General officers commanding the several brigades kept the troops under their command respectively close to the infantry to support them, and they were most active in the pursuit of the enemy after they had been driven through Vitoria.

I send this dispatch by my aide de camp Capt. Fremantle, whom I beg leave to recommend to your Lordship's protection. He will have the honor of laying at the feet of His Royal Highness the colors of the 4th batt. 100th regt., and Marshal Jourdan's bâton of a Marshal of France, taken by the 87th regt.

I enclose a return of the killed and wounded in the late operations, and a return of the ordnance, carriages, and ammunition taken from the enemy in the action of the 21st inst.

Return of the killed, wounded, and missing, of the allied army at Vitoria, on the 21st June, 1813.

	Officers.	Serjeants.	R. and F.	Total loss of officers, non-commissioned officers, and R. and F.	British.	Spanish.	Portuguese.	Horses.
Killed .	33	19	688	740	501	89	150	92
Wounded	230	158	3782	4174	2807	464	899	68
Missing .	—	1	265	266	—	—	—	26

1 serjeant, 2 drummers, and 263 R. and F. have been returned missing by the several corps of the army, British and Portuguese. It is supposed that the greater number of them lost their regiments in the course of the night, and that very few of them have fallen into the hands of the enemy.

Return of Ordnance, Carriages, and Ammunition, captured from the enemy in the action at Vitoria, on the 21st June, 1813.

151	Brass Ordnance, on travelling carriages.
415	Caissons.
14,249	Rounds of ammunition.
1,973,400	Musket Ball cartridges.
40,668	lbs. of Gunpowder.
56	Forage waggons.
44	Forge waggons.

A. DICKSON, Lieut. Col. commanding the Artillery.

To Earl Bathurst.

Caseda, on the river Aragon, 29th June, 1813.

It is desirable that any reinforcements of infantry which you may send to this army may come to Santander, notwithstanding that I am very apprehensive of the consequence of marching our vagabond soldiers through the province of Biscay in that state of discipline in which they and their officers generally come out to us. It may be depended upon, that the people of this province will shoot them as they would the French, if they should misbehave.

We started with the army in the highest order, and up to the day of the battle nothing could get on better; but that event has, as usual, totally annihilated all order and discipline. The soldiers of the army have got among them about a million sterling in money, with the exception of about 100,000 dollars, which were got for the military chest. The night of the battle, instead of being passed in getting rest and food to prepare them for the pursuit of the following day, was passed by the soldiers in looking for plunder. The consequence was, that they were incapable of marching in pursuit of the enemy, and were totally knocked up. The rain came on and increased their fatigue, and I am quite convinced that we have now out of the ranks double the amount of our loss in the battle; and that we have lost more men in the pursuit than the enemy have; and have never in any one day made more than an ordinary march.

This is the consequence of the state of discipline of the British army. We may gain the greatest victories; but we shall do no good until we shall so far alter our system, as to force all ranks to perform their duty. The new regiments are, as usual, the worst of all. The [Eighteenth Hussars] are a disgrace to the name of a soldier, in action as well as elsewhere; and I propose to draft their horses from them, and to send the men to England, if I can't get the better of them in any other manner.

To Lieut. Gen. the Earl of Dalhousie.

Huarte, 2d July, 1813.

I am anxious to establish a strict and close blockade of Pamplona, preparatory to any other measures for the capture of the place which it may be expedient to adopt, of which I request your Lordship to take charge, and to arrange the details with Col. Sir R. Fletcher, who has received my directions upon the subject.

It is my opinion that the principle on which the blockade ought to be established is, that redoubts should be constructed on certain favorable spots which Col. Sir R. Fletcher will point out, at the distance of 1000 and 1200 yards from the place, to serve as points of support to the piquets by which the blockade should be maintained by day and night. These should be posted by day, in posts to be fixed for them and numbered. At night they should be closed to within 600 yards of the place, and ought to communicate. Measures should be taken to strengthen the village on the north side of the fort, so as to render it a secure post.

It is my wish to render the duty of the blockade as light as possible to the several divisions which shall come up; and I request your Lordship to order them to occupy such positions in the neighbourhood of the place as may best enable them to form the blockade, and to execute the works which it will be necessary to make. Hereafter I propose that the blockade should be held by the Spanish troops, when I shall relieve your Lordship from the trouble with which I am now charging you.

It is desirable to cut the corn as close to the fort as possible, and at all events to prevent the enemy from cutting it. It might be possible, perhaps, after a few dry days, to burn that close to the fort, which will not be under the fire of our day piquets, or of the guns in the situations of our redoubts. The guns attached to the divisions might be in these situations till those intended for them shall arrive from Vitoria.

To Earl Bathurst.

Huarte, 2d July, 1813.

I enclose the copy of a letter from the Governor of Vitoria, which shows how our men are going on in that neighbourhood. These men are detachments from the different regiments of the army who were sent to Vitoria the day after the battle, each under officers, in order to collect the wounded and their arms and accoutrements. It is quite impossible for me or any other man to command a British army under the existing system. We have in the service the scum of the earth as common soldiers; and of late years we have been doing every thing in our power, both by law and by publications, to relax the discipline by which alone such men can be kept in order. The officers of the lower ranks will not perform the duty required from them for the purpose of keeping their soldiers in order; and it is next to impossible to punish any officer for neglects of this description. As to the non-commissioned officers, as I have repeatedly stated, they are as bad as the men, and too near them, in point of pay and situation, by the regulations of late years, for us to expect them to do any thing to keep the men in order. It is really a disgrace to have any thing to say to such men as some of our soldiers are.

I now beg to draw your attention to the mode in which these irregularities affect our numbers. On the 17th June the total British and Portuguese force was 67,036 R. and F.; on the 29th June it is 58,694 R. and F.: diminution 8342 R. and F. The British on the 17th June were 41,547 R. and F.; on the 29th June 35,650 R. and F.: diminution 5897. The loss of British R. and F. in the battle was 3164, including 200 missing; so that the diminution from irregularities, straggling, &c., since, for plunder, is 2733. The loss of Portuguese R. and F. in the battle was 1022, including 73 missing; and their diminution from the same causes is 1423.

While we were pursuing the enemy by the valley of Araquil towards Pamplona, finding so many men straggling from their ranks, I ordered that an hospital might be established to receive them; and, although there are so many men absent from their regiments, there are only 160 in that hospital. The others are plundering the country in different directions.

To Earl Bathurst.

Ostiz, 3d July, 1813.

Gen. Clausel having retired towards Logroño, after finding our troops at Vitoria on the 22d June, and having ascertained the result of the action of the 21st, still remained in the neighbour-hood of Logroño on the 24th, and till late on the 25th, and had not marched for Tudela, as I had been informed when I wrote my dispatch of the 24th June: I conceived, therefore, that there was some prospect of intercepting his retreat; and after sending the light troops towards Roncesvalles in pursuit of the army under King Joseph, I moved the Light, 3d, 4th, and 7th divi-sions, and Col. Grant's and Col. Ponsonby's brigades of cavalry, towards Tudela; and the 5th and 6th divisions, and the House-hold and the Conde de la Bisbal's cavalry, from Vitoria and Salvatierra towards Logroño, in hopes that I should be able to intercept Gen. Clausel. He made some extraordinary forced marches, followed by Gen. Mina with his own cavalry, and the regiment of Spanish cavalry under the command of Don Julian Sanchez, and arrived at Tudela on the evening of the 27th. He there crossed the Ebro; but the Alcalde having informed him that we were upon the road, he immediately recrossed, and marched towards Zaragoza, where I understand from Gen. Alava that he has since arrived.

I then turned off to Caseda on the Aragon, where I arrived on the 28th; but, finding that the enemy had already advanced so far upon their march as to render it impossible for me to cut them off from Jaca, and thinking it probable that my farther advance in that direction would force Gen. Clausel to avoid the road of Jaca, and to seek a junction with Marshal Suchet, which he would otherwise seek to avoid, and which I had no means of preventing, I discontinued the pursuit with the allied British and Portuguese troops; and they are on their return towards Pamplona. Those under Gen. Mina are still following the enemy; and he has taken from them 2 pieces of cannon and some stores in Tudela, and 300 prisoners. Lieut. Gen. H. Clinton has also taken possession of 5 pieces which the enemy left at Logroño.

In the mean time the troops under the command of Lieut. Gen. Sir R. Hill have kept the blockade of Pamplona, and have moved through the mountains to the head of the Bidasoa, the enemy having entirely retired into France on that side.

I enclose the report which I have received from Lieut. Gen. Sir T. Graham of his actions with the enemy on the 24th and 25th June, which appear to have been more serious than I had imagined when I addressed your Lordship on the 26th ult.

Gen. Foy had with him the garrison of Bilbao, and those of Mondragon and Tolosa, besides his division of the army of Portugal, and his force was considerable. It gives me great satisfaction to see that the Spanish and Portuguese troops, mentioned by Sir T. Graham, have conducted themselves so well. The General has continued to push on the enemy by the high road, and has dislodged them from all strong positions which they have taken; and yesterday a brigade of the army of Galicia, under the command of Gen. Castaños, attacked and drove the enemy across the Bidasoa, by the bridge of Irun. The enemy still maintained a post in a strong stone blockhouse, which served as a head to the bridge, and some troops in some loop-holed houses on the right of the Bidasoa; but Gen. Don P. A. Giron having sent for some Spanish artillery, and Capt. Dubourdieu's brigade of 9 pounders having been sent to their support, the fire of these guns obliged the enemy to evacuate; and they blew up the blockhouse and burnt the bridge. Sir T. Graham reports that in all these affairs the Spanish troops have conducted themselves remarkably well.

The garrison at Pasages, consisting of 150 men, surrendered on the 30th to the troops under Col. Longa.

The enemy, on seeing some of our ships off Deba, evacuated

the fort and town of Guetaria on the 1st inst.; and the garrison went by sea to San Sebastian. This place is blockaded by land by a detachment of Spanish troops. They have likewise evacuated Castro Urdiales, and the garrison have gone by sea to Santoña.

In my former reports I have made your Lordship acquainted with the progress of the army of reserve of Andalusia, under Gen. the Conde de la Bisbal, to join the army; and he arrived at Burgos on the 25th and 26th ult.

When the enemy retired across the Ebro, previous to the battle at Vitoria, they left a garrison of about 700 men in the castle of Pancorbo, by which they commanded, and rendered it impossible for us to use, the great communication from Vitoria to Burgos. I therefore requested the Conde de la Bisbal, on his march to Miranda, to make himself master of the town and lower works, and to blockade the place as closely as he could. I have not received the report of his first operations, but I understand that he carried the town and lower fort by assault on the 28th; and I have now the pleasure to enclose his report of the final success of this operation, and the copy of the capitulation by which the garrison have surrendered. The decision and dispatch with which this place has been subdued are highly creditable to the Conde de la Bisbal and the officers and troops under his command.

I am concerned to inform your Lordship that Lieut. Gen. Sir J. Murray raised the siege of Tarragona, I cannot say on what day, and embarked his troops: a great portion of the artillery and stores were left in the batteries. It appears that Marshal Suchet, with a considerable body of troops, had moved from Valencia by Tortosa, and Gen. Maurice Mathieu with another corps from the neighbourhood of Barcelona, for the purpose of impeding Sir J. Murray's operations, which he did not think himself sufficiently strong to continue. I have not yet received from Sir J. Murray the detailed account of these transactions.

Lieut. Gen. Lord W. Bentinck, however, who had joined and taken the command of the army at the Coll de Balaguer on the 17th, had brought it back to Alicante, where he arrived himself on the 23rd, and was proceeding to carry into execution my instructions.

When Marshal Suchet marched into Catalonia, the Duque del Parque had advanced, and had established his head quarters at San Felipe de Xativa, and his troops on the Jucar, where he still was on the 24th; but I believe that he will have retired upon Suchet's return to Valencia.

I am not informed of the extent of the loss of the heavy artillery at Tarragona, nor whether it will cripple the operations of the troops on the eastern coast. Considering, however, the nature of the enemy's position in Valencia and Catalonia, and his possession of the numerous fortified posts in these provinces, which render it scarcely possible for the allied troops to carry on any operation until they shall become masters of some of them, I am apprehensive that the enemy will be induced to withdraw his active army from thence, in order to throw them upon our right flank, in the confidence that, in the existing state of our equipment, we can effect nothing against any of the fortresses; and that, without some at least of the fortresses, the operations of our troops in the field must be very confined.

Before I had received intelligence of the last state of affairs on the eastern coast, I had doubted the expediency of laying siege to Pamplona, which I had at first intended, upon finding that the place was of such a description, and in such a state of defence, as to require a much larger equipment of heavy ordnance than I had immediately at command; and that it would require an operation of from 5 to 6 weeks' duration, which could not even be commenced for a fortnight or 3 weeks, and the employment of from 15,000 to 20,000 men of our best troops; whereas the blockade could be held by troops of inferior numbers, and of not so good a description; and it is probable that, in point of time, the place would be obliged to surrender within 12 weeks. The disasters at Tarragona, and my view of their probable consequences, have induced me to determine only to blockade Pamplona, for which the necessary works are now constructing; and I shall now have the whole army at liberty for any operation that I may think it proper to carry on.

To Lieut. Gen. Sir T. Graham, K. B.

Lanz, 4th July, 1813.

From the account which I have received from Major Smith of the state of San Sebastian, and in a view to the general situation of our affairs, I feel very anxious to attack that place. Although our train, which was framed with a view to the siege of Burgos, is not quite sufficient for that of Pamplona, it appears to me, from all accounts, that it is fully so for that of San Sebastian. It is now at Bilbao, and I have desired that it may be ordered forthwith to Pasages. I have likewise written to Sir G. Collier, who commands the squadron on the coast, to request him to station himself off or in Pasages, in order the better to keep the maritime blockade of San Sebastian at all events, and to assist eventually at the siege. I have likewise written to England for an increase of the maritime force on the coast.

I shall be much obliged to you if you will desire Major Smith to have the necessary preparations made of fascines, gabions, &c., for this operation. I write to Sir R. Fletcher, to desire he would let you know the prices which I had agreed to pay for these for the siege of Pamplona.

Sir R. Fletcher is now employed in the arrangement and construction of the works for the blockade of Pamplona; but as soon as these shall be arranged, I will send him to San Sebastian. In the mean time, Major Smith might act for him. I shall likewise send Lieut. Col. Dickson, and all the means in artillery, sappers, &c.

I shall be very much obliged to you if you will let me know your opinion whether the Spanish troops could carry on this concern, with a few English to assist occasionally to lead an assault, &c. It will be very desirable if this should be practicable, as it will save our English and Portuguese troops, of whom we have lost more since the 21st, I am very certain, than the enemy have lost. However, as the loss is to be attributed in a great measure to their own irregularity, I am in hopes it is not quite irretrievable.

I understand that San Sebastian is now blockaded by the Spanish troops; but if any more than the mere blockade should be thought necessary by Major Smith, before I can receive your answer, and can settle what troops shall carry on the siege, I shall be obliged to you if you will settle that it may be done by any troops you may think proper.

Hill is in Berrueta; Byng close to St Jean Pied de Port; and the 7th division will be to-morrow through the Puerto de Arraiz. Clausel was at Zaragoza on the 1st.

P. S. I believe I informed you yesterday that the Conde de la Bisbal had taken Pancorbo, with 700 prisoners.

To Earl Bathurst.

Zubieta, 10th July, 1813.

Since I addressed your Lordship on the 3d inst., I have received reports from Gen. Mina, stating that Gen. Clausel had marched from Zaragoza towards Jaca. I have not yet heard of his arrival at that place.

On their right the enemy have remained nearly in the same situation since they crossed the Bidasoa, and destroyed the bridge of Irun. Preparations are making, and are already in great forwardness, to attack the fort of San Sebastian, of which I am in hopes that we shall obtain possession in a short time after we shall have broken ground.

Notwithstanding that the enemy had withdrawn their right and left quite into France, they still maintained their centre in strength in the valley of Baztan; of which, on account of its riches, and the strong positions it affords, they appeared determined to keep possession, and had assembled there 3 divisions of the army of the South, under the command of Gen. Gazan. Lieut. Gen. Sir R. Hill, having been relieved from the blockade of Pamplona, dislodged them successively from all their positions on the 4th, 5th, and 7th inst., with two brigades of British, and one of Portuguese infantry of the 2d division, under the command of Lieut. Gen. the Hon. W. Stewart, and with one brigade of Portuguese infantry of the Conde de Amarante's division, under the command of the Conde.

The last post which the enemy occupied in the Puerto de Maya, between that village and Urdax, was remarkably strong; and the fog was so thick in the afternoon, that it was impossible for the troops to advance beyond the point at which they found themselves when it came on. The enemy, however, had been pushed so vigorously up to that point, that they were obliged to abandon their post in the night, and to retire into France. In all these affairs the troops conducted themselves remarkably well; and Lieut. Gen. Sir R. Hill was much satisfied with the conduct of Lieut. Gen. the Hon. W. Stewart, and of the Conde de Amarante.

The whole of our right being thus established on the frontier, I am proceeding to the left, in order to superintend the operations there.

In proportion as the troops have returned from the movement which they made last week to intercept the retreat of Gen. Clausel, I have employed them in the blockade of Pamplona, a measure which, at the same time that it has enabled me to increase our force in the mountains, gives those troops some repose, which they require after the marches which they have made in the last 2 months. The 3d, 4th, and 6th divisions are now employed in the blockade, and in the construction of the works, to enable me to maintain it with a reduced body of troops.

I have not yet heard of the progress of the Conde de la Bisbal since the fall of Pancorbo; but as soon as he shall arrive I propose to give his troops a few days' rest in the same manner, and by that time I hope that I shall not only have brought to a termination the operations of the siege of San Sebastian, but shall have heard of the result of the armistice in Germany.

Since I addressed your Lordship last, I have received from Lieut. Gen. Lord W. Bentinck a letter of the 30th ult. It appears from other accounts, that the Duque del Parque had retired from the Jucar on the 25th, without loss, and had taken up again the position of Castalla. Lord W. Bentinck had received accounts of the battle of the 21st June, and proposed to move forward as soon as it should be in his power.

It is unfortunate that when Lieut. Gen. Sir J. Murray raised the siege of Tarragona and embarked his army, leaving his cannon, he did not proceed immediately to Valencia, according to the orders which I had given him, instead of disembarking again, and remaining at the Coll de Balaguer.

Return of the killed, wounded, and missing,
from the 4th to the 8th July, 1813.

	Officers.	Serjeants.	R. and F.	Total loss of officers, non-commissioned officers, and R. & F.
Killed	—	1	7	8
Wounded	5	4	110	119
Missing	—	—	2	2

Portuguese loss included.

To Earl Bathurst.

Lesaca, 19th July, 1813.

Having examined our situation on the great road from Vitoria to Irun, and our prospects for the siege of San Sebastian, it appeared to me to be desirable to obtain possession of the *débouchés* of the mountains towards Vera; and I accordingly returned to San Estevan on the 14th, and on the 15th moved forward the 7th and Light divisions, which are now posted on the heights overlooking Sarre and Vera, and the latter occupy Vera. The enemy made but a trifling resistance, and withdrew their posts to the top of the Puerto de Vera.

We established a battery of four 18 pounders against a convent, which the enemy had fortified and occupied in force, about 600 yards from the works of San Sebastian, the

possession of which was necessary, previous to the commencement of any further operations against the place. This battery
opened on the morning of the 14th, and the convent was so far
destroyed that Lieut. Gen. Sir T. Graham ordered that the
building, and a redoubt which protected its left flank, might be
stormed on the 17th. I have not yet received his report of the
details of this operation, which, however, was successful; and
our troops were established at the convent, and at the village
immediately below it, which the enemy had burnt. Our works
have been since continued with great activity; and I understand
from Sir T. Graham that the batteries will open to destroy and
enfilade the defences of the point of attack to-morrow. The
same batteries will answer to effect a breach in the town wall.

I have every reason to believe that Gen. Clausel has marched
from Jaca into France. I have received a report from Gen. Mina of
the 12th, in which he informs me that Gen. Duran had joined him
in the neighbourhood of Zaragoza, and that he had attacked, on
the 8th, Gen. Paris, who had for some time commanded a division
in Aragon. Gen. Paris had retired on the night of the 9th, leaving
a garrison in a redoubt in the neighbourhood of Zaragoza, which
Gen. Mina had left Gen. Duran to attack while he followed the
enemy with his own division and the cavalry under Brigadier Don
Julian Sanchez. He had taken a considerable number of prisoners
and a good deal of baggage from Gen. Paris; and a convoy on the
11th. It is impossible to applaud too highly the activity, intelligence, and gallantry with which these operations have been
carried on. I have since heard that Gen. Paris had arrived at Jaca
on the 14th, and that he had brought with him the garrisons of
Ayerbe, Huesca, &c., and was about to retire into France.

Marshal Suchet evacuated Valencia on the 5th inst., and Gen.
Elio entered that city at the head of the 2d army on the 7th. I
have a letter from Lord W. Bentinck of the 7th, from San Felipe,
in which he informs me that he expected to arrive at Valencia on
the 10th.

I have not heard of Marshal Suchet's retreat beyond Castel-
lon. But the garrison of Segorbe has been withdrawn; and I
understand that on the instant Gen. Severoli blew up the fort of
Alcañiz and marched upon Mequinenza by Caspe.

The Conde de la Bisbal's corps relieved the British and Portuguese troops in the blockade of Pamplona on the 17th inst. The enemy made two sorties on the 11th and 15th inst., in both of which they were repulsed, and suffered considerably. I enclose a list of killed and wounded on those occasions.

P. S. Since writing the above, I have received a dispatch from Sir T. Graham, of which the enclosed is a copy, containing his report on the attack of the convent near San Sebastian.

To Earl Bathurst.

San Estevan, 1st Aug. 1813.

Two practicable breaches having been effected at San Sebastian on the 24th July, orders were given that they should be attacked on the morning of the 25th. I am concerned to have to report that this attempt to obtain possession of the place failed, and that our loss was very considerable.

I went to the siege on the 25th, and, having conferred with Lieut. Gen. Sir T. Graham and the officers of the engineers and artillery, it appeared to me that it would be necessary to increase the facilities of the attack before it should be repeated. But, upon adverting to the state of our ammunition, I found that we had not a sufficiency to do anything effectual till that should arrive for which I had written on the 26th June, which I had reason to believe was embarked at Portsmouth, and to expect every hour. I therefore desired that the siege should for the moment be converted into a blockade, a measure which I found to be the more desirable when I returned to Lesaca in the evening.

Marshal Soult had been appointed *Lieutenant de l'Empereur*, and Commander in Chief of the French armies in Spain and the southern provinces of France, by a *Décret Impérial* on the 1st July; and he joined and took the command of the army on the 13th July, which having been joined nearly about the same time by the corps which had been in Spain under the command of Gen. Clausel, and by other reinforcements, was called *L'armée d'Espagne*, and re-formed into 9 divisions of infantry, forming the right, centre, and left, under the command of Gen. Reille, the Comte d'Erlon, and Gen. Clausel, as Lieut. Generals, and a reserve under Gen. Villatte, and 2 divisions of dragoons and one of light cavalry, the two former under the command of Gens. Treillard and Tilly, and the latter under the command of Gen. Pierre Soult. There was besides allotted to the army a large proportion of artillery, and a considerable number of guns had already joined.

The allied army was posted, as I have already informed your Lordship, in the passes of the mountains, with a view to cover the blockade of Pamplona and the siege of San Sebastian. Major Gen. Byng's brigade of British infantry, and Gen. Morillo's division of Spanish infantry, were on the right in the pass of Roncesvalles; Lieut. Gen. Sir L. Cole was posted at Viscarret to support those troops; and Lieut. Gen. Sir T. Picton, with the 3d division, at Olague in reserve. Lieut. Gen. Sir R. Hill occupied the valley of Baztan with the remainder of the 2d division, and the Portuguese division under the Conde de Amarante, detaching Gen. Campbell's Portuguese brigade to Les Alduides, within the French territory. The Light and 7th occupied the heights of Sta Barbara and the town of Vera, and the Puerto de Echalar, and kept the communication with the valley of Baztan; and the 6th division was in reserve at San Estevan. Gen. Longa's division kept the communication between the troops at Vera and those under Lieut. Gen. Sir T. Graham and Mariscal de Campo Don P. A. Giron on the great road. The Conde de la Bisbal blockaded Pamplona.

The defect of this position was that the communication between the several divisions was very tedious and difficult, while the communications of the enemy in front of the passes were easy and short; and in case of attack those in the front line could not support each other, and could look for support only from their rear.

On the 24th Marshal Soult collected the right and left wings of his army, with one division of the centre and 2 divisions of cavalry, at St Jean Pied de Port; and on the 25th attacked, with between 30,000 and 40,000 men, Gen. Byng's post at

Roncesvalles. Lieut. Gen. Sir L. Cole moved up to his support with the 4th division, and these officers were enabled to maintain their post throughout the day; but the enemy turned it in the afternoon, and Lieut. Gen. Sir L. Cole considered it to be necessary to withdraw in the night; and he marched to the neighbourhood of Zubiri. In the actions which took place on this day the 20th regt. distinguished themselves.

Two divisions of the centre of the enemy's army attacked Sir R. Hill's position in the Puerto de Maya, at the head of the valley of Baztan, in the afternoon of the same day. The brunt of the action fell upon Major Gen. Pringle's and Major Gen. Walker's brigades, in the 2d division, under the command of Lieut. Gen. the Hon. W. Stewart. These troops were at first obliged to give way, but having been supported by Major Gen. Barnes's brigade of the 7th division, they regained that part of their post which was the key of the whole, and which would have enabled them to reassume it if circumstances had permitted it. But Sir R. Hill having been apprised of the necessity that Sir L. Cole should retire, deemed it expedient to withdraw his troops likewise to Irurita, and the enemy did not advance on the following day beyond the Puerto de Maya.

Notwithstanding the enemy's superiority of numbers, they acquired but little advantage over these brave troops during the 7 hours they were engaged. All the regiments charged with the bayonet. The conduct of the 82d regt., which moved up with Major Gen. Barnes's brigade, is particularly reported. Lieut. Gen. the Hon. W. Stewart was slightly wounded.

I was not apprised of these events till late in the night of the 25th and 26th; and I adopted immediate measures to concentrate the army to the right, still providing for the siege of San Sebastian, and for the blockade of Pamplona.

This would have been effected early on the 27th, only that Lieut. Gen. Sir L. Cole and Lieut. Gen. Sir T. Picton concurred in thinking their post at Zubiri not tenable for the time during which it would have been necessary for them to wait in it. They therefore retired early on the 27th, and took up a position to cover the blockade of Pamplona, having the right, consisting of the 3d division, in front of Huarte, and extending to the hills beyond Olaz; the left, consisting of the 4th division, Major Gen. Byng's brigade of the 2d division, and Brig. Gen. Campbell's (Portuguese) brigade of the Conde de Amarante's Portuguese division, on the heights in front of Villaba, having their left at a chapel behind Sorauren, on the high road from Ostiz to Pamplona, and their right resting upon a height which defended the high road from Zubiri and Roncesvalles. Gen. Morillo's division of Spanish infantry, and that part of the Conde de la Bisbal's corps not engaged in the blockade, were in reserve. From the latter the regiment of *Pravia* and that of *El Principe* were detached to occupy part of the hill on the right of the 4th division, by which the road from Zubiri was defended.

The British cavalry under Lieut. Gen. Sir S. Cotton were placed near Huarte on the right, being the only ground on which it was possible to use the cavalry.

The river Lanz runs in the valley which was on the left of the allied, and on the right of the French army, along the road to Ostiz; beyond this river there is another range of mountains connected with Lizaso and Marcalain, by which places it was now necessary to communicate with the rest of the army.

I joined the 3d and 4th divisions just as they were taking up their ground on the 27th, and shortly afterwards the enemy formed their army on a mountain, the front of which extends from the high road to Ostiz to the high road to Zubiri; and they placed one division on the left of that road on a height, and in some villages in front of the 3d division: they had here also a large body of cavalry.

In a short time after they had taken up their ground, the enemy attacked the hill on the right of the 4th division, which was then occupied by one battalion of the 4th Portuguese regt., and by the Spanish regiment of *Pravia*. These troops defended their ground, and drove the enemy from it with the bayonet. Seeing the importance of this hill to our position, I reinforced it with the 40th regt., and this regiment, with the Spanish regiments *El Principe* and *Pravia*, held it from this time, notwithstanding the repeated efforts of the enemy during the 27th and 28th to obtain possession of it. Nearly at the same time that the enemy attacked this height on the 27th, they took possession of the village of Sorauren on the road to Ostiz, by which they acquired the communication by that road, and they kept up a fire of musketry along the line till it was dark.

We were joined on the morning of the 28th by the 6th division of infantry, and I directed that the heights should be occupied on the left of the valley of the Lanz, and that the 6th division should form across the valley in rear of the left of the 4th division, resting their right on Oricain, and their left on the heights above mentioned. The 6th division had scarcely taken their position when they were attacked by a very large force of the enemy which had been assembled in the village of Sorauren. Their front was, however, so well defended by the fire of their own light troops, from the heights on their left, and by the fire from the heights occupied by the 4th division and Brig. Gen. Campbell's Portuguese brigade, that the enemy were soon driven back with immense loss from a fire on their front, both flanks, and rear.

In order to extricate their troops from the difficulty in which they found themselves in their situation in the valley of the Lanz, the enemy now attacked the height on which the left of the 4th division stood, which was occupied by the 7th caçadores, of which they obtained a momentary possession. They were attacked, however, again by the 7th caçadores, supported by Major Gen. Ross with his brigade of the 4th division, and were driven down with great loss.

The battle now became general along the whole front of the heights occupied by the 4th division, and in every part in our favor, excepting where one battalion of the 10th Portuguese regt. of Major Gen. Campbell's brigade was posted. This battalion having been overpowered, and having been obliged to give way immediately on the right of Major Gen. Ross's brigade, the enemy established themselves on our line, and Major Gen. Ross was obliged to withdraw from his post. I however ordered the 27th and 48th regts. to charge, first, that body of the enemy which had first established themselves on the height, and next, those on the left. Both attacks succeeded, and the enemy were driven down with immense loss; and the 6th division having moved forward at the same time to a situation in the valley nearer to the left of the 4th, the attack upon this front ceased entirely, and was continued but faintly on other points of our line.

In the course of this contest, the gallant 4th division, which had so frequently been distinguished in this army, surpassed their former good conduct. Every regiment charged with the bayonet, and the 40th, 7th, 20th, and 23d, four different times. Their officers set them the example, and Major Gen. Ross had two horses shot under him. The Portuguese troops likewise behaved admirably; and I had every reason to be satisfied with the conduct of the Spanish regiments *El Principe* and *Pravia*.

I had ordered Lieut. Gen. Sir R. Hill to march by Lanz upon Lizaso, as soon as I found that Lieut. Gens. Sir T. Picton and Sir L. Cole had moved from Zubiri, and Lieut. Gen. the Earl of Dalhousie from San Estevan to the same place, where both arrived on the 28th, and the 7th division came to Marcalain.

The enemy's force which had been in front of Sir R. Hill, followed his march, and arrived at Ostiz on the 29th. The enemy thus reinforced, and occupying a position on the mountains which appeared little liable to attack, and finding that they could make no impression on our front, determined to endeavor to turn our left by an attack on Sir R. Hill's corps. They reinforced with one division the troops which had been already opposed to him, still occupying the same points in the mountain on which was formed their principal force; but they drew in to their left the troops which occupied the heights opposite the 3d division; and they had, during the night of the 29th and 30th, occupied in strength the crest of the mountain on our left of the Lanz opposite to the 6th and 7th divisions; thus connecting their right in their position with the divisions detached to attack Lieut. Gen. Sir R. Hill.

I, however, determined to attack their position, and ordered Lieut. Gen. the Earl of Dalhousie to possess himself of the top of the mountain in his front, by which the enemy's right would be turned; and Lieut. Gen. Sir T. Picton to cross the heights on which the enemy's left had stood, and to turn their left by the road to Roncesvalles. All the arrangements were made to attack the front of the enemy's position, as soon as the effect of these movements on their flanks should begin to appear. Major Gen. the Hon. E. Pakenham, whom I had sent to take the command of the 6th division, Major Gen. Pack having been wounded, turned the village of Sorauren as soon as the Earl of Dalhousie had driven the enemy from the mountain by which that flank was defended; and the 6th division, and Major Gen. Byng's brigade, which had relieved the 4th division on the left of our position on the road to Ostiz, instantly attacked and carried that village. Lieut. Gen. Sir L. Cole likewise attacked the front of the enemy's main position with the 7th caçadores, supported by the 11th Portuguese regt., the 40th, and the battalion under Col. Bingham, consisting of the 53d and Queen's regt. All these operations obliged the enemy to abandon a position which is one of the strongest and most difficult of access that I have yet seen occupied by troops.

In their retreat from this position, the enemy lost a great number of prisoners. I cannot sufficiently applaud the conduct of all the General officers, officers, and troops throughout these operations. The attack made by Lieut. Gen. the Earl of Dalhousie was admirably conducted by his Lordship, and executed by Major Gen. Inglis and the troops composing his brigade; and that by Major Gen. the Hon. E. Pakenham, and Major Gen. Byng, and that by Lieut. Gen. Sir L. Cole; and the movement made by Sir T. Picton merited my highest commendation. The latter officer co-operated in the attack of the mountain, by detaching troops to his left, in which Lieut. Col. the Hon. R. Trench was wounded, but I hope not seriously.

While these operations were going on, and in proportion as I observed their success, I detached troops to the support of Lieut. Gen. Sir R. Hill. The enemy appeared in his front late in the morning, and immediately commenced an extended manœuvre upon his left flank, which obliged him to withdraw from the height which he occupied behind Lizaso to the next range. He there, however, maintained himself; and I enclose his report of the conduct of the troops.

I continued the pursuit of the enemy after their retreat from the mountain to Olague, where I was at sunset immediately in the rear of their attack upon Lieut. Gen. Sir R. Hill. They withdrew from his front in the night; and yesterday took up a

strong position with 2 divisions to cover their rear on the pass
of Doña Maria. Lieut. Gen. Sir R. Hill and the Earl of Dalhousie attacked and carried the pass, notwithstanding the vigorous
resistance of the enemy, and the strength of their position. I am
concerned to add that Lieut. Gen. the Hon. W. Stewart was
wounded upon this occasion. I enclose Lieut. Gen. Sir R. Hill's
report.

In the mean time, I moved with Major Gen. Byng's brigade,
and the 4th division, under Lieut. Gen. the Hon. Sir L. Cole, by
the pass of Velate, upon Irurita, in order to turn the enemy's
position on Doña Maria. Major Gen. Byng took in Elizondo a
large convoy going to the enemy, and made many prisoners.
We have this day continued the pursuit of the enemy in the valley of the Bidasoa, and many prisoners and much baggage have
been taken. Major Gen. Byng has possessed himself of the
valley of Baztan, and of the position on the Puerto de Maya,
and the army will be this night nearly in the same positions
which they occupied on the 25th July.

I trust that H. R. H. the Prince Regent will be satisfied with
the conduct of the troops of His Majesty, and of his allies, on
this occasion. The enemy having been considerably reinforced
and re-equipped, after their late defeat, made a most formidable attempt to relieve the blockade of Pamplona, with the
whole of their forces, excepting the reserve under Gen. Villatte,
which remained in front of our troops on the great road from
Irun. This attempt has been entirely frustrated by the operations
of a part only of the allied army; and the enemy has sustained
a defeat, and suffered a severe loss in officers and men.

The enemy's expectations of success beyond the point of
raising the blockade of Pamplona, were certainly very sanguine. They brought into Spain a large body of cavalry, and a
great number of guns; neither of which arms could be used to
any great extent by either party in the battle which took place.
They sent off the guns to St Jean Pied de Port, on the evening of
the 28th, which have thus returned to France in safety.

The detail of the operations will show your Lordship how
much reason I have to be satisfied with the conduct of all the
General officers, officers, and troops. It is impossible to describe

the enthusiastic bravery of the 4th division; and I was much indebted to Lieut. Gen. Sir L. Cole for the manner in which he directed their operations; to Major Gen. Ross, Major Gen. Anson, Major Gen. Byng, and Brig. Gen. Campbell, of the Portuguese service. All the officers commanding, and the officers of the regiments, were remarkable for their gallantry; but I particularly observed Lieut. Col. O'Toole, of the 7th caçadores, in the charge upon the enemy on our left on the 28th; and Capt. J. Telles Jurdão, of the 11th Portuguese regt., in the attack of the mountain on the 30th.

I beg to draw your Lordship's attention likewise to the valuable assistance I received throughout these operations from Lieut. Gen. Sir R. Hill; and from Lieut. Gen. the Earl of Dalhousie, and Lieut. Gen. Sir T. Picton, in those of the 30th and 31st July. To the Conde de la Bisbal, likewise, I am indebted for every assistance it was in his power to give consistently with his attention to the blockade. I have already mentioned the conduct of the regiments of *Pravia* and *El Principe*, belonging to the army of reserve of Andalusia, in a most trying situation; and the whole corps appeared animated by the same zealous spirit which pervaded all the troops in that position.

Marshal Sir W. Beresford was with me throughout these operations; and I received from him all the assistance which his talents so well qualify him to afford me. The good conduct of the Portuguese officers and troops in all the operations of the present campaign, and the spirit which they show on every occasion, are not less honorable to that nation than they are to the military character of the officer who, by his judicious measures, has re-established discipline, and renewed a military spirit in the army.

I have again to draw your Lordship's attention to the valuable assistance I received throughout these operations from Major Gen. Murray, the Q. M. G., and Major Gen. Pakenham, the Adj. Gen., and the officers of those departments respectively; from Lord FitzRoy Somerset, Lieut. Col. Campbell, and the officers of my personal Staff.

Although our wounded are numerous, I am happy to say that the cases in general are slight; and I have great pleasure in reporting to your Lordship, that the utmost attention has been paid to them by the Inspector General, Dr M'Grigor, and by the officers of the department under his direction.

Adverting to the extent and nature of our operations, and the difficulties of our communications at all times, I have reason to be extremely well satisfied with the zeal and exertions of Sir R. Kennedy, the Commissary Gen., and the officers of his department, throughout the campaign; which, upon the whole, have been more successful in supplying the troops than could have been expected.

I transmit this dispatch to your Lordship by H. S. H. the Hereditary Prince of Orange, who is perfectly acquainted with all that has passed, and with the situation of the army; and will be able to inform your Lordship of many details relating to this series of operations, for which a dispatch does not afford scope. His Highness had a horse shot under him in the battle near Sorauren on the 28th July.

P. S. I have omitted to inform your Lordship in the body of the dispatch, that the troops in the Puerto de Maya lost there 4 Portuguese guns on the 25th July. Major Gen. Pringle, who commanded when the attack commenced, had ordered them to retire towards Maya; and when Lieut. Gen. Stewart came up, he ordered that they might return, and retire by the mountain road to Elizondo. In the mean time, the enemy were in possession of the pass, and the communication with that road was lost, and they could not reach it.

I enclose returns of the loss before San Sebastian, from the 7th to the 27th July, and returns of the killed, wounded, and missing, in the operations from the 25th ult. to the 1st inst.

To Lieut. Gen. Sir T. Graham, K. B.

Lesaca, 4th Aug. 1813, 9 A.M.

I have received your letters to the 3d inst., which I have been obliged to delay acknowledging till this moment. The troops are of course a good deal fatigued, and we have suffered very considerably, particularly the English troops in the 2d division, in the affair in the Puerto de Maya, which, with the existing want of shoes and of musket ammunition, induces me to delay for a day or two any forward movement, and to doubt the expediency of making one at all. I keep every thing in readiness, however. I am perfectly aware of the objections to our positions in the Pyrenees; but if we should not be able to advance from them without incurring more loss than we ought, or than we can well afford, I am afraid that we cannot well retire from them.

Many events turned out unfortunately for us on the 1st inst., each of which ought to have been in our favor; and we should have done the enemy a great deal more mischief than we did in his passage down this valley. But as it is, I hope that Soult will not feel an inclination to renew his expedition, on this side at least. The French army must have suffered terribly. Between the 25th of last month and 2d of this, they were engaged seriously not less than 10 times; on many occasions in attacking very strong positions, in others beat from them or pursued. I understand that the officers say they have lost 15,000 men. I thought so; but as they say so, I now think more. I believe we have about 4000 prisoners. It is strange enough that our diminution of strength to the 31st does not exceed 1500 men; although I believe our casualties are 6000.

I propose to resume the operations of the siege as soon as the train and stores shall arrive from England; and I gave orders to the Commissary Gen. to give compensation as is proposed for the loss of boats, and to have the boats repaired. I shall be much obliged to you if you will give directions, if you have not already given them, that the road from Pasages to the wharf, and the wharf itself, may be repaired according to the memorandums, Nos. 3 and 4, in Col. Dickson's letter to you of the 1st inst. Also, if you will apply to Sir G. Collier to have a derrick erected on the wharf according to his memorandum No. 5.

I shall have the boats called from the different harbours, but I will not answer for their coming.

I have written several times to England, and I write again by this occasion, to have our naval force increased; which is the only mode of having either an efficient blockade, or means to carry on the siege as we ought.

I shall be much obliged to you if you will order Col. May, of the artillery, to head quarters, to arrange the ammunition concerns of the army, which are now in my hands.

I have received from Sir R. Fletcher a plan for the recommencement and prosecution of the siege; and he appears to think it necessary that more works should be constructed. If that be the case, he had better commence them immediately, and Col. Dickson had better commence the re-landing of the guns, &c., and re-arming the batteries, at least so far as to protect Sir R. Fletcher's works.

To Earl Bathurst.

Lesaca, 8th Aug. 1813.

I enclose you the copy of a letter which I have received from the Duc de Berri; and as the answer will involve the discussion of some military and political questions, upon which you may wish to know my opinion, and upon which government must determine, and as I write with more facility in English than in French, I think it best to write it to your Lordship, and to refer the Duc de Berri to you.

It is a very common error, among those unacquainted with military affairs, to believe that there are no limits to military success. After having driven the French from the frontiers of Portugal and Madrid to the frontiers of France, it is generally expected that we shall immediately invade France; and some even here expect that we shall be at Paris in a month. None appear to have taken a correct view of our situation on the frontier, of which the enemy still possess all the strongholds within Spain itself; of which strongholds, or at least some of them, we must get possession before the season closes, or we shall have no communication whatever with the interior of Spain.

Then in France, on the same great communications, there are other strongholds, of which we must likewise get possession.

An army which has made such marches, and has fought such battles, as that under my command has, is necessarily much deteriorated. Independently of the actual loss of numbers by death, wounds, and sickness, many men and officers are out of the ranks for various causes. The equipment of the army, their ammunition, the soldiers' shoes, &c., require renewal; the magazines for the new operations require to be collected and formed, and many arrangements to be made, without which the army could not exist a day, but which are not generally understood by those who have not had the direction of such concerns in their hands. Then observe, that this new operation is the invasion of France, in which country every body is a soldier, where the whole population is armed and organised, under persons, not, as in other countries, inexperienced in arms, but men who, in the course of the last 25 years, in which France has been engaged in war with all Europe, must, the majority of them, at least, have served somewhere.

I entertain no doubt that I could to-morrow enter France, and establish the army on the Adour, but I could go no farther certainly. If peace should be made by the Powers of the North, I must necessarily withdraw into Spain, and the retreat, however short, would be difficult, on account of the hostility and the warlike disposition of the inhabitants, particularly of this part of the country, and the military direction they would receive from the gentry their leaders. To this add, that the difficulty of all that must be done to set the army to rights, after its late severe battles and victories, will be much increased by its removal into France at an early period; and that it must stop short in the autumn if it now moves at too early a period.

So far for the immediate invasion of France, which, from what I have seen of the state of the negotiations in the north of Europe, I have determined to consider only in reference to the convenience of my own operations.

The next point for consideration is the proposal of the Duc de Berri to join this army, taking the command of the 20,000 men who he says are ready, organised, and even armed, in order to act with us. My opinion is, that the interests of the House of Bourbon and of all Europe are the same, viz., in some manner or other, to get the better and rid of Buonaparte.

Although, therefore, the allies in the north of Europe, and even Great Britain and Spain, might not be prepared to go the length of declaring that they would not lay down their arms till Buonaparte should be dethroned, they would be justified in taking this assistance from the House of Bourbon, and their French party who are dissatisfied with the government of Buonaparte. It might be a question with the House of Bourbon, whether they would involve their partisans in France upon any thing not short of such a declaration, but none with the allies whether they would receive such assistance. Indeed, there would scarcely be a question for the Princes of the House of Bourbon, if they are acquainted with the real nature and extent of Buonaparte's power. He rests internally upon the most extensive and expensive system of corruption that was ever established in any country, and externally upon his military power, which is supported almost exclusively by foreign contributions. If he can be confined to the limits of France by any means, his system must fall. He cannot bear the expense of his internal government and of his army; and the reduction of either would be fatal to him. Any measures, therefore, which should go only to confine him to France would forward, and ultimately attain, the objects of the House of Bourbon and of their partisans.

If the House of Bourbon and the allies, however, don't concur in this reasoning, we must then, before the Duc de Berri is allowed to join the army, get from the allies in the north of Europe a declaration how far they will persevere in the contest with a view to dethrone Buonaparte; and the British government must make up their minds on the question, and come to an understanding upon it with those of the Peninsula.

To Earl Bathurst.

Lesaca, 14th Aug. 1813.

I have received your letter of the 5th inst., enclosing Lord Cathcart's dispatch of the 12th July, and one from Mr Hamilton of the same date, with the copy of Mr Thornton's letter of the 12th July.

I confess that I am not satisfied with the state of affairs in the north of Germany, which, however, is probably owing to my not knowing what has passed between the King's government and the allies on the Continent, in regard either to peace, or to carrying on the war.

It appears to me that Buonaparte has the allies, including Austria, exactly in the state in which he would wish to have them. In regard to peace, it appears that the Austrians propose a basis to which the Russians and Prussians don't agree; and that these powers don't make common cause with England and Spain, as to peace: and as to the Prince Royal of Sweden, he appears to stand alone likewise, and that his hopes of the peace, for which he wishes, are confined to an engagement by the Emperor of Russia that he will not guarantee the dominions of Denmark in the negotiations about to be entered upon.

There may therefore be fairly counted four parties among the allies, by concession to any one of which Buonaparte would gain such an advantage as would place the game in his hands, if the accounts given of the relative force of the French and the allies be correct: or it would require great firmness and conduct to carry on the war, supposing Mr Thornton's notion to be correct, that there would still remain a sufficient force for the contest, even if the Austrians were to be satisfied, and to withdraw their assistance. In this notion, however, I should doubt Mr Thornton's having taken into consideration the possibility that the concession to the Austrians should be such as to induce them to take part in the war against the allies to compel them to a peace, which would not be inconsistent with the Austrian character of mediator; or, what is more probable, should adopt a system of neutrality hostile to the allies, and friendly to France.

There appears, therefore, no concert or common cause in the negotiations for peace; and as for the operations of the war, there may be something better, as Lord Cathcart has not gone into details at all; but there does not appear to exist any thing, in writing or any where, excepting in loose conversations among Princes. For my part, I would not march even a corporal's guard upon such a system.

Probably what I am about to write has already occurred to the King's government, and that matters are not ripe for such a scheme; or that the notions and claims of some of the allies are so wild and unreasonable, or so selfish, that they cannot be reconciled to the general interest, at the same time that the forces and resources, particularly of the greater powers, cannot be spared.

There are some leading principles, however, in the political state of Europe on which the interests of all parties would coincide, such as the independence of Spain, Germany, Italy, and Holland, of France; the restoration of Hanover to the King's family; the re-establishment of the Prussian frontier, and of the Prussian influence over Saxony and Hesse; a frontier for the Austrian monarchy, and influence in Germany to balance that of Prussia; the re-establishment of the independence of the Hanse Towns, &c.; an understanding between England and Russia; and the powers less immediately interested might bring the others to take a general view of the common interests, without which all may depend upon it that they cannot make peace with security, or war with honor or advantage.

The object of each should be to diminish the power and influence of France, by which alone the peace of the world can be restored and maintained: and although the aggrandisement and security of the power of one's own country is the duty of every man, all nations may depend upon it that the best security for power, and for every advantage now possessed, or to be acquired, is to be found in the reduction of the power and influence of the grand disturber; and in the adoption of some scheme for that object, to be acted upon by the allies in concert, whether in the negotiation for peace, or in the operations of war. For my part, I repeat what I told you before, I shall enter France, or not, (unless I should be ordered,) according to what I think best for my own operations, as I have no reliance whatever upon what is doing in the north.

To Earl Bathurst.

Lesaca, 2d Sept. 1813.

The fire against the fort of San Sebastian was opened on the 26th Aug., and directed against the towers which flanked the bastion on the eastern face; against the demi bastion on the south east angle, and the termination of the curtain of the south face.

Lieut. Gen. Sir T. Graham had directed that an establishment should be formed on the island of Sta Clara, which was effected on the night of the 26th, and the enemy's detachment on the island were made prisoners. Capt. Cameron of the 9th had the command of the detachment which effected this operation, and Lieut. Gen. Sir T. Graham particularly applauds his conduct, and that of Lieut. Chadwick, of the Royal Engineers. The conduct of Lieut. the Hon. J. Arbuthnot, of the Royal Navy, who commanded the boats, was highly meritorious, as likewise that of Lieut. Bell, of the Royal Marines. All that was deemed practicable to carry into execution in order to facilitate the approach to the breaches before made in the wall of San Sebastian, having been effected on the 30th Aug., and the breach having been made at the termination of the bastion, the place was stormed at 11 o'clock in the day on the 31st, and carried.

The loss on our side has been severe. Lieut. Gen. Sir J. Leith, who had joined the army only two days before, and Major Gens. Oswald and Robinson, were unfortunately wounded in the breach; and Col. Sir R. Fletcher was killed by a musket ball at the mouth of the trenches. In this officer, and in Lieut. Col.

Craufurd of the 9th regt., His Majesty's service has sustained a serious loss.

I have the honor to enclose Lieut. Gen. Sir T. Graham's report of this operation, in which your Lordship will observe with pleasure another distinguished instance of the gallantry and perseverance of His Majesty's officers and troops under the most trying difficulties.

All reports concur in praise of the conduct of the detachment from the 10th Portuguese brigade, under Major Snodgrass, which crossed the river Urumea, and stormed the breach on the right under all the fire which could be directed upon them from the castle and town.

The garrison retired to the castle, leaving about 270 prisoners in our hands; and I hope that I shall soon have the pleasure to inform your Lordship that we have possession of that post.

Since the fire against San Sebastian had been recommenced, the enemy had drawn the greatest part of their force to the camp of Urrugne; and there was every reason to believe that they would make an attempt to relieve the place. Three divisions of the 4th Spanish army, commanded by Gen. Don M. Freyre, occupied the heights of San Marcial and the town of Irun, by which the approach to San Sebastian by the high road was covered and protected; and they were supported by the 1st division of British infantry under Gen. Howard, and Lord Aylmer's brigade, on their left and in the rear of Irun; and by Gen. Longa's division, encamped near the Sierra de Aya, in rear of their right. In order to secure them still further, I moved 2 brigades of the 4th division, on the 30th, to the Convent of San Antonio, one of which (Gen. Ross'), under Lieut. Gen. Sir L. Cole, the same day, afterwards moved up to the Sierra de Aya, and the other on the morning of the 31st; leaving the 9th Portuguese brigade on the heights between the Convent of Vera and Lesaca. Major Gen. Inglis's brigade of the 7th division was moved on the 30th to the bridge of Lesaca; and I gave orders for the troops in the Puertos of Echalar, Zugarramurdi, and Maya, to attack the enemy's weakened posts in front of these positions.

The enemy crossed the Bidasoa by the fords between Andarra

and the destroyed bridge on the high road, before daylight on the morning of the 30th, with a very large force, with which they made a most desperate attack along the whole front of the position of the Spanish troops on the heights of San Marcial. They were beat back, some of them even across the river, in the most gallant style, by the Spanish troops, whose conduct was equal to that of any troops that I have ever seen engaged, and the attack, having been frequently repeated, was upon every occasion defeated with the same gallantry and determination. The course of the river being immediately under the heights on the French side, on which the enemy had placed a considerable quantity of cannon, they were enabled to throw a bridge across the river three quarters of a mile above the high road, over which, in the afternoon, they marched again a considerable body, who, with those who had crossed the fords, again made a desperate attack upon the Spanish positions. This was equally beat back; and at length, finding all their efforts on that side fruitless, the enemy took advantage of the darkness of a violent storm to retire their troops from this front entirely.

Notwithstanding that, as I have above informed your Lordship, I had a British division on each flank of the 4th Spanish army, I am happy to be able to report that the conduct of the latter was so conspicuously good, and they were so capable of defending their post without assistance, in spite of the desperate efforts of the enemy to carry it, that, finding that the ground did not allow of my making use of the 1st or 4th divisions on the flanks of the enemy's attacking corps, neither of them were in the least engaged during the action.

Nearly at the same time that the enemy crossed the Bidasoa in front of the heights of San Marcial, they likewise crossed that river with about 3 divisions of infantry in 2 columns, by the fords below Salain, in front of the position occupied by the 9th Portuguese brigade. I ordered Gen. Inglis to support this brigade with that of the 7th division under his command; and as soon as I was informed of the course of the enemy's attack, I sent to Lieut. Gen. the Earl of Dalhousie, to request that he would likewise move towards the Bidasoa with the 7th division; and to the Light division to support Major Gen. Inglis by every means in their power. Major Gen. Inglis found it impossible to maintain the heights between Lesaca and the Bidasoa, and he withdrew to those in front of the Convent of San Antonio, which he maintained. In the mean time Major Gen. Kempt moved one brigade of the Light division to Lesaca; by which he kept the enemy in check, and covered the march of the Earl of Dalhousie to join Gen. Inglis.

The enemy, however, having completely failed in their attempt upon the position of the Spanish army on the heights of San Marcial, and finding that Major Gen. Inglis had taken a position from which they could not drive him, at the same time that it covered and protected the right of the Spanish army, and the approaches to San Sebastian by Oyarzun, and that their situation on the left of the Bidasoa was becoming at every moment more critical, retired during the night.

The fall of rain during the evening and night had so swollen the Bidasoa that the rear of their column was obliged to cross the bridge of Vera. In order to effect this object, they attacked the posts of Major Gen. Skerrett's brigade of the Light division, at about 3 in the morning, both from the Puerto de Vera, and from the left of the Bidasoa. Although the nature of the ground rendered it impossible to prevent entirely the passage of the bridge after daylight, it was made under the fire of a great part of Major Gen. Skerrett's brigade, and the enemy's loss in the operation must have been very considerable.

While this was going on upon the left of the army, Mariscal de Campo Don P. A. Giron attacked the enemy's posts in front of the pass of Echalar on the 30th and 31st. Lieut. Gen. the Earl of Dalhousie made Gen. Le Cor attack those in front of Zugarramurdi with the 6th Portuguese brigade on the 31st, and Major Gen. the Hon. C. Colville made Col. Douglas attack the enemy's posts in front of the pass of Maya on the same day, with the 7th Portuguese brigade. All these troops conducted themselves well.

The attack made by the Earl of Dalhousie delayed his march till late in the afternoon of the 31st; but he was in the evening in a favorable situation for his further progress; and in the morning of the 1st in that allotted for him.

In these operations, in which a second attempt by the enemy

to prevent the establishment of the Allies upon the frontier has been defeated by the operations of a part only of the allied army, at the very moment at which the fort of San Sebastian was taken by storm, I have had great satisfaction in observing the zeal and ability of the officers, and the gallantry and discipline of the troops.

The different reports which I have transmitted to your Lordship, from Lieut. Gen. Sir T. Graham, will have shown the ability and perseverance with which he has conducted the arduous enterprise intrusted to his direction, and the zeal and exertion of all the officers employed under him.

I fully concur in the Lieut. General's report of the cordial assistance which he has received from Capt. Sir G. Collier and the officers, seamen, and marines under his command, who have done every thing in their power to facilitate and insure our success. The seamen have served with the artillery in the batteries, and have, upon every occasion, manifested that spirit which is characteristic of the British navy.

I cannot sufficiently applaud the conduct of Mariscal de Campo Don M. Freyre, the Commander in Chief of the 4th Spanish army, who, whilst he made every disposition which was proper for the troops under his command, set them an example of gallantry which, having been followed by the General officers and chiefs, and other officers of the regiments, insured the success of the day. In his report, in which I concur, the General expresses the difficulty which he finds of selecting particular instances of gallantry, in a case in which all have conducted themselves so well; but he has particularly mentioned Gen. Mendizabal, who volunteered his assistance, and commanded on the height of San Marcial; Mariscal de Campo Losada, who commanded in the centre, and was wounded; Mariscal de Campo Don José Garcia de Paredes, the Commanding officer of the artillery; Brig. Gen. Don Juan Diaz Porlier; Don Josef Maria Espeleta; Don Stanislas Sanchez Salvador, the Chief of the Staff of the 4th army; and Don Antonio Roselló; and Cols. Fuente Pita, the commanding engineer; Don Juan Loarte, of the regiment de la Constitucion, and Don Juan Ugarte Mendia.

Major Gen. Inglis and the regiments in his brigade, of the

7th division, conducted themselves remarkably well. The 51st regt., under Col. Mitchell, and the 68th, under Lieut. Col. Hawkins, covered the change of position by the troops from the heights between the Bidasoa and Lesaca to those of San Antonio; and these corps were distinguished.

Throughout these operations I have received every assistance from the Adj. Gen., Major Gen. Pakenham, and the Q. M. G., Major Gen. Murray, and all the officers of the Staff, and of my own family.

I transmit this dispatch by Major Hare, acting Assist. Adj. General with this army, attached to Lieut. Gen. Sir T. Graham, whom I beg leave to recommend to your Lordship's protection.

P. S. I enclose a return of the killed and wounded in the operations of the 31st ult. and 1st inst., and returns of the loss before San Sebastian, from the 28th July to the 31st Aug.

Return of the killed, wounded, and missing,
on the 31st Aug. and 1st Sept. 1813.

	Officers.	Serjeants.	R. and F.	Total loss of officers, non-commissioned officers, and R. and F.	British.	Spanish.	Portuguese.	Horses.
Killed .	29	20	351	400	51	261	88	2
Wounded	159	115	1823	2067	334	1347	386	4
Missing .	5	3	148	156	32	71	53	—

To the Rt. Hon. Sir H. Wellesley, K. B.

Lesaca, 9th Oct. 1813.

I enclose a letter which I have received from the Minister at War, of the 28th Sept., in which he has enclosed the copy of one of the 5th Sept. from the Conde de Villa Fuentes, the *Xefe*

Politico of the province of Guipuzcoa, complaining of the conduct of the allied British and Portuguese army in the storm of the town of San Sebastian; and, as I received at the same time the enclosed newspaper, which contains the same charges against that army in a more amplified style, and both appear to proceed from the same authority, I shall proceed to reply to both complaints; and I trouble your Excellency on this subject, as it is one upon which your Excellency will recollect that I have orders to correspond with His Majesty's minister alone.

I should have wished to adopt another mode of justifying the officers concerned on this occasion; but as there is no redress by the law for a libel, I must be satisfied with that which is in my hands.

I shall begin with that charge which the enclosed newspaper contains, and which is not made in direct terms in the letter from the *Xefe Politico*, though it is directly charged against Lieut. Gen. Sir T. Graham that he intended to burn the town; viz., that the town of San Sebastian was thus ill treated, because its former trade had been exclusively with the French nation, and to the disadvantage of Great Britain.

This charge cannot be intended to apply to the common soldiers, who cannot be supposed to know or to reflect much upon what passed before they attacked the place. This infamous charge applies exclusively to the principal officers, who, from motives, not of commercial policy, but of commercial revenge, are supposed so far to have forgotten their duty as to have ordered or suffered the sack of this unfortunate town, and thus to have risked the loss of all they had acquired by their labors and their gallantry; and you will more readily conceive, than I can venture to describe, the feelings of indignation with which I proceed to justify the General and other officers of this army from a charge officially made by a person in a high office, that they designed to plunder and burn the town of San Sebastian.

I need not assure you that this charge is most positively untrue. Every thing was done that was in my power to suggest to save the town. Several persons urged me, in the strongest manner, to allow it to be bombarded, as the most certain mode of forcing the enemy to give it up. This I positively would not allow, for the same reasons that I did not allow Ciudad Rodrigo or Badajoz to be bombarded; and yet if I had harbored so infamous a wish as to destroy this town from motives of commercial revenge, or any other, I could not have adopted a more certain method than to allow it to be bombarded.

Neither is it true that the town was set on fire by the English and Portuguese troops. To set fire to the town was part of the enemy's defence. It was set on fire by the enemy on the 22d July, before the final attempt was made to take it by storm; and it is a fact that the fire was so violent on the 24th July, that the storm, which was to have taken place on that day, was necessarily deferred till the 25th, and, as it is well known, failed.

I was at the siege of San Sebastian on the 30th Aug., and I aver that the town was then on fire. It must have been set on fire by the enemy, as I repeat that our batteries, by positive order, threw no shells into the town; and I saw the town on fire on the morning of the 31st Aug., before the storm took place.

It is well known that the enemy had prepared for a serious resistance, not only on the ramparts, but in the streets of the town; that traverses were established in the streets, formed of combustibles, with the intention of setting fire to and exploding them during the contest with the assailants. It is equally known that there was a most severe contest in the streets of the town between the assailants and the garrison; that many of these traverses were exploded, by which many lives on both sides were lost; and it is a fact that these explosions set fire to many of the houses.

The *Xefe Politico*, the author of these complaints, must have been as well aware of these facts as I am, and he ought not to have concealed them. In truth, the fire in the town was the greatest evil that could befall the assailants, who did every thing in their power to get the better of it; and it is a fact that, owing to the difficulty and danger of communicating through the fire with the advanced posts in the town, it had very nearly become necessary at one time to withdraw those posts entirely.

In regard to the plunder of the town by the soldiers, I am the last man who will deny it, because I know that it is true. It has fallen to my lot to take many towns by storm; and I am concerned to add that I never saw or heard of one so taken, by any troops, that it was not plundered. It is one of the evil consequences attending the necessity of storming a town, which every officer laments, not only on account of the evil thereby inflicted on the unfortunate inhabitants, but on account of the injury it does to discipline, and the risk which is incurred of the loss of all the advantages of victory, at the very moment they are gained.

It is hard that I and my General officers are to be so treated as we have been by the *Xefe Politico*, and unrestrained libellers, because an unavoidable evil has occurred in the accomplishment of a great service, and in the acquirement of a great advantage. The fault does not lie with us; it is with those who lost the fort, and obliged us at great risk and loss to regain it for the Spanish nation by storm.

Notwithstanding that I am convinced it is impossible to prevent a town in such a situation from being plundered, I can prove that upon this occasion particular pains were taken to prevent it. I gave most positive orders upon the subject, and desired that the officers might be warned of the peculiar situation of the place, the garrison having the castle to retire to, and of the danger that they would attempt to retake the town if they found the assailants were engaged in plunder.

If it had not been for the fire, which certainly augmented the confusion, and afforded greater facilities for irregularity; and if by far the greatest proportion of the officers and non-commissioned officers, particularly of the principal officers who stormed the breach, had not been killed or wounded in the performance of their duty in the service of Spain, to the number of 170 out of about 250, I believe that the plunder would have been in a great measure, though not entirely, prevented.

Indeed, one of the subjects of complaint, that sentries were placed on every house, shows the desire at least of the officers to preserve order. These sentries must have been placed by order; and unless it is supposed, as charged, that the officers intended that the town should be plundered and burned, and placed the sentries to secure that object, it must be admitted that their intention in placing these sentries was good.

It likewise most unfortunately happened that it was impossible to relieve the troops which stormed the town till the 2d inst., instead of immediately after the town was in our possession. Those who make these complaints forget that on the 31st Aug., the day this town was stormed, the whole of the left of the army was attacked by the enemy.

I don't believe that I should have been congratulated and thanked for having successfully done my duty on that occasion, if I had either risked the blockade of Pamplona, or the loss of the battle fought on the 31st Aug., by keeping at San Sebastian troops to relieve those which had stormed, in order that the inhabitants of San Sebastian might suffer rather less by their irregularities. In fact, it was not possible to allot troops to relieve them till the 2d; at which time I assert that all irregularity had ceased, as I was at San Sebastian on that day.

In regard to the injuries done to the inhabitants by the soldiers with their fire arms and bayonets, in return for their applause and congratulations, it appears to me extraordinary that it did not occur to the complainants that these injuries, if they were really done, were done by accident, during the contest in the streets with the enemy, and not by design.

In regard to the charge of kindness to the enemy, I am afraid it is but too well founded; and that till it is positively ordered by authority, in return for the *Ordonnance* of the French government, adverted to in my dispatch of the 10th Sept., that all enemy's troops in a place taken by storm shall be put to death, it will be difficult to prevail upon British officers and soldiers to treat an enemy, when their prisoners, otherwise than well.

I wish that the *Xefe Politico* had not made the charge against so respectable a character as Lieut. Gen. Sir T. Graham, that he omitted to apply for his assistance to extinguish the fire in the town till it was entirely destroyed, leaving the inference to be drawn that he therefore wished that the town should be destroyed, as it would have saved me the pain of observing, that the total neglect of the Spanish authorities to furnish any

assistance whatever that was required from them to carry on
the operations against San Sebastian did not encourage Sir
Thomas to apply for the assistance of the *Xefe Politico* in any
shape. In fact, every thing was done that could be done to
extinguish the fire by our own soldiers; and I believe that the
truth is, that the assistance was asked by me, not only to
endeavor to extinguish the fire, but to bury the dead bodies
lying about the town and ramparts; and it was not made sooner,
because the want of it was not felt at an earlier period.

I certainly lament as much as any man can the evils sustained by this unfortunate town, and those who have reason to
complain of their fate, and deserve the relief of government;
but a person in the situation of a *Xefe Politico* should take
care, in forwarding these complaints, not to attack the charac-
ters of honorable and brave men, who are as incapable of
entertaining a design to injure the peaceable inhabitants of any
town, as they are of allowing their conduct to be influenced by
the infamous motives attributed to them in the enclosed libel.

I hear frequently of the union of the two nations; but I am
quite certain that nothing is so little likely to promote that
union as the encouragement given to such unfounded charges,
and the allowing such infamous libels to pass unpunished.

I have only to add, to what I have already stated in this letter, in answer to the Minister at War's inquiries regarding the
punishment of the offenders on this occasion, that several soldiers were punished. How many, it is not in my power at
present to state.

To Earl Bathurst.

Lesaca, 9th Oct. 1813.

Having deemed it expedient to cross Bidasoa with the left of
the army, I have the pleasure to inform your Lordship that that
object was effected on the 7th inst. Lieut. Gen. Sir T. Graham
directed the 1st and 5th divisions, and the 1st Portuguese

brigade under Brig. Gen. Wilson, to cross that river in three columns below, and in one above, the site of the bridge, under the command of Major Gen. Hay, Col. the Hon. C. Greville, Major Gen. the Hon. E. Stopford, and Major Gen. Howard; and Lieut. Gen. Don M. Freyre directed that part of the 4th Spanish army, under his immediate command, to cross in three columns at fords above those at which the allied British and Portuguese troops passed. The former were destined to carry the enemy's intrenchments about and above Andaye; while the latter should carry those on the Montagne Verte, and on the height of Mandale, by which they were to turn the enemy's left.

The operations of both bodies of troops succeeded in every point; the British and Portuguese troops took 7 pieces of canon in the redoubts and batteries which they carried, and Spanish troops one piece of cannon in those carried by them.

I had particular satisfaction in observing the steadiness and gallantry of all the troops. The 9th British regt. were very strongly opposed, charged with bayonets more than once, and have suffered; but I am happy to add, that in other parts of these corps, our loss has not been severe. The Spanish troops, under Lieut. Gen. Don M. Freyre, behaved admirably, and turned and carried the enemy's intrenchments in the hills with great dexterity and gallantry; and I am much indebted to the Lieut. General, and to Lieut. Gen. Sir T. Graham, and to the General and Staff officers of both corps, for the execution of the arrangements for this operation.

Lieut. Gen. Sir T. Graham, having thus established within the French territory the troops of the allied British and Portuguese army, which had been so frequently distinguished under his command, resigned the command to Lieut. Gen. Sir J. Hope, who had arrived from Ireland on the preceding day.

While this was going on upon the left, Major Gen. C. Baron Alten attacked, with the Light division, the enemy's intrenchments in the Puerto de Vera, supported by the Spanish division under Brig. Gen. Longa; and the Mariscal de Campo Don P. A. Giron attacked the enemy's intrenchments and posts on the mountain called La Rhune immediately on the right of the Light division, with the army of reserve of Andalusia.

Col. Colborne, of the 52d regt., who commanded Major Gen. Skerrett's brigade in the absence of the Major General on account of his health, attacked the enemy's right in a camp which they had strongly intrenched. The 52d regt., under the command of Major Mein, charged, in a most gallant style, and carried the intrenchment with the bayonet. The 1st and 3d caçadores, and the 2d batt. 95th regt., as well as the 52d regt., distinguished themselves in this attack. Major Gen. Kempt's brigade attacked by the Puerto, where the opposition was not so severe; and Major Gen. C. Alten has reported his sense of the judgment displayed both by the Major General and by Col. Colborne in these attacks. The Light division took 22 officers, and 400 prisoners, and 3 pieces of cannon; and I am particularly indebted to Major Gen. C. Baron Alten, for the manner in which he executed this service.

On the right, the troops of the army of reserve of Andalusia, under the command of Don P. A. Giron, attacked the enemy's posts and intrenchments on the mountain of La Rhune in two columns, under the command of Spaniards only.

These troops carried every thing before them in the most gallant style, till they arrived at the foot of the rock on which the hermitage stands; and they made repeated attempts to take even that post by storm; but it was impossible to get up; and the enemy remained during the night in possession of the hermitage, and on a rock on the same range of the mountain with the right of the Spanish troops. Some time elapsed yesterday morning before the fog cleared away sufficiently to enable me to reconnaitre the mountain, which I found to be least inaccessible by its right, and that the attack of it might be connected with advantage with the attack of the enemy's works in front of the camp of Sarre. I accordingly ordered the army of reserve to concentrate to their right, and as soon as the concentration commenced, Mariscal de Campo Don P. A. Giron ordered the battalion *de Las Ordenes* to attack the enemy's post on the rock, on the right of the position occupied by his troops, which was instantly carried in the most gallant style. These troops followed up their success, and carried an intrenchment on a hill, which protected the right of the camp of Sarre; and the enemy immediately evacuated all their works to defend the approaches to the camp, which were taken possession of by detachments from the 7th division, sent by Lieut. Gen. the Earl of Dalhousie through the Puerto de Echalar for this purpose.

Don P. A. Giron then established the battalion of *Las Ordenes* on the enemy's left, on the rock of the hermitage. It was too late to proceed farther last night; and the enemy withdrew from their post at the hermitage, and from the camp of Sarre, during the night.

It gives me singular satisfaction to report the good conduct of the officers and troops of the army of reserve of Andalusia, as well in the operations of the 7th inst. as in those of yesterday. The attack made by the battalion of *Las Ordenes*, under the command of Col. Hore, yesterday, was made in as good order and with as much spirit as any that I have seen made by any troops; and I was much satisfied with the spirit and discipline of the whole of this corps.

I cannot applaud too highly the execution of the arrangements for these attacks, by the Mariscal de Campo Don P. A. Giron, and the General and Staff officers under his directions.

I omitted to report to your Lordship, in my dispatch of the 4th inst., that when on my way to Roncesvalles, on the 1st inst., I directed Brig. Gen. Campbell to endeavor to carry off the enemy's piquets in his front, which he attacked on that night; and completely succeeded, with the Portuguese troops under his command, in carrying the whole of one piquet, consisting of 70 men. A fortified post, on the mountain of Airola, was likewise stormed, and the whole garrison put to the sword.

Since I addressed your Lordship last, I have received dispatches from Lieut. Gen. Clinton in Catalonia, to the 3d inst. The General was still at Tarragona, and the enemy were in their old position on the Llobregat. Lieut. Gen. Lord W. Bentinck had embarked for Sicily, on the 23d Sept.

I send this dispatch by my aide de camp, Captain the Earl of March, whom I beg leave to recommend to your Lordship's protection.

Return of the killed, wounded, and missing,
on the 7th and 8th Oct. 1813.

	Officers.	Serjeants.	R. and F.	Total loss of officers, non-commissioned officers, and R. & F.	British.	Portuguese.
Killed	4	5	70	127	79	48
Wounded ...	40	33	422	674	495	179
Missing ...	—	—	5	13	5	8

To Earl Bathurst.

St Pé, 13th Nov. 1813.

The enemy had since the beginning of August occupied a position with their right upon the sea in front of St Jean de Luz, and on the left of the Nivelle, their centre on La Petite Rhune, and on the heights behind that village; and their left consisting of two divisions of infantry under the Comte d'Erlon on the right of that river, on a strong height in rear of Ainhoué, and on the mountain of Mondarrain, which protected the approach to that village. They had had one division under Gen. Foy at St Jean Pied de Port, which was joined by one of the army of Aragon under Gen. Paris, at the time the left of the allied army crossed the Bidasoa. Gen. Foy's division joined those on the heights behind Ainhoué, when Sir R. Hill moved into the valley of Baztan. The enemy, not satisfied with the natural strength of this position, had the whole of it fortified; and their right in particular had been made so strong that I did not deem it expedient to attack it in front.

Pamplona having surrendered on the 31st Oct., and the right of the army having been disengaged from covering the blockade of that place, I moved Lieut. Gen. Sir R. Hill on the 6th and 7th into the valley of Baztan, as soon as the state of the roads, after the recent rains, would permit, intending to attack the enemy on the 8th; but the rain which fell on the 7th having again rendered the roads impracticable, I was obliged to defer the attack till the 10th, when we completely succeeded in carrying all the positions on the enemy's left and centre, in separating the former from the latter, and by these means turning the enemy's strong positions occupied by their right on the lower Nivelle, which they were obliged to evacuate during the night; having taken 51 pieces of cannon, and 1400 prisoners.

The object of the attack being to force the enemy's centre, and to establish our army in rear of their right, the attack was made in columns of divisions, each led by the General officer commanding it, and each forming its own reserve. Lieut. Gen. Sir R. Hill directed the movements of the right, consisting of the 2d division under Lieut. Gen. the Hon. Sir W. Stewart; the 6th division under Lieut. Gen. Sir H. Clinton; a Portuguese division under Lieut. Gen. Sir J. Hamilton, and a Spanish division under Gen. Morillo, and Col. Grant's brigade of cavalry and a brigade of Portuguese artillery under Lieut. Col. Tulloh, and 3 mountain guns under Lieut. Robe, which attacked the positions of the enemy behind Ainhoué.

Marshal Sir W. Beresford directed the movements of the right of the centre, consisting of the 3d division under Major Gen. the Hon. C. Colville, the 7th division under Mariscal de Campo Le Cor, and the 4th division under Lieut. Gen. the Hon. Sir L. Cole.

The latter attacked the redoubts in front of Sarre, that village, and the heights behind it, supported on their left by the Army of Reserve of Andalusia, under the command of Mariscal de Campo Don P. A. Giron, which attacked the enemy's positions on the right of Sarre, on the slopes of La Petite Rhune, and the heights behind the village on the left of the 4th division.

Major Gen. C. Baron Alten attacked, with the Light division and Gen. Longa's Spanish division, the enemy's positions on La Petite Rhune; and, having carried them, co-operated with the right of the centre in the attack of the heights behind Sarre.

Gen. V. Alten's brigade of cavalry, under the direction of Lieut. Gen. Sir S. Cotton, followed the movements of the centre; and there were 3 brigades of British artillery with this part of the army, and 3 mountain guns with Gen. Giron, and 3 with Major Gen. C. Alten.

Lieut. Gen. Don M. Freyre moved in two columns from the heights of Mandale towards Ascain, in order to take advantage of any movement the enemy might make from the right of their position towards their centre; and Lieut. Gen. Sir J. Hope with the left of the army drove in the enemy's outposts in front of their intrenchments on the lower Nivelle, carried the redoubt above Urrugne, and established himself on the heights immediately opposite Siboure, in readiness to take advantage of any movement made by the enemy's right.

The attack began at daylight; and Lieut. Gen. Sir L. Cole having obliged the enemy to evacuate the redoubt on their right in front of Sarre by a cannonade, and that in front of the left of the village having been likewise evacuated on the approach of the 7th division under Gen. Le Cor to attack it, Lieut. Gen. Sir L. Cole attacked and possessed himself of the village, which was turned on its left by the 3d division, under Major Gen. the Hon. C. Colville; and on its right, by the reserve of Andalusia under Don P. A. Giron; and Major Gen. C. Baron Alten carried the positions on La Petite Rhune. The whole then co-operated in the attack of the enemy's main position behind the village. The 3d and 7th divisions immediately carried the redoubts on the left of the enemy's centre, and the Light division those on the right, while the 4th division, with the reserve of Andalusia on their left, attacked their positions in their centre. By these attacks the enemy were obliged to abandon their strong positions which they had fortified with much care and labor; and they left in the principal redoubt on the height the 1st batt. 88th regt., which immediately surrendered.

While these operations were going on in the centre, I had the pleasure of seeing the 6th division, under Lieut. Gen. Sir H. Clinton, after having crossed the Nivelle, and having driven in the enemy's piquets on both banks, and having covered the passage of the Portuguese division under Lieut. Gen. Sir J. Hamilton on its right, make a most handsome attack upon the right of the enemy's position behind Ainhoué and on the right of the Nivelle, and carry all the intrenchments, and the redoubt on that flank. Lieut. Gen. Sir J. Hamilton supported, with the Portuguese division, the 6th division on its right; and both co-operated in the attack of the second redoubt, which was immediately carried.

Major Gen. Pringle's brigade of the 2d division, under the command of Lieut. Gen. Sir W. Stewart, drove in the enemy's piquets on the Nivelle and in front of Ainhoué, and Major Gen. Byng's brigade of the 2d division carried the intrenchments and a redoubt further on the enemy's left; in which attack, the Major General and these troops distinguished themselves. Major Gen. Morillo covered the advance of the whole to the heights behind Ainhoué, by attacking the enemy's posts on the slopes of Mondarrain, and following them towards Itsassu. The troops on the heights behind Ainhoué were, by these operations, under the direction of Lieut. Gen. Sir R. Hill, forced to retire towards the bridge of Cambo, on the Nive, with the exception of the division on Mondarrain, which, by the march of a part of the 2d division, under Lieut. Gen. Sir W. Stewart, was pushed into the mountains towards Baygorry.

As soon as the heights were carried on both banks of the Nivelle, I directed the 3d and 7th divisions, being the right of our centre, to move by the left of that river upon St Pé, and the 6th division by the right of the river on the same place, while the 4th and Light divisions, and Gen. Giron's reserve, held the heights above Ascain, and covered this movement on that side, and Lieut. Gen. Sir R. Hill covered it on the other. A part of the enemy's troops had retired from their centre and had crossed the Nivelle at St Pé; and as soon as the 6th division approached, the 3d division, under Major Gen. the Hon. C. Colville, and the 7th division, under Gen. Le Cor, crossed that river, and attacked, and immediately gained possession of, the heights beyond it. We were thus established in the rear of the enemy's right; but so much of the day was now spent, that it was impossible to make any further movement; and I was obliged to defer our further operations till the following morning.

The enemy evacuated Ascain in the afternoon, of which

village Lieut. Gen. Don M. Freyre took possession, and quitted all their works and positions in front of St Jean de Luz during the night, and retired upon Bidart, destroying all the bridges on the lower Nivelle. Lieut. Gen. Sir J. Hope followed them with the left of the army as soon as he could cross the river; and Marshal Sir W. Beresford moved the centre of the army as far as the state of the roads, after a violent fall of rain, would allow; and the enemy retired again on the night of the 11th into an intrenched camp in front of Bayonne.

In the course of the operations, of which I have given your Lordship an outline, in which we have driven the enemy from positions which they had been fortifying with great labor and care for 3 months, in which we have taken 51 pieces of cannon and 6 tumbrils of ammunition, and 1400 prisoners, I have great satisfaction in reporting the good conduct of all the officers and troops. The report itself will show how much reason I had to be satisfied with the conduct of Marshal Sir W. Beresford, and of Lieut. Gen. Sir R. Hill, who directed the attacks of the centre and right of the army; and with that of Lieut. Gens. Sir L. Cole, Sir W. Stewart, Sir J. Hamilton, and Sir H. Clinton; Major Gens. the Hon. C. Colville and C. Baron Alten; Mariscal de Campo F. Le Cor, and Mariscal de Campo Don P. Morillo, commanding divisions of infantry; and with that of Don P. A. Giron, commanding the reserve of Andalusia.

Lieut. Gen. Sir R. Hill, and Marshal Sir W. Beresford, and these General officers, have reported their sense of the conduct of the Generals and troops under their command respectively; and I particularly request your Lordship's attention to the conduct of Major Gen. Byng, and of Major Gen. Lambert, who conducted the attack of the 6th division. I likewise particularly observed the gallant conduct of the 51st and 68th regts., under the command of Major Rice and Lieut. Col. Hawkins, in Major Gen. Inglis's brigade, in the attack of the heights above St Pé, in the afternoon of the 10th. The 8th Portuguese brigade, in the 3d division, under Major Gen. Power, likewise distinguished themselves in the attack of the left of the enemy's centre; and Major Gen. Anson's brigade of the 4th division, in the village of Sarre and the centre of the heights.

Although the most brilliant part of this service did not fall to the lot of Lieut. Gen. Sir J. Hope and Lieut. Gen. Don M. Freyre, I had every reason to be satisfied with the mode in which these General officers conducted the service of which they had the direction.

Our loss, although severe, has not been so great as might have been expected, considering the strength of the positions attacked, and the length of time, from daylight in the morning till night, during which the troops were engaged; but I am concerned to add that Col. Barnard, of the 95th, has been severely, though I hope not dangerously, wounded; and that we have lost in Lieut. Col. Lloyd, of the 94th, an officer who had frequently distinguished himself, and was of great promise.

I received the greatest assistance in forming the plan for this attack, and throughout the operations, from the Q. M. G., Sir G. Murray, and the Adj. Gen., the Hon. Sir E. Pakenham; and from Lieut. Cols. Lord FitzRoy Somerset and Campbell, and all the officers of my personal staff, and H. S. H. the Prince of Orange.

The artillery, which was in the field, was of great use to us; and I cannot sufficiently acknowledge the intelligence and activity with which it was brought to the point of attack under the directions of Col. Dickson, over the bad roads through the mountains in this season of the year.

I send this dispatch by my aide de camp, Lieut. the Marquis of Worcester, whom I beg leave to recommend to your Lordship.

Return of the killed, wounded, and missing, in the passage of the Nivelle, on the 10th Nov. 1813.

	Officers.	Serjeants.	R. and F.	Horses.	Total loss of officers, non-commissioned officers, and R. & F.
Killed	26	28	289	16	343
Wounded	155	132	1991	25	2278
Missing	3	1	69	—	73

To Earl Bathurst.

St Jean de Luz, 21st Nov. 1813.

I have received your letter of the 5th, enclosing one from Lord Aberdeen, containing his Lordship's opinion of the sentiments of the Austrian Court respecting the House of Bourbon.

I enclose you the Proclamation which I have issued since I have been in France, which will show you that I have acted exactly according to your wishes and the sentiments contained in His Royal Highness' speech from the throne, which I have since received. I am happy to add that the conduct of the Portuguese and British troops has been exactly what I wished; and that the natives of this part of the country are not only reconciled to the invasion, but wish us success, afford us all the supplies in their power, and exert themselves to get intelligence for us. In no part of Spain have we been better, I might say so well, received; because we really draw more supply from the country than we ever did from any part of Spain. The inhabitants, who had at first left their habitations, have in general returned to them, many of them at the risk of their lives, having been fired at by the French sentries at the outposts; and they are living very comfortably and quietly with our soldiers cantoned in their houses.

The Spaniards plundered a good deal, and did a good deal of mischief, in the first two days; but even this misfortune has been of service to us. Some were executed, and many punished; and I sent all the Spanish troops back into Spain to be cantoned, which has convinced the French of our desire not to injure individuals.

I have had a good deal of conversation with people here, and at St Pé, regarding the sentiments of the people of France in general respecting Buonaparte and his government; and I have found it to be exactly what might be supposed from all that we have heard and know of his system. They all agree in one opinion, viz., that the sentiment throughout France is the same as I have found it here, an earnest desire to get rid of him, from a conviction that as long as he governs they will have no peace.

The language common to all is, that although the grievous hardships and oppression under which they suffer are intolerable, they dare not have the satisfaction even of complaining; that, on the contrary, they are obliged to pretend to rejoice, and that they are allowed only to lament in secret and in silence their hard fate.

I enclose you an original address which has been presented to me by the constituted authorities and notables here (which I hope your Lordship will do me the favor not to make public), which will show the strong sentiment here respecting the war; the same prevailed at St Pé, and I hear of the same opinions in all parts of the country.

I have not myself heard any opinion in favor of the House of Bourbon. The opinion stated to me upon that point is, that 20 years have elapsed since the Princes of that House have quitted France; that they are equally, if not more, unknown to France than the Princes of any other Royal House in Europe; but that the allies ought to agree to propose a Sovereign to France instead of Napoleon, who must be got rid of, if it is hoped or intended that Europe should ever enjoy peace; and that it was not material whether it was of the House of Bourbon or of any other Royal Family.

I have taken measures to open correspondence with the interior, by which I hope to know what passes, and the sentiments of the people, and I will take care to keep your Lordship acquainted with all that I may learn. In the mean time, I am convinced more than ever that Napoleon's power stands upon corruption, that he has no adherents in France but the principal officers of his army, and the *employés civils* of the government, and possibly some of the new proprietors; but even these last I consider doubtful.

Notwithstanding this state of things, I recommend to your Lordship to make peace with him if you can acquire all the objects which you have a right to expect. All the powers of Europe require peace possibly more than France, and it would not do to found a new system of war upon the speculations of any individual on what he sees and learns in one corner of France. If Buonaparte becomes moderate, he is probably as good a Sovereign as we can desire in France; if he does not, we shall have another war in a few years; but if my speculations are well founded, we shall have all France against him; time will have been given for the supposed disaffection to his government to produce its effect; his diminished resources will have decreased his means of corruption, and it may be hoped that he will be engaged singlehanded against insurgent France and all Europe.

There is another view of this subject, however, and that is, the continuance of the existing war, and the line to be adopted in that case. At the present moment it is quite impossible for me to move at all: although the army was never in such health, heart, and condition as at present, and it is probably the most complete machine for its numbers now existing in Europe, the rain has so completely destroyed the roads that I cannot move; and, at all events, it is desirable, before I go farther forward, that I should know what the allies propose to do in the winter, which I conclude I shall learn from your Lordship as soon as the King's government shall be made acquainted with their intentions by the King's diplomatic servants abroad. As I shall move forward, whether in the winter or the spring, I can inquire and ascertain more fully the sentiments of the people, and the government can either empower me to decide to raise the Bourbon standard, or can decide the question hereafter themselves, after they shall have all the information before them which I can send them of the sentiments and wishes of the people.

I can only tell you that, if I were a Prince of the House of Bourbon, nothing should prevent me from now coming forward, not in a good house in London, but in the field in France; and if Great Britain would stand by him, I am certain he would succeed. This success would be much more certain in a month or more hence, when Napoleon commences to carry into execution the oppressive measures which he must adopt in order to try to retrieve his fortunes.

I must tell your Lordship, however, that our success, and every thing, depends upon our moderation and justice, and upon the good conduct and discipline of our troops. Hitherto these have behaved well, and there appears a new spirit among the officers, which I hope will continue, to keep the troops in order. But I despair of the Spaniards. They are in so miserable a state, that it is really hardly fair to expect that they will refrain from plundering a beautiful country, into which they enter as conquerors; particularly, adverting to the miseries which their own country has suffered from its invaders. I cannot, therefore, venture to bring them back into France, unless I can feed and pay them; and the official letter which will go to your Lordship by this post will show you the state of our finances, and our prospects. If I could now bring forward 20,000 good Spaniards, paid and fed, I should have Bayonne. If I could bring forward 40,000, I don't know where I should stop. Now I have both the 20,000 and the 40,000 at my command, upon this frontier, but I cannot venture to bring forward any for want of means of paying and supporting them. Without pay and food, they must plunder; and if they plunder, they will ruin us all.

I think I can make an arrangement of the subsidy to cover the expense of 20,000 Spaniards; but all these arrangements are easily settled, if we could get the money. Where we are to get the money, excepting from England, it is impossible for me to devise; as the patriotic gentlemen at Lisbon, now that they can buy no Commissariat debts, will give us no money, or very little, for the drafts on the Treasury, and the yellow fever has put a stop to the communication with Cadiz and Gibraltar; and if we had millions at all three, we could not get a shilling for want of ships to bring it.

To Earl Bathurst.

St Jean de Luz, 14th Dec. 1813.

Since the enemy's retreat from the Nivelle they had occupied a position in front of Bayonne, which had been intrenched with great labor since the battle fought at Vitoria in June last. It appears to be under the fire of the works of the place: the right rests upon the Adour; and the front in this part is covered by a morass occasioned by a rivulet which falls into the Adour. The right of the centre rests upon this same morass, and its left upon the river Nive; the left is between the Nive and the Adour, on which river the left rests. They had their advanced posts from their right in front of Anglet and towards Biaritz. With their left they defended the river Nive, and communicated with Gen. Paris' division of the army of Catalonia, which was at St Jean Pied de Port; and they had a considerable corps cantoned in Ville Franque and Mouguerre.

It was impossible to attack the enemy in this position, as long as they remained in force in it, without the certainty of great loss, at the same time that success was not very probable, as the camp is so immediately protected by the works of the place. It appeared to me, therefore, that the best mode of obliging the enemy either to abandon the position altogether, or at least so to weaken his force in it as to offer a more favorable opportunity of attacking it, was to pass the Nive, and to place our right upon the Adour; by which operation the enemy, already distressed for provisions, would lose the means of communication with the interior afforded by that river, and would become still more distressed. The passage of the Nive was likewise calculated to give us other advantages; to open to us a communication with the interior of France for intelligence, &c., and to enable us to draw some supplies from the country.

I had determined to pass the Nive immediately after the passage of the Nivelle, but was prevented by the bad state of the roads, and the swelling of all the rivulets occasioned by the fall of rain in the beginning of that month; but the state of the weather and roads having at length enabled me to collect the materials, and make the preparations for forming bridges for the passage of that river, I moved the troops out of their cantonments on the 8th, and ordered that the right of the army, under Lieut. Gen. Sir R. Hill, should pass on the 9th at and in the neighbourhood of Cambo, while Marshal Sir W. Beresford should favor and support his operation by passing the 6th division, under Lieut. Gen. Sir H. Clinton, at Ustaritz. Both operations succeeded completely. The enemy were immediately driven from the right bank of the river, and retired towards Bayonne by the great road of St Jean Pied de Port. Those posted opposite Cambo were nearly intercepted by the 6th division; and one regiment was driven from the road and obliged to march across the country.

The enemy assembled in considerable force on a range of heights running parallel with the Adour, and still keeping Ville Franque by their right. The 8th Portuguese regt., under Col. Douglas, and the 9th caçadores, under Col. Brown, and the British light infantry battalion of the 6th division, carried this village and the heights in the neighbourhood. The rain which had fallen the preceding night, and on the morning of the 8th, had so destroyed the road, that the day had nearly elapsed before the whole of Sir R. Hill's corps had come up; and I was therefore satisfied with the possession of the ground which we occupied.

On the same day Lieut. Gen. Sir J. Hope, with the left of the army under his command, moved forward by the great road from St Jean de Luz towards Bayonne, and reconnaitred the right of the intrenched camp under Bayonne, and the course of the Adour below the town, after driving in the enemy's posts from the neighbourhood of Biaritz and Anglet. The Light division, under Major Gen. C. Alten, likewise moved forward from Bassussarry, and reconnaitred that part of the enemy's intrenchments. Sir J. Hope and Major Gen. Alten retired in the evening to the ground they had before occupied.

On the morning of the 10th Lieut. Gen. Sir R. Hill found that the enemy had retired from the position which they had occupied the day before on the heights, into the intrenched camp on that side of the Nive; and he therefore occupied the position intended for him, with his right towards the Adour, and his left at Ville Franque, and communicating with the centre of the army under Marshall Sir W. Beresford by a bridge laid over the Nive; and the troops under the Marshal were again drawn to the left of that river.

Gen. Morillo's division of Spanish infantry, which had remained with Sir R. Hill when the other Spanish troops went into cantonments within the Spanish frontier, was placed at

Urcuray, with Col. Vivian's brigade of light dragoons at Hasparren, in order to observe the movements of the enemy's division under Gen. Paris, which upon our passage of the Nive had retired towards St Palais.

On the 10th in the morning the enemy moved out of the intrenched camp with their whole army, with the exception only of what occupied the works opposite to Sir R. Hill's position, and drove in the piquets of the Light division and of Sir J. Hope's corps, and made a most desperate attack upon the post of the former at the château and church of Arcangues, and upon the advanced posts of the latter on the high road from Bayonne to St Jean de Luz, near the Mayor's house of Biaritz. Both attacks were repulsed in the most gallant style by the troops, and Sir J. Hope's corps took about 500 prisoners. The brunt of the action with Sir J. Hope's advanced post fell upon the 1st Portuguese brigade, under Major Gen. Arch. Campbell, which were on duty, and upon Major Gen. Robinson's brigade of the 5th division, which moved up to their support.

Lieut. Gen. Sir J. Hope reports most favorably of the conduct of these, and of all the other troops engaged; and I had great satisfaction in finding that this attempt made by the enemy upon our left, in order to oblige us to draw in our right, was completely defeated by a comparatively small part of our force.

I cannot sufficiently applaud the ability, coolness, and judgment of Lieut. Gen. Sir J. Hope, who, with the General and Staff officers under his command, showed the troops an example of gallantry which must have tended to produce the favorable result of the day. Sir J. Hope received a severe contusion, which, however, I am happy to say, has not deprived me for a moment of the benefit of his assistance.

After the action was over, the regiments of Nassau and Francfort, under the command of Col. Krüse, came over to the posts of Major Gen. Ross' brigade of the 4th division, which were formed for the support of the centre.

When the night closed, the enemy were still in large force in front of our posts, on the ground from which they had driven the piquets. They retired, however, during the night, from Lieut. Gen. Sir J. Hope's front, leaving small posts, which were immediately driven in. They still occupied in force the bridge on which the piquets of the Light division had stood, and it was obvious that the whole army was still in front of our left; and about 3 in the afternoon they again drove in Lieut. Gen. Sir J. Hope's piquets, and attacked his post. They were again repulsed with considerable loss. The attack was recommenced on the morning of the 12th, with the same want of success. The 1st division, under Major Gen. Howard, having relieved the 5th division, the enemy discontinued it in the afternoon, and retired entirely within the intrenched camp on that night. They never renewed the attack on the posts of the Light division after the 10th.

Lieut. Gen. Sir J. Hope reports most favorably of the conduct of all the officers and troops, particularly of the Portuguese brigade under Gen. Arch. Campbell, and of Gen. Robinson's and Gen. Hay's brigades of the 5th division, under the command of Col. the Hon. C. Greville. He mentions particularly Major Gen. Hay, commanding the 5th division; Major Gens. Robinson and Bradford, Brig. Gen. Campbell, Cols. do Rego and Greville, commanding the several brigades; Lieut. Col. Lloyd, of the 84th, who was unfortunately killed; Lieut. Cols. Barns of the Royals, and Cameron of the 9th; Capt. Ramsay, of the Royal horse artillery; Col. De Lancey, the D. Q. M. G.; Lieut. Col. Macdonald, the A. A. G. attached to Sir J. Hope's corps; and the officers of his personal Staff.

The 1st division, under Major Gen. Howard, were not engaged till the 12th, when the enemy's attack was more feeble; but the Guards conducted themselves with their usual spirit.

The enemy, having thus failed in all their attacks with their whole force upon our left, withdrew into their intrenchments on the night of the 12th, and passed a large force through Bayonne; with which, on the morning of the 13th, they made a most desperate attack upon Lieut. Gen. Sir R. Hill. In expectation of this attack, I had requested Marshal Sir W. Beresford to reinforce the Lieut. General with the 6th division, which crossed the Nive at daylight in the morning; and I further reinforced him by the 4th division, and 2 brigades of the 3d.

The expected arrival of the 6th division gave the Lieut.

General great facility in making his movements; but the troops under his own immediate command had defeated and repulsed the enemy with immense loss before their arrival. The principal attack having been made along the high road from Bayonne to St Jean Pied de Port, Major Gen. Barnes' brigade of British infantry, and the 5th brigade of Portuguese infantry under Brig. Gen. Ashworth, were particularly engaged in the contest with the enemy on that point; and these troops conducted themselves admirably. The Portuguese division of infantry, under the command of Mariscal de Campo F. Le Cor, moved to their support on their left in a very gallant style, and regained an important position between those troops and Major Gen. Pringle's brigade engaged with the enemy in front of Ville Franque. I had great satisfaction also in observing the conduct of Major Gen. Byng's brigade of British infantry, supported by the Portuguese brigade under the command of Major Gen. Buchan, in carrying an important height from the enemy on the right of our position, and maintaining it against all their efforts to regain it.

Two guns and some prisoners were taken from the enemy, who, being beat in all points, and having suffered considerable loss, were obliged to retire upon their intrenchments.

It gives me the greatest satisfaction to have another opportunity of reporting my sense of the services and merits of Lieut. Gen. Sir R. Hill upon this occasion, as well as of those of Lieut. Gen. the Hon. Sir W. Stewart, commanding the 2d division of infantry, Major Gens. Barnes, Byng, and Pringle, Mariscal de Campo F. Le Cor, Major Gens. Buchan and Da Costa, and Brig. Gen. Ashworth. The British artillery under Lieut. Col. Ross, and the Portuguese artillery under Col. Tulloh, distinguished themselves; and Lieut. Gen. Sir R. Hill reports particularly the assistance he received from Lieut. Cols. Bouverie, A. A. G., and Jackson, A. Q. M. G., attached to his corps, Lieut. Col. Goldfinch of the Royal engineers, and from the officers of his personal Staff.

The enemy marched a large body of cavalry across the bridge of the Adour yesterday evening, and retired their force opposite to Sir R. Hill this morning towards Bayonne.

Throughout these various operations I have received every assistance from Sir G. Murray, Q. M. G., and Sir E. Pakenham, A. G., and Lord FitzRoy Somerset, Lieut. Col. Campbell, and the officers of my personal Staff.

I send this dispatch by Major Hill, the aide de camp of Lieut. Gen. Sir R. Hill, whom I beg leave to recommend to your Lordship's protection.

Return of the killed, wounded, and missing, in the operations of the Nive, from the 9th to the 13th Dec. 1813.

	Officers.	Serjeants.	R. and F.	Horses.	Total loss of officers, non-commissioned officers, and R. & F.
Killed	32	15	603	13	650
Wounded	233	215	3459	21	3907
Missing	17	14	473	1	504

SEVEN

THE CAMPAIGNS OF 1814

The story of the campaign of 1814 does not take long to tell. Following the battle of the River Nive, Wellington's forces remained quiet for a little while, not least because the British commander was not prepared to advance farther into France until he could be quite certain that there was no possibility of a separate peace between the eastern powers and Napoleon (however unlikely the prospect, given the French emperor's refusal to contemplate anything resembling a compromise settlement, even in the aftermath of the battle of Leipzig such an eventuality could not entirely be ruled out). Operations, then, were not resumed till 14 February. In brief, Sir John Hope crossed the River Adour to complete the investment of Bayonne, while Wellington himself pushed east to engage the forces of Marshal Soult. A fierce battle followed at Orthez on 27 February, whereupon Soult fell back towards Toulouse, leaving Wellington free to detach a large force under Marshal Beresford to capture the important port of Bordeaux, from whence had come rumours of a royalist uprising. Having made up the gap that this had caused in his ranks by summoning two divisions of Spanish troops to his assistance (hitherto almost all the Spanish forces had been kept back behind the frontier for fear that they would ravage the French countryside and spark off a guerrilla war against the invaders), in late March Wellington resumed his operations and closed in on Toulouse. Here he found that Soult had adopted a strong defensive position on the heights that overlooked the city, and on 10 April there followed a bloody battle which saw Wellington's troops launch repeated assaults on Soult's positions under heavy fire.

Casualties were very severe while the day did not pass without a variety of setbacks, but by nightfall the French were everywhere falling back into the city itself. Unmolested by Wellington's shaken troops, Soult evacuated the place the following day, but in the event, other than a fierce sortie at Bayonne on 14 April, there was no more fighting, for news arrived that Napoleon had abdicated. Moving on to Bordeaux, where it received a hero's welcome, the Anglo-Portuguese army was then finally broken up, many of its British units being sent to the United States to take part in the War of 1812, whilst their Portuguese counterparts set off on the long march to their home country. Their sacrifices, however, should not be forgotten. Since 1808 some 40,000 British troops – roughly one fifth of those who had taken part in the Peninsular War – had fallen in action or died of sickness or disease, whilst Portuguese losses had amounted to another 20,000. As Wellington was to observe of the battle of Waterloo a year later, next to a battle lost, there is nothing sadder than a battle won.

To Earl Bathurst.

St Jean de Luz, 20th Feb. 1814.

In conformity with the intention which I communicated to your Lordship in my last dispatch, I moved the right of the army, under Lieut. Gen. Sir R. Hill, on the 14th. He drove in the enemy's piquets on the Joyeuse river, and attacked their position at Hellette, from which he obliged Gen. Harispe to retire with some loss towards St Martin. I made the detachment of Gen. Mina's troops in the valley of Baztan advance on the same day upon Baygorry and Bidarry; and the direct communication of the enemy with St Jean Pied de Port being cut off by Lieut. Gen. Sir R. Hill's success at Hellette, that fort has been blockaded by the Spanish troops above mentioned.

On the following morning (the 15th) the troops under Lieut.

Gen. Sir R. Hill continued the pursuit of the enemy, who had retired to a strong position in front of Garris; where Gen. Harispe was joined by Gen. Paris' division, which had been recalled from the march it had commenced for the interior of France; and by other troops from the enemy's centre.

Gen. Morillo's Spanish division, after driving in the enemy's advanced posts, was ordered to move towards St Palais, by a ridge parallel to that on which was the enemy's position, in order to turn their left, and cut off their retreat by that road; while the 2d division, under Lieut. Gen. Sir W. Stewart, should attack in front. Those troops made a most gallant attack upon the enemy's position, which was remarkably strong, but which was carried without very considerable loss. Much of the day had elapsed before the attack could be commenced; and the action lasted till after dark, the enemy having made repeated attempts to regain the position, particularly in two attacks, which were most gallantly received and repulsed by the 39th regt., under the command of the Hon. Col. O'Callaghan, in Major Gen. Pringle's brigade. The Major General, and Lieut. Col. Bruce, of the 39th, were unfortunately wounded. We took 10 officers and about 200 prisoners.

The right of the centre of the army made a corresponding movement with the right on these days; and our posts were on the Bidouze river on the evening of the 15th.

The enemy retired across the river at St Palais, in the night, destroying the bridges; which, however, were repaired, so that the troops under Lieut. Gen. Sir R. Hill crossed on the 16th; and on the 17th the enemy were driven across the Gave de Mauleon, &c. They attempted to destroy the bridge at Arriver-ete, but they had not time to complete its destruction; and a ford having been discovered above the bridge, the 92d regt., under the command of Col. Cameron, supported by the fire of Capt. Bean's troop of horse artillery, crossed the ford, and made a most gallant attack upon two battalions of French infantry posted in the village, from which the latter were driven with considerable loss. The enemy retired in the night across the Gave d'Oléron, and took up a strong position in the neighbourhood of Sauveterre, in which they were joined by other troops.

On the 18th our posts were established on the Gave d'Oléron, and measures are in preparation to enable Lieut. Gen. Sir R. Hill to cross that river as soon as the pontoon train shall arrive.

In all the actions which I have above detailed to your Lordship, the troops have conducted themselves remarkably well; and I had great satisfaction in observing the good conduct of those under Gen. Morillo, in the attack of Hellette, on the 14th, and in driving in the enemy's advanced posts in front of their position at Garris, on the 15th.

Since the 14th the enemy have considerably weakened their force in Bayonne; and they have withdrawn from the right of the Adour above the town. Their whole force appears collected on the Gave; and they still hold their bridge at Peyrehorade.

I returned from Lieut. Gen. Sir R. Hill's corps yesterday, in order to put in motion the left of the army, which I was in hopes I should have been able to have passed across the Adour below Bayonne, for which operation a bridge has been prepared by the assistance of the navy.

The weather is so unfavorable, however, that it is impossible to attempt this operation at the present moment; and I therefore return to Sir R. Hill's corps to-morrow morning, in order to superintend the further operations in that quarter; and I leave to Lieut. Gen. Sir J. Hope to cross the Adour whenever the weather will permit.

I have received no intelligence from Catalonia since I addressed your Lordship last; but I have this day received a report from the Governor of Pamplona, stating that the fort of Jaca had surrendered to Gen. Mina by capitulation on the 17th inst. I am not acquainted with the particulars of this event; but I know that the place contained 84 pieces of brass cannon.

Return of the killed, wounded, and missing in the
various operations from the 14th to the 17th Feb.

	Officers.	Serjeants.	R. and F.	Total loss of officers, non-commissioned officers, and R. & F.
Killed	1	2	28	31
Wounded	22	12	155	189
Missing	—	—	12	12

Portuguese loss included.

To Earl Bathurst.

St Sever, 1st March, 1814.

The sense which I had of the difficulties attending the movement of the army by its right, across so many rivers as must
have been and as have lately been passed in its progress, induced
me to determine to pass the Adour below the town of Bayonne,
notwithstanding the difficulties which opposed this operation;
and I was the more induced to adopt this plan, as, whatever might
be the mode in which I should eventually move upon the enemy,
it was obvious that I could depend upon no communication
with Spain and the seaports of that kingdom, and with St Jean
de Luz, excepting that alone which is practicable in the winter,
viz., by the high roads leading to and from Bayonne. I likewise
hoped that the establishment of a bridge below Bayonne would
give me the use of the Adour as a harbour.

The movements of the right of the army, which I detailed to
your Lordship in my last dispatch, were intended to divert the
enemy's attention from the preparations at St Jean de Luz and
Pasages for the passage of the Adour below Bayonne, and to
induce the enemy to move his force to his left, in which objects

they succeeded completely; but upon my return to St Jean de Luz, on the 19th, I found the weather so unfavorable at sea, and so uncertain, that I determined to push forward my operations on the right, notwithstanding that I had still the Gave d'Oléron, the Gave de Pau, and the Adour to pass.

Accordingly, I returned to Garris on the 21st, and ordered the 6th and Light divisions to break up from the blockade of Bayonne; and Gen. Don M. Freyre to close up the cantonments of his corps towards Irun, and to be prepared to move when the left of the army should cross the Adour.

I found the pontoons collected at Garris, and they were moved forward on the following days to and across the Gave de Mauleon, and the troops of the centre of the army arrived.

On the 24th, Lieut. Gen. Sir R. Hill passed the Gave d'Oléron at Villenave, with the Light, 2d, and Portuguese divisions, under the command of Major Gen. Baron C. Alten, Lieut. Gen. Sir W. Stewart, and Mariscal de Campo Le Cor; while Lieut. Gen. Sir H. Clinton passed with the 6th division between Monfort and Laas; and Lieut. Gen. Sir T. Picton made demonstrations, with the 3d division, of an intention to attack the enemy's position at the bridge of Sauveterre, which induced the enemy to blow up the bridge.

Mariscal de Campo Don P. Morillo drove in the enemy's posts near Navarreins, and blockaded that place.

Marshal Sir W. Beresford likewise, who, since the movement of Sir R. Hill on the 14th and 15th, had remained with the 4th and 7th divisions, and Col. Vivian's brigade, in observation on the Lower Bidouze, attacked the enemy on the 23rd in their fortified posts at Hastingues and Oeyregave, on the left of the Gave de Pau, and obliged them to retire within the *tête de pont* at Peyrehorade.

Immediately after the passage of the Gave d'Oléron was effected, Sir R. Hill and Sir H. Clinton moved towards Orthez and the great road leading from Sauveterre to that town; and the enemy retired in the night from Sauveterre across the Gave de Pau, and assembled their army near Orthez on the 25th, having destroyed all the bridges on the river.

The right and right of the centre of the army assembled opposite Orthez; Lieut. Gen. Sir S. Cotton, with Lord E. Somerset's brigade of cavalry, and the 3d division, under Lieut. Gen. Sir T. Picton, were near the destroyed bridge of Berenx; and Marshal Sir W. Beresford, with the 4th and 7th divisions, under Lieut. Gen. Sir G. L. Cole and Major Gen. Walker, and Col. Vivian's brigade, towards the junction of the Gave de Pau with the Gave d'Oléron.

The troops opposed to the Marshal having moved on the 25th, he crossed the Gave de Pau below the junction of the Gave d'Oléron on the morning of the 26th, and moved along the high road from Peyrehorade towards Orthez, on the enemy's right. As he approached, Lieut. Gen. Sir S. Cotton crossed with the cavalry, and Lieut. Gen. Sir T. Picton with the 3d division, below the bridge of Berenx; and I moved the 6th and Light divisions to the same point; and Lieut. Gen. Sir R. Hill occupied the heights opposite Orthez and the high road leading to Sauveterre.

The 6th and Light divisions crossed in the morning of the 27th at daylight, and we found the enemy in a strong position near Orthez, with his right on a height on the high road to Dax, and occupying the village of St Boés, and his left on the heights above Orthez and that town, and opposing the passage of the river by Sir R. Hill.

The course of the heights on which the enemy had placed his army necessarily retired his centre, while the strength of the position gave extraordinary advantages to the flanks.

I ordered Marshal Sir W. Beresford to turn and attack the enemy's right with the 4th division under Lieut. Gen. Sir G. L. Cole, and the 7th division under Major Gen. Walker, and Col. Vivian's brigade of cavalry; while Lieut. Gen. Sir T. Picton should move along the great road leading from Peyrehorade to Orthez, and attack the heights on which the enemy's centre and left stood, with the 3d and 6th divisions under Lieut. Gen. Sir H. Clinton, supported by Sir S. Cotton, with Lord E. Somerset's brigade of cavalry. Major Gen. Baron C. Alten, with the Light division, kept the communication, and was in reserve between these two attacks. I likewise desired Lieut. Gen. Sir R. Hill to cross the Gave, and to turn and attack the enemy's left.

Marshal Sir W. Beresford carried the village of St Boés with the 4th division, under the command of Lieut. Gen. Sir G. L. Cole, after an obstinate resistance by the enemy; but the ground was so narrow that the troops could not deploy to attack the heights, notwithstanding the repeated attempts of Major Gen. Ross and Brig. Gen. Vasconcellos' Portuguese brigade; and it was impossible to turn them by the enemy's right without an excessive extension of our line.

I therefore so far altered the plan of the action as to order the immediate advance of the 3d and 6th divisions, and I moved forward Col. Barnard's brigade of the Light division to attack the left of the height on which the enemy's right stood.

This attack, led by the 52d regt. under Lieut. Col. Colborne, and supported on their right by Major Gen. Brisbane's and Col. Keane's brigades of the 3d division, and by simultaneous attacks on the left by Major Gen. Anson's brigade of the 4th division, and on the right by Lieut. Gen. Sir T. Picton, with the remainder of the 3d division and the 6th division, under Lieut. Gen. Sir H. Clinton, dislodged the enemy from the heights and gave us the victory.

In the mean time, Lieut. Gen. Sir R. Hill had forced the passage of the Gave above Orthez, and seeing the state of the action he moved immediately, with the 2d division of infantry under Lieut. Gen. Sir W. Stewart and Major Gen. Fane's brigade of cavalry, direct for the great road from Orthez to St Sever, thus keeping upon the enemy's left.

The enemy retired at first in admirable order, taking every advantage of the numerous good positions which the country afforded him. The losses, however, which he sustained in the continued attacks of our troops, and the danger with which he was threatened by Lieut. Gen. Sir R. Hill's corps, soon accelerated his movements, and the retreat at last became a flight, and the troops were in the utmost confusion.

Lieut. Gen. Sir S. Cotton took advantage of the only opportunity which offered to charge with Major Gen. Lord E. Somerset's brigade, in the neighbourhood of Sault de Navailles, where the enemy had been driven from the high road by Lieut. Gen. Sir R. Hill. The 7th hussars distinguished themselves upon this occasion, and made many prisoners.

We continued the pursuit till it was dusk; and I halted the army in the neighbourhood of Sault de Navailles. I cannot estimate the extent of the enemy's loss: we have taken 6 pieces of cannon and a great many prisoners; the numbers I cannot at present report. The whole country is covered by their dead. The army was in the utmost confusion when I last saw it passing the heights near Sault de Navailles, and many soldiers had thrown away their arms. The desertion has since been immense.

We followed the enemy on the 28th to this place; and we this day passed the Adour. Marshal Sir W. Beresford marched with the Light division and Gen. Vivian's brigade upon Mont de Marsan, where he has taken a very large magazine of provisions. Lieut. Gen. Sir R. Hill has moved upon Aire, and the advanced posts of the centre are at Cazères.

The enemy are apparently retiring upon Agen, and have left open the direct road towards Bordeaux.

While the operations of which I have above given the report were carrying on on the right of the army, Lieut. Gen. Sir J. Hope, in concert with Rear Adm. Penrose, availed himself of an opportunity which offered on the 23d Feb. to cross the Adour below Bayonne, and to take possession of both banks of the river at its mouth. The vessels destined to form the bridge could not get in till the 24th, when the difficult, and at this season of the year dangerous, operation of bringing them in was effected with a degree of gallantry and skill seldom equalled. Lieut. Gen. Sir J. Hope particularly mentions Capt. O'Reilly, Lieut. Cheshire, Lieut. Douglas, and Lieut. Collins, of the navy, and also Lieut. Debenham, Agent of Transports; and I am infinitely indebted to Rear Adm. Penrose for the cordial assistance I received from him in preparing for this plan, and for that which he gave Lieut. Gen. Sir J. Hope in carrying it into execution.

The enemy, conceiving that the means of crossing the river which Lieut. Gen. Sir J. Hope had at his command, viz., rafts made of pontoons, had not enabled him to cross a large force in the course of the 23d, attacked the corps which he had sent over on that evening. This corps consisted of 600 men of the 2d brigade of Guards, under the command of Major Gen. the Hon. E. Stopford, who repulsed the enemy immediately. The Rocket brigade was of great use upon this occasion.

Three of the enemy's gun boats were destroyed this day; and a frigate lying in the Adour received considerable damage from the fire of a battery of 18 pounders, and was obliged to go higher up the river to the neighbourhood of the bridge.

Lieut. Gen. Sir J. Hope invested the citadel of Bayonne on the 25th; and Lieut. Gen. Don M. Freyre moved forward with the 4th Spanish army in consequence of directions which I had left for him.

On the 27th, the bridge having been completed, Lieut. Gen. Sir J. Hope deemed it expedient to invest the citadel of Bayonne more closely than he had done before; and he attacked the village of St Etienne, which he carried, having taken a gun and some prisoners from the enemy; and his posts are now within 900 yards of the outworks of the place.

The result of the operations which I have detailed to your Lordship is, that Bayonne, St Jean Pied de Port, and Navarreins, are invested; and the army, having passed the Adour, are in possession of all the great communications across that river, after having beaten the enemy, and taken their magazines.

I have ordered forward the Spanish troops under Gen. Freyre, and the heavy British cavalry and artillery, and the Portuguese artillery.

Your Lordship will have observed with satisfaction the able assistance which I have received in these operations from Marshal Sir W. Beresford, Lieut. Gens. Sir R. Hill, Sir J. Hope, and Sir S. Cotton; and from all the General officers, officers, and troops acting under their orders respectively. It is impossible for me sufficiently to express my sense of their merits, or of the degree in which the country is indebted to their zeal and ability for the situation in which the army now finds itself.

All the troops distinguished themselves; the 4th division, under Lieut. Gen. Sir G. L. Cole, in the attack of St Boés, and the subsequent endeavors to carry the right of the heights; the 3d, 6th, and Light divisions, under the command of Lieut. Gen. Sir T. Picton, Sir H. Clinton, and Major Gen. Baron C. Alten, in the attack of the enemy's position on the heights: and these, and the 7th division under Major Gen. Walker, in the various operations and attacks on the enemy's retreat.

The charge made by the 7th hussars under Lord E. Somerset was highly meritorious.

The conduct of the artillery throughout the day deserved my highest approbation.

I am likewise much indebted to Sir G. Murray, the Q. M. G., and Sir E. Pakenham, the A. G., for the assistance I have received from them; and to Lord FitzRoy Somerset, and the officers of my personal Staff; and to the Mariscal de Campo Don M. de Alava.

The last accounts which I have received from Catalonia are of the 20th. The French commanders of the garrisons of Llerida, Mequinenza, and Monzon, had been induced to evacuate those places by orders sent to them by the Baron de Eroles in Marshal Suchet's cipher, of which he had got possession.

The troops composing these garrisons, having joined, were afterwards surrounded in the pass Martorell, on their march towards the French frontier, by a detachment from the 1st Spanish army, and by a detachment from the Anglo-Sicilian corps. Lieut. Gen. Copons allowed them to capitulate; but I have not yet received from him any report on this subject, nor do I yet know what is the result.

It was expected in Catalonia that Marshal Suchet would immediately evacuate that province; and I have heard here that he is to join Marshal Soult.

I have not yet received the detailed report of the capitulation of Jaca.

I enclose the returns of killed and wounded upon the late occasion. I send this dispatch by my aide de camp Major Fremantle, whom I beg leave to recommend to your Lordship's protection.

Return of the killed, wounded, and missing, on the 27th Feb., at Orthez.

	Officers.	Serjeants.	R. and F.	Horses.	Total loss of officers, non-commissioned officers, and R. & F.
Killed	18	25	234	7	277
Wounded	134	89	1700	33	1923
Missing	1	5	64	51	70

To Earl Bathurst.

Aire, 11th March, 1814.

I have received your Lordship's letter of the 1st inst., with the draft of the proposed preliminary treaty. If Napoleon is to continue as a sovereign, I should be glad to see him reduced to make such a treaty: but I confess that I never thought he was so reduced; and, if I can give any credit to the facts stated in the French papers to the 1st inst., he certainly is not so. Indeed things were in such a state, that I hope the treaty will not have been proposed; as, if it is, Buonaparte will certainly publish it; and the interests of Spain, the only country which it appears has had an opportunity, and has refused, to make a separate treaty, are entirely forgotten; and when every fortress in Germany is to be given up by the preliminary treaty, the enemy is to remain in possession of the fortresses in Spain till the definitive treaty shall be signed. It is very desirable that the King's minister should be instructed what to say upon this point at Madrid.

I am not sufficiently informed of the state of affairs and of opinions at the Imperial head quarters in the middle of February, or of the real facts of the misfortunes upon the Seine and Marne, and of the causes of the subsequent movements, to be able to form any judgment of the state of affairs. I should think that the armies are falling back to concentrate a little; and it is possible that Augereau's movement from Lyons, the object of which is certainly to bring the Viceroy out of Italy, may have had some influence over them. In this case, more particularly if what M. de Viel Castel says of the Prince Royal's movement be true, the Allies may still be able to hold their ground within the French territory; and Napoleon may be confined to a small space round Paris.

Whenever the Congress at Châtillon is broken up, we have a fine Royalist game in our hands here, if the Allies can hold their ground within the French territory, and if I can in any manner get rid of M. de Viel Castel. With strong professions in favor of the Bourbons, he has contrived to circulate a whisper that Monsieur was not received at the Imperial head quarters, and had been desired to remain in Switzerland; and, between the misfortunes of the Allies and this secret, the stability of Napoleon's throne seems to be very sufficiently provided for. In the mean time, Marshal Beresford has marched with 2 divisions upon Bordeaux, and I wait the result of that movement, and the arrival of my cavalry and cannon.

I beg your Lordship's attention to the enclosed state of the army. I take it, there are not much less than 7000 Portuguese, and double the number of British, destined to join us, some of whom ought to have joined long ago.

In the mean time, however, if Suchet joins Soult with his whole force, we shall be very weak, particularly in British troops, which must be the foundation of every thing. I can bring more Spaniards into the field, but I have not the means of maintaining both them and the additional British and Portuguese. Necessity has no law, however, and I must bring them forward, if the expected British and Portuguese troops should not soon arrive.

To Earl Bathurst.

Tarbes, 20th March, 1814.

The enemy collected their force at Conchez on the 13th, as I reported to your Lordship in my dispatch of that date, which induced me to concentrate the army in the neighbourhood of Aire. The various detachments which I had sent out, and the reserves of cavalry and artillery moving out of Spain, did not join till the 17th.

In the mean time, the enemy, not finding his situation at Conchez very secure, retired on the 15th to Lembège, keeping his advanced posts towards Conchez.

The army marched on the 18th, and Lieut. Gen. Sir R. Hill drove in the enemy's outposts upon Lembège. The enemy retired in the night upon Vic Bigorre; and on the following day, the 19th, held a strong rear guard in the vineyards in front of the town. Lieut. Gen. Sir T. Picton, with the 3d division, and Major

Gen. Bock's brigade, made a very handsome movement upon this rear guard, and drove them through the vineyards and town; and the army assembled at Vic Bigorre and Rabastens.

The enemy retired in the night upon Tarbes. We found them this morning with the advanced posts of their left in the town, and their right upon the heights near the windmill of Oleac. Their centre and left were retired, the latter being upon the heights near Audos. We marched in two columns from Vic Bigorre and Rabastens; and I made Lieut. Gen. Sir H. Clinton turn and attack the right with the 6th division, through the village of Dours; while Lieut. Gen. Sir R. Hill attacked the town by the high road from Vic Bigorre.

Lieut. Gen. Sir H. Clinton's movement was very ably made, and was completely successful. The Light division under Major Gen. C. Baron Alten likewise drove the enemy from the heights above Orleix; and Lieut. Gen. Sir R. Hill having moved through the town and disposed his columns for the attack, the enemy retired in all directions. The enemy's loss was considerable in the attack made by the Light division; ours has not been considerable in any of these operations.

Our troops are encamped this night upon the Larret and the Arroz; Lieut. Gen. Sir H. Clinton with the 6th division, and Lieut. Gen. Sir S. Cotton, with Major Gen. Ponsonby's and Lord E. Somerset's brigades, being well advanced upon their right.

Although the enemy's opposition has not been of a nature to try the troops, I have had every reason to be satisfied with their conduct in all these affairs, particularly with that of the 3d division in the attack of the vineyards and town of Vic Bigorre yesterday, and with that of the 6th and Light divisions this day.

In all the partial affairs of the cavalry, ours have shown their superiority; and 2 squadrons of the 14th dragoons under Capt. Milles on the 14th, and one squadron of the 15th on the 16th, conducted themselves most gallantly, and took a great number of prisoners. The 4th Portuguese dragoons under Col. Campbell likewise conducted themselves remarkably well in a charge on the 13th.

I have not received any recent intelligence from Catalonia.

To Earl Bathurst.

Seysses, 1st April, 1814.

The enemy retired into Toulouse upon the approach of our troops on the 28th ult. They had fortified the suburb on the left of the Garonne as a *tête de pont*, which they occupy in considerable force; and the remainder of the army is in the town or immediately behind it. The great fall of rain in the course of the last and the beginning of this week, and the melting of the snow in the mountains, has increased the river to such a degree, and rendered the current so rapid, as to frustrate all our endeavors to lay our bridge below the town. I made Sir R. Hill cross the Garonne, above the junction of the Arriège, yesterday morning, and march upon Cintegabelle, where there is a bridge over the latter river. But the same causes have so entirely destroyed the roads on the right of the Arriège, as to render it impracticable to manœuvre the army on that side of Toulouse. I have, therefore, ordered Sir Rowland to return; and I hope to be able to cross the river below Toulouse in a few days.

According to my last accounts from Bordeaux, of the 26th, His Majesty's ships had not yet entered the river.

Nothing of importance has occurred lately in Catalonia.

To Earl Bathurst.

Toulouse, 12th April, 1814.

I have the pleasure to inform your Lordship that I entered this town this morning, which the enemy evacuated during the night, retiring by the road of Carcassonne.

The continued fall of rain and the state of the river prevented me from laying the bridge till the morning of the 8th, when the Spanish corps and the Portuguese artillery, under the immediate orders of Gen. Don M. Freyre, and the head quarters, crossed the Garonne.

We immediately moved forward to the neighbourhood of the town; and the 18th hussars, under the immediate command of Col. Vivian, had an opportunity of making a most gallant attack upon a superior body of the enemy's cavalry, which they drove through the village of Croix Dorade, and took about 100 prisoners, and gave us possession of an important bridge over the river Ers, by which it was necessary to pass, in order to attack the enemy's position. Col. Vivian was unfortunately wounded upon this occasion; and I am afraid that I shall lose the benefit of his assistance for some time.

The town of Toulouse is surrounded on three sides by the canal of Languedoc and the Garonne. On the left of that river, the suburb, which the enemy had fortified with strong field works in front of the ancient wall, formed a good *tête de pont*. They had likewise formed a *tête de pont* at each bridge of the canal, which was besides defended by the fire in some places of musketry, and in all of artillery from the ancient wall of the town. Beyond the canal to the eastward, and between that and the river Ers, is a height which extends as far as Montaudran, and over which pass all the approaches to the canal and town from the eastward, which it defends; and the enemy, in addition to the *têtes de pont* on the bridges of the canal, had fortified this height with five redoubts, connected by lines of intrenchments, and had, with extraordinary diligence, made every preparation for defence. They had likewise broken all the bridges over the Ers within our reach, by which the right of their position could be approached. The roads, however, from the Arriège to Toulouse being impracticable for cavalry or artillery, and nearly so for infantry, as reported in my dispatch to your Lordship of the 1st inst., I had no alternative, excepting to attack the enemy in this formidable position.

It was necessary to move the pontoon bridge higher up the Garonne, in order to shorten the communication with Lieut. Gen. Sir R. Hill's corps, as soon as the Spanish corps had passed; and this operation was not effected till so late an hour on the 9th as to induce me to defer the attack till the following morning.

The plan, according to which I determined to attack the enemy, was for Marshal Sir W. Beresford, who was on the right of the Ers with the 4th and 6th divisions, to cross that river at the bridge of Croix Dorade, to gain possession of Montblanc, and to march up the left of the Ers to turn the enemy's right, while Gen. Don M. Freyre, with the Spanish corps under his command, supported by the British cavalry, should attack the front. Lieut. Gen. Sir S. Cotton was to follow the Marshal's movement with Major Gen. Lord E. Somerset's brigade of hussars; and Col. Vivian's brigade, under the command of Col. Arentschildt, was to observe the movements of the enemy's cavalry on both banks of the Ers beyond our left.

The 3d and Light divisions, under the command of Lieut. Gen. Sir T. Picton and Major Gen. C. Baron Alten, and the brigade of German cavalry, were to observe the enemy on the lower part of the canal, and to draw their attention to that quarter by threatening the *têtes de pont*, while Lieut. Gen. Sir R. Hill was to do the same on the suburb on the left of the Garonne.

Marshal Sir W. Beresford crossed the Ers, and formed his corps in 3 columns of lines in the village of Croix Dorade, the 4th division leading, with which he immediately carried Montblanc. He then moved up the Ers in the same order, over most difficult ground, in a direction parallel to the enemy's fortified position; and as soon as he reached the point at which he turned it, he formed his lines and moved to the attack. During these operations, Gen. Don M. Freyre moved along the left of the Ers to the front of Croix Dorade where he formed his corps in 2 lines with a reserve on a height in front of the left of the enemy's position, on which height the Portuguese artillery was placed; and Major Gen. Ponsonby's brigade of cavalry in reserve in the rear.

As soon as formed, and that it was seen that Marshal Sir W. Beresford was ready, Gen. Don M. Freyre moved forward to the attack. The troops marched in good order, under a very heavy fire of musketry and artillery, and showed great spirit, the General and all his Staff being at their head; and the two lines were soon lodged under some banks immediately under the enemy's intrenchments; the reserve and Portuguese artillery, and British cavalry, continuing on the height on which the troops had first formed. The enemy, however, repulsed the movement of the right of Gen. Freyre's line round their left flank; and having followed up their success, and turned our right by both sides of the high road leading from Toulouse to Croix Dorade, they soon compelled the whole corps to retire. It gave me great satisfaction to see that, although they suffered considerably in retiring, the troops rallied again as soon as the Light division, which was immediately on their right, moved up; and I cannot sufficiently applaud the exertions of Gen. Don M. Freyre, the officers of the Staff of the 4th Spanish army, and of the officers of the General Staff, to rally and form them again.

Lieut. Gen. Mendizabal, who was in the field as a volunteer, Gen. Ezpeleta, and several officers of the Staff and chiefs of corps, were wounded upon this occasion; but Gen. Mendizabal continued in the field. The regiment de *Tiradores de Cantabria*, under the command of Col. Leon de Sicilia, kept its position, under the enemy's intrenchments, until I ordered it to retire.

In the mean time, Marshal Sir W. Beresford, with the 4th division, under the command of Lieut. Gen. Sir G. L. Cole, and the 6th division, under the command of Lieut. Gen. Sir H. Clinton, attacked and carried the heights on the enemy's right, and the redoubt which covered and protected that flank; and he lodged those troops on the same height with the enemy; who were, however, still in possession of 4 redoubts, and of the intrenchments and fortified houses.

The badness of the roads had induced the Marshal to leave his artillery in the village of Montblanc; and some time elapsed before it could be brought to him, and before Gen. Don M. Freyre's corps could be reformed and brought back to the attack. As soon as this was effected the Marshal continued his movement along the ridge, and carried, with Gen. Pack's brigade of the 6th division, the two principal redoubts and fortified houses in the enemy's centre. The enemy made a desperate effort from the canal to regain these redoubts, but they were repulsed with considerable loss; and the 6th division continuing its movement along the ridge of the height, and the Spanish troops continuing a corresponding movement upon the front, the enemy were driven from the two redoubts and intrenchments on their left;

and the whole range of heights were in our possession. We did not gain this advantage, however, without severe loss; particularly in the brave 6th division. Lieut. Col. Coghlan of the 61st, an officer of great merit and promise, was unfortunately killed in the attack of the heights. Major Gen. Pack was wounded, but was enabled to remain in the field; and Col. Douglas, of the 8th Portuguese regt., lost his leg, and I am afraid that I shall be deprived for a considerable time of his assistance.

The 36th, 42d, 79th, and 61st, lost considerable numbers, and were highly distinguished throughout the day.

I cannot sufficiently applaud the ability and conduct of Marshal Sir W. Beresford throughout the operations of the day; nor that of Lieut. Gens. Sir G. L. Cole, Sir H. Clinton, Major Gens. Pack and Lambert, and the troops under their command. Marshal Sir W. Beresford particularly reports the good conduct of Brig. Gen. d'Urban, the Q. M. G., and Gen. Brito Mozinho, the A. G. to the Portuguese army.

The 4th division, although exposed on their march along the enemy's front to a galling fire, were not so much engaged as the 6th, and did not suffer so much; but they conducted themselves with their usual gallantry.

I had also every reason to be satisfied with the conduct of Gen. Don M. Freyre, Lieut. Gen. Don G. Mendizabal, Mariscal de Campo Don Pedro Bárcenas, Brig. Don J. de Ezpeleta, Mariscal de Campo Don A. G. de Marcilla, and the Chief of the Staff Don E. S. Salvador, and the officers of the Staff of the 4th army. The officers and troops conducted themselves well in all the attacks which they made subsequent to their being re-formed.

The ground not having admitted of the operations of the cavalry, they had no opportunity of charging.

While the operations above detailed were going on, on the left of the army, Lieut. Gen. Sir R. Hill drove the enemy from their exterior works in the suburb, on the left of the Garonne, within the ancient wall. Lieut. Gen. Sir T. Picton likewise, with the 3d division, drove the enemy within the *tête de pont* on the bridge of the canal nearest to the Garonne; but the troops having made an effort to carry it, they were repulsed, and some loss was sustained. Major Gen. Brisbane was wounded, but I hope not so as to deprive me for any length of time of his assistance; and Lieut. Col. Forbes, of the 45th, an officer of great merit, was killed.

The army being thus established on three sides of Toulouse, I immediately detached our light cavalry to cut off the communication by the only road practicable for carriages which remained to the enemy, till I should be enabled to make arrangements to establish the troops between the canal and the Garonne.

The enemy, however, retired last night, leaving in our hands Gen. Harispe, Gen. Baurot, Gen. St Hilaire, and 1600 prisoners. One piece of cannon was taken on the field of battle; and others, and large quantities of stores of all descriptions, in the town.

Since I sent my last report, I have received an account from Rear Adm. Penrose of the successes in the Gironde of the boats of the squadron under his command.

Lieut. Gen. the Earl of Dalhousie crossed the Garonne nearly about the time that Adm. Penrose entered the river, and pushed the enemy's parties under Gen. Lhuillier beyond the Dordogne. He then crossed the Dordogne on the 4th, near St André de Cubzac, with a detachment of the troops under his command, with a view to the attack of the fort of Blaye. His Lordship found Gen. Lhuillier and Gen. Desbareaux posted near Etauliers, and made his disposition to attack them, when they retired, leaving about 300 prisoners in his hands. I enclose the Earl of Dalhousie's report of this affair.

In the operations which I have now reported, I have had every reason to be satisfied with the assistance I received from the Quarter Master and Adjutant General, and the officers of those departments respectively; from Mariscal de Campo Don Luis Wimpffen and the officers of the Spanish Staff, and from Mariscal de Campo Don M. de Alava; from Col. Dickson, commanding the allied artillery; and from Lieut. Col. Lord FitzRoy Somerset and the officers of my personal Staff.

I send this dispatch by my aide de camp, Major Lord W. Russell, whom I beg leave to recommend to your Lordship's protection.

P. S. I enclose a return of the killed and wounded in the late operations.

Return of the killed, wounded, and missing,
at the battle of Toulouse, 10th April, 1814.

	Officers.	Serjeants.	R. and F.	Total loss of officers, non-commissioned officers, and R. and F.	British.	Spanish.	Portuguese.	Horses.
Killed	31	21	543	595	312	205	78	62
Wounded	248	123	3675	4046	1795	1722	529	59
Missing	3	—	15	18	17	1	—	2

To Lieut. Gen. Sir J. Hope, K. B.

Toulouse, 16th April, 1814.

I have been so much occupied since I entered this town on the 12th inst., that I have not had leisure to write to you; and I am apprehensive that you will not have heard of the great events that have occurred. I will therefore give you an account of them in the order of their occurrence.

We beat Marshal Soult on the 10th, in the strong position which he took to maintain Toulouse. The 11th was spent in reconnaissances towards the road of Carcassonne, and in the arrangements to be adopted for shutting him in Toulouse entirely. The 11th at night he evacuated the town, and marched by the road of Carcassonne.

I entered the town about noon, and found the white flag flying, every body wearing white cockades, Buonaparte's statue thrown out of the window of the Capitol, and the eagles pulled down, &c. The *adjoint* of the mayor addressed me as in the enclosed paper (No. 1), which I answered as in the enclosed (No. 2).

In the afternoon Col. Cooke and Col. St Simon arrived from Paris; the former sent by His Majesty's minister with the King of Prussia to apprise me, and the latter sent by the Provisional government of France to apprise Marshal Soult, of the events which had occurred in the capital to the night of the 7th, when they quitted it.

Shortly after the entry of the Allies, the Emperor Alexander published a proclamation, in which he declared the determination of the Allies not to make peace with Buonaparte. The Senate immediately assembled, and decreed *la Déchéance de Buonaparte;* a Provisional government has been appointed; and a constitution has been framed, under which Louis XVIII. is called to the throne of his ancestors; and Buonaparte has abdicated, accepting an establishment in the island of Elba and a pension of 6,000,000 *livres*, of which half for himself and the remainder for his family.

These are the principal events which have occurred, of which you will find the details in the enclosed newspapers.

In consequence of these events, and finding that the Allies had agreed with the Provisional government for a suspension of hostilities, I have had a correspondence with Marshal Soult, of which I enclose you the copies, intending, if he should declare his submission to the Provisional government, and to the constitution of the 6th April, to agree to a suspension of hostilities with him. But you will see, from his last letter, that he does not submit to that government; the reason for which he stated to Col. Gordon to be, that he could not give entire credit to Col. St Simon; and that he wished to have time to receive from some of the ministers of Napoleon an account of the events which had occurred. He was informed, however, both by Col. Cooke and Col. St Simon, that they had been stopped at Blois by the gendarmerie attending the court of the Empress; and that, having been brought before the Minister at War, the Duc de Feltre, this person had backed their passports in order that their mission might not be interrupted; at the same time declaring that his functions had ceased with the government of his late

Sovereign. The conduct of Marshal Soult, therefore, can be considered in no other light than as prolonging the miseries of war without an object, excepting that of promoting a civil war in the country.

The garrison and corps of troops posted at Montauban, under the command of Gen. Loverdo, having submitted to the Provisional government, I have concluded a treaty to suspend hostilities with them; and I march to-morrow to follow Marshal Soult, and to prevent his army from becoming the *noyau* of a civil war in France.

I recommend to you to send this letter and all its enclosures to the Governor of Bayonne, in order that he may be made acquainted with the state of affairs at Paris and elsewhere in France; and that he may choose the line he will adopt. If he will acknowledge the Provisional government, I have no objection to allow of a suspension of hostilities at Bayonne.

EIGHT

WATERLOO

Of all Wellington's many fights, the battle of Waterloo of 18 June 1815 is by far the most famous, witnessing, as it did, the final defeat of Napoleon Bonaparte. Yet the campaign itself only lasted for four days, and many Peninsular veterans who had not been there felt for ever afterwards that the years of hardship and suffering that they had endured in the far harsher conditions of the Iberian Peninsula had been unfairly eclipsed (particular anger was occasioned by the fact that all those officers and men who had been at Waterloo received a special campaign medal, this being a favour that was not extended to veterans of the Peninsular War until 1847). That said, the battles of the Hundred Days were bloody in the extreme, while Wellington was subjected to as severe a test as anything he had faced in the course of his military career. In brief, everything revolved around the sudden escape of Napoleon from the island of Elba, where he had been sent into exile in April 1814. Landing on the Mediterranean coast of France on 1 March 1815, Napoleon quickly moved to Paris where he arrived on 20 March, virtually the entire French army having gone over to his cause without a shot. The powers of Europe, whose representatives were all gathered at Vienna in order to negotiate the remodelling of Europe necessitated by the end of the Napoleonic Wars, having declared him an outlaw. Napoleon mobilised for war, and in mid-June marched to attack his nearest opponents, these being the Anglo-Dutch army commanded by the Duke of Wellington and the Prussian army of Marshal Blücher. Arrayed to defend the frontiers of Belgium, the Allied commanders were taken unawares by his approach, and Napoleon was able to win an initial victory over Blücher on 16 June. At Quatre Bras, however, Marshal Ney proved less successful when he came up against Wellington's forces, and the Allied armies were able to remain in contact with one another and to fall back on fresh defensive positions at Mont Saint Jean and Wavre. Two days later fighting resumed with Napoleon launching a series of ferocious attacks on Wellington's forces, but, despite what he later called hard pounding, the British commander was able to hold the line, and at length the Prussians arrived from Wavre, the forces that Napoleon had sent against them having signally failed to stay their march. After one last attack by part of the Imperial Guard, which Wellington played a direct part in repelling, the Anglo-Dutch forces went over to the offensive, whereupon the exhausted French collapsed and fled the field. It was the end of an era, and, with it, the military career of the Duke of Wellington.

To the Rt. Hon. Sir H. Wellesley, G. C. B.

Bruxelles, 2d June, 1815.

I enclose copies of letters received yesterday from Cooke, which will show you the state of affairs in Italy, upon which I sincerely congratulate you.

We have as yet done nothing here. The Russians are not yet arrived upon the Rhine; but I believe that Woronzoff's advanced guard entered Francfort this day. The whole of Schwarzenberg's army will not be collected on the Upper Rhine till towards the 16th, at about which time I hope we shall begin.

I shall enter France with between 70,000 and 80,000 men; the Prussians near me with twice as many. There is certainly a serious insurrection in La Vendée, and the French have already moved some of their force from the frontier; but I don't think we can move till we shall be certain of the movements of Prince Schwarzenberg.

To Lieut. Col. Sir H. Hardinge, K. C. B.

Bruxelles, 6th June, 1815, 7 P.M.

All accounts which I receive from the frontier appear again to concur in the notion of a collection of troops about Maubeuge.

Buonaparte was expected to be at Laon on the 6th; and there were on all parts of the road between Paris and the frontier extraordinary preparations for the movement of troops in carriages. The numbers of the latter collected are immense in some of the towns.

I shall be obliged to you to mention these facts to the Marshal.

I shall likewise be obliged to you to mention to him that I have had a letter from the King of Saxony, in which he desires me to take the command of the Saxon troops. This is in consequence of an arrangement of the Allies. But I beg you to tell the Marshal that I shall not take any command of these troops till I shall learn from him that he has directed them to place themselves under my orders.

To Earl Bathurst.

Waterloo, 19th June, 1815.

Buonaparte, having collected the 1st, 2d, 3d, 4th, and 6th corps of the French army, and the Imperial Guard, and nearly all the cavalry, on the Sambre, and between that river and the Meuse, between the 10th and 14th of the month, advanced on the 15th and attacked the Prussian posts at Thuin and Lobbes, on the Sambre, at day-light in the morning.

I did not hear of these events till in the evening of the 15th; and I immediately ordered the troops to prepare to march, and afterwards to march to their left, as soon as I had intelligence from other quarters to prove that the enemy's movement upon Charleroi was the real attack.

The enemy drove the Prussian posts from the Sambre on that day; and Gen. Ziethen, who commanded the corps which had been at Charleroi, retired upon Fleurus; and Marshal Prince Blücher concentrated the Prussian army upon Sombref, holding the villages in front of his position of St Amand and Ligny.

The enemy continued his march along the road from Charleroi towards Bruxelles; and, on the same evening, the 15th, attacked a brigade of the army of the Netherlands, under the Prince de Weimar, posted at Frasne, and forced it back to the farm house, on the same road, called Les Quatre Bras.

The Prince of Orange immediately reinforced this brigade with another of the same division, under Gen. Perponcher, and, in the morning early, regained part of the ground which had been lost, so as to have the command of the communication leading from Nivelles and Bruxelles with Marshal Blücher's position.

In the mean time, I had directed the whole army to march upon Les Quatre Bras; and the 5th division, under Lieut. Gen. Sir T. Picton, arrived at about 2½ P.M. in the day, followed by the corps of troops under the Duke of Brunswick, and afterwards by the contingent of Nassau.

At this time the enemy commenced an attack upon Prince Blücher with his whole force, excepting the 1st and 2d corps, and a corps of cavalry under Gen. Kellermann, with which he attacked our post at Les Quatre Bras.

The Prussian army maintained their position with their usual gallantry and perseverance against a great disparity of numbers, as the 4th corps of their army, under Gen. Bülow, had not joined; and I was not able to assist them as I wished, as I was attacked myself, and the troops, the cavalry in particular, which had a long distance to march, had not arrived.

We maintained our position also, and completely defeated and repulsed all the enemy's attempts to get possession of it. The enemy repeatedly attacked us with a large body of infantry and cavalry, supported by a numerous and powerful artillery. He made several charges with the cavalry upon our infantry, but all were repulsed in the steadiest manner.

In this affair, H. R. H. the Prince of Orange, the Duke of Brunswick, and Lieut. Gen. Sir T. Picton, and Major Gens. Sir J. Kempt and Sir D. Pack, who were engaged from the commencement of the enemy's attack, highly distinguished themselves, as well as Lieut. Gen. C. Baron Alten, Major Gen. Sir C. Halkett, Lieut. Gen. Cooke, and Major Gens. Maitland and Byng, as they successively arrived. The troops of the 5th division, and those of the Brunswick corps, were long and severely engaged, and conducted themselves with the utmost gallantry. I must particularly mention the 28th, 42d, 79th, and 92d regts., and the battalion of Hanoverians. Our loss was great, as your Lordship will perceive by the enclosed return; and I have particularly to regret H. S. H. the Duke of Brunswick, who fell fighting gallantly at the head of his troops.

Although Marshal Blücher had maintained his position at Sombref, he still found himself much weakened by the severity of the contest in which he had been engaged, and, as the 4th corps had not arrived, he determined to fall back and to concentrate his army upon Wavre; and he marched in the night, after the action was over. This movement of the Marshal rendered necessary a corresponding one upon my part; and I retired from the farm of Quatre Bras upon Genappe, and thence upon Waterloo, the next morning, the 17th, at 10 o'clock.

The enemy made no effort to pursue Marshal Blücher. On the contrary, a patrole which I sent to Sombref in the morning found all quiet; and the enemy's vedettes fell back as the patrole advanced. Neither did he attempt to molest our march to the rear, although made in the middle of the day, excepting by following, with a large body of cavalry brought from his right, the cavalry under the Earl of Uxbridge. This gave Lord Uxbridge an opportunity of charging them with the 1st Life Guards, upon their *débouché* from the village of Genappe, upon which occasion his Lordship has declared himself to be well satisfied with that regiment.

The position which I took up in front of Waterloo crossed the high roads from Charleroi and Nivelles, and had its right thrown back to a ravine near Merke Braine, which was occupied, and its left extended to a height above the hamlet Ter la

Haye, which was likewise occupied. In front of the right centre, and near the Nivelles road, we occupied the house and gardens of Hougoumont, which covered the return of that flank; and in front of the left centre we occupied the farm of La Haye Sainte. By our left we communicated with Marshal Prince Blücher at Wavre through Ohain; and the Marshal had promised me that, in case we should be attacked, he would support me with one or more corps, as might be necessary.

The enemy collected his army, with the exception of the 3d corps, which had been sent to observe Marshal Blücher, on a range of heights in our front, in the course of the night of the 17th and yesterday morning, and at about 10 o'clock he commenced a furious attack upon our post at Hougoumont. I had occupied that post with a detachment from Gen. Byng's brigade of Guards, which was in position in its rear; and it was for some time under the command of Lieut. Col. Macdonell, and afterwards of Col. Home; and I am happy to add that it was maintained throughout the day with the utmost gallantry by these brave troops, notwithstanding the repeated efforts of large bodies of the enemy to obtain possession of it.

This attack upon the right of our centre was accompanied by a very heavy cannonade upon our whole line, which was destined to support the repeated attacks of cavalry and infantry, occasionally mixed, but sometimes separate, which were made upon it. In one of these the enemy carried the farm house of La Haye Sainte, as the detachment of the light battalion of the German Legion, which occupied it, had expended all its ammunition; and the enemy occupied the only communication there was with them.

The enemy repeatedly charged our infantry with his cavalry, but these attacks were uniformly unsuccessful; and they afforded opportunities to our cavalry to charge, in one of which Lord E. Somerset's brigade, consisting of the Life Guards, the Royal Horse Guards, and 1st dragoon guards, highly distinguished themselves, as did that of Major Gen. Sir W. Ponsonby, having taken many prisoners and an eagle.

These attacks were repeated till about 7 in the evening, when the enemy made a desperate effort with cavalry and infantry, supported by the fire of artillery, to force our left centre, near the farm of La Haye Sainte, which, after a severe contest, was defeated; and, having observed that the troops retired from this attack in great confusion, and that the march of Gen. Bülow's corps, by Frischermont, upon Planchenois and La Belle Alliance, had begun to take effect, and as I could perceive the fire of his cannon, and as Marshal Prince Blücher had joined in person with a corps of his army to the left of our line by Ohain, I determined to attack the enemy, and immediately advanced the whole line of infantry, supported by the cavalry and artillery. The attack succeeded in every point: the enemy was forced from his positions on the heights, and fled in the utmost confusion, leaving behind him, as far as I could judge, 150 pieces of cannon, with their ammunition, which fell into our hands.

I continued the pursuit till long after dark, and then discontinued it only on account of the fatigue of our troops, who had been engaged during twelve hours, and because I found myself on the same road with Marshal Blücher, who assured me of his intention to follow the enemy throughout the night. He has sent me word this morning that he had taken 60 pieces of cannon belonging to the Imperial Guard, and several carriages, baggage, &c., belonging to Buonaparte, in Genappe.

I propose to move this morning upon Nivelles, and not to discontinue my operations.

Your Lordship will observe that such a desperate action could not be fought, and such advantages could not be gained, without great loss; and I am sorry to add that ours has been immense. In Lieut. Gen. Sir T. Picton His Majesty has sustained the loss of an officer who has frequently distinguished himself in his service; and he fell gloriously leading his division to a charge with bayonets, by which one of the most serious attacks made by the enemy on our position was repulsed. The Earl of Uxbridge, after having successfully got through this arduous day, received a wound by almost the last shot fired, which will, I am afraid, deprive His Majesty for some time of his services.

H. R. H. the Prince of Orange distinguished himself by his gallantry and conduct, till he received a wound from a musket ball through the shoulder, which obliged him to quit the field.

It gives me the greatest satisfaction to assure your Lordship that the army never, upon any occasion, conducted itself better. The division of Guards under Lieut. Gen. Cooke, who is severely wounded, Major Gen. Maitland, and Major Gen. Byng, set an example which was followed by all; and there is no officer nor description of troops that did not behave well.

I must, however, particularly mention, for His Royal Highness' approbation, Lieut. Gen. Sir H. Clinton, Major Gen. Adam, Lieut. Gen. C. Baron Alten (severely wounded), Major Gen. Sir C. Halkett (severely wounded), Col. Ompteda, Col. Mitchell (commanding a brigade of the 4th division), Major Gens. Sir J. Kempt and Sir D. Pack, Major Gen. Lambert, Major Gen. Lord E. Somerset, Major Gen. Sir W. Ponsonby, Major Gen. Sir C. Grant, and Major Gen. Sir H. Vivian, Major Gen. Sir O. Vandeleur, and Major Gen. Count Dornberg.

I am also particularly indebted to Gen. Lord Hill for his assistance and conduct upon this, as upon all former occasions.

The artillery and engineer departments were conducted much to my satisfaction by Col. Sir G. Wood and Col. Smyth; and I had every reason to be satisfied with the conduct of the Adj. Gen., Major Gen. Barnes, who was wounded, and of the Q. M. G., Col. de Lancey, who was killed by a cannon shot in the middle of the action. This officer is a serious loss to His Majesty's service, and to me at this moment.

I was likewise much indebted to the assistance of Lieut. Col. Lord FitzRoy Somerset, who was severely wounded, and of the officers composing my personal staff, who have suffered severely in this action. Lieut. Col. the Hon. Sir Alex. Gordon, who has died of his wounds, was a most promising officer, and is a serious loss to His Majesty's service.

Gen. Kruse, of the Nassau service, likewise conducted himself much to my satisfaction; as did Gen. Tripp, commanding the heavy brigade of cavalry, and Gen. Vanhope, commanding a brigade of infantry in the service of the King of the Netherlands.

Gen. Pozzo di Borgo, Gen. Baron Vincent, Gen. Müffling, and Gen. Alava, were in the field during the action, and rendered me every assistance in their power. Baron Vincent is wounded, but I hope not severely; and Gen. Pozzo di Borgo received a contusion.

I should not do justice to my own feelings, or to Marshal Blücher and the Prussian army, if I did not attribute the successful result of this arduous day to the cordial and timely assistance I received from them. The operation of Gen. Bülow upon the enemy's flank was a most decisive one; and, even if I had not found myself in a situation to make the attack which produced the final result, it would have forced the enemy to retire if his attacks should have failed, and would have prevented him from taking advantage of them if they should unfortunately have succeeded.

Since writing the above, I have received a report that Major Gen. Sir W. Ponsonby is killed; and in announcing this intelligence to your Lordship, I have to add the expression of my grief for the fate of an officer who had already rendered very brilliant and important services, and was an ornament to his profession.

I send with this dispatch 3 eagles, taken by the troops in this action, which Major Percy will have the honor of laying at the feet of His Royal Highness. I beg leave to recommend him to your Lordship's protection.

Return* of the killed, wounded, and missing of the British and Hanoverian army under the command of Field Marshal the Duke of Wellington, K. G., in the battle fought at Quatre Bras on the 16th June, 1815.

	Officers.	Serjeants.	R. and F.	Total loss of officers, non-commissioned officers, and R. and F.	British.	Hanoverians.	Horses.
Killed ...	29	19	302	350	316	34	19
Wounded ..	126	111	2143	2380	2156	224	14
Missing ...	4	6	171	181	32	149	1

* The returns of the killed and wounded of the Dutch, Belgian, Brunswick, and Nassau troops are not among the papers of the Duke of Wellington.

Return of the killed, wounded, and missing on the retreat from Quatre Bras to Waterloo, on the 17th June, 1815.

	Officers.	Serjeants.	R. and F.	Total loss of officers, non-commissioned officers, and R. and F.	British.	Hanoverians.	Horses.
Killed ...	1	1	33	35	26	9	45
Wounded ..	7	13	112	132	52	80	20
Missing ...	4	3	64	71	30	32	33

Return of the killed, wounded, and missing in the battle fought at Waterloo on the 18th June, 1815.

	Officers.	Serjeants.	R. and F.	Total loss of officers, non-commissioned officers, and R. and F.	British.	Hanoverians.	Horses.
Killed ...	116	109	1822	2047	1759	288	1495
Wounded ..	504	364	6148	7016	5892	1124	891
Missing ...	20	29	1574	1623	807	816	773

	Killed.	Wounded.	Missing.
Total	2432	9528	1875

The greater number of the men returned missing had
gone to the rear with wounded officers and soldiers,
and joined afterwards. The officers are supposed killed.

To the Earl of Aberdeen, K. T.

Bruxelles, 19th June, 1815.

You will readily give credit to the existence of the extreme grief with which I announce to you the death of your gallant brother, in consequence of a wound received in our great battle of yesterday. He had served me most zealously and usefully for many years, and on many trying occasions; but he had never rendered himself more useful, and had never distinguished himself more, than in our late actions. He received the wound which occasioned his death when rallying one of the Brunswick battalions which was shaking a little; and he lived long enough to be informed by myself of the glorious result of our actions, to which he had so much contributed by his active and zealous assistance.

I cannot express to you the regret and sorrow with which I look round me, and contemplate the loss which I have sustained, particularly in your brother. The glory resulting from such actions, so dearly bought, is no consolation to me, and I cannot suggest it as any to you and his friends; but I hope that it may be expected that this last one has been so decisive, as that no doubt remains that our exertions and our individual losses will be rewarded by the early attainment of our just object. It is then that the glory of the actions in which our friends and relations have fallen will be some consolation for their loss.

P. S. Your brother had a black horse, given to him, I believe, by Lord Ashburnham, which I will keep till I hear from you what you wish should be done with it.

Sources

WD J. Gurwood (ed.), *The Dispatches of Field Marshal the Duke of Wellington during his Various Campaigns in India, Denmark, Portugal, Spain, the Low Countries and France from 1789 to 1815* (London, 1852)

SD Second Duke of Wellington (ed.), *Supplementary Despatches, Correspondence and Memoranda of Field Marshal Arthur, Duke of Wellington* (London, 1858–72)

One: The Campaigns of 1808

Wellington to Castlereagh, 21 July 1808, WD, III, pp. 31–4
Wellington to Castlereagh, 25 July 1808, WD, III, pp. 36–7
Wellington to Castlereagh, 1 August 1808, WD, III, pp. 42–6
Wellington to Castlereagh, 1 August 1808, WD, III, pp. 46–7
Wellington to Burrard, 8 August 1808, WD, III, pp. 57–61
Wellington to Castlereagh, 8 August 1808, WD, III, p. 62
Wellington to Castlereagh, 16 August 1808, WD, III, pp. 77–80
Wellington to Castlereagh, 17 August 1808, WD, III, pp. 80–83
Wellington to Castlereagh, 22 August 1808, WD, III, pp. 94–5
Wellington to Richmond, 22 August 1808, WD, III, p. 95
Wellington to Stuart, 25 August 1808, WD, III, pp. 97–8
Wellington to Richmond, 27 August 1808, WD, III, pp. 102–3
Wellington to Castlereagh, 5 September 1808, WD, III, pp. 112–17

Two: The Campaigns of 1809

Memorandum on the defence of Portugal, 7 March 1809, WD, III, pp. 181–3
Wellington to Castlereagh, 24 April 1809, WD, III, pp. 189–90

Wellington to Cuesta, 29 April 1809, WD, III, pp. 197–8
Wellington to Beresford, 12 May 1809, WD, III, p. 230
Wellington to Castlereagh, 18 May 1809, WD, III, pp. 239–41
Wellington to Beresford, 17 July 1809, WD, III, pp. 361–2
Wellington to Frere, 24 July 1809, WD, III, pp. 366–7
Wellington to Castlereagh, 24 July 1809, WD, III, pp. 368–9
Wellington to Villiers, 29 July 1809, WD, III, p. 378
Wellington to Frere, 31 July 1809, WD, III, pp. 383–4
Wellington to Castlereagh, 1 August 1809, WD, III, pp. 386–7
Wellington to Castlereagh, 8 August 1809, WD, III, pp. 397–400
Wellington to Castlereagh, 21 August 1809, WD, III, pp. 440–42
Wellington to Castlereagh, 25 August 1809, WD, III, pp. 449–54

Three: The Campaigns of 1810

Memorandum for Lieutenant Colonel Fletcher, 20 October 1809,
    WD, III, pp. 556–60
Wellington to Liverpool, 11 July 1810, WD, IV, pp. 161–2
Wellington to H. Wellesley, 27 July 1810, WD, IV, pp. 190–91
Wellington to Liverpool, 29 August 1810, WD, IV, pp. 247–9
Wellington to Stuart, 9 September 1810, WD, IV, pp. 269–71
Wellington to Stuart, 11 September 1810, WD, IV, pp. 273–4
Wellington to Liverpool, 20 September 1810, WD, IV, pp. 291–4
Wellington to Liverpool, 30 September 1810, WD, IV, pp. 304–8
Wellington to Liverpool, 13 October 1810, WD, IV, pp. 329–32

Four: The Campaigns of 1811

Wellington to Liverpool, 14 March 1811, WD, IV, pp. 661–70
Wellington to Beresford, 25 March 1811, WD, IV, p. 695
Wellington to Beresford, 4 April 1811, WD, IV, pp. 722–4
Wellington to Liverpool, 1 May 1811, WD, IV, pp. 781–2
Wellington to Liverpool, 7 May 2011, WD, IV, pp. 787–90
Wellington to Liverpool, 8 May 1811, WD, IV, pp. 794–8
Wellington to Liverpool, 15 May 1811, WD, V, pp. 20–22
Wellington to H. Wellesley, 22 May 1811, WD, V, pp. 30–31
Wellington to Liverpool, 23 May 1811, WD, V, pp. 42–3
Wellington to Gordon, 12 June 1811, WD, V, pp. 84–7
Wellington to Liverpool, 13 June 1811, WD, V, pp. 88–93

Wellington to Liverpool, 11 July 1811, WD, V, pp. 147–8
Wellington to Graham, 27 July 1811, WD, V, pp. 190–91
Wellington to Liverpool, 27 August 1811, WD, V, pp. 238–40
Wellington to Liverpool, 29 September 1811, WD, V, pp. 292–6

Five: The Campaigns of 1812

Wellington to Liverpool, 1 January 1812, WD, V, p. 453
Wellington to Liverpool, 20 January 1812, WD, V, pp. 472–6
Wellington to Richmond, 29 January 1812, WD, V, pp. 493–4
Wellington to Liverpool, 20 March 1812, WD, V, pp. 552–4
Wellington to Liverpool, 20 March 1812, WD, V, p. 554
Wellington to Liverpool, 27 March 1812, WD, V, pp. 560–63
Wellington to Liverpool, 7 April 1812, WD, V, pp. 576–81
Wellington to Liverpool, 18 June 1812, WD, V, pp. 713–16
Wellington to Liverpool, 25 June 1812, WD, V, pp. 721–3
Wellington to Liverpool, 30 June 1812, WD, V, pp. 726–8
Wellington to Bathurst, 7 July 1812, WD, V, pp. 735–6
Wellington to Bathurst, 21 July 1812, WD, V, pp. 749–52
Wellington to Bathurst, 24 July 1812, WD, V, pp. 753–8
Wellington to Bathurst, 24 July 1812, WD, V, pp. 758–9
Wellington to Graham, 25 July 1812, WD, V, pp. 759–60
Wellington to Bathurst, 28 July 1812, WD, V, pp. 765–6
Wellington to Bathurst, 4 August 1812, WD, VI, pp. 10–11
Wellington to Bathurst, 13 August 1812, WD, VI, pp. 21–4
Wellington to Bathurst, 18 August 1812, WD, VI, pp. 35–6
Wellington to H. Wellesley, 23 August 1812, WD, VI, pp. 37–40
Wellington to Bathurst, 30 August 1812, WD, VI, pp. 48–9
Wellington to Bathurst, 7 September 1812, WD, VI, pp. 57–8
Wellington to Paget, 20 September 1812, WD, VI, pp. 81–2
Wellington to Bathurst, 27 September 1812, WD, VI, pp. 93–4
Wellington to Bathurst, 5 October 1812, WD, VI, pp. 106–7
Wellington to Bathurst, 11 October 1812, WD, VI, pp. 114–15
Wellington to Bathurst, 26 October 1812, WD, VI, pp. 133–7
Wellington to Bathurst, 28 October 1812, WD, VI, pp. 138–40
Wellington to H. Wellesley, 1 November 1812, WD, VI, pp. 144–5
Wellington to Bathurst, 3 November 1812, WD, VI, pp. 148–9
Wellington to Bathurst, 19 November 1812, WD, VI, pp. 164–7
Wellington to Liverpool, 23 November 1812, WD, VI, pp. 172–5
Wellington to Cooke, 25 November 1812, SD, VII, pp. 476–8

Six: The Campaigns of 1813

Wellington to Bathurst, 11 May 1813, WD, VI, pp. 479–80
Wellington to Bathurst, 31 May 1813, WD, VI, pp. 507–8
Wellington to Bathurst, 6 June 1813, WD, VI, pp. 516–17
Wellington to Bourke, 10 June 1813, WD, VI, p. 521
Wellington to Bathurst, 13 June 1813, WD, VI, pp. 525–6
Wellington to Bathurst, 19 June 1813, WD, VI, pp. 534–6
Wellington to Bathurst, 22 June 1813, WD, VI, pp. 539–43
Wellington to Bathurst, 29 June 1813, WD, VI, pp. 558–9
Wellington to Dalhousie, 2 July 1813, WD, VI, pp. 571–2
Wellington to Bathurst, 2 July 1813, WD, VI, pp. 575–6
Wellington to Bathurst, 3 July 1813, WD, VI, pp. 578–82
Wellington to Graham, 4 July 1813, WD, VI, pp. 584–5
Wellington to Bathurst, 10 July 1813, WD, VI, pp. 591–3
Wellington to Bathurst, 19 July 1813, WD, VI, pp. 608–9
Wellington to Bathurst, 1 August 1813, WD, VI, pp. 636–45
Wellington to Graham, 4 August 1813, WD, VI, pp. 646–7
Wellington to Bathurst, 8 August 1813, WD, VI, pp. 663–5
Wellington to Bathurst, 14 August 1813, WD, VI, pp. 680–82
Wellington to Bathurst, 2 September 1813, WD, VI, pp. 726–33
Wellington to H. Wellesley, 9 October 1813, WD, VII, pp. 46–9
Wellington to Bathurst, 9 October 1813, WD, VII, pp. 49–51
Wellington to Bathurst, 13 November 1813, WD, VII, pp. 131–5
Wellington to Bathurst, 21 November 1813, WD, VII, pp. 151–3
Wellington to Bathurst, 14 December 1813, WD, VII, pp. 194–201

Seven: The Campaigns of 1814

Wellington to Bathurst, 20 February 1814, WD, VII, pp. 324–5
Wellington to Bathurst, 1 March 1814, WD, VII, pp. 336–41
Wellington to Bathurst, 11 March 1814, WD, VII, pp. 364–5
Wellington to Bathurst, 20 March 1814, WD, VII, pp. 384–6
Wellington to Bathurst, 1 April 1814, WD, VII, pp. 409–10
Wellington to Bathurst, 12 April 1814, WD, VII, pp. 425–30
Wellington to Hope, 16 April 1814, WD, VII, pp. 445–7

Eight: Waterloo

Wellington to H. Wellesley, 2 June 1815, WD, VIII, p. 118
Wellington to H. Hardinge, 6 June 1815, WD, VIII, p. 126
Wellington to Bathurst, 19 June 1815, WD, VIII, pp. 146–50
Wellington to Aberdeen, 19 June 1815, WD, VIII, pp. 154–5

PENGUIN CLASSICS

THE FEDERALIST PAPERS
JAMES MADISON, ALEXANDER HAMILTON AND JOHN JAY

'The establishment of a Constitution, in a time of profound peace,
by the voluntary consent of a whole people, is a PRODIGY'

Written at a time when furious arguments were raging about the best way to govern America, *The Federalist Papers* had the immediate practical aim of persuading New Yorkers to accept the newly drafted Constitution in 1787. In this they were supremely successful, but their influence also transcended contemporary debate to win them a lasting place in discussions of American political theory. Acclaimed by Thomas Jefferson as 'the best commentary on the principles of government which ever was written', *The Federalist Papers* make a powerful case for power-sharing between State and Federal authorities and for a Constitution that has endured largely unchanged for two hundred years.

In a brilliantly detailed introduction Isaac Kramnick sets the *Papers* in their historical and political context. This edition also contains the American Constitution as an appendix.

'The introduction is an outstanding piece of work. I am strongly recommending its reading' Warren Burger, the former Chief Justice, Supreme Court of the United States

Edited with an introduction by Isaac Kramnick

PENGUIN CLASSICS

A SHORT ACCOUNT OF THE DESTRUCTION OF THE INDIES
BARTOLOMÉ DE LAS CASAS

'Oh, would that I could describe even one hundredth part of the afflictions and calamities wrought among these innocent people by the benighted Spanish!'

Bartolomé de Las Casas was the first and fiercest critic of Spanish colonialism in the New World. An early traveller to the Americas who sailed on one of Columbus's voyages, Las Casas was so horrified by the wholesale massacre he witnessed that he dedicated his life to protecting the Indian community. He wrote *A Short Account of the Destruction of the Indies* in 1542, a shocking catalogue of mass slaughter, torture and slavery, which showed that the evangelizing vision of Columbus had descended under later conquistadors into genocide. Dedicated to Philip II to alert the Castilian Crown to these atrocities and demand that the Indians be entitled to the basic rights of humankind, this passionate work of documentary vividness outraged Europe and contributed to the idea of the Spanish 'Black Legend' that would last for centuries.

Nigel Griffin's powerful translation conveys the compelling immediacy of Las Casas's writing. This edition also contains an introduction discussing his life, work and political legacy.

Translated by Nigel Griffin with an introduction by Anthony Pagden

PENGUIN CLASSICS

MADAME BOVARY
GUSTAVE FLAUBERT

'Oh, why, dear God, did I marry him?'

Emma Bovary is beautiful and bored, trapped in her marriage to a mediocre doctor and stifled by the banality of provincial life. An ardent devourer of sentimental novels, she longs for passion and seeks escape in fantasies of high romance, in voracious spending and, eventually, in adultery. But even her affairs bring her disappointment, and when real life continues to fail to live up to her romantic expectations the consequences are devastating. Flaubert's erotically charged and psychologically acute portrayal of Emma Bovary caused a moral outcry on its publication in 1857. It was deemed so lifelike that many women claimed they were the model for his heroine; but Flaubert insisted: 'Madame Bovary, c'est moi'.

This modern translation by Flaubert's biographer, Geoffrey Wall, retains all the delicacy and precision of the French original. This edition also contains a preface by the novelist Michèle Roberts.

'A masterpiece' Julian Barnes

'A supremely beautiful novel' Michèle Roberts

Translated and edited with an introduction by Geoffrey Wall
With a Preface by Michèle Roberts

PENGUIN CLASSICS

THE CONQUEST OF GAUL
CAESAR

> 'The enemy were overpowered and took to flight.
> The Romans pursued as far as their strength enabled them to run'

Between 58 and 50 BC Julius Caesar conquered most of the area now covered by France, Belgium and Switzerland, and invaded Britain twice, and *The Conquest of Gaul* is his record of these campaigns. Caesar's narrative offers insights into his military strategy and paints a fascinating picture of his encounters with the inhabitants of Gaul and Britain, as well as lively portraits of the rebel leader Vercingetorix and other Gallic chieftains. *The Conquest of Gaul* can also be read as a piece of political propaganda, as Caesar sets down his version of events for the Roman public, knowing he faces civil war on his return to Rome.

Revised and updated by Jane Gardner, S. A. Handford's translation brings Caesar's lucid and exciting account to life for modern readers. This volume includes a glossary of persons and places, maps, appendices and suggestions for further reading.

Translated by S. A. Handford
Revised with a new introduction by Jane F. Gardner

PENGUIN CLASSICS

THE PROFESSOR
CHARLOTTE BRONTË

'She was not handsome, she was not rich, she was not even accomplished,
yet she was my life's treasure; I must then be a man of peculiar discernment'

Working as a professor in M Pelet's establishment in Brussels, William
Crimsworth meets the fascinating Directrice of the neighbouring school, Mlle
Zoräide Reuter and, recognizing her as an intellectual equal, becomes powerfully
attracted to her. Despite her betrothal to M Pelet, Mlle Reuter will not release her
hold over William, and she tries to stand in the way of his finding love elsewhere.
But new possibilities open up to him and he is not to be so easily deterred.
Published two years after the author's death, *The Professor* draws on Charlotte
Brontë's own professional and personal experiences as a teacher in Brussels. Like
Jane Eyre and *Villette* it is the intimate first-person account of a life that brings
extremes of despair and joy.

In her introduction, Heather Glen examines the character of William in the context
of love of wealth and the importance of moral and social propriety, and considers
him as the model of a self-made man.

Edited with an introduction and notes by Heather Glen

PENGUIN CLASSICS

ECCLESIASTICAL HISTORY OF THE ENGLISH PEOPLE
BEDE

> 'With God's help, I, Bede ... have assembled these facts about the history of
> the Church in Britain ... from the traditions of our forebears, and from my own
> personal knowledge'

Written in ad 731, Bede's *Ecclesiastical History of the English People* is the
first account of Anglo-Saxon England ever written, and remains our single most
valuable source for this period. It begins with Julius Caesar's invasion in the first
century bc and goes on to tell of the kings and bishops, monks and nuns who
helped to develop government and convert the people to Christianity during these
crucial formative years. This is a rich, vivid portrait of an emerging church and
nation by the 'Father of English History'.

Leo Sherley-Price's translation from the Latin brings us an accurate and readable
version of Bede's *History*. This edition includes *Bede's Letter to Egbert*, denouncing
false monasteries; and *The Death of Bede*, an admirable eye-witness account by
Cuthbert, monk and later Abbot of Jarrow, both translated by D. H. Farmer.

Translated by Leo Sherley-Price
Edited with an introduction and notes by D. H. Farmer

THE STORY OF PENGUIN CLASSICS

Before 1946 ... 'Classics' are mainly the domain of academics and students; readable editions for everyone else are almost unheard of. This all changes when a little-known classicist, E. V. Rieu, presents Penguin founder Allen Lane with the translation of Homer's *Odyssey* that he has been working on in his spare time.

1946 Penguin Classics debuts with *The Odyssey*, which promptly sells three million copies. Suddenly, classics are no longer for the privileged few.

1950s Rieu, now series editor, turns to professional writers for the best modern, readable translations, including Dorothy L. Sayers's *Inferno* and Robert Graves's unexpurgated *Twelve Caesars*.

1960s The Classics are given the distinctive black covers that have remained a constant throughout the life of the series. Rieu retires in 1964, hailing the Penguin Classics list as 'the greatest educative force of the twentieth century.'

1970s A new generation of translators swells the Penguin Classics ranks, introducing readers of English to classics of world literature from more than twenty languages. The list grows to encompass more history, philosophy, science, religion and politics.

1980s The Penguin American Library launches with titles such as *Uncle Tom's Cabin*, and joins forces with Penguin Classics to provide the most comprehensive library of world literature available from any paperback publisher.

1990s The launch of Penguin Audiobooks brings the classics to a listening audience for the first time, and in 1999 the worldwide launch of the Penguin Classics website extends their reach to the global online community.

The 21st Century Penguin Classics are completely redesigned for the first time in nearly twenty years. This world-famous series now consists of more than 1300 titles, making the widest range of the best books ever written available to millions – and constantly redefining what makes a 'classic'.

The Odyssey continues ...

The best books ever written

P E N G U I N (🐧) C L A S S I C S

SINCE 1946

Find out more at www.penguinclassics.com